HIRED!
The Job-Hunting/
Life-Planning Guide

HIRED!
The Job-Hunting/
Life-Planning Guide

CONNIE HARRIS

PRENTICE HALL
Upper Saddle River, New Jersey 07458

Library of Congress Cataloging-in-Publication Data

Harris, Connie
   Hired! : the job-hunting/life-planning guide / Connie Harris.
     p. cm.
   Includes bibliographical references (p.   ).
   ISBN 0-13-226812-4
   1. Job hunting—Handbooks, manuals, etc.   2. Career development—
Handbooks, manuals, etc.   I. Title.
HF5382.7.H366   1996
650.14—dc20
                                         95-23348
                                           CIP

Acquisitions editor: Elizabeth Sugg
Editorial/production supervision: Linda Zuk, WordCrafters Editorial Services, Inc.
Cover design: Wendy Alling Judy
Prepress/manufacturing buyer: Ed O'Dougherty
Marketing manager: Frank Mortimer
Editorial assistant: Kahdijah Bell

This book was set in Meridien by Pine Tree Composition Inc., and was printed and bound by Banta. The cover was printed by Banta-Harrisonburg.

© 1996 by Harris Espérance Incorporated

Published by Prentice Hall
Simon & Schuster/A Viacom Company
Upper Saddle River, New Jersey 07458

Text Credits:

p. xiv: *My Creed* by Dean Alfange, reprinted by permission of JII Promotion Associates, Inc., Coshocton, OH.

p. 73: Terrence E. Deal and Allen A. Kennedy, *Corporate Cultures* (pp. 107–108), © 1982 by Addison-Wesley Publishing Company, Inc. Reprinted by permission of the publisher.

p. 76: Table from *1984 Information Please Almanac.* Copyright © 1993 Houghton Mifflin Co. Reprinted by permission of Houghton Mifflin Co. All rights reserved.

p. 103: Robert Half, *The Robert Half Way to Get Hired in Today's Job Market* (New York: Rawson, Wade Publishers, Inc. © 1981), pp. 75–76. Reprinted by permission of Simon & Schuster, Inc. New York, NY.

pp. 157–58: Gabriele Lusser Rico, *Writing the Natural Way* (Los Angeles, CA: Jeremy P. Tarcher, Inc., © 1983), pp. 35–36. Reprinted by permission of The Putnam Publishing Group and Jeremy P. Tarcher, Inc.

pp. 242–43: Genie Z. Laborde, *Influencing with Integrity* (Redwood City, CA: Syntony Publishing, © 1983). Reprinted by permission of Genie Z. Laborde, International Dialogue Education Association, Redwood, CA.

p. 267: Anthony Robbins, *Unlimited Power* (New York: Ballantine Books, Inc., © 1986), pp. 218–220. Reprinted by permission of Robbins Research International, San Diego, CA.

p. 371: David Kersey and Marilyn Bates, *Please Understand Me* (Del Mar, CA: Prometheus Nemesis Book Company, ©1978). p. 1.

Computer-generated graphics from Image Gallery, *Presentation Task Force CGM, Release 4.0* by New Vision Technologies Inc., Nepean, Ontario, Canada K2E 8A5 (613–727–8183).

Computer-generated graphics from *WordPerfect 6.0,* Novell, Inc., Orem, VT.

Printed in the United States of America

10 9 8 7 6 5 4 3 2 1

ISBN 0-13-226812-4

Prentice Hall International (UK) Limited, *London*
Prentice Hall of Australia Pty. Limited, *Sydney*
Prentice Hall Canada, Inc., *Toronto*
Prentice Hall Hispanoamericana, S.A., *Mexico*
Prentice Hall of India Private Limited, *New Delhi*
Prentice Hall of Japan, Inc., *Tokyo*
Simon & Schuster Asia, Pte. Ltd., *Singapore*
Editora Prentice Hall do Brasil, Ltda., *Rio de Janeiro*

To my students, clients, friends, and family,
who have shared so much with me.
It is because of them
that this book has become a reality.
Thank you.

CONTENTS

Chapter 7
Master Job Applications: The Employer Screening Process   179

Chapter 8
Write Power Letters: The Great Door Openers   201

Chapter 9
Create a Confident You: The Finished Product   227

UNIT 3   MARKET   249

Chapter 10
Develop a Master Plan: The Self-Paced Schedule   251

Chapter 11
Land Interviews: A Marketing Game   261

PREFACE

I hear and I forget.
I see and I remember.
I do and I understand.
        —Confucius

HIRED! is the wholistic approach to job hunting, incorporating life planning into the job search process. It is comprehensive in scope but not difficult in practice. It is a practical text, not a scholarly tome. *HIRED!* is exercise-driven and filled with examples. The exercises build skills through doing. The examples provide understanding through seeing. The goal of *HIRED!* is to motivate you to become personally responsible for your life.

HIRED! is a practical how-to manual with a companion planner that provides the organization for job hunting and life planning. This planner, which is flexible and expandable, has a place for everything, allowing for lifelong use. It is the job-hunting/life-planning system that "goes and grows with you."

HIRED! examines your life. Its goal is **wholeness,** the bringing of balance and harmony into your four life zones: personal, social, professional, and financial. With the whole-life approach, you can backtrack from the future into the present and make reasoned decisions concerning your career and life directions. For example, today, as you market yourself for a specific job, you discover a new insight about yourself. Tomorrow, as you work on your job, you complete a noteworthy project. These insights and projects are recorded in your data file for future reference. Thus, *HIRED!* becomes an ongoing, continuous system that works for you throughout the years.

HIRED!'s four units, "Discover," "Package," "Market," and "Hired," are designed to feed on and interact with each other. Each unit builds on the one before it, allowing you to practice what you have learned in the preceding unit. Each unit is developed to build expression, inspiration, and direction.

The goals of "Discover" are **awareness** and **direction** (knowing what you want to do, what you have to offer, and where you want to go with your career life). As you complete the exercises in this unit, you will be motivated to move into the detailed work of the next unit.

The goals in "Package" are **expression** and **creation** (capturing your true essence on paper, in person, and through others). Completion of this unit prepares you for the action of Unit 3.

The goals of "Market" are **implementation** and **realization** (planning and executing the step-by-step job-hunting process). Once achieved, you will be on your way to realizing the career and life fulfillment goals presented in Unit 4.

The goals of "Hired" are **growth** and **harmony** (continuous learning and wholeness). Establishing balance and harmony throughout your life brings you back, full circle, to "Discover."

As you begin your journey into *HIRED!*, relax and enjoy the creative energy and the awareness found by doing the exercises. Apply the new knowledge and skills to all areas of your life. Then as you realize your dreams and experience the fulfillment of achievement, savor the wholeness of life.

My Creed

I do not choose to be a common man. It is my right to be uncommon, if I can. I seek opportunity, not security. I do not wish to be a kept citizen, humbled and dulled by having the state look after me. I want to take the calculated risk; to dream and to build, to fail and to succeed. I refuse to barter incentive for a dole. I prefer the challenges of life to the guaranteed existence; the thrill of fulfillment to the stale calm of utopia. I will not trade freedom for beneficence, nor my dignity for a handout. It is my heritage to think and act for myself, enjoy the benefit of my creations, and to face the world boldly and say, "This I have done." All this is what it means to be an American.

—Dean Alfange

H = HARMONY

Many do not know that we are here in this world to live in harmony.
—Dhammapada

Harmony brings wholeness to your life. Harmony, as defined by Webster, is the "consistent, orderly or pleasing arrangement of parts, forming a pleasingly consistent whole." Think of the finer things in life. Believe in the positives, the beautiful, the goodness of employers. Employers struggle with life just as you do. Reach for harmony through your imagination

I = IMAGINATION

Imagination is more important than knowledge.
—Albert Einstein

Imagination is the fuel for creativity. Napolean believed that imagination ruled the world. Imagination is the ability to create an idea or mental picture in your mind. All creations were first created in the mind. What you can create in your mind you can recreate in reality. Imagine yourself as already possessing all that you dream. Imagine finding the job and living the life you really want. Fulfillment of imagination begins with responsibility.

R = RESPONSIBILITY

. . . we are responsible for our own lives. Our behavior is a function of our decisions, not our conditions.
—Stephen R. Covey

Once you have imagined your life, it is then important to take **responsibility** for achieving it. Your mental creation will not come to fruition unless you take responsibility for your life and do the work of bringing it to fulfillment. Your life, happiness, and success are your responsibility only. Blaming others serves only one purpose: it keeps you from realizing your potential. Take responsibility for your life, your successes, and your failures.

E = ENTHUSIASM

Nothing great was ever achieved without enthusiasm.
—Emerson

Enthusiasm is a magic potion that spreads like morning sunshine, warming all it touches. John Paul Getty ranks enthusiasm "well ahead of business acumen, ambition, and even imagination." Enthusiasm puts a smile on your face, a spring in your walk. Knowing your dream and taking responsibility for it fuels your soul with the positive energy called enthusiasm. It will not be willpower or hard determination that achieves your dreams; it will be imagination, responsibility, and enthusiasm. Enthusiasm gives energy and direction.

D = DIRECTION

Be a "meaningful specific" not a "wandering generality."
—Zig Ziglar

Direction is the key to success. It's the guiding light that keeps you going. Direction provides you with decision-making tools. You can ask yourself, Does this action take me closer to or farther away from my goal? By staying with answers that take you closer to your goals, you will find your path quickly. Add $H + I + R + E + D$, and reach for all life has to offer.

HIRED's GOLDEN RULES

Always do your best.
Expect good things to happen.
Appreciate employers' needs and points of view.

SEVEN FACTORS AFFECTING THE JOB HUNT

Read each of the seven factors. In the column, indicate whether you believe this is a positive (+) or a negative (−) factor for you. In the space at the right, write specific steps you can take to improve all negative and positive factors.

Factor	±	Steps for Improving
1. Personal appearance		
2. Work history		
3. Health		
4. Personal situation		
5. Education		
6. Marketing ability		
7. Personal attitude and perception		

The factors listed above are presented in random order. The factor most critical to *you* during your job search may not be the most critical for another job hunter. For example, work history may be the negative factor for one job applicant, while education may be the critical element for another. Identify the factors that need improving in your job search, and then take specific steps to make the necessary improvements.

EXPANDING PERCEPTIONS

If you believe there are no jobs, few jobs, or abundant jobs, you're right.

What you believe to be true about the job-hunting process is true for you. Whether your belief is based on fact, hearsay, opinion, or the national news media (which is often sensationalism), the fact that you believe it to be true will affect all you do during your job hunt. As you begin your job hunt, it is important to look at how perceptions of the job market are formed. Perceptions limit and restrict imagination. Following are two exercises to demonstrate the point.

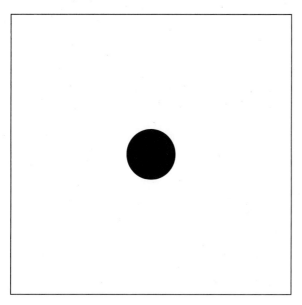

Exercise 1

What do you see in the box above? Write your answer in the blank box:

Exercise 2

Using only four straight lines, connect all four dots. Do not lift your pencil. Write what you have learned about this lesson in the blank box.

For answers to these exercises, turn to Appendix B on page 389.

**JOB HUNTING SUCCESS IS NOT A SECRET—JOB HUNTING
SUCCESS IS A SYSTEM**

The steps of the system feed on and interact with each other.
No one part stands alone. You stand in the center.
The system is:

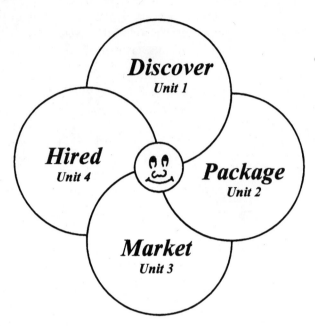

HIRED! AND ITS *COMPANION PLANNER*

HIRED! is a "system" and your *Companion Planner* is what makes the
system work. The *Planner* is flexible, expandable, and portable. It goes
and grows with you. It meets the needs you have for life planning and
job hunting. You will use it now, in the coming years, and for the rest of
your working life.

THE UNITS

HIRED! is divided into four units: "Discover," "Package," "Market," and
"Hired." Behind each unit are category dividers to keep the system
organized. As you use the *Companion Planner,* you may find it necessary
to add alphabetical (A–Z) or name dividers. For example, when there are
numerous employers, you will want to add name dividers in the
"Employer" section for each employer. This keeps the file organized and
makes it easier to use. Another example would be to add alphabetical
and/or name dividers in the "Network Records" section because your
network system has become large and complex.

You may find it necessary to expand into more than one notebook.
My system now comprises four notebooks, one for each unit. This has
allowed me to use the system efficiently and to keep it organized.

To make the *HIRED!* system work, a three-ring, two-inch notebook is required. Below is a diagram of the dividers necessary for each unit.

DISCOVER DIVIDERS

OTHER ACTIVITIES	EMPLOYERS	EDUCATION	PERSONAL	SELF-AWARENESS

PACKAGE DIVIDERS

LETTERS	APPLICATIONS	REFERENCES	RESUMES

MARKET DIVIDERS

EMPLOYER RECORDS	NETWORK RECORDS	INTERVIEW INFORMATION	ACTION PLAN

HIRED DIVIDERS

FINANCIAL MANAGEMENT	LIFE MANAGEMENT	CAREER MANAGEMENT

WORKING FORMS AND MASTER FORMS

The forms are designed to cover each topic thoroughly. There are sets of working forms and master forms. You should complete the working forms. **Do not write on the master forms.** They are provided so you can make more copies when needed.

The forms may be completed using pen, typewriter, or computer. You can create your own computer system by duplicating the forms. Be sure to include all the areas on each form since each form was specifically developed to provide a complete detailed record for you.

DO A COMPLETE JOB

You are encouraged to do a thorough and complete job on the first twelve forms that make up your data file. This is your history—your record of who you are. Take time. Complete all your assignments, filing in all the details now. There will never be a better time. The extra effort you put forth today will prove to be a great time saver in the future. So let's get started. Do the very best you can. You will be glad you did.

MASTER FORMS FOR THE *COMPANION PLANNER*

Following is a list of all the forms used for the *Companion Planner*. A master set of forms is included with the *Companion Planner*.

Unit Divider	Section Divider	Form No.	Form Description
DISCOVER	Personal	1	Vitals
DISCOVER	Personal	2	Other Names and Relatives
DISCOVER	Personal	3	Addresses
DISCOVER	Education	4	Education Summary
DISCOVER	Education	5	Education Course Record
DISCOVER	Education	6	Licenses and Certifications
DISCOVER	Employers	7	Employer Summary
DISCOVER	Employers	8	Employer Record
DISCOVER	Employers	9	Description by Job Title
DISCOVER	Other	10	Summary of Other Activities
DISCOVER	Other	11	Description by Activity
DISCOVER	Other	12	Miscellaneous Activities
PACKAGE	Resumes	13	Job Objective
PACKAGE	Resumes	14	Personal Check List
PACKAGE	Resumes	15	Historical Resume Draft (4 pages)
PACKAGE	Resumes	16	Combination Resume Draft (4 pages)
PACKAGE	References	17	Reference List
PACKAGE	References	18	Employment Verification Request (2 pages)
PACKAGE	References	19	Education Verification and Transcript Request
PACKAGE	References	20	Personal Reference Request
PACKAGE	References	21	Authorization to Release Information
PACKAGE	References	22	Reference Contact Record
PACKAGE	References	23	Draft Reference List
PACKAGE	Applications	24	Job Application (6 pages)
MARKET	Action Plan	25	Action Plan
MARKET	Action Plan	26	Monthly Planner
MARKET	Action Plan	27	Weekly Planner
MARKET	Network Records	28	Network Contact List
MARKET	Network Records	29	Network Contact Record
MARKET	Employer Records	30	Employer Contact Record (2 pages)
MARKET	Employer Records	31	Interview Self-Evaluation (2 pages)
MARKET	Employer Records	32	Employer Rating Matrix
HIRED	Career Management	33	Performance Review (2 pages)
HIRED	Career Management	34	
HIRED	Career Management	35	
HIRED	Career Management	36	
HIRED	Life Management	37	Goals—Long-Term and Short-Term (2 pages)
HIRED	Life Management	38	
HIRED	Financial Management	39	Budget Work Sheet
HIRED	Financial Management	40	Cash Flow Statement
HIRED	Financial Management	41	Assets and Liabilities
HIRED	Financial Management	42	Income and Expenses
HIRED	Financial Management	43	Job Search Expenses

ACKNOWLEDGMENTS

Grateful acknowledgment is made for permission to reproduce examples of student and client work throughout the text. Without these examples and the permission from the individuals involved, this text would not have been possible. In almost all cases, the names, places, and dates have been altered to protect the privacy of the individuals. In some instances, the examples are compilations. My students and clients have been the best teachers, and I will be forever in their debt.

I also wish to thank the following individuals:

- Judy Bowie, DeVry Institute of Technology; Earl Wilkie, Pennsylvania Institute of Technology; Marvin Copes, American Institute of Commerce; Carolyn Robbins, Denver Business Institute; and John Wiltbank, ECPI, for their insights.

- Professor Bern Wisner, Central Oregon Community College, who provided me with the opportunity to develop the Getting Hired class and the text for that class. Without Bern's belief in me and the class, this text would not exist.

- All my students and clients. Each one taught me new ways to job hunt, communicate better, teach, and live a fuller life.

- My encouraging and steadfast friends: Howard Becker, Ida Becker, Dee Berman, Velma Bond, Michele Hoppes-Daum, Arlene Deitz, Betty Fitzpatrick, Linda Galbraith, Frances Gnose, Ken Harman, Brian Hole, Beverlee Jackson, Jeanne Littleton, Josephine Manes, Alice McCullough, Jennifer Miller, Martin Morisette, Jo Powell, Terry Pridemore, Kathy Stahancyk, Elaine Thompson, and Robert E. Trappe.

- My wonderful, supporting husband, Marvin Harris, without whom the finishing touches of the text would not have come to fruition.

- Elizabeth Sugg, my editor at Prentice Hall; Kim Miller; and Linda Zuk, whose faith in the content of this volume made its publication possible.

DISCOVER

Thoroughly to know oneself, is above all art, for it is the highest art.
—Theologia Germanica

Awareness and **direction**—knowing what you want to do, where you want to go, and what you have to offer—are the goals of "Discover." Once awareness and direction are achieved, the job-hunting process can be carefully planned and implemented.

The exercises in this unit serve as a catalyst for reasoned career decision making. They are not intended to be a replacement for the comprehensive career and personality assessments provided by the college career education center or by other professionals.

"Discover" is an experience and an experiment into the known and unknown realms of your mind and background. In the beginning, it is carefree and speculative. You have fun, go with the flow, and are spontaneous and childlike. At the end, you come full circle (from the fanciful to the realistic, from dreams of your past to realities of your future) and arrive with a defined career direction and job objective.

In Chapter 1, "Know Thyself—A Self-Awareness Journey," you do exercises in a spontaneous manner and are not concerned about logic or results. Through these exercises, you find the hidden treasures buried in the unknown crevices of your mind, the clues to the meaning and direction of life. These gems are concealed in your dreams, aspirations, and desires. They are the jewels to your future. *Discover* yourself and the path to self-awareness.

In Chapter 2, "Capture the Past—A Data File That Goes and Grows with You," it's your job to uncover and record the details of the past. As you capture the past, you find the golden threads of life that bring fulfillment and satisfaction. These threads are woven and entwined throughout your life experiences. They are buried in your skills, abilities, and desires, and they illuminate the road to the future. *Discover* your past and the path to successful tomorrows.

In Chapter 3, "Explore Jobs and Employers—Work and Its Environment," you examine job functions and employer environments—the foundation for identifying fulfilling careers and suitable employers. You learn that jobs have futures and lead to fulfillment. You learn that employer environments are as important as the job itself. *Discover* the jobs and employers that best fit your needs and desires.

How much of what passes for grief in the world is really nothing more than regret?
—Elizabeth Forsythe Hailey

1

In Chapter 4, "Chart the Future—Goal Setting for Life," you identify long-term career and life goals. You set these goals into a master plan covering life's four zones: personal, social, professional, and financial. These goals take you to your job objective, your next "right" job. *Discover* your future and bring satisfaction and fulfillment and balance and harmony to your life.

As you travel the path to self-awareness, you walk through valleys and climb mountains of the known, unknown, unexpected, and unfamiliar. There are surprises and sudden twists in this journey. You search, explore, discover, and record the real and the surreal (your dreams, aspirations, and visions). You create a record for self-analysis and awareness. You come full circle from uncertainty to certainty with a career direction and your next job objective. You will arrive with confidence at the beginning of Unit 2, "Package."

As you uncover the truths of the past and the directions of the future, you will have either a quiet awakening or a sudden "aha" experience. Through the exercises in "Discover," you will find that you're pointed in the right direction or, more disturbingly, that you're traveling far afield from your true wants and desires. Whatever the case, rest assured that all your experiences establish a strong base for building the future you want, deserve, and can create. So relax, do each exercise, and allow the experience of each to build a crescendo of full awareness and understanding. *Discover* your direction for life.

Look within. Within is the foundation of good, and it will ever bubble up, if thou wilt ever dig.
—Marcus Aurelius

KNOW THYSELF
A Self-Awareness Journey

Life is either a daring adventure or it is nothing.
—Helen Keller

Recently I was talking to Janice who was in a career crisis. She was close to being fired and was considering walking off the job. The consequences of either event would be devestating. Everything was wrong, and she felt totally out of control.

I asked her questions designed to make her think: "Why are you in this job? Why do you work for this company? What was your major? Why this major? Why did you pick this school? What do *you* really want to do?"

Her replies were familiar. They went like this: "Well, I don't know. I really never thought about it. My boss suggested it."

Janice looked at me amazed. She had never thought about what she really wanted, what she liked, or what caused her present circumstances. She isn't unusual but very typical. Janice had listened to teachers, parents, bosses, and friends but had never taken time to think about or listen to herself. She had actually made all her life and career decisions by default, based solely on other people's ideas and circumstances.

After close examination, you, too, may find that you are living your life similar to Janice, by default. You may have never stopped to think for yourself. Now is the time to get to know yourself—to know what *you* enjoy, where *you* want to be, and with whom.

How do you get to know yourself? It's easy—take the phone off the hook, turn off the TV, and tell everyone to stay away. Then take paper and pencil and start working through the exercises in this chapter. Go back into your memory—back as far as you can go. Look for the good things in your life—the activities that made you feel good, that gave you a sense of achievement.

Begin today to know thyself. Begin today to think and to plan for yourself.

USING THE SELF-AWARENESS SECTION
OF THE *COMPANION PLANNER*

Follow the instructions for each exercise in Chapter 1, and then file the completed exercises in the SELF-AWARENESS section. Chapter 1 exercises include:

Exercise 1-1: What I Really Want to Do

Exercise 1-2: Childhood Dreams

Exercise 1-3: Twenty-Five Things I Love to Do

Exercise 1-4: Twelve Things I'm Good At

Exercise 1-5: My Weekend Retreat

Exercise 1-6: My Five Greatest Achievements

Exercise 1-7: Create the Future

Exercise 1-8: Putting It All Together

Exercise 1-9: A Perfect Job

Exercise 1-10: A Self-Assessment Summary

Exercise 1-11: Greener Pastures? A Reality Check

Exercise 1-12: Spontaneous Creations

If you do other self-awareness exercises, keep them here. It's the perfect place for them.

As the years go by, you may find it necessary to repeat these exercises. It is helpful and informative for you to compare the answers from a prior time to your current answers. So keep these exercises and any other ones for future reference.

If the SELF-AWARENESS section becomes large and cumbersome, you can add dividers for each exercise. Since these exercises are very personal, you may want to put this section in a separate notebook.

Good luck. Have fun. Enjoy discovering your "best" self.

Author's Note:
The exercises in this chapter serve as a catalyst for reasoned, career decision-making. They are not intended to be a replacement for the comprehensive career or personality assessments provided by college career education centers or by other professionals.

Despite several decades of research, the most efficient way to predict vocation choice is simply to ask the person what he wants to be.

—Dr. John T. Holland

Take a piece of paper and head it like the following example. Then begin writing as fast as you can. Write everything you can think of concerning the job you would really like. Don't censor your thoughts or writing. Don't be concerned with whether or not it seems possible. Just write about what you would really like to do.

Exercise 1-1 - What I Really Want to Do   September 7, 19xx

I wanted to be a singer—country-western music. I've enjoyed the music since I was young, still prefer country.

Writing was always a way to "get away," let feelings out that I otherwise kept hidden. Wanted to write books, but now I lean more toward poetry. Sometimes I can "hear" my poems as a song.

Teaching was a goal for many years, even up until about 10 years ago, until I discovered kids make me nervous. Perhaps I still could teach but the students would be different and the classroom would be different—music, poetry, adults eager to learn.

As a lawyer, I could help people like me, underprivileged, used women—tired of the system.

I still love country music. It speaks to me. What I really want to do is sing and write country music. Now if I can only combine my loves with my work...what a miracle that would be.

...we do not write in order to be understood; we write in order to understand.

—C. Day Lewis

Figure 1-1   What I Really Want to Do. Courtesy of a student

Dreams are the seedlings of realities.
—James Allen, *As a Man Thinketh*

Childhood dreams include both the dreams you held as a child and the dreams you hold as an adult. Childhood is your total past. First look at your early years, and then proceed to the present.

Grab a pencil and paper. Head the page like the example and begin writing. Don't worry about making sense; just write what comes to mind. It's as simple as that.

Exercise 1-2 - Childhood Dreams   *September 7, 19xx*

1. Fly like a bird
2. Be a teacher
3. Climb mountains
4. Help people
5. Be a missionary
6. Be a violinist
7. Play the piano
8. Get hired at Tek
9. Become an electronic assembler
10. Get promoted to buyer
11. Get promoted to purchasing agent
12. Be promoted ot purchasing manager
13. Become a travel writer
14. Become rich and famous
15. Travel the world (world traveler)
16.
17.
18.
19.
20.
21.

Step 1
List the dreams you had as a child. Play "When I grow up, I want to be . . ."

Step 2
List the jobs and promotions you once dreamed of and got. These jobs were once just dreams. Follow your work history.

Step 3
List your next dream promotions or jobs.

Step 4
List all current fantasy dream jobs, anything you would like to do—take the stops out. Don't worry about training requirements or whether the job is practical.

In the example, Debbie listed seven childhood dreams, her first important job and the promotions she earned. Her last three dreams are the jobs she wants in the future.

Are you still having dreams of things you want to be? I hope so. Have fun. Dream big!

Figure 1-2   Childhood Dreams.

> **To be successful, you must love what you do.**
> **—Dottie Walters**

One day I asked students to share what they had written for this exercise. Picking students and numbers at random I asked Betty what she had listed for number three. Betty looked a little sheepish but replied, "This is embarrassing. I wrote, 'making love to my husband.'"

As you can see, your list can cover all the activities you love. These are your private thoughts, so write them the way life really is. Don't try to write what you think is important or what might impress someone else, just write all the things you enjoy doing. Cover all areas of your life.

Exercise 1-3 - 25 Things I Love to Do   September 7, 19xx

1. Write poetry
2. Read science fiction
3. Hike in the woods
4. Watch the ocean/walk on the beach
5. Build my nest egg
6. Organize parties/conventions
7. Sing with the radio/tapes
8. Tell jokes and stories
9. Visit friends
10. Go dancing
11. Eat pizza
12. Play Nintendo
13. Shop when I have money
14. Walk in the snow
15. Help other people
16. Fish in the ocean
17. Drive fast
18. Watch snow falling
19. Sleep in
20. Cuddle the cat
21. Fight the "system" and win
22. Improve the environment
23. Play games
24. Go to school
25. Sit in the park and watch the ducks

I found this exercise very ...

Grab a piece of paper and head it like the example. It doesn't matter what you like to do, why you like doing it, or how minor or trivial it seems to be—just write it down.

Step 1

Begin writing your random thoughts. Write as fast as you can, and don't stop until you have listed twenty-five things you love to do. If you think of more, make the list longer; but record at least twenty-five. Don't rank these activities in order of preference. Just write as fast as you can.

The example shows a variety of activities. There's no relevant factor other than that they are things Carl enjoys and loves doing.

Step 2

Write your feelings about this exercise.

Figure 1-3 Twenty-Five Things I Love to Do. Courtesy of a student

The first work of the Artist is herself.
—Laurence G. Boldt, *ZEN and the Art of Making a Living*

Grab a piece of paper and head it like the example. Your goal is to make a list of things you do well. Do not censor your thoughts. Write down everything that you do well.

Step 1
List twelve things you are good at. List more if possible—as many as you can think of—but no less than twelve.

If you have difficulty coming up with this list, ask a friend, a loved one, a teacher, or your boss. But first make an effort to do it on your own.

Step 2
Write your feelings about this exercise.

Exercise 1-4 - 12 Things I'm Good At   September 7, 19xx

1. Talking   I found this exercise ...

2. Telling jokes and stories

3. Dancing

4. Listening

5. Sharing

6. Synthesizing ideas/concepts

7. Writing

8. Organizing things, people, systems

9. Photography

10. Repairing cars

11. Thinking up ideas/developing them

12. Eating fast

Don't be modest or shy. Brag a little!

Figure 1-4   Twelve Things I'm Good At.

Relationships are everything.
—Anthony Robbins

Imagine you are having a weekend retreat at your favorite place. Your budget is unlimited; your agenda is whatever you desire. You can invite twelve guests, and everyone wants to come. Who will you invite? Your guests can be anyone—dead or alive, real or imaginary, famous or infamous. They can be great leaders, influential people, personal friends, fictional characters.

Head up a page like the one below. Then begin listing your guests.

Step 1
List your twelve guests.

Step 2
Now tell me WHY. List one reason why you invited each guest.

Exercise 1-5 - My Weekend Retreat	September 7, 19xx
1. Stephen King	1. & 2. I'm fascinated with their books. Interested in how they get ideas.
2. Dean Koontz	
3. My son Rich	3. Loves to do comedy/entertaining
4. Susie M.	4. My Italian friend — fascinating lady!
5. Rusty R.	5. & 6. My best friends. Lots of fun to be around. Funny, intelligent, motivated.
6. Norma G.	
7. Garth Brooks	7. & 8. Country singers. I love their music because it touches my soul.
8. Reba McIntyre	
9. Buddha	9. Want to know what he thinks of the world today.
10. Mr. "X"	10. The mystery lover — every retreat needs romance.
11. My father	11. I'd like to get to know him.
12. Garfield	12. I love cats and he would add a lot of humor and mischief to the weekend.

Be wild.
Use your imagination.
Make it a real party. Have a great weekend.

Figure 1-5   My Weekend Retreat. Courtesy of a student

The splendid achievements of the intellect, like the soul, are everlasting.
                                                                —Sallust

What is an achievement? It's an activity that gave you a sense of pride, a feeling of fulfillment. Where do achievements come from? Everywhere! Look for achievements at home, at school, on the job, in a hobby, or in a club or organization.

Step 1
Describe five accomplishments that you feel good about.

Include the value or benefit in your description; for example, improved the environment, helped the homeless, saved money, protected lives, improved morale.

If you have worked, look for work experiences that gave you real satisfaction. Concentrate on specific projects. Spend some time on writing specific results. Include percentages, numbers, dollars, or dates. These provide real meaning and credibility.

If you have not worked, look for achievements from home, school, and community activities. Use action verbs; be explicit. Write what you did and put in the details.

This is no time to be bashful. Don't take accomplishments for granted.

Step 2
Record your feelings about this exercise.

Exercise 1-6 - My 5 Greatest Achievements   September 7, 19XX

1. I organized 2 dances for the high school choir. Each raised nearly $4,500.

2. Wrote and circulated a petition for stop sign on unsafe corner. After lots of debate, the city installed sign. There hasn't been an accident since it was installed (over 3 years).

3. As partner with brother, age 18, bought and completely remodeled an old house (500 square-foot addition). Replaced all old roofing, siding, flooring, wiring, plumbing, sheetrock, and windows. Completed landscaping, including a new sidewalk and lawn. All financial planning and work, except sheetrocking, was done by us with no previous experience. Sold house for sizable profit.

4. Organized fund-raising projects that allowed construction of the bicentennial amphitheater in City Park.

5. Over a period of 6 years, sold $5,000 in magazine subscriptions for Music Boosters. Top salesperson in Boosters' history.

I'm feeling rather...

Figure 1-6   **My Five Greatest Achievements.** Courtesy of a student

Begin with the person you really want to become.

This exercise is visionary, so find a place where you can be alone. Clear your mind of everything. Relax.

You're going away on a long trip and will probably never be able to return. It's an adventure you've chosen. You're excited but know you will miss everyone and they will miss you. In your mind's eye, attend your "going away" party five years from today.

Many people have come to honor you, to express feelings of love and appreciation for your life. See the faces of loved ones, friends, neighbors, and work associates as they join the party. Listen to what they say about you. Feel their excitement, sorrow, feelings, loss. Feel their joy for having known you.

The party will feature six speakers, people who have come to honor you. The speakers may be people you know now or plan to know in the future.

- The first speaker is a family member.

- The second speaker is a friend, someone who can provide a sense of who you are as a person.

- The third speaker is someone from your work or profession.

- The fourth speaker is your banker or financial planner.

- The fifth speaker is your doctor.

- The sixth speaker is a neighbor or community member, someone who can talk about the service you have given to your community.

Ask yourself: If I were to leave five years from today, what would I want said about me and my accomplishments?

Exercise 1-7 - Create the Future - My "Going Away" Party   _September 7, 19xx_

Speaker # 1: Family Member

My son Rich would speak. He would say that I was there for my children in spirit, if not physically. That I would listen to their hopes, dreams, and problems. They could call me or come over at any time of the night or day and I was never too busy to listen. I encouraged them to follow their dreams and to be the best they could be. I taught them to be honest and to stand up for what they believed in. I taught them ...

Speaker #2: Friend

My best friend Rusty would say that I was funny. I could be depended on to listen and offer comments but was never judgmental. I was there to help whenever and in whatever way I could. I treated my friends as members of my family. I was ...

Speaker #3: Work Associate

My coworker Susie would say that I was dedicated and professional. I performed my duties quickly and competently. I shared my job knowledge with other workers and was a patient teacher. I treated customers and employees with respect and friendliness. I explained the importance of doing a job correctly, rather than yelling at people's mistakes. I was always available ...

Figure 1-7   My "Going Away" Party. Courtesy of a student

What would I have wanted to accomplish? What would I like each of these speakers to say about me and my life? What kind of spouse, parent, or child would I like their words to reflect? What kind of friend was I? What kind of employee or business associate was I? How did I manage my finances? What kind of physical and mental condition did I keep?

What character would you like each to have seen in you? What contributions and achievements would you want each to remember? Look carefully at the people around you. What difference did you make in each one's life? What legacy did you leave behind?

These speakers are in essence creating the person you want to become. When you reread what each has said, make sure that they have said the words that describe the person you really want to be, not necessarily the person who exists today. You can become whatever you want to be in this exercise.

This exercise increases your personal understanding of what's really important to you in life. So take plenty of time. Go back over what you've written several days later and add or change what the speakers say.

The example format provides you with the number of replies you need. You will likely use several pages.

In this exercise, you are to leave the bad behind and take only the good with you. The difficulty in forgetting the negative past is that we're not used to doing it. We're used to remembering mistakes and hardships instead of successes and achievements. There are enough people out there reminding you of your failures; you do not need to be one of them.

Now take a few minutes and several sheets of paper and being writing. Leave a three-inch column at the right.

Exercise 1-8 - Create the Future - My "Going Away" Party   _September 7, 19xx_

Speaker # 4: Banker

My banker would say that when he first met me, I kept control of my money and managed to save for emergencies. I gave what I could to charities to help the less fortunate than I. He would then go on and tell you how I began to save and manage my money more. That I had accumulated a large investment portfolio while still giving generously to many worthwhile causes. He would tell you ...

Speaker #5: Doctor

My doctor would tell you that when I first came to her office I was overweight, a nervous wreck, and a true physical disaster. But she would go on to tell you that I learned to take care of myself and my body. That I followed a regular program of exercise and ate balanced meals. She would tell you that I stopped smoking and had prolonged my life by several years ...

Speaker #6: Neighbor or Community Member

My neighbor would speak of my role as a promoter of tenants' rights. My work as the president of the Tenants' Action Committee and organizer of our neighborhood watch program. He would say that I was active in ...

Capture the real you, the one you want to become.

Figure I-8   My "Going Away" Party. Courtesy of a student

The exercises you have just completed are only a sample of what you can do in self-awareness and in getting to know yourself. The following exercise is to help you put it together. Head one sheet of paper like the following example. Divide the page into six blocks as shown.

Step 1

Review Exercise 1-2, "Childhood Dreams." Circle all dreams you would enjoy doing in your work. Record them in the right-hand column. Now select three to five of your favorite dreams and record them in block 1 on your sheet of paper.

Step 2

Review Exercise 1-3, "Twenty-five Things I Love to Do." Identify and circle three to five activities you want to incorporate into your work. Record them in block 2.

Step 3

Review Exercise 1-4, "Things I'm Good At." Circle five things that you are good at and would like to do at work. Choose items that you really enjoy. Record these in block 3.

Step 4

Review Exercise 1-5, "My Weekend Retreat." Consider the type of people you wish to be around. What are their personal characteristics? Ages? Education? Personalities? Record these in block 4.

Step 5

Review Exercise 1-6, "My Five Greatest Achievements." Circle skill words, for example, *organized, wrote, developed*. Choose the five skills you enjoy most and record them in block 5.

Step 6

Review Exercise 1-7, "Create the Future." Circle the personal qualities and values you want to incorporate in your work. For example: "She always had time to give a helping hand." Record five characteristics or values in block 6.

Exercise 1-9 - Putting It All Together   September 7, 19xx

Ex 1-2. Dream jobs
Writer
Singer
Lawyer
Dance club owner
General manager of motel or resort

Ex 1-3. Things I Love To Do
Read
Go to school
Fight the "system"
Help other people
Walk on the beach

Ex 1-4. Skills I'm Good At
Teaching/training
Persuading people
Finances
Helping people
My job (front desk)

Ex 1-5. Type of People I Enjoy
Ages 30 to 50
Open
Funny/musically inclined
Intelligent
Wise in the ways of the world

Ex 1-6. Skills from Achievements
Listening
Organizing
Writing
Financial planning
Selling

Ex 1-7. Values Important to Me
Understanding
Honesty
Sense of humor
Dedicated to helping others
Good stewards of finances/resources

Figure 1-9 Putting It All Together. Courtesy of a student

Choose a job you love and you will never have to work a day in your life.
—Confucius

Step 1
Head a page like the example.

Step 2
Review Exercise 1-8, "Putting It All Together." Then list five jobs that combine all or most of the key elements you listed in Exercise 1-8. These jobs should be ones that you are qualified to apply for today.

If you have difficulty with this part, brainstorm with friends. Identify at least five jobs that incorporate the things you enjoy doing most.

Step 3
List 5 jobs that would be appropriate for you in five years. Again, use the help of friends or family to identify job ideas. Be creative in your answers. Ask several friends. No suggestion should be ruled out.

Step 4
Write a description of your next job, the perfect job for you, and another description of an appropriate job you could hold five years from now. Incorporate the ideas listed in Exercise 1-8, and tie them to one of the perfect jobs you identified.

Answer these questions: (1) What is my job title? (2) What skills do I use? (3) What is my boss like? (4) What is the geographic location? (5) What is the management style? (6) What kind of people do I work with? (7) What is the office, plant, environment like?

Exercise 1-9 - The Perfect Jobs for Me   September 7, 19xx

Today

1. Front desk manager
2. Western singer
3. Poetry writer
4. Assistant manager of motel
5. Band organizer/manager

5 Years from Now

1. Entertainment lawyer
2. Famous country singer
3. Dance club owner
4. General manager of large resort
5. Owner of large resort

General Job Description—Today

Assistant manager of large motel/resort area overseeing all phases of operations. Today it is in central Oregon, a mountain retreat. I see Sunriver, the Inn of the Seventh Mountain, Black Butte, or the Riverhouse as a possibility. I train and teach my staff how to help other people, provide quality service ...

General Job Description—5 Years from Now

General manager for a large resort on the Oregon or California coast. This resort will feature big-name entertainment groups whose bookings I am personally involved in. The management team is really a team—highly motivated, energetic, fun, intelligent, and wise in the ways of the world, particularly the business world ...

Figure 1-10   **The Perfect Job.** Courtesy of a student

Describe your dream job. Begin writing now.

Resolve to be thyself, and know that he who finds himself loses his misery.
—Coventry Patmore

Use the information you developed in this chapter to complete the following questions. Write your answers here in the text or use notebook paper and file behind the SELF-ASSESSMENT divider.

1. My education is strongest in these areas:

_____

_____

_____

2. The skills and knowledge I possess are in these areas:

_____

_____

_____

3. Five things I enjoy and do best are:

_____

_____

_____

4. I would like to have a boss like:

_____

_____

_____

5. The perfect work environment and conditions for me are:

_____

_____

_____

6. My short-term goals are:
    Example A: Full-time career opportunity in the retail management field.
    Example B: Part-time sales position with flexible working hours to pay for college.

    _____

    _____

    _____

7.   My long-term job goal is:

    _____

    _____

    _____

    _____

Do what you can with what you have, where you are.
—Theodore Roosevelt

This exercise is designed for those individuals who are currently employed and are considering changing jobs, careers, or employers. The following questions are to stimulate your thinking.

- Why do you want to make a change?

- What do you want to change?

- How do you plan on making these changes?

- Do you really need to change your job, career, or employer to achieve what you really want?

- What's the *real* problem? Is it you? How's your attitude? Can you see the situation from your boss's viewpoint?

Step 1
Write whatever thoughts you have. There are no right or wrong answers here. Capture your feelings, your thoughts.

Step 2
Answer the following questions:

- Is the WHY strong enough to motivate me to action?

- Is the HOW detailed enough to get me going?

- Are there real problems, or am I the problem? Problems often follow the person. Can you make changes without jumping ship?

Seriously consider all these questions. Now write . . .

Exercise 1-11 - Greener Pastures   September 7, 19xx
_____

I want to make these changes because . . .

In order to make these changes I need to do . . .

As I write this, I'm beginning to realize . . .

Figure 1-11   Greener Pastures?

Spontaneous painting and modeling are ways of channeling a 'force' which can change a person's attitude and hence his personal outlook and behavior. . . . [It] can be the most direct expression of your unconscious world which lies buried beneath our daily actions and which erupts in symbolism of our dreams and fantasies.

—E. M. Lyddiatt, *Spontaneous Painting and Modeling*

What are "spontaneous creations"? They are creativeness in art, whether in writing, dancing, drawing, or using color. They are a means of seeing and expressing yourself in a very different way.

There are no rules here. Your creation can be realistic or abstract. Don't be self-conscious; most of us operate with the artistic ability of a ten-year-old. Do whatever feels right for you. Take as much time as you need to complete the picture. If you're having difficulty starting, pick up a color and begin. Once started, it will flow to completion.

Step 1
Gather the materials—one sheet of $8\frac{1}{2}$-by-11-inch white paper (card stock is best) and twelve colored markers. (If these are not available, a box of crayons will suffice.)

Step 2
Imagine yourself as a color or colors; now spontaneously create yourself on paper.

Step 3
After completing the picture, list each color in the sequence used. If you used only one color, your job is easy. The last color on your list should be white. Whether you were aware of it or not, you used white unless all the white was covered with color.

Step 4
Next write several descriptive words for each color describing what the color means to you.

Figure 1-12   Realistic Creation. Courtesy of a client

Step 5

Now write a short description of what the picture means to you. Concentrate on the picture as a whole.

Step 6

Finally, share the picture in a group. This works best with four other "artists." Take turns having each tell the order of the colors and what they mean. Explain how the picture came into being. Share what the picture as a whole means to you. Then ask the others in the group to make comments and share what they see and experience. Remember, this is your picture; take the words of others into consideration. However, it's not necessary to incorporate their interpretation into your picture, although many of the comments will be meaningful and helpful. Record relevant comments.

Step 7

File this picture in your notebook. You will want to refer back to it over time. As times passes, you will be surprised by what you really captured on paper.

Here are some of the thoughts the client in Figure 1-12 wrote about his picture:

Colors

Black—heavy, hiding, defeat, sad, weight

Brown—warm, safe, secure

Yellow—light, happy, smart, glowing

Red—sharp, angry, fire

White—empty space

An overweight, caring man—arms wide to embrace . . . smart and sharp, some inner anger, with base in heavy, worldly defeat, facts—attitudes.

Here is what the student in Figure 1-13 discovered in her picture:

Colors

Blue—for dreaming
Green—for growing
White—for uncomfortable space
Reversed OK
Blue —for sky or sea
Green—for growing things
Undulating lines . . . ??

Another student commented, ". . . appears scattered, but trying to pull things together."

Figure 1-13 Abstract Creation. Courtesy of a student

The picture you paint is like a parable. Its meanings are many . . . its interpretations are vast. Only you can decide its truths.

CAPTURE THE PAST
A Data File That Goes and Grows with You

Nothing changes more consistently than the past; for the past that influences our lives consists, not of what actually happened, but of what men believed happened.

—Gerald White Johnson, *American Heroes and Hero Worship*

A few years ago I made a record of all my past experiences. As I searched my memory and files, I was amazed at how much I had forgotten. I was also surprised by the amount and variety of my experiences. Even now, I'm surprised when reviewing my file.

I've found it to be an exciting experience to review and record one's past. It is encouraging to relive life and realize what you have achieved. For the job hunt it's helpful and critical to have a complete and accurate record, because one really does forget so much.

How do you begin to record your past? There really isn't any mystery to it. You simply start at the beginning and systematically travel through each year, noting your activities.

Begin preparing for your future today. Capture the best and brightest experiences in your past. It's truly an adventure in history.

Start by completing all the forms and compiling your own data file record.

It is easier to capture your past now than to wait until you're under the gun of job hunting. Complete the information today and update it annually or each time you begin a new job hunt or think about starting one.

The forms may be handwritten, typed, or computer generated.

The following forms and records are kept in the PERSONAL section of the *Companion Planner:*

- Form 1: Vitals
  This form captures basic vital information. It provides quick access to data that may be required during your job search.

- Form 2: Other Names and Relatives
  Even though it may seem rather ridiculous to maintain this type of information for your job hunt, complete it anyway. You never know when you might need it.

- Form 3: Address Record
  A list of all addresses for the past fifteen years can be useful for many activities: job, credit card, and loan applications. It's smart to keep it up to date.

- Other Documents
  You may choose to file copies of other important documents in this section. Keep your originals in a safe place. Examples of documents you may wish to include are:

  Birth certificate
  Social Security card
  Military discharge papers
  Alien status card
  Work permit

Some of the information requested may seem unimportant or frivolous. But there are job applications and requests from employers for such data. For example, it's required information for government top security positions. You may think you'll never work in such a position, but life moves in strange ways. Complete all the information to the best of your ability. It won't be any easier later.

It's not where you've been but where you're going that counts.
—Unknown

Complete the forms, filling in all information that's applicable to your situation. The forms may be handwritten, typed, or computer generated. Then file them behind the Personal divider in the DISCOVER section of your *Companion Planner*. Let's get started.

STEP I: COMPLETE FORM I, VITALS

Fill in your complete name. Write in your Social Security number. Fill in your date and place of birth.

Check the appropriate box and complete the portion that follows if you are a citizen by naturalization.

Complete the "If Alien" portion only if you were not born in the United States.

Fill in any military service information.

VITALS

Name (Last, First, Middle) Haverstall, Henry James	Social Security Number 999-87-8899
Date of Birth 06/29/64	Place of Birth (City, County, State, Country) Eugene, Lane County, Oregon United States of America

If U.S. CITIZEN: By Birth **X**   By Naturalization __

Derivative	Alien Registration Number
Date	Petition Number
Certificate Number	Date
Place	Certification Number
	Place

If ALIEN, Indicate:

Alien Registration Number	Present Citizenship
Date of Entry	Port of Entry

MILITARY SERVICE (Past or Present)

Serial Number	Branch	Dates (From - To)
540-06-5555	U.S. Marines	4/25/83 - 4/25/86

© 1995 Harris Espérance Incorporated   Form 1/95

Figure 2-1   FORM I, Vitals

STEP 2: COMPLETE FORM 2, OTHER NAMES/RELATIVES

Self esteem comes from within, not from without.
—Unknown

This form allows you to maintain a file of the names you have used and the names, addresses, and birth dates of relatives. This may seem unimportant, but if you were to complete a job application for a top security position with the government, this information would be required. It is a lot easier to begin today to acquire this information than to wait until you need it.

OTHER NAMES
Include names from birth, marriages, and other name changes. List dates each was used.

Dates	Names
01/31/43 - 09/24/61	Ann Marie Jones
09/24/64 - 06/30/83	Ann Marie Davidson
06/30/83 -	Ann Marie Conley

RELATIVES
List the following relatives: parents, stepparents, spouse, divorced spouse(s), children stepchildren, brothers, sisters, stepbrothers, stepsisters, father- and mother-in-law.

Relationship	Full Name	Date of Birth	Address/Telephone
Father	William Dale Jones	06/23/11 06/24/39 Married 05/27/90 Married	1689 Elm Drive Springfield, OR 97477 (503) 555-7963
Mother	Victoria Cecilia Watts-Jones	04/29/18 06/24/39 Married 06/12/87-Died	Deceased
Stepmother	Jane (Lawton) Jones	07/24/29 05/27/90 Married	1689 Elm Drive Springfield, OR 97477 (503) 555-6428
Former Spouse	Raymond D. Davidson	06/14/33	2250 Filbert Drive Stamps, AR 71860 (501) 555-8172
Spouse	James R. Conley	11/27/37	265 Knowledge Sumter, SC 29150 (803) 555-4368
Brother	Curtis V. Jones	07/05/40	636 SE 43rd Avenue Syracuse, NY 13206 (315) 555-9056
Brother	Robert L. Jones	07/03/44	P O Box 1937 Fort Bragg, CA 95437 (707) 555-6073

© 1995 Harris Espérance Incorporated   Form 2/95

Figure 2-2 FORM 2, Other Names

Other Names
Include your:

- Birth name
- Maiden name
- Names by former marriages
- Other name changes

Relatives
List:

- Parents
- Stepparents
- Spouse
- Former spouse(s)
- Children
- Stepchildren
- Brothers
- Sisters
- Stepbrothers
- Stepsisters
- Father-in-law
- Mother-in-law

Fill in all information. Use additional pages if necessary.

STEP 3: COMPLETE FORM 3, ADDRESSES

Think globally; act locally.
—Unknown

Old addresses may seem unimportant at this time; but if you were to apply for a top security position with the government, you would be required to provide them. It is far easier to maintain an address record beginning now than to go back and rebuild one. You may not think you'll ever need old addresses, but you never know what the future may hold. This information is also useful when completing credit and home mortgage applications.

List all addresses for the past fifteen years. Record the oldest address first and proceed to your current address.

Complete the form to the best of your ability. But don't spend too much time on this form now; there's a lot more work ahead of you. If you get hung up on an old address, move on.

ADDRESSES

Page __ of __

List all addresses for the past 15 years.
Record the oldest address first and proceed to your current address.

Dates	Street/Mailing Addresses	City	State	Zip	Telephone
02/05/61	1351 South 3rd Street	Fort Worth	TX	76101	(817) 555-6498
09/10/80	43 South 10 Place	Dallas	TX	75006	(214) 555-7651
11/19/84	3387 Bear Creek Road	Decatur	GA	30035	(404) 555-3478
06/21/91	666 South 14th Street	Dayton	OH	14203	(513) 555-3892

Form 3/95

Figure 2-3 FORM 3, Addresses

Reality is a puzzle each of us puts together.
—Genie Laborde, *Influencing with Integrity*

You may choose to keep copies of your birth certificate, Social Security card, work permit, alien status card, and other personal documents in your notebook. Make photocopies of the originals to file here. Keep originals in a safe place at home or in a safe-deposit box at a bank.

File these documents behind the Personal divider in the DISCOVER section of your *Companion Planner.*

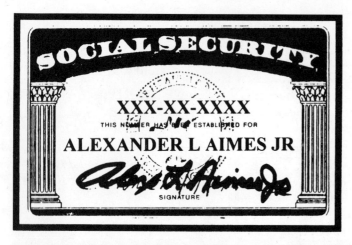

Figure 2-4   Personal Documents

Education is the best provision for old age.
—Aristotle

Having a detailed record of all your educational experiences will help you over the years as you analyze your career directions, loves, and experiences. Getting the information on paper, in an organized system, will prove valuable. Take the time to get the details now. It's amazing how often you will use your record for a variety of tasks. For example, you may want to review your college records when you're writing a resume. These records serve as a "tickler" (reminder) for the mind.

The forms may be handwritten, typed, or computer generated. The following forms make up the EDUCATION section of the *Companion Planner.*

- Form 4: Education Summary
  Record all schools attended in chronological order. Include kindergarten, grade school, high school, colleges, trade school, military, and vocational schools.

  Also include: training provided by employers, educational workshops and seminars and any other training provided by recognized training or educational institutions.

- Form 5: Education Detail Record
  Complete a detailed form for each school or training institution.

- Form 6: Licenses and Certificates
  All licenses or certificates should be listed here. Keep a photocopy of each.

- Other Documents
  You may choose to file *copies* of other important documents in this section. Some of the possible documents are:

  High school transcripts, diplomas and report cards
  College transcripts and diplomas
  Trade school or business school transcripts, diplomas, certificates of completion
  Military school records
  Seminar or course certificates
  Class syllabi
  Scholarship awards
  Extracurricular activities
  Special recognitions (news articles, certificates of appreciation, etc.)

- INDIVIDUAL EDUCATION Dividers
  If the detail in this section becomes cumbersome, add dividers for each school. This will make it easier to handle and to use.

I use the word *gather* because that's probably exactly what you'll need to do, since most of us have odds and ends of educational history stored in sundry places. This exercise organizes all your educational experiences and stores it for you in a convenient spot. The EDUCATION section of your *Companion Planner* contains Form 4, Education Summary; Form 5, Education— Detailed Record; and Form 6, Licenses and Certifications. When you've completed the forms, file them behind the EDUCATION divider in the DISCOVER section.

EDUCATION SUMMARY
List all schools attended in chronological order. Begin with kindergarten or preschool.

Dates Attended	School Name	Mailing Address City State Zip	Type of School Course of study
09/69 – 06/70	Green Valley Preschool	Post Office Box 894 Yardley, PA 19067	Kindergarten General Studies
09/71 – 06/75	Griffen Elementary School	145 Georgia Street Belmont, MA 02178	1st through 4th General Studies
09/75 – 06/79	Washington Middle School	1993 Fieldmont Road Belmont, MA 02178	5th through 8th General Studies
09/79 – 06/83	Crook County High School	East First and Knowledge Streets Prineville, OR 97754	9th through 12th College Prep.
09/83 – 06/85	Central Oregon Community College	2600 NW College Way Bend, OR 97701-4998	Community College AA Business Admin.
09/85 – 06/88	University of Washington	Seattle, WA 98103	University B.S. Business Admin.
07/88 – 10/90	U.S. Air Force Military School		Military
11/90 – 12/90	Dale Carnegie & Assoc. Garden City, NY 11530	Presented in Eugene, OR 97401 By Mr. Art Chevez	Effective Speaking and Human Relations

© 1995 Harris Espérance Incorporated   Form 4/95

Figure 2-5   FORM 4, Education Summary

STEP 1: COMPLETE FORM 4, EDUCATION SUMMARY

Record schools attended in chronological order. Include all schooling:

- Kindergarten
- Grade Schools
- High Schools
- Colleges
- Trade Schools
- Military Schools
- Vocational Schools

Also include:

- Company training programs
- Community college classes
- Training provided by recognized training or educational institutions
- Other educational workshops and seminars

Include training provided by employers.

STEP 2: COMPLETE FORM 5 FOR HIGH SCHOOL EDUCATION

Begin with the last high school you attended, whether or not you graduated. Complete the form to the best of your ability.

File copies of your transcript and diploma with this form. Any special recognitions, scholarships, etc., that you received can also be filed here.

<table>
<tr><td colspan="2" align="center">EDUCATION — DETAILED RECORD
Attach copies of support documents: diploma, transcript, certificates, awards.</td></tr>
<tr><td colspan="2">Name of School or Organization
Springfield Senior High School</td></tr>
<tr><td>Address
875 North Seventh Street, Springfield, OR 97477</td><td>Telephone
(503) 555-1263</td></tr>
<tr><td>Type of Degree
General Studies/ College Preparatory</td><td>Date Earned
06/07/91</td></tr>
<tr><td colspan="2">Grade Point Average 3.41   Class Size 260   Class Rank Top 10%</td></tr>
<tr><td colspan="2">Key Personnel

Name with Courtesy Title   Job Title   Address/Location   Telephone Number
Ms. Leona James   Principal   Same as above
Mr. Dean W. Lopez   Assistant Principal   "   "   "</td></tr>
<tr><td colspan="2">Key Courses

See transcript
       Mechanical Drawing, Bookkeeping 1, Typing 1, Journalism, Volleyball</td></tr>
<tr><td colspan="2">Special Awards/Achievements

•   Received full-ride athletic scholarship

•   Voted Most Valuable Player and Player of the Year in State AAA High School Volleyball championship playoffs</td></tr>
<tr><td colspan="2">Clubs/Other Activities

•   Student body treasurer, senior year

•   Yearbook staff and sports editor</td></tr>
<tr><td>© 1995 Harris Espérance Incorporated</td><td align="right">Form 5/95</td></tr>
</table>

Figure 2-6   FORM 5, High School Education

Record the name, address, and phone number of the school, the type of degree, and the date earned.

Record key personnel. Be sure to spell each name correctly.

List your grade point average, class size, and ranking.

List key courses.

Record all awards and achievements.

Include extracurricular activities, such as clubs or sports. This may include paid employment as well.

Make a complete record. Use as many pages or forms as necessary.

STEP 3: COMPLETE FORM 5 FOR COLLEGE EDUCATION

Next complete a Form 5 for each college, trade, or business school you've attended. Begin with the current or last school you attended.

File copies of your transcript, diploma, and certificates of completion with this form.

Fill in all the information to make a complete record. Use as many pages or forms as necessary.

EDUCATION — DETAILED RECORD
Attach copies of support documents: diploma, transcript, certificates, awards.

Name of School or Organization
The University of Wyoming

Address 3414 University Station, Laramie, WY 82071	**Telephone** (307) 555-9167
Type of Degree Bachelor of Science—Broadcasting major	**Date Earned** 12/20/xx

Grade Point Average 2.81 Major: 3.18	**Class Size**	**Class Rank**

Key Personnel

Name with Courtesy Title	Job Title Address/Location	Telephone Number
Mr. Charles Evans	Head Coach Women's Basketball, U of W	(307) 555-9155
Dr. Joyce McDonald	Intercollegiate Athletics/Academic Counselor, U of W	(307) 555-9166

Key Courses
See transcripts

Special Awards/Achievements
- Achieved all-time career leading rebounder and scorer for U of W
- Nominated for Kodiak All-American Basketball Team
- Selected 4 times for the High Country Athletic All-Conference First Team
- Chosen 2 times for a Converse All-American College Basketball Team (84, 86)
- Received a NCAA Sixth Year Grant to complete college education
- Played professionally overseas (Luxembourg) for 1 year while earning degree.
- Voted Player of the Year. Averaged 29 points per game.
- Team won country championship. (87-88)

Clubs/Other Activities
- In 1988, narrated video recruiting tape for the University of Wyoming women's basketball team. Assisted in script creation and advised on production. Received many compliments from viewers. Comments from letters of recommendation referring to tape include "Great presence on camera," and "Her voice, the accent and tone are what we in the general public have learned to expect from the electronic media." Tape still being used for recruiting.
- Hosted a University of Wyoming television production for the 1989 NCAA ski championships in Jackson Hole, Wyoming. Conducted live interviews of skiers and organizational sponsors. Updated competition results daily on live broadcasts.
- Anchored weather and sports sections of student television news broadcasts.
- Was floor director for the television productions of the Cowboy coaches shows (the Voice of the Wyoming Cowboys) for two years.
- Set up and operated dollies, camera mounting heads, and related equipment for network broadcasting. Covered football and basketball games. Assisted camera operators in acquiring the "perfect" shot.

© 1995 Harris Espérance Incorporated   Form 5/95

Figure 2-7 FORM 5, College Education. Courtesy of a student·

STEP 4: COMPLETE FORM 5 FOR MILITARY EDUCATION

If you were in the military, complete a Form 5 for each military school you've attended.

File a copy of your military school transcript with this form.

Fill in all the information to make a complete record. Use as many pages or forms as necessary.

EDUCATION — DETAILED RECORD
Attach copies of support documents: diploma, transcript, certificates, awards.

Name of School or Organization
Defense Intelligence College

Address Washington, D.C.	**Telephone** (202) 555-4691
Type of Degree Mobile Counter Narcotics Analytical Methodologies	**Date Earned** 12/12/91

Grade Point Average	**Class Size** 100	**Class Rank** N/A

Key Personnel

Name with Courtesy Title	**Job Title**	**Address/Location**	**Telephone Number**
Mr. Ronald R. Matheson	Commandant	Washington, D.C.	

Key Courses

- Studied various forms of conceptual tools used to identify trends, patterns, and details in criminal activity.

Special Awards/Achievements

- Certificate of Completion

Clubs/Other Activities

None

© 1995 Harris Espérance Incorporated   Form 5/95

Figure 2-8 FORM 5, Military Education. Courtesy of a student

STEP 5: COMPLETE FORM 5 FOR TRAINING COURSES, WORKSHOPS, AND OTHER CLASSES

Complete a Form 5 for workshops and training seminars you've attended. The training may be conducted by consultants, schools, or employers.

File copies of all training certificates with this form.

Fill in all the information to make a complete record. Use as many pages or forms as necessary to cover all your training.

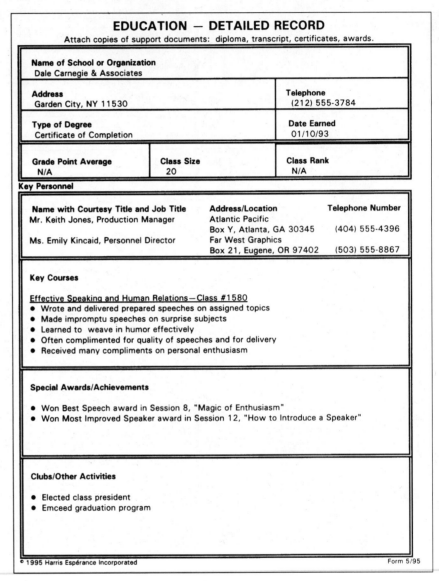

Figure 2-9 FORM 5, Other Education

STEP 6: COMPLETE FORM 6, LICENSES AND CERTIFICATIONS

List all licenses and certifications, such as your state driver's license, first aid card, CPR certificate, beverage server certification, apprenticeship card, journeyman card.

File copies of all licenses and certifications with this form.

Complete Form 6 by filling in all pertinent information, such as type of license, issuing agent, license number, issue date, and expiration date.

LICENSES AND CERTIFICATIONS
List all licenses and certifications including driver's license, first aid, CPR certification, etc.

Type of License	Issuing Agent	License #	Issue Date	Expiration Date
Driver's	State of Oregon	#765749	01/03/91	01/31/95
First Aid	American Red Cross		11/12/89	11/12/94
Industrial Audiometric Technician	State of Oregon Worker's Comp. Dept. Accident Prevention Div.	Certificate # 1065	03/24/90	06/30/93
First Aid Instructor/ Trainer	American Red Cross		02/19/91	12/31/92

© 1995 Harris Espérance Incorporated   Form 6/96

Figure 2-10   FORM 6, Licenses and Certifications

You may choose to file copies of the following documents in this section: diplomas, transcripts, military records, course descriptions/syllabi, report cards, course certificates, licenses, scholarship awards, special recognitions.

File these documents with the proper form in the EDUCATION section of your *Companion Planner*.

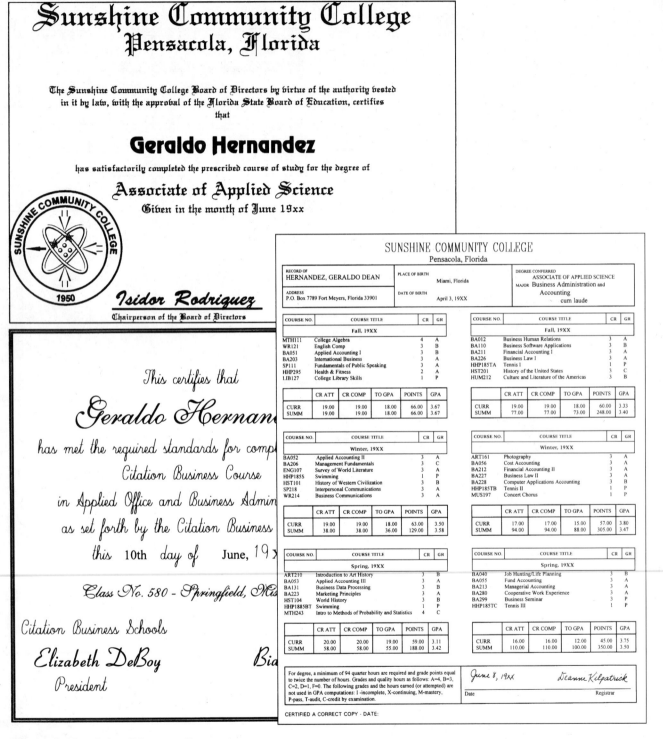

Figure 2-11   Other Education Documents

USING THE EMPLOYER'S SECTION
OF THE *COMPANION PLANNER*

When men are employed, they are best contented.
—Benjamin Franklin

This section refers to paid employment only. This includes self employment and military service. Volunteer work is covered under the Other Activities section.

The forms may be handwritten, typed, or computer generated.

The following forms and records are kept in the EMPLOYER section of the *Companion Planner*.

- Form 7: Employer Summary
  Record all employers in chronological order, beginning with your first paid employment and continuing to your last or current employer. Number each employer, with your first paid employer being number one.

- Form 8: Employer Record
  Complete this form in as much detail as possible. The information requested becomes more valuable as time passes. It is too easy to forget details such as your supervisor's name. During the job hunt, it is essential that accuracy prevail at all times. The effort it takes to complete this information will prove to be worthwhile in the future.

  If you cannot acquire this information for past employers, fill in as much as possible. Be sure to complete the form in detail for your current employer and then update your file as you move to new employers.

- Form 9: Description by Job Title (to be filed with Form 8)
  You may need several of these forms, depending on the number of positions you have held. Give serious thought to all the areas and write a finite, detailed reply. Attach this form to the appropriate Employer Record, Form 8.

- Other Documents
  You may choose to file *copies* of other important documents in this section. Some of the possible documents are:

  Performance reviews
  Reference letters
  Awards, rewards or special recognitions
  Samples of work (projects)

- INDIVIDUAL EMPLOYER Dividers
  Add dividers for each employer if you have had more than three employers. This will make it easier to maintain organization and to use.

Your employment data should include all **paid** employment. Volunteer work will be covered in Exercise 2-4. The EMPLOYERS section of your *Companion Planner* contains these forms: Form 2-7, Employer Summary; Form 2-8, Employer Record; and Form 2-9, Description by Job Title. When you've completed these forms, file them behind the Employers divider in the DISCOVER section.

STEP 1: COMPLETE FORM 7, EMPLOYER SUMMARY

Record all employers in chronological order.

EMPLOYER SUMMARY   Page _1_ of _1_

No.	Dates Employed	Employer Name/Telephone/ Mailing/Street Address City State Zip	Supervisor's Name Courtesy Title Job Title	Job Title Start and End Pay Rates
1	02/13/60 to 06/17/61	Jumbo Cafe 7th and Main Streets Springfield, OR 97477 (503) 555-4763	Mr. Victor Plouvier Owner/Operator	Waitress and Fry Cook $0.85/hour to $1.05/hour plus tips
2	08/27/61 to 09/18/61	Timber Topper 2nd and Main Streets Springfield, OR 97477 (503) 555-4396	Mr. Charles Jones Manager	Waitress $1.25/hour plus tips
3	09/16/61 to 04/13/62	Rubenstein's Furniture 1115 West Eighth Eugene, OR 97401 (503) 555-5688	Mr. Herb Williams Office Manager Mr. Lester Wheeler Controller	Office Clerk $192/month $202/month
4	04/16/62 to 01/19/79	Radison Lumber Corp. Springfield Division 4th and C Streets Springfield, OR 97754 (503) 555-6348 Eastern Division Atlanta, GA 30345 (404) 555-9617	Mr. W. H. Anders Accounting Dept. Supervisor Mr. Alex J. Simons Controller	General Accounting Clerk $ 225/month $2,700/year Office Mgr. and Accounting Supervisor $ 1,630/month $19,560/year
5	10/10/79 to 05/30/83	Cone Lumber Company Post Office Box 768 Combs Flat Road Springfield, OR 97477 (503) 555-6487	Mr. Ray Hammon, Jr. Operating General Manager	Director of Personnel and Safety $ 1,500/month $18,000/year $ 2,083/month $25,000/year
6				

© 1995 Harris Espérance Incorporated   Form 7/95

Figure 2-12   FORM 7, Employer Summary

Begin with your first employer and continue to your last employer.

Number each employer in sequence. This number is used as a reference number in the detailed record.

Fill in hire and termination dates. Include the month, day, and year.

Fill in the employer's name, address, and telephone number to the best of your ability.

Include job titles and courtesy titles with the supervisor's name.

List your beginning and ending titles with their respective rates.

STEP 2: COMPLETE FORM 8, EMPLOYER RECORD

Complete a Form 2-8 for each employer. Fill in as much data as possible.

Employer Name/Address/Telephone
Record complete information. Include FAX numbers.

Employer Number
This number corresponds to the number on the Employer Summary form.

```
EMPLOYER RECORD

Employer Name                                          Employer No.
U.S. National Bank of Oregon                              12

Address: Mailing, Street, City, State, Zip, Country    Telephone No.
314 SW 6th Street, Redmond, OR 97756, U.S.A.           (503) 555-5638

Key Personnel

Name with Courtesy Title    Job Title                      Telephone No.
Ms. Janet Provost           Operations Manager             (503) 555-6472
Mrs. Debra Jenkins          Assistant Operations Manager   (503) 555-4367
Mr. Kenneth L. Rankin       V-P, Central Oregon Operations (503) 555-1963

Description of Business

Type of Product or Service:   Banking, loans, investments
Profit _x_  Nonprofit ___  Not-for-Profit ___ Government Agency ___  Union ___  Nonunion _x_
Co-op ___  Public _x_  Private ___  Corporation _x_  Partnership ___  Other ___
Number of Employees: Hourly _20_   Salaried _7_   Locations _Redmond_
Annual Sales $_____   Annual Production—Unit/Volume_____
Other_____

Employee Benefits  (Describe)

Major Medical ___yes___   Dental ___yes___   Vision ___yes___  Life _$25,000_
Disability ___Long-term and partial___   Retirement _yes, vesting 5 years_
Vacation ___1 week; 2 weeks after 1st year___   Holidays _10_
Other ___Bonus incentives—vary with promotions; education assistance_

Record of Job History
Hire/Promotion/
Termination Dates   Pay Rate        Job Title           Name of Supervisor

Hired: 06/01/89     $5.00/hour      Bank Teller         Ms. Diana Keeting
Raise: 06/01/89     $5.55/hour
Promoted: 12/01/89  $6.25/hour      Head Bank Teller

Reason for Leaving

Voluntarily resigned. Chose to move to West Coast and to make a major career change (from
banking services to sales).

© 1995 Harris Espérance Incorporated                              Form 8/95
```

Figure 2-13 FORM 8, Employer Record

Key Personnel
List the names of anyone who may be important to remember later on. Do not include supervisors listed on the Employer Summary form.

Description of Business
This information provides data useful for resume writing, interviewing, and negotiating.

Employee Benefits
This information is helpful when determining and negotiating employment packages.

Record of Job History
Make a complete record here. Be as detailed and exact as possible.

Reason for Leaving
It's important to list an honest, positive reply here. If you are having difficulty, refer to Chapter 6 on references.

EXAMPLE OF FORM 8 FOR U.S. MILITARY SERVICE

Complete a form similar to this one for military service. Fill in as much information as possible.

File a photocopy of your military service record and discharge papers with this form. Keep the originals in a safe place.

EMPLOYER RECORD

Employer Name U. S. Marines	Employer No. 6
Address: Mailing, Street, City, State, Zip Code, Country Bremerton, WA 98315	Telephone No. (206) 555-4931

Key Personnel

Name with Courtesy Title	Job Title	Telephone No.
Sgt. Snyder		(206) 555-4637
Sgt. Forrel		(206) 555-4623
Lt. Foldetti	Guard Officer	(206) 555-2179
Capt. Black	Guard Officer	(206) 555-8724

Description of Business

Type of Product or Service_____Military service—security_____
Profit ___ Nonprofit ___ Not-for-Profit ___ Government Agency _x_ Union ___ Nonunion ___
Co-op ___ Public ___ Private ___ Corporation ___ Partnership ___ Other _____
Number of Employees: Hourly _____ Salaried _____ Locations _____
Annual Sales $_____ Annual Production—Unit/Volume_____
Other_____

Employee Benefits (Describe)

Major Medical ____yes____ Dental ____yes____ Vision ____yes____ Life ____$ 50,000____
Disability _yes_ Retirement _after 20 years_
Vacation _31.5 days/year_ Holidays _0_
Other _____

Record of Job History

Hire/Promotion/ Termination Dates	Pay Rate	Job Title	Name of Supervisor
4/26/83 Enlisted	$573/mo.	Boot Camp	Drill Instructor
10/1/83	$658/mo.	E-2 Security Guard	Sgt. Snyder
3/2/84	$695/mo.	E-3 Security Guard	Sgt. Snyder
9/2/85	$720/mo.	E-4 Security Guard	Sgt. Snyder
4/25/86	Discharged		

Reason for Leaving

End of enlistment—Honorable Discharge

© 1995 Harris Espérance Incorporated   Form 8/95

Figure 2-14 FORM 8, Military Service. Courtesy of a student

STEP 3: COMPLETE FORM 9, DESCRIPTION BY JOB TITLE

Divide—Support—Rank . . . the secret to writing job descriptions.

DESCRIPTION BY JOB TITLE

Employer No. 3	Employer Name The River's Edge, Highway 97, Bend, OR 97701 (503) 555-3984		
Job Title Server	**Hire Date** 03/01/89	**Beg. Wage** $4.25/hr. + tips	**Supervisor** Ms. Julie Carlson, Head Server
Job Title Head Server	**Term. Date** 09/15/91	**End Wage** $5.75/hr. + tips	**Supervisor** Mr. Jerry Olson, Restaurant Manager

Job Description (Functional/Achievement Narrative)

- <u>Restaurant and Banquet Management Skills</u>: Supervised up to 10 hourly employees. Coordinated activities of dining room. Trained dining-room employees in fine-dining service. Resolved and adjusted complaints regarding food and/or service. Scheduled dining reservations and table assignments. Planned details for banquets, receptions, and other social functions. Hired, trained, and supervised banquet staff. Directed setup and decoration of tables and room.
- <u>Tableside and Beverage Service</u>: Carved and served dinners on chafing dishes at tableside include steak Diane, rack of lamb and chateaubriand. Set up and prepared salads (Caesar and wilted spinach), desserts (bananas Foster and cherries jubilee), and flaming drinks (coffee royale) at tableside.
- <u>Waiting Service</u>: Served meals to patrons in formal and informal settings. Presented verbal and printed menus. Recommended dinner courses, appropriate beverages, and desserts. Answered questions regarding food preparations and wine selections. Memorized and wrote orders. Observed diners to fulfill any additional requests and to perceive when course was completed to deliver next course or check. Relayed orders to kitchen and lounge through NCE computerized firing system.
- <u>Customer Service</u>: Provided travel directions, weather, what's-happening-in-our-town information to patrons.

Quotable Quotes/Special Recognitions/Awards

- Chosen employee of the year (1990) and received $100 bonus with plaque.
- Chosen employee of the month three times (March, September, December 1990)
- Received repeated requests by frequent patrons for my service. Took great pride in making sure children had an exceptionally fun experience while parents enjoyed a pleasant dining experience.
- Often complimented by customers on having a great smile and wonderful attitude. Received many compliments from supervisors on efficiency and quality of service provided.
- Coworkers enjoyed my ability to make them laugh at appropriate times.

Licenses

- Food and Alcohol Server (Expiration 12/31/92)

What I Liked Best about this Job . . .

- Working with the public and coworkers. Doing tasks to help others and meeting new people.
- My favorite work experience happened last week. I was helping the cooks sweep the floors in the kitchen when I came around the corner and found the employees and owners standing in a row singing "Happy Birthday" to me. They had a cake with candles. No one else had ever received a cake or been sung to. It made me feel great.

What I Liked Least about this Job . . .

- Making a mistake on an order. Always felt personally responsible no matter where the mistake may have originated.

Job Description Summary

- Served food and beverages to customers in a lively, fast-paced gourmet restaurant.

© 1995 Harris Espérance Incorporated   Form 9/95

Figure 2-15   FORM 9, Description by Job Title of Head Server

Job Descriptions

Divide each job into functional areas. **Support** each area with skill statements. **Rank** each skill statement. There are helpful tips on how to write effective job descriptions on the next few pages.

Quotable Quotes

Check performance reviews and reference letters for quotes. Verbal comments are permissible if they can be verified.

Licenses

List license, licensing agent, and expiration date if applicable.

Liked Best/Least About Job

Record an honest answer that is relevant to the job but that is also one the employer wants to hear. Be careful with your "least" answer.

Job Description Summary

Write two or three concise and descriptive sentences that adequately describe what you did. This will be used for job applications, which often provide very little space.

LEARN TO WRITE EFFECTIVE JOB DESCRIPTIONS

Writing effective job descriptions is one of the most difficult parts of capturing your past. If you learn to do this, resume writing and job application completion become a snap. Following are some suggestions to make the writing of job descriptions easier for you and informative for the employer.

Since most of us are not professional writers and lack the skills to effectively present ourselves on paper, it's imperative to find a method to improve and help us write. That's where *cribs* come in. Cribs are lists of answers or other illicit aids. They're useful even for good writers.

Crib #1: The *Dictionary of Occupational Titles* (DOT)

You will find over twenty thousand job descriptions in the *Dictionary of Occupational Titles* (DOT). Use it as a guide in writing work experiences. Following is the description for a head waiter/waitress in a hotel or restaurant.

311.137-022 WAITER/WAITRESS, HEAD (hotel & rest.)
Supervises and coordinates activities of dining-room employees engaged in providing courteous and rapid service to diners: Greets guests and escorts them to tables. Schedules dining reservations. Arranges parties for patrons. Adjusts complaints regarding food or service. Hires and trains dining-room employees. Notifies payroll department regarding work schedules and time records. May assist in preparing menus. May plan and execute details for banquets. [STEWARD/STEWARDESS, BANQUET (hotel & rest.); MANAGER, CATERING (hotel & rest.)]. May supervise WAITERS/WAITRESSES, ROOM SERVICE (hotel & rest.) and be designated CAPTAIN, ROOM SERVICE (hotel & rest.).

When using the DOT to write functional job descriptions, change verbs from the present tense to the past tense; for example, *supervises* becomes *supervised*.

Use a Verb–Object–Results/Comments format to write all your skill narratives.

Following is an example of how to write your skill statement using the DOT descriptions.

Verb(s)	Object(s)	Results/Comments
Supervised and coordinated	dining-room employees	in providing courteous and rapid service to diners.
Greeted and escorted Scheduled	guests dining reservations.	to tables.

You can see how easy it is to write a functional job narrative by using descriptions from the DOT.

PRACTICE WRITING FUNCTIONAL JOB DESCRIPTIONS USING DOT

Following are examples of job descriptions from the DOT. Select one that fits your experience. Read the description, then rewrite it in a format that describes your experiences. Remember to change the verbs from present tense to past tense.

211.462-010 CASHIER II (clerical) cash clerk; cashier, general; cashier, office; ticket clerk

Receives cash from customers or employees in payment for goods or services and records amounts received. Recomputes or computes bill, itemized lists, and tickets showing amount due, using adding machine or cash register. Makes change, cashes checks, and issues receipts or tickets to customers. Records amounts received and prepares reports of transactions. Reads and records totals shown on cash register tape and verifies against cash on hand. May be required to know value of features of items for which money is received. May give cash refunds or issue credit memorandums to customers for returned merchandise. May operate ticket dispensing machine. May sell candy, cigarettes, gum, or gift certificates, and issue trading stamps. . . .

Verb(s)	Object(s)	Results/Comments

293.357-022 MEMBERSHIP SOLICITOR (any ind.)

Solicits membership for club or trade association: Visits or contacts prospective members to explain benefits and costs of membership and to describe organization and objectives of club or association. May collect dues and payments for publications from members. May solicit funds for club or association. May speak to members at meetings about services available. . . .

Verb(s)	Object(s)	Results/Comments

620.261-010 AUTOMOBILE MECHANIC (auto. ser.) garage mechanic

Repairs and overhauls automobiles, buses, trucks, and other automotive vehicles. Examines vehicle and discusses with customer or AUTOMOBILE REPAIR-SERVICE ESTIMATOR . . . nature and extent of damage or malfunction. Plans work procedure, using charts, technical manuals, and experience. Raises vehicle . . . to gain access to mechanical units bolted to underside of vehicle. Removes unit, such as engine . . . using wrenches, and hoist. Disassembles unit and inspects parts for wear, using micrometers, calipers . . . Repairs and replaces parts, such as pistons, rods, gears . . . Overhauls or replaces carburetors, . . . Rebuilds parts such as crankshafts . . . Rewires ignition system . . . Relines and adjusts brakes. . . .

Verb(s)	Object(s)	Results/Comments

293.157-010 FUND RAISER (nonprofit organ.)

Plans fund-raising program for charities or other causes and writes to, telephones, or visits individuals or establishments to solicit funds: Compiles and analyzes information about potential contributors to develop mailing or contact list and to plan selling approach. Writes, telephones, or visits potential contributors and persuades them to contribute funds by explaining purposes and benefits of fund-raising program. Takes pledges or funds from contributors. Records expenses incurred and contributions received. May organize volunteers and plan social functions to raise funds. May prepare fund-raising brochures for mail-solicitation programs. May sell emblems or other tokens of organization represented.

Verb(s)	Object(s)	Results/Comments

EXAMPLE OF FORM 9 FOR A MANUFACTURING JOB

Divide—Support—Rank . . . the secret to writing job descriptions.

Sherry used the *Dictionary of Occupational Titles* to write her skill statements. She divided her job into functional skill areas and then supported each area with specific skill statements. She selected skills that were applicable and transferrable to her new accounting career. From a millworker to an accountant, Sherry found it easy to transfer skills by using the DOT.

DESCRIPTION BY JOB TITLE

Employer No. 6	Employer Name	Bend Millwork Company 62845 Boyd Acres Road Bend OR 97701	503-555-1444

Job Title Board Patcher	Hire Date 09/25/79	Beg. Wage $6.00/hour	Supervisor Mr. Tom Adams
Job Title Shipping Tally	Term. Date 06/30/94	End. Wage $10.14/hour	Supervisor Mr. Leon Savage

Job Description (Functional/achievement Narrative)

- **Shipping Tally:** Verified and maintained records of incoming and outgoing shipments. Compared identifying information, counted and measured items, and verified against bills of lading, invoices, and orders.
- **Production Tally:** Compiled and recorded production data from customer orders, work tickets, and product specifications. Calculated quantities of items produced, materials used, amount of waste, and frequency of defects.
- **Inventory Control:** Processed data using computer, and reconciled with actual physical inventory. Solved inventory problems through troubleshooting, using computer-generated information and hand-recorded documentation.
- **Freight:** Used knowledge of shipping procedures and transportation routes and rates to find the "best way" to ship.
- **Supervised:** Often in light of Supervisor's absence in the Shipping Department. Oversaw a crew of 3 people.
- **Volunteered:** In various offices throughout company. Acquired knowledge in many departments, such as invoicing, AR & AP, Cost Accounting, and Scheduling. Acquired computer and clerical skills.

Quotable Quotes/Special Recognitions/Awards

- Was often told of my amazing ability to learn quickly with a high degree of accuracy, very dependable.

Licenses

- None

What I Liked Best about this Job

- The knowledge I gained through working in the various offices throughout the company, and the experience of using different computer programs in each of those departments.

What I Liked Least about this Job

- The lack of communication between management and employees—I worked hard to ensure that the communications flowed.

Job Description Summary

- Kept accurate production and shipping records. Tracked production and shipment of products using customer orders, product specifications, and computers.

© 1995 Harris Espérance Incorporated   Form 9/95

Figure 2-16   FORM 9, Mill Worker. Courtesy of a student

Job Description
Divide each job into functional areas. **Support** each area with skill statements. **Rank** each skill statement.

Quotable Quotes
Check performance reviews and reference letters for quotes. Verbal comments are permissible if they can be verified.

Licenses
List license, licensing agent, and expiration date if applicable.

Liked Best/Least About Job
Record an honest answer that is relevant to the job but that is also one the employer wants to hear. Be careful with your "least" answer.

Job Description Summary
Write two or three concise and descriptive sentences that adequately describe what you did. This will be used for job applications, which often provide very little space.

Crib #2: Employer Job Descriptions

Obtain a copy of the employer's job description. The following example shows a job description for one employer.

PRESENTATION SERVICES MANAGER

Manage all preparations, scheduling, and coordination of corporate events and related activities locally and nationally. Coordinate and technically prepare corporate showroom for all booked events. Schedule, coordinate, and operate all aspects of showroom and conference areas for corporate events. Hire and supervise professional staff within department and temporary labor for specific events. Possess high degree of technical skills, including staging, lighting, and audiovisual expertise. Organize and manage multiple projects within aggressive time frames. Possess excellent interpersonal skills and proven ability to work in team environment. Negotiate contracts for labor, supplies, and training. Develop and maintain vendor relationships. Develop, administer, and monitor department budgets.

Avoid phrases like *duties are* and *responsible for*. Replace these phrases with action verbs such as *managed, constructed, administered, supervised*.

Remember that the skill is in the verb, not the noun. Use active past-tense verbs to describe what you've done . . . to describe your job.

Personalize the descriptions by naming the projects completed, specifying the dollars saved, indicating the number and type of employees supervised, and so forth.

Use a Verb–Object–Results/Comments format when writing job descriptions.

Verb(s)	Object(s)	Results/Comments
Coordinated and operated	all aspects of showroom and conference areas.	
Hired and supervised	professional staff and temporary labor	for special events.
Organized and managed	multiple projects	within aggressive time frames.
Developed and maintained	vendor relationships.	

With an employer's job description, you can see how easy it becomes to capture what you have done on the job.

Crib #3: Your Greatest Achievements

It's the stories you tell that sell.

Another way to tell what you have done is to write achievement narratives. Write about your accomplishments rather than using job titles, duties, responsibilities, or functional descriptions. You are hired for what you can do, not for a list of job duties. Stories capture the essence of your capabilities.

- Write short stories depicting your successes.

- Begin your story with a short one-line title.

- Study the examples that follow, and review Exercise 1-6, "My Five Greatest Achievements," in Chapter 1 for ideas.

IMPROVED PHONE SYSTEM
Discussed with supervisor the advantages of installing com-lines on the telephone and designating one person to answer the phones, for which I volunteered. These changes reduced the noise level, added privacy, and created a more workable atmosphere.

IMPROVED WORKING CONDITIONS
Meticulously kept production sheds clean and cleared of all scraps and debris. By own initiative, improved yard efficiency by reorganizing and/or discarding several years' accumulation of unattended stock and debris. Upon leaving for college, supervisor stated, "I hate to see you go. This is the cleanest this place has ever been."

REMODELED OLD HOUSE
As partner with brother, age 18, bought and completely remodeled an old house and added a 500-square-foot addition.
- Replaced all roofing, siding, flooring, wiring, plumbing, sheetrock, and windows. Poured new sidewalk. Planted new lawn and completed landscaping.
- All financial planning and work, except sheetrocking, was done by us. Received many compliments on quality of work. One carpenter said, "When you first got this place, I thought it would be a real mess when you finished; but now I'm really impressed. You boys did a super job."
- Sold house for an $8,000 profit.

Use the following guidelines for writing achievement narratives:

- Write a one-line header; then follow up with the story.

- List the highest or most relevant skill first. End the narrative with the lowest level skill statements.

- Use strong active verbs and precise nouns. The skill is in the verb, not the noun; so begin your sentences with verbs.

  - Initiated and wrote customized employee handbook for EZ Products Inc.

- Use explicit examples to build credibility.

  - Over a period of 6 years, sold $5,000 of magazine subscriptions for booster club.

  - Recognized as top salesperson in Boosters' 25-year history.

- Choose examples to illustrate personal qualities, such as showing stick-to-itiveness or competitiveness, being a team player, going the extra mile, having the ability to get along with others.

  - Played starting center and strong forward for Sporting Luxembourg.

  - Voted Player of the Year. Averaged 29 points per game.

- Team won country championship.

- Show results. Get to the bottom line by demonstrating how hiring you will impact the company. Use dollar amounts, percentages.

  - Developed and implemented a new accident prevention program. Reduced last year's lost-time accidents by 40% and total accidents by 28%. Saved $350,000 in worker compensation insurance premiums.

- Use numbers to quantify accomplishments.

  - Screened 380 scholarship applicants and selected 10 recipients.

- Prioritize support statements. Prioritize words. Prioritize skills. Prioritize every thought.

  - Prepared annual, quarterly, and monthly operating budgets with annual sales of $150,000,000.

  - Managed and maintained accounts receivable for over 3,700 accounts with average active monthly balance over $400,000.

  - Converted accounts receivable to in-house computerized system that handles all billings and ages accounts.

- Describe the value or benefit derived.

  - Organized 2 Dance-a-Thons for high school choir. Each raised nearly $4,500.

- Use colorful expressions that provide a feel for the job, the environment, and you as a person.

  - Served food and beverages to patrons in a fast-paced, western-style atmosphere. Took pride in making sure children had an exceptionally fun time while parents enjoyed a pleasant dining experience. Received many compliments from customers on my friendly, efficient service.

- Use verbal or written testimonials found in reference letters, performance reviews.

  - Margie McDonald, Executive Director of High Country Athletics Conference, writes, "You will find Michele very upbeat and excited about what she is doing, and her enthusiasm permeates everyone with whom she comes into contact." (Quote from reference letter)

- Tell the truth. Never exaggerate; it's not necessary. Don't be cute or clever.

EXAMPLE OF FORM 9 FOR A U.S. GOVERNMENT JOB

Divide—Support—Rank

Notice the use of headers with the skill statements. Headers make skill statements easier to read and comprehend. They break up the grey print.

DESCRIPTION BY JOB TITLE

Employer No. 5	Employer Name U.S. Forest Service		
Job Title Archeological Technician	**Hire Date** 08/01/88	**Beg. Wage** $6.26/hr.	**Supervisor** Mr. James Ford
Job Title Archeological Technician	**Term. Date** 12/31/88	**End Wage** $6.26/hr.	**Supervisor** Mr. James Ford

Job Description (Functional/Achievement Narrative)
- **Planning**: Researched historic and archeological documents. Interviewed district personnel familiar with the location of sites in project areas. Studied USGS and FS maps and aerial photos to determine areas likely to contain archeological sites. Proposed survey intensity based on probability. Previewed soil and vegetation overlays to predict site locations. Planned survey strategy and coverage intensity and mapped probability areas.
- **Budgeting**: Estimated budget needs for the 1988 field season.
- **Fieldwork**: Completed 2 timber sale surveys. Recorded 3 prehistoric and 6 historic sites. Conducted subsurface test probes at one site.
- **Analysis**: Collated field data and assessed site function and age. Measured and described artifacts and debris.
- **Communication Skills**: Completed site forms and project reports. Determined eligibility for all sites. Proposed mitigation measures. Gained concurrence from SHPO. Prepared cultural resources sections of EAs. Provided cultural resource input for 3 ERs. Presented an analysis of the potential for archeological sites in the project areas. Coordinated mitigation measures with district resource personnel and received approval.
- **Other**: Summarized annual cultural resource accomplishments for the regional and Washington offices. Updated district TRI mapping system and maintained cultural resource files. Drafted large- and small-scale maps.

Quotable Quotes/Special Recognitions/Awards
- Received many compliments from superiors about quality/quantity of work and my personal attitude and work habits. (See performance review.)

Licenses
- Government GS193-09 Archeologist Grade; MA specializing in Zoology, Archeology, and Anthropology
- CPR and First aid certified. Excellent driver's record.

What I Liked Best about this Job . . .
- Hands-on experience working in the field.
- Working with other professionals.

What I Liked Least about this Job . . .
- It was a temporary position.

Job Description Summary
- Conducted fieldwork on 2 timber sale surveys. Recorded 3 prehistoric and 6 historic sites including subsurface test probe for one site. Completed site forms and project reports. Provided budget estimates for 1988 field season.

© 1995 Harris Espérance Incorporated

Form 9/95

Divide each job into major functional skill areas.

Support each functional area with skill statements. Be specific with your details.

- Use strong active verbs.
- Show results.
- Quantify accomplishments.
- Use numbers and names.
- Use colorful expressions.
- Tell the truth.
- Use testimonials.
- Choose examples to demonstrate personal qualities, such as being organized, a go-getter, or a team player.

Rank each skill statement according to the highest skill level or most relevant skill for your career goal.

Figure 2-17 FORM 9, Archeological Technician. Courtesy of a client

EXAMPLE OF FORM 9 FOR SELF-EMPLOYMENT

Divide—Support—Rank

Remember to use headers with the skill statements. Headers make skill statements easier to read and comprehend, and they break up the grey print.

DESCRIPTION BY JOB TITLE

Employer No.	Employer Name		
11	Green Thumb Nursery, 5580 Highway 20, Bend, OR 97701		(503) 555-4458

Job Title	Hire Date	Beg. Wage	Supervisor
Owner/Operator	02/01/84	Net profit first year, $5,000	Self/Owner

Job Title	Term. Date	End Wage	Supervisor

Job Description (Functional/Achievement Narrative)
- **Supervision**: Supervised up to 6 nursery workers. Trained employees in nursery tasks, concepts behind work, and the scientific basis of plant propagation, transplanting, and growing-on. Interviewed, screened, and hired employees. Wrote job descriptions. Planned weekly work schedules and yearly personnel requirements Fostered an open and productive work environment. Encouraged employees to return year after year even though work was seasonal. Most employees did return.
- **Budget Management**: Analyzed annual start-up costs and secured financing. Developed operating budgets for advertising, physical plant overhead, payroll, and supplies. Generated increased profits through careful monitoring of budgets. Calculated downtime expenses and budgeted funds for them. Figured profit margins, break-even points, and department cost analysis.
- **Planning**: Coordinated annual ordering and shipment dates. Researched new varieties of vegetables, flowers, shrubs, and trees suited for climate. Received enthusiastic support of selections from customers. Scheduled seeding times and amounts. Projected increased growth in sales, and increased orders to match demand. Researched and designed 2 greenhouses. Supervised construction. Realized a 75% savings on each structure using nontraditional materials and construction methods.
- **Business Promotion**: Enhanced business reputation through involvement in civic projects. Designed and landscaped highway interchange for community. Organized beautification program in downtown. Planted flower barrels annually. Sought and gained approval from city government for planting trees in downtown area. Committed nursery to annual tree care program. Donated over 100 flower planters to county fairgrounds annually. Gave nursery products to charitable organizations.
- Business Accomplishments: Increased gross sales from $21,000 in 1984 to over $100,000 in 1988. Expanded from ¼ acre to 2 acres. Increased greenhouse production from 1,100 square feet to over 5,000 square feet. Improved profit figures from a $5,000 loss to over $17,000 profit.

Quotable Quotes/Special Recognitions/Awards
- Received Business of the Year award and President's award in 1987 from the county Chamber of Commerce for beautification work.
- Received many compliments from customers for providing expert advice on plant selection, planting, disease control, and general plant care.
- Received Superior Instructor rating from community college students and program coordinator.

Licenses
- CPR and First Aid certified. Chauffeur's license.

What I Liked Best about this Job
- Working with the community, customers and our dedicated, capable employees.

What I Liked Least about this Job
- Terminating employees when season ended.

Job Description Summary
- Owned and operated full-scale profitable nursery supplying a wholesale and retail customer base. Built a returning customer base.

© 1995 Harris Espérance Incorporated   Form 9/95

Divide each job into major functional skills areas.

Support each functional area with skill statements. Be specific with your details.

- Use strong active verbs.
- Show results.
- Quantify accomplishments.
- Use numbers and names.
- Use colorful expressions.
- Tell the truth.
- Use testimonials.
- Choose examples to demonstrate personal qualities, such as being organized, a go-getter, or a team player.

Rank each skill statement according to the highest skill level or most relevant skill for your career goal.

Figure 2-18 FORM 9, Small Business. Courtesy of a client

EXAMPLE OF FORM 9 FOR MILITARY SERVICE

Divide—Support—Rank

DESCRIPTION BY JOB TITLE

Employer No. 3	Employer Name U.S. Marines, Bremerton, WA		
Job Title E2 Security Guard	Hire Date 04/06/82	Beg. Wage $573/month	Supervisor Corp. Snyder
Job Title E4 Security Guard	Term. Date 04/25/86	End Wage $720/month	Supervisor Sgt. Wynenski

Job Description (Functional/Achievement Narrative)

- **Supervision:** Oversaw at times conduct of entire guard force of up to 100 men guarding undisclosable materials or places vital to the national security.

- **Physical Fitness:** Trained 10 men into top physical condition. Awarded citation for fitness.

- **Communications:** Supervised and gave concise orders to 10 men. Resolved personal problems and disagreements between men to ensure team coordination, good communications, morale, and mental health.

- **Leadership:** Led by example and instilled gung ho attitude in 10 men through trying hardships.

Quotable Quotes/Special Recognitions/Awards
- Received average 4.5 and up proficiency conduct marks through enlistment.
- Received Meritorious Mast on 2/9/84 for being February's Marine of the Month.
- Received GLM on 4/26/86 for 3 years of good service.
- Received Meritorious Mast for outstanding IF inspection.
- Selected from entire barracks (300 men) to train marines from California on alarm systems and guard procedures.

Licenses
- Government top-security clearance

What I Liked Best about this Job
- The challenge of leadership and supervision

What I Liked Least about this Job
- Inability to change jobs or location and government waste

Job Description Summary
- Led and supervised squad of 10 men in most aspects of guard life. Guarded various government sites and materials vital to national security.

© 1995 Harris Espérance Incorporated   Form 9/95

Figure 2-19 FORM 9, Military Service. Courtesy of a student

Divide each job into major functional skill areas.

Support each functional area with skill statements. Be specific with your details.

- Use strong active verbs.
- Show results.
- Quantify accomplishments.
- Use numbers and names.
- Use colorful expressions.
- Tell the truth.
- Use testimonials.
- Choose examples to demonstrate personal qualities, such as being organized, a go-getter, or a team player.

Rank each skill statement according to the highest skill level or most relevant skill for your career goal.

STEP 4: GATHER OTHER DOCUMENTS

You may choose to file copies of the following documents in this section:

- Performance reviews
- Reference letters
- Special recognitions, such as cash rewards, ribbons, and awards
- Thank-you notes and letters

File these documents with the appropriate employer form.

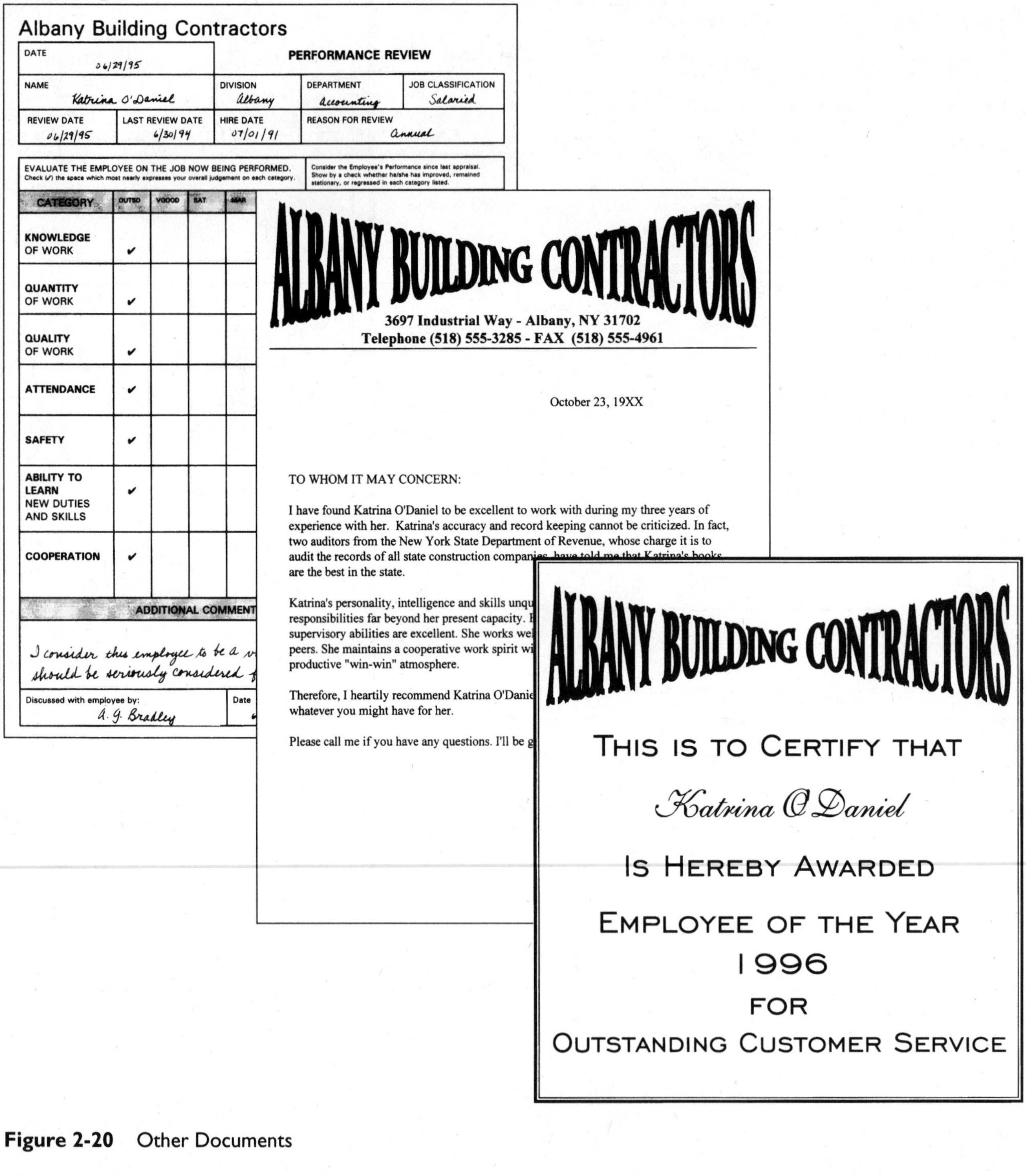

Albany Building Contractors

DATE 06/29/95	PERFORMANCE REVIEW		
NAME Katrina O'Daniel	DIVISION Albany	DEPARTMENT Accounting	JOB CLASSIFICATION Salaried
REVIEW DATE 06/29/95 / LAST REVIEW DATE 6/30/94	HIRE DATE 07/01/91	REASON FOR REVIEW Annual	

EVALUATE THE EMPLOYEE ON THE JOB NOW BEING PERFORMED. Check (✓) the space which most nearly expresses your overall judgement on each category.

Consider the Employee's Performance since last appraisal. Show by a check whether he/she has improved, remained stationary, or regressed in each category listed.

CATEGORY	OUTSD	VGOOD	SAT	MAR
KNOWLEDGE OF WORK	✓			
QUANTITY OF WORK	✓			
QUALITY OF WORK	✓			
ATTENDANCE	✓			
SAFETY	✓			
ABILITY TO LEARN NEW DUTIES AND SKILLS	✓			
COOPERATION	✓			

ADDITIONAL COMMENT

I consider this employee to be a v… should be seriously considered f…

Discussed with employee by: A. G. Bradley — Date

ALBANY BUILDING CONTRACTORS
3697 Industrial Way - Albany, NY 31702
Telephone (518) 555-3285 - FAX (518) 555-4961

October 23, 19XX

TO WHOM IT MAY CONCERN:

I have found Katrina O'Daniel to be excellent to work with during my three years of experience with her. Katrina's accuracy and record keeping cannot be criticized. In fact, two auditors from the New York State Department of Revenue, whose charge it is to audit the records of all state construction compan… are the best in the state.

Katrina's personality, intelligence and skills unqu… responsibilities far beyond her present capacity. … supervisory abilities are excellent. She works we… peers. She maintains a cooperative work spirit wi… productive "win-win" atmosphere.

Therefore, I heartily recommend Katrina O'Danie… whatever you might have for her.

Please call me if you have any questions. I'll be g…

ALBANY BUILDING CONTRACTORS

THIS IS TO CERTIFY THAT

Katrina O'Daniel

IS HEREBY AWARDED

EMPLOYEE OF THE YEAR

1996

FOR

OUTSTANDING CUSTOMER SERVICE

Figure 2-20 Other Documents

USING THE OTHER ACTIVITIES SECTION
OF THE *COMPANION PLANNER*

Your life consists of many activities besides work and formal educational experiences. Often the skills you need for a job come from such outside activities. Don't judge the value of your experience, simply record the activity here. You should have a complete record. A wealth of skills may be acquired from activities completely unrelated to work or school. Use the following forms to capture the "rest" of your life.

The forms may be handwritten, typed, or computer generated. The following forms and records are maintained in the Other Activities section of the *Companion Planner*.

- Form 10: Summary of Other Activities
  Record all your outside activities in chronological order on this form. Begin with early activities and continue to the present. Include activities such as:

    - Memberships in professional, community, political, religious, and social organizations

    - Volunteer work

    - Home activities such as cooking, childcare, gardening, landscaping, auto mechanics, wiring, painting, wallpapering

    - Hobbies such as photography, calligraphy, stamp collecting, traveling, public speaking, reading, entertaining . . . activities that provide skills that may be valuable to an employer.

- Form 11: Description by Activity
  Use this form to record your activities in detail. Cover major activities or projects that provide skills viable in the job market. Use the same techniques you used in writing employment skill narratives. Write achievement and/or functional narratives to describe what you did.

- Form 12: Miscellaneous Activities
  Use this form to capture an activity that is repeated often but the details are few, for example: books read, travels, public speaking, movies watched.

- Other Documents
  File *copies* of other related documents in this section, including:

    - Awards and rewards

    - Newspaper and magazine articles

    - Thank-you letters and notes

    - Certificates of recognition or appreciation

- INDIVIDUAL ACTIVITY dividers
  Add separate dividers for major activities when this section becomes cumbersome.

> Every man's work, whether it be literature or music or pictures or architecture or anything else, is always a portrait of himself.
>
> —Mark Twain

The OTHER ACTIVITIES section of your *Companion Planner* should contain these forms: Form 10, Summary of Other Activities; Form 11, Description by Activity, and Form 12, Miscellaneous Activities. When you've completed these forms, file them behind the Other Activities divider in the DISCOVER section.

SUMMARY OF OTHER ACTIVITIES

Record all other activities in chronological order.   Page ___ of ___

No.	Dates of Activity	Activity or Organization Mailing/Street Address City State Zip	Description of Activity
1	01/81 to 08/81	Veteran's Administration Hospital 16111 Plummer Road Sepulveda, CA 91343 (714) 555-9816	Volunteer hospital attendant and pharmacy aide
2	2/87 to 9/90	Redmond Baby-Sitting Cooperative 3012 SW Timber Street Redmond, OR 97756 (503) 555-5480	Set up and organized a baby-sitting exchange
3	9/88 to 6/90	M.A. Lynch School 14th and Kalama Redmond, OR 97756 (503) 555-4264	Teacher's assistant
4	2/89 to 10/91	Redmond Little League 3012 SW Timber Street Redmond, OR 97756 (503) 555-3872	Restructured and reorganized Redmond Little League Baseball
5	05/90 to present	Redmond Toastmasters Redmond, OR 97756	Self-improvement group dedicated to improving leadership and communication skills

© 1995 Harris Espérance Incorporated   Form 10/95

Figure 2-21   FORM 10, Summary of Other Activities

STEP 1: COMPLETE FORM 10, SUMMARY OF OTHER ACTIVITIES

Record other activities in chronological order.

Begin with early activities and continue to the present.

Include activities such as:

- Memberships in clubs and organizations—professional, social, community, political, religious
- Volunteer work
- Entrepreneurial pursuits—self-employment if not full-time and not part of your employer records.
- Home activities—cooking, childcare, gardening, landscaping, auto mechanics, wiring, painting, wallpapering
- Hobbies/interests—other activities not listed elsewhere

STEP 2: COMPLETE FORM 11, DESCRIPTION BY ACTIVITY

Use Form 11 to record your other activities in detail. Cover all major activities and projects not included in the employment section.

Use the *Dictionary of Occupational Titles* (DOT) as a guide when writing functional skill narratives.

DESCRIPTION BY ACTIVITY

Activity No.	Name of Organization or Activity (include Address and Telephone No.)
1	Veteran's Administration Hospital 16111 Plummer Road (714) 555-0583 Sepulveda, CA 91343

Length of Activity From: 01/81 To: 08/81	Purpose of Organization or Activity Volunteered to assist in Veteran's Hospital as a hospital attendant and pharmacy aide.

Offices Held	Dates Held
• Hospital Attendant	01/82 - 04/81
• Pharmacy Aide	05/81 - 08/81

Awards, Special Recognitions, Etc.

• Offered full-time employment.
• Voted Best Volunteer of the Month.

Quotable Quotes
• Received many compliments from customers and from hospital staff.
• "David performed his duties in an efficient and enthusiastic manner. He got along with all the customers and hospital staff. His smile and great attitude were contagious." Quote from reference letter from Ms. Alicia Solomon.

Description of Activities/Accomplishments

Hospital Attendant:
• Directed and escorted incoming patients and visitors from hospital admitting office to designated areas in hospital.
• Assisted patients in walking to prevent accidents from falling.
• Transported non-ambulatory patients using a wheelchair.
• Delivered messages and filed papers for office staff.

Pharmacy Aide:
• Mixed pharmaceutical preparations under direction of pharmacist.
• Received and placed supplies in stock.
• Delivered drug orders and ran errands.
• Labeled drugs, chemicals, and other pharmaceutical preparations as directed by pharmacist.
• Computed charges for drugs and engaged in other duties designated by and under the supervision of pharmacist.
• Procured, stored, and issued pharmaceutical materials and supplies.
• Dispensed prescribed medicines.

© 1995 Harris Espérance Incorporated   Form F11/95

Figure 2-22 FORM 11, Hospital Volunteer

David was a hospital volunteer. In the example, he described his duties in a functional format by using the *Dictionary of Occupational Titles* for descriptive sentences.

Use the techniques you learned in writing your job descriptions in Step 3 of the previous section.

Complete a detailed record for each major activity.

- Use headers to make reading and comprehension easier.

- Use bullets with skill statements to improve readability.

- Use white space to break up the gray print.

Include special accomplishments and awards in your narrative. Describe your accomplishments, skills, and experiences. Your club's management manual should provide a detailed listing of duties for all officers. Use it to write your functional skills.

Complete a detailed record for each major activity.

DESCRIPTION BY ACTIVITY

Activity No. 5	Name of Organization or Activity (include Address and Telephone No.) Redmond Toastmasters, Redmond, OR 97756
Length of Activity From: 05/90 To:	Purpose of Organization or Activity Self-improvement—to improve communication and leadership skills.

Offices Held	Dates Held
• Area Governor	1992-93
• Club Treasurer	1991, 1994

Awards, Special Recognitions, Etc.
• Received Toastmaster of the Year award from district, division, area, and club ('92).
• Received highest rating out of 24 presenters—awarded Best Presenter award ('92).

Quotable Quotes
• "Janice, we've never had an Area Governor accomplish so much in such a short time. You've inspired your area beyond all imagination." Quote from District Governor Harry Livingstone.

Description of Activities/Accomplishments

Special Accomplishments:
• Sponsored 9 new members in 3 months—highest in club history ('92).
• Sponsored new club in Madras.
• Wrote monthly newsletter for past 3 years. Received many compliments from district officers. Many of them preferred this newsletter over the district one because of its informative and uplifting format.
• Presented "Educational Opportunities for the Working Adult" at fall district conference. Received highest rating out of 24 presenters. Awarded Best Presenter award ('92).

Club Treasurer:
• Received and disbursed funds: Completed and forwarded new bank signature cards to authorize withdrawals. Notified club members in writing of dues payable. Collected payable dues and fees on a timely basis. Paid bills promptly. Reconciled bank account monthly. Made deposits and wrote checks for disbursements.
• Prepared records and reports: Prepared budgets and cash flow projections, annually and quarterly. Monitored budget for compliance. Maintained complete and accurate records of all financial transactions. Presented verbal and written financial reports monthly. Submitted club accounts for audit at year-end. Received compliments from accountant for quality and accurate work. Trained successor.

Figure 2-23 FORM 11, Club Membership

In the example, Janice used the Toastmasters' club management handbook as a crib for writing her skill narratives. The duties were easily translated to functional skill narratives.

Do not take for granted the skills you acquire in activities not related to a job. Often the skills you need for a new job may come from an outside activity. Skills acquired from home and community activities are just as important as skills learned from employment.

■ Use headers to make reading and comprehension easier.

■ Use bullets with skill statements to improve readability.

■ Use white space to break up the gray print.

EXAMPLE OF FORM II FOR VOLUNTEER WORK

Job descriptions from the *Dictionary of Occupational Titles* were used for writing the functional narratives in this example.

DESCRIPTION BY ACTIVITY

Activity No. 4	Name of Organization or Activity (include Address and Telephone No.) Redmond Little League, Redmond, OR 97756
Length of Activity From: 02/89 To: 10/91	**Purpose of Organization or Activity** To provide recreational baseball to youngsters in the community.

Offices Held	Dates Held
• Secretary, Bookkeeper, • Fund-Raiser, Public Relations	February 1, 1989 – October 9, 1991

Awards, Special Recognitions, Etc.
- Received Volunteer of the Year award in 1989 and 1990.
- Received many compliments from parents and children for the work given to the program.

Quotable Quotes
- "I've never worked with anyone who gave so much to this program. The kids have all grown from the experience. The fine example you provide for others is a great inspiration to all of us."
Quote from letter by Mr. Daniel Wysocki, a parent of a Little Leaguer

Description of Activities/Accomplishments

- **Secretary:** Scheduled appointments, gave information to callers, and relieved officials of clerical work and minor administrative and business details. Composed and typed routine correspondence. Compiled and typed statistical reports. Recorded minutes of board meetings. Compiled financial reports. Prepared outgoing mail using postage metering machine. Located and attached appropriate files to correspondence to be answered by employer. Answered phones and provided callers with information, or routed call to appropriate official. Greeted visitors, ascertained nature of business, and conducted visitors to appropriate person.

- **Bookkeeper:** Maintained complete set of finance transactions and records. Verified and entered details of transactions as they occurred in account and cash journals from items such as sales slips, invoices, check stubs, inventory records, and acquisitions. Summarized details on separate ledgers and transferred data to general ledger. Balanced books and compiled reports to show statistics such as cash receipts and expenditures, accounts payable and receivable, profit and loss. Paid all incoming bills.

- **Fund-Raising Coordinator:** Planned fund-raising events for league. Organized volunteers and planned social functions. Wrote to, telephoned, and visited individuals and businesses to solicit funds. Compiled and analyzed information about potential contributors to develop mailing and contact lists. Prepared market strategy and sale approach. Wrote, telephoned, and visited potential contributors and persuaded them to contribute funds by explaining purpose and benefits of fund-raising program. Took pledges and fees from contributors. Recorded expenses incurred and contributions received.

- **Sponsor Coordinator:** Solicited sponsors from community. Compiled and maintained sponsor lists and contribution records. Explained privileges and obligations of sponsorship.

- **Concessions Coordinator:** Supervised and coordinated activities of concession personnel. Hired and discharged employees. Supervised employees engaged in cooking, serving and ordering food and related supplies. Planned menus, prepared and apportioned foods and used surpluses and leftovers. Specified number of servings to be made. Set prices.

- **Public Relations:** Planned and conducted public relations program designed to create and maintain favorable public image for league. Planned and directed development of information designed to keep public informed of league programs. Prepared and distributed fact sheets and news releases to media and other interested parties. Purchased advertising space and time. Arranged media events to highlight programs and individuals.

Form F11/95

Figure 2-24 FORM II, Volunteer Activities

STEP 3: COMPLETE FORM 12, MISCELLANEOUS ACTIVITIES

Use this form when an activity is repeated often and the detail is short.

Examples of miscellaneous activities include books read, movies watched, and speeches given, photo credits, as well as travels, cooking, competitions, and awards.

Complete a record for each repetitive activity.

MISCELLANEOUS ACTIVITIES

Year	Name of Activity: Books Read
1992	Bradshaw, John. Home Coming—Reclaiming and Championing Your Inner Child. Bantum Books, a division of Bantam Doubleday Deli Publishing Group, Inc., 666 Fifth Avenue, New York, NY 10103. Copyright 1990 by John Bradshaw.
	Clawson, James G., John P. Kotter, Victor A. Faux, and Charles C. McArthur. Self-Assessment and Career Development, 3rd Edition. Prentice Hall, Englewood Cliffs, NJ 07632. Copyright 1992, 1985, 1978 by Prentice Hall. ISBN 0-13-803180-0.
	Dawson, Kenneth M. and Sheryl N. Job Search—The Total System. John Wiley & Sons, Inc., New York, NY. Copyright 1988 by Dawson & Dawson Management, Consultants.
	Frankl, Viktor E. Man's Search for Meaning. A Washington Square Press publication of Pocket Books, a division of Simon & Schuster Inc., 1230 Avenue of the Americas, New York, NY 10020. Copyright 1984, 1962, 1959. ISBN 0-671-66736-X. First Washington Square Printing February 1985. $6.95.
	Otte, Fred L., and Peggy G. Hutcheson. Helping Employees Manage Careers. Prentice Hall, Englewood Cliffs, NJ 07632. Copyright 1992 by Prentice Hall. ISBN 0-13-385287-3.
	Poole, Bernard John, Stephanie Urchick Lashway, and Paul W. Layne. The Resume Writer— Writing It Right. Prentice Hall, Englewood Cliffs, NJ 07632. Copyright 1992 by Bernard John Poole, Stephanie Urchick Lashway, Paul W. Layne. ISBN 0-13-775388-8.
	Sadat, Jehan. A Woman of Egypt. Pocket Books, a division of Simon & Schuster Inc., 1230 Avenue of the Americas, New York, NY 10020. Copyright 1987 by Simon & Schuster Inc. ISBN 0-671-72996-9. LCCCN 87-12697. $10.95. Jehan Sadat's intimate story of her love for Anwar Sadat and for her country.
1993	Heller, Joseph. God Knows. Alfred A. Knopf, Inc., New York, NY. Copyright 1984 by Scapegoat Productions, Inc. ISBN 0-394-52919-7.
	McCullough, David. Truman. Simon & Schuster, New York, NY. Copyright 1992. ISBN 0-671-45654-7.
	Segal, Eric. Acts of Faith. Bantam Books, New York, NY. Copyright 1992 by Plays Inc. ISBN 0-553-07034-7.
	Sher, Barbara. Wishcraft—How to Get What You Really Want. Ballantine Books, New York, NY. Copyright 1979 by Barbara Sher. ISBN 345-34089-2. $7.95.
	Talbot, Michael. The Holographic Universe. Harper Perennial, HarperCollins Publishers, Inc., New York, NY 10022. Copyright 1991 by Michael Talbot. ISBN 0-06-092258-3. $10.

 Form 12/95

Figure 2-25 FORM 12, Books Read

This form can also be used as a catchall of activities. If you have hobbies or special interests that demonstrate specific skills, and if these skills are not recorded elsewhere, list them on this form. Following are some example narratives written by students.

Year	Miscellaneous Activities
1989–1991	Pulled green, dry, and planer chains in lumber mill for 3 years without any lost time due to accidents or illnesses. Perfect attendance record.
1993	Operated D-10, Terex, Skookum overhead log crane, Hysters, and lift trucks. Excellent safety record on all equipment.
1986–1988	Was pack leader for boy scout troop. Increased local pack membership from 7 to 35. Enlisted parents' support and involvement for all programs.
1981–1995	Traveled extensively—visited the Orient, Europe, Africa, India.
1988–	Licensed pilot. F.A.A. Commercial Pilot Certificate No. 0035062. ▪ Rated for single-engine and multiengine airplane and rotocraft helicopter. ▪ Instrument certified. Over 5,000 hours flying time. ▪ 750 hours helicopter. 350 hours navigating. ▪ 76 transoceanic flights as aircraft commander.
1981–1988	Former army captain and helicopter pilot. ▪ Aviation section leader and company commander. ▪ Graduated first in officer candidate school and flight school.
1995	Certified American Red Cross CPR and first aid instructor.
1993	Called and visited customers regarding past-due accounts. Often complimented on personal ability to work with a variety of people on delicate financial matters.
1990–	Drove 18-wheeler for 5 years, averaging 100,000 per year without a single accident. Received best driver of the year award for all 5 years.
1990–	Taught budgeting and low-cost food preparation to low-income families through local county extension agency. Prepared income taxes for senior citizens through community volunteer program.

STEP 4: COPY AND FILE OTHER DOCUMENTS

You may choose to file copies of supporting documents with each form in this section. Other documents may include: newspaper clippings, awards or rewards, certificates of recognition, letters of appreciation, thank-you cards and letters, ribbons. File these records with the appropriate activity form.

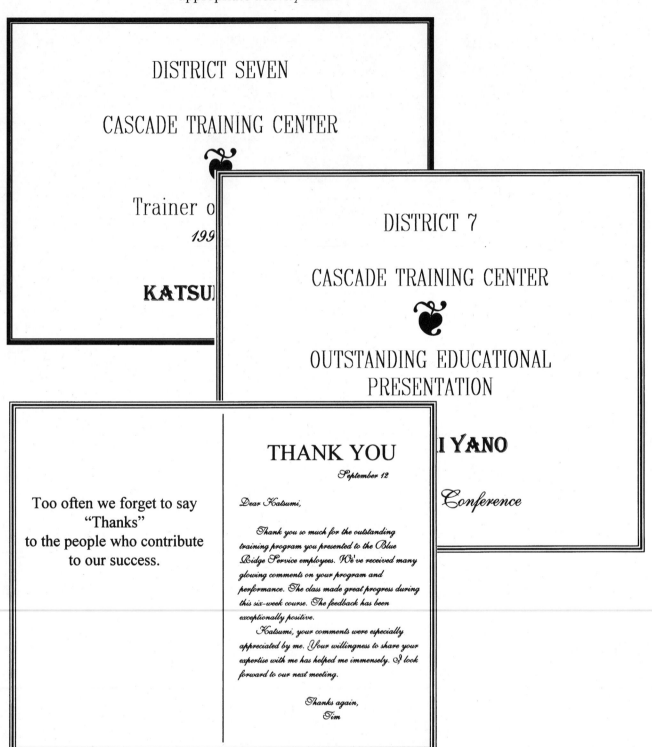

Figure 2-26   Other Documents

Here is a refresher on the writing techniques you want to use. Think of an activity, a job, a project, or an achievement that you did well, feel good about, and enjoyed. Then write an achievement or functional narrative about it. When writing skill narratives, begin by choosing action words (verbs) like the ones listed here. Then add the object(s)—fill in the details; add results, testimonials, comments. Prioritize every verb, date, concept, sentence, and word.

To help get you started, here's a list of action verbs.

Adapted	Distributed	Launched	Reinforced
Addressed	Drafted	Lectured	Represented
Adjusted	Drew	Maintained	Reshaped
Administered	Edited	Managed	Resolved
Advised	Eliminated	Measured	Responded to
Analyzed	Established	Moderated	Retrieved
Answered	Evaluated	Monitored	Revamped
Applied	Examined	Moved	Reviewed
Approved	Expanded	Negotiated	Revised
Arranged	Explained	Obtained	Saved
Audited	Expressed	Officiated	Scheduled
Cataloged	Filed	Operated	Screened
Chaired	Followed	Ordered	Selected
Charted	Formulated	Organized	Solved
Coded	Founded	Originated	Sorted
Compiled	Gathered	Performed	Streamlined
Completed	Generated	Persuaded	Strengthened
Computed	Governed	Pinpointed	Submitted
Conceived	Graphed	Planned	Supervised
Conducted	Guided	Prepared	Synthesized
Consulted	Implemented	Presented	Systematized
Contracted	Improved	Presided	Taught
Controlled	Increased	Processed	Trained
Coordinated	Indexed	Produced	Transcribed
Created	Influenced	Programmed	Treated
Cut (costs)	Initiated	Proposed	Updated
Delegated	Installed	Provided	Used
Demonstrated	Interviewed	Recommended	Validated
Designed	Introduced	Reconciled	Verified
Developed	Invented	Recorded	Volunteered
Directed	Investigated	Recruited	Wrote
	Issued	Reduced	X-rayed

The following examples were written for the job objective of MEDICAL RECORDS. Are you able to write in a similar manner?

Skill/Verb	Object	Results/Comments
Transcribed	physician's written orders.	
Charted, graphed, and recorded	data in patient medical records,	including patient identification, vital signs, prescriptions, and scheduled and canceled appointments.

Now write some experience narratives of your own using verbs from the list on page 59.

_____

_____

_____

_____

_____

_____

_____

_____

_____

_____

_____

_____

EXPLORE JOBS AND EMPLOYERS
Work and Its Environment

The wrong job or environment is like shoes two sizes too small; it's deforming.

Patty served me breakfast early one morning in a New York City restaurant. She turned this meal into a pleasant dining experience. She had worked all over the world as a waitress. Patty loved her work, and it showed.

Later I met Gary, a garbage collector with a mission. He had the most important job in the world—to clean up the environment. He gave speeches and introduced projects to his community to make it a better world.

These two people do jobs that some might find unsatisfying, yet both Patty and Gary have found satisfaction in their work and in their environment. Why? Because they have matched what they do with an environment they enjoy. Both have found happiness in their world and brought professionalism to their job.

Richard Nelson Bolles provides a basis for job and environment selection in *What Color Is Your Parachute?* He asks you to think of yourself as a plant—In what environment would you thrive? He writes, "It is easier to make the environment conform to you, rather than you to the environment."

In this chapter, you will look at both the elements of a job and its environment. Any combination other than the right job and the right environment can be detrimental to your career, self-esteem, and health. So it is important to consider these factors.

How do you know what's right for you? You continue on the path of self-awareness. You build on the exercises you began in Chapter 1. Only you can decide what is right for you.

In this chapter, you will learn first about jobs and what elements you enjoy most. Then you will learn about employers and their diverse work environments. The exercises that you do on separate pages can be filed in the SELF-AWARENESS section of your *Companion Planner*.

Both a person's desires and his abilities need to be considered in finding the rightness of a career . . . most people often mismatch both areas.

—Gunn

You have already become familiar with the *Dictionary of Occupational Titles*. Now you are going to use it to find jobs that you would enjoy and that fit you as a person.

Step 1

Imagine the *Dictionary of Occupational Titles* as a large college campus. On this campus are ten large buildings. You are to survey each of the buildings to determine which ones interest you the most. Following is a "picture" of this campus. Review the campus, and select the buildings (categories) and floors (divisions) that interest you.

LISTING OF OCCUPATIONAL CATEGORIES AND DIVISIONS

0 PROFESSIONAL, TECHNICAL, MANAGERIAL	**1 PROFESSIONAL, TECHNICAL, MANAGERIAL**
Architecture	Museum, library and archival sciences
Engineering: aeronautical, electrical/electronic, civil, ceramic, mechanical, chemical, mining and petroleum, metallurgy and metallurgical, industrial, agricultural, marine, nuclear	Law and jurisprudence
	Religion and theology
	Writing
	Art
Drafting	Entertainment and recreation
Surveying/cartographic	Administrative specializations
Mathematics and physical sciences	Managers and officials
Computer related	Other professional, technical and managerial occupations not listed elsewhere
Life sciences	
Social sciences	
Medicine and health	
Education	

2 CLERICAL AND SALES	**3 SERVICE**
Stenography, typing, and filing	Domestic service
Computing and account-recording	Food and beverage preparation and service
Production and stock clerks	Lodging and related occupations
Information and message distribution	Barbering, cosmetology and related occupations
Miscellaneous clerical occupations	Amusement and recreation
Sales occupations, services,	Miscellaneous personal services
Sales occupations, consumable commodities	Apparel and furnishings services
Sales occupations, commodities	Protective services
Miscellaneous sales occupations	Building and related service occupations

4 AGRICULTURAL, FISHERY, FORESTRY	5 PROCESSING
Plant farming Animal farming Miscellaneous agriculture Fishery Forestry Hunting and trapping	Processing metals, food, tobacco, paper, petroleum, coal, natural and manufactured gas, chemicals, plastics, synthetics, rubber, paint, wood and wood products, stone, clay, glass, leather, or textiles Ore refining and foundry
6 MACHINE TRADES	**7 BENCH WORK**
Metal machining Metalworking Mechanics and machinery repairing Paper working. Printing. Wood Machining. Machining stone, clay, or glass. Textiles	Fabrication, assembly, and repair of metal products; scientific, medical, photographic, optical, horological equipment; electrical equipment; plastics, synthetics, rubber, wood products, stone, sand, clay, glass, textiles, and leather Painting and decorating. Other
8—STRUCTURAL	**9—MISCELLANEOUS**
Fabricating metals Welding, cutting Assembling, installing, and repairing electrical Painting, plastering, waterproofing, and cementing Excavating, grading, and paving Construction and structural	Motor freight. Transportation Packaging and materials handling Extraction of minerals Production and distribution of utilities Motion picture, radio, and television production Graphic arts

Step 2

Record your choices here.

Category	Division

Step 3

Now study the *Dictionary of Occupational Titles*, and identify jobs that fit you. When you find a job title that seems right, read the job descriptions above and below it. Now list five jobs that you would enjoy doing.

1. _____

2. _____

3. _____

4. _____

5. _____

The *Dictionary of Occupational Titles* (DOT) is published by the U.S. Department of Labor, Employment and Training Administration, Washington, D.C. It lists over twenty thousand occupations with detailed descriptions and can be found at your local library.

Every job requires a worker to function in some degree to data, things, and people. Much of the information in the *Dictionary of Occupation Titles* (DOT) is based on this premise. The functions in the following listings are arranged from the relatively simple to the complex.

Step 1

Review the lists and identify the worker functions you enjoy most.

DATA

Data include information, knowledge, and conceptions related to data, people, or things and obtained by observation, investigation, interpretation, visualization, and mental creation. Data are intangible and include numbers, words, symbols, ideas, concepts, and oral verbalization. (4th Digit of the Occupation Code in the DOT)

0 Synthesizing	Combining, creating, developing, planning, designing.
1 Coordinating	Organizing.
2 Analyzing	Evaluating, interpreting.
3 Compiling	Researching, collecting, gathering.
4 Computing	Performing arithmetic operations.
5 Copying	Retrieving, entering, posting, transcribing, storing data.
6 Comparing	Examining or observing data, people, or things.

THINGS

Things are inanimate objects, substances, or materials. They include machines, tools, equipment, and products. A thing is tangible and has shape, form, and other physical characteristics. (6th Digit of the Occupational Code in the DOT)

0 Setting up	Installing, building, constructing, repairing, restoring, diagnosing, fixing, inventing, creating, designing, improving.
1 Precision Working	Shaping, fitting, guiding, fashioning, appraising, drawing, cutting, lettering, setting.
2 Controlling	(Operating machines or machinery) Adjusting, changing, starting, stopping, checking, cleaning, refilling.
3 Driving	(Operating equipment) Steering, guiding.
4 Manipulating	(Tools, objects, computers) Using.
5 Tending	Minding, watching.
6 Feeding	(Off-bearing) Loading, emptying.
7 Handling	Lifting, shipping, moving, pushing, pulling, feeling, planting; working with objects, things, earth, or nature; being athletic.

PEOPLE

People include human beings and animals dealt with on an individual basis as if they were human. (5th Digit of the Occupational Code in the DOT)

0 Mentoring	Advising, guiding, consulting, counseling with regard to legal, scientific, clinical, or spiritual problems; founding or leading.
1 Negotiating	Exchanging ideas to reach joint decisions and/or formulate policies or programs.
2 Instructing	Teaching, training, coaching; working with animals; teaching through explanation, demonstration, and supervised practice; making recommendations on the basis of technical disciplines.
3 Supervising	Determining work procedures and assigning duties to workers; maintaining harmonious relations; promoting efficiency and production.
4 Diverting	Performing, amusing, distracting, usually through stage, screen, TV, or radio.
5 Persuading	Influencing others in favor of a product, service, or point of view; selling; urging.
6 Speaking/ signaling	Talking; communicating with people or animals; sensing; feeling; listening.
7 Serving	Attending to needs or requests of people or animals; responding to immediately; caring for; treating.
8 Helping	(Taking instructions) No variety of responsibility is involved in this function.

Step 2

Rank the categories Data, Things, and People using the following codes: 1 = Most Favorite, 2 = Next Favorite, and 3 = Least Favorite. Now record the rank on the blank line in the following table.

Step 3

Review the lists and record the worker functions you enjoy most. You may have several choices in one group and only a few in another.

Data Rank #_____	People Rank #_____	Things Rank #_____

The *Occupational Outlook Handbook* (OOH) is another resource that can help you with your career decision. This book groups jobs into different categories than the DOT and provides another way to look at occupational choices.

DOT Codes

Nature of the Work

Working Conditions

Employment Statistics

Training, Other Qualifications, and Advancement

Job Outlook

Earnings Potential

Related Occupations

Sources of Additional Information

Handlers, Equipment Cleaners, Helpers, and Laborers

Construction Trades Helpers

(D.O.T. 709.687-018; 821.667, 684-014; 822.664, .684-014; 825.684-010; 829.684-022, -026; 840.687; 844.687; 850.684-014, -850.687; 860.664-014, -018; 861.664, .687; 862.684-018, -022; 864.687-010, 860.567-010, .664-014, .687-010, -026, -034, -042; 899.664-010; 911.667-018; 930.664-014, .666-010, .667-010, .687-010, -014; 939.364, .663; 953.687)

Nature of the Work

Construction trades helpers, also known as construction laborers, provide much of the routine physical labor at building sites. They supply tools, materials, and equipment to carpenters, electricians, masons, plumbers, and other construction workers. They also dig trenches, set braces to support the sides of excavations, operate earth tamping equipment, and clean up rubble and debris.

Some construction laborers have job titles that indicate the work they do. Bricklayers' tenders and plasterers' tenders, both commonly known as hod carriers, mix and supply materials for bricklayers and plasterers, set up and move scaffolding, and provide many other services. Hod carriers must be familiar with the work of bricklayers and plasterers and know the materials and tools they use. Construction

laborers also place concrete for cement masons, who do the finishing work..

Laborers may operate motorized equipment such as cement mixers, buggies, front-end loaders, "walk-behind" ditchdiggers, small mechanical hoists, and laser beam equipment to align and grade ditches and tunnels.

Working Conditions

Construction work is physically strenuous. It requires frequent bending, climbing, and heavy lifting. Much of the work is performed outdoors. Construction helpers, like most other workers in construction, are subject to falls; cuts, burns, and abrasions from tools and equipment; and sore or strained muscles from heavy lifting.

Employment

Construction trades helpers held about 519,000 jobs in 1986. Construction contractors were their major employers. Construction laborers work throughout the country, but most jobs are concentrated in metropolitan areas.

Training, Other Qualifications, and Advancement

For most construction helpers' jobs, little or no formal training or experience is needed. For some jobs, like plumbers' and electricians' helpers, experience and familiarity with construction methods, materials, and operations are needed. Generally, helpers must be at least 18 years old, in good physical condition, and willing to work hard.

Beginners usually do simple jobs, such as unloading trucks or picking up debris, and learn skills informally from craft workers and more experienced helpers. As laborers gain experience, job assignments become more complex. In order to better prepare laborers for job tasks, contractors and unions have established 4- to 8-week entry level training programs in many States to teach basic construction techniques, safety practices, and machinery operation. In addition, some programs offer training to help experienced laborers keep abreast of technological advances. For instance, two subjects currently being emphasized are asbestos removal and abatement, and the handling, control, removal, and disposal of toxic and hazardous wastes.

Some laborers become supervisors and direct the work of laborer crews.

Job Outlook

Employment of construction trades helpers is expected to grow more slowly than the average

for all occupations through the year 2000. Nevertheless, job openings should be plentiful because the occupation is large and turnover is high. Many people take laborer jobs in order to earn money for a specific purpose—for example, a college education—and then quit. Others quickly move into construction trades jobs such as carpenter, bricklayer, or cement mason, or decide they don't like construction work.

Growth in population and economic activity will spur construction work in the years ahead. Employment of laborers will not grow as fast, however, as continued mechanization and technological advances limit the need for human labor. Mechanization has affected helpers more than construction trades occupations and will likely continue to do so.

Employment of construction laborers is highly sensitive to cyclical swings in construction activity, and layoffs are common in downturns.

Earnings

Median weekly earnings for construction trades helpers working full time were about $275 in 1986. One-half earned between $200 and $390 weekly; the highest 10 percent earned more than $520 a week. Earnings for construction trades helpers may be reduced on occasion because poor weather and downturns in construction activity limit the amount of time they can work.

Many construction laborers are members of the Laborers' International Union of North America.

Related Occupations

Construction trades helpers need strength and stamina. Other occupations in which work is arduous are refuse collectors, machine feeders and offbearers, and hand freight, stock, and material movers.

Sources of Additional Information

For information about jobs, contact local building or construction contractors, local construction associations, a local of the Laborers' International Union of North America, or the local office of the State employment service.

For general information about the work of construction laborers, contact:

Laborers' International Union of North America, 905 16th St. NW., Washington, DC 20006.

Laborers'—Associated General Contractors' Education and Training Fund, P.O. Box 37, Pomfret Center, CT 06259.

A bricklayer helper uses brick tongs to move brick.

Figure 3-1   Occupational Outlook Handbook, 1988–89 Edition (Washington, D.C.: U.S. Department of Labor), p. 400

The *Occupational Outlook Handbook* is filled with information. The preceding example shows the type of information available for each job category. The code numbers are identical to those used in the *Dictionary of Occupational Titles*. Reading about jobs that interest you is helpful during your decision making.

Step 1
Review this list of job categories.

Managerial and management-related occupations	Health-diagnosing and health-treating practitioners	Marketing and sales occupations	Construction trades and extractive occupations
Engineers, Surveyors, and Architects	Registered nurses, pharmacists, dieticians, therapists, and physician assistants	Administrative support occupations	Production occupations
Natural, computer, and mathematical occupations	Health technologists and technicians	Service occupations	Transportation and materials-moving occupations
Lawyers, social scientists, social workers, and religious workers	Writers, artists, and entertainers	Agriculture, forestry, fishing, and related occupations	Handlers, equipment cleaners, helpers, and laborers
Teachers, librarians, and counselors	Technologists and technicians (except health)	Mechanics, installers, and repairers	Job opportunities in the armed forces

Step 2
Choose three occupational categories that fit you best, and record the choices here.

1. _____

2. _____

3. _____

Step 3
Now look up and read the job descriptions within the OOH category you have chosen. Do they still fit your needs? If yes, continue on to the next exercise. If no, redo this exercise until you have found at least one job that fits your interests.

The *Occupational Outlook Handbook* is published every other year by the U.S. Department of Labor, Bureau of Labor Statistics, Washington, D.C. It describes 850 occupations in thirty-five major industries and can be found at your local library.

Record the skills you enjoy most from your data file. There are many. Review each section carefully. For convenience, draw circles around all skills you enjoy. Classify every skill according to type (Data, People, or Things), and record each on a form similar to the following sample.

Education
The skills I enjoy using most while going to school are:

Data	People	Things

Employers
The skills I enjoy using most while working are:

Data	People	Things

Other
The skills I enjoy using most while doing other activities are:

Data	People	Things

Summary Recap
The skills I enjoy most are:

Data	People	Things

I've heard many people talk about their dead-end jobs. I would like to go on the record and state: "There are no dead-end jobs; only dead-end thinking." To illustrate the point, I've listed some of the jobs I've held over the years and the path that each has taken. With some thought, one could continue each initial job down a career path and find that each leads somewhere. It all depends on one's personal initiative and imagination.

JOBS AND CAREER PATHS

Bean picker/ field-worker	Baby-sitter	Carhop	General acct./ office clerk	Personnel director	Career consultant
Row checker/ bag weigher	Nursery worker	Waitress	Log/sawmilll timber clerk	Safety director	College instructor
Picker supervisor	Nursery supervisor	Fry cook	Timber accountant	Affirmative action mgr.	Corporate trainer
Irrigation/ field hand	Nursery manager	Cafe manager	Timber dept. accting. mgr.	Benefits manager	
Field owner/ employer	Nursery owner	Cafe owner/ employer			

Step 1
List four jobs you have held, and create a career path for each.

Step 2
In the last two columns, list two jobs you would love to have, and create a career path for each.

Let's look now at employers and the environments that surround them. We will begin by choosing the type of environment.

Would you prefer welding bomb casings or baby carriages?
— Richard Nelson Bolles

Step 1
Check the environment that best fits you.

I prefer working for a company that produces a:

    Product _____   Describe the kind of product: _____

    Service _____   Describe the type of service: _____

I prefer working with these types of people: _____

I prefer a profit _____, nonprofit _____, or a not-for-profit _____ organization.

I prefer a local _____, national _____, or an international _____ business.

I prefer a union _____ or a nonunion _____ operation.

I prefer working with a public _____, private _____, self- _____, or cooperative ownership.

I prefer working for the government: city _____, county _____, state _____, or federal _____ .

Step 2
Now describe the environment in the space that follows.

It is far easier to make the environment conform to you, rather than you to the environment.

Step 1
Choose and then describe the size of the organization you would prefer.

_____ Very small (under 50 employees)
_____ Medium (101–500 employees)
_____ Super large (over 5,000 employees)
_____ Small (50–100 employees)
_____ Large (501–5,000 employees)

Step 2
Describe the geographic location you would prefer.

Step 3
Choose the distance from home you prefer and then describe your commute.

Close to home: _____ blocks
Far from home: _____ miles

Culture is defined by *Webster's New Collegiate Dictionary* as "the customary beliefs, social forms . . . and material traits of a group." It is further defined as "the integrated pattern of human behavior that includes thought, speech, action, and artifacts and depends upon [one's] capacity for learning and transmitting knowledge to succeeding generations."

Culture shock may be one of the major reasons why people supposedly "fail" when they leave one organization for another. For example, consider the differences in the cultural environment of your local home-owned bank and the Bank of America.

Step 1
Following is a recap of culture types as depicted in *Corporate Cultures,* by Terrence E. Deal and Allen A. Kennedy. Read the culture styles and decide which culture fits you best; then look for this culture in each employer environment.

Tough-Guy/ Macho:	Work Hard/ Play Hard:	Bet-Your Company:	Process:
A world of individualists who regularly take high risks and get quick feedback on whether their actions were right or wrong.	Fun and action are the rule here, and employees take few risks, all with quick feedback; to succeed, the culture encourages them to maintain a high level of relatively low-risk activity.	Cultures with big-stakes decisions, where years pass before employees know whether decisions have paid off; a high-risk, slow-feedback environment.	A world of little or no feedback where employees find it hard to measure what they do; instead, they concentrate on how it's done . . . another name for this culture when the processes get out of control—bureaucracy!

Step 2
Describe the culture that fits you best.

Step 3

Described here are four basic types of management styles. Read them; then complete the two unfinished sentences that follow.

Authoritarian:	Paternalistic:	Participative:	Laissez-Faire:
The decision-making power is concentrated in one person or an elite group; this style is not constitutionally responsible to the people.	The authority figure undertakes to supply the needs or regulate the conduct of those under his or her control in matters affecting them as individuals as well as in their employment	This style provides the individual and/or group the opportunity to participate in the decision-making process.	This style is characterized by deliberate abstention from direction or decision making or interference with individual freedom of choice and action.

The management style I use most is:

The management style I enjoy working with most is:

From the following list, select three industrial classification codes that interest you, and list them here.

1. _____

2. _____

3. _____

Standard Industrial Classification (Sic) Code List

DIVISION A. AGRICULTURE, FORESTRY & FISHERIES
0100 Agricultural Production--Crops
0200 Agricultural Production-Livestock
0700 Agricultural Services
0800 Forestry
0910 Commercial Fishing
0920 Fish Hatcheries, Game Propagation
0970 Hunting, Trapping, Game Propagation

DIVISION B: MINING
1000 Metal Mining
1200 Coal Mining
1300 Oil and Gas Extraction
1400 Nonmetallic Minerals, Except Fuels

DIVISION C: CONSTRUCTION
1520 Residential Building Construction
1530 Operative Builders
1540 Nonresidential Building Construction
1610 Highway and Street Construction
1620 Heavy Construction, Except Highway
1710 Plumbing, Heating, Air-Conditioning
1730 Electrical Work
1740 Masonry, Stonework and Plastering
1750 Carpentry and Floor Work
1760 Roofing, Siding and Sheet Metal Work
1770 Concrete Work
1780 Water Well Drilling
1790 Misc. Special Trade Contractors

DIVISION D: MANUFACTURING
2010 Meat Products
2020 Dairy Products
2030 Preserved Fruits and Vegetables
2040 Grain Mill Products
2050 Bakery Products
2060 Sugar and Confectionery Products
2070 Fats and Oils
2080 Beverages
2090 Misc. Food and Kindred Products
2100 Tobacco Products
2200 Textile Mill Products
2300 Apparel and Other Textile Products
2400 Lumber and Wood Products/Logging
2500 Furniture and Fixtures
2600 Paper and Allied Products
2700 Printing and Publishing
2810 Industrial Inorganic Chemicals
2820 Plastics Materials and Synthetics
2830 Drugs
2840 Soap, Cleaners, and Toilet Goods
2850 Paints and Allied Products
2860 Industrial Organic Chemicals
2870 Agricultural Chemicals
2890 Miscellaneous Chemical Products
2910 Petroleum Refining
2950 Asphalt Paving and Roofing Materials
2990 Misc. Petroleum and Coal Products
3000 Rubber and Misc. Plastic Products
3100 Leather and Leather Products
3200 Stone, Clay and Glass Products
3300 Primary Metal Industries
3400 Fabricated Metal Products
3500 Industrial Machinery and Equipment
3600 Electronic & Other Electric Equipment
3710 Motor Vehicles and Equipment
3720 Aircraft and Parts
3730 Ship and Boat Building and Repairing
3740 Railroad Equipment
3750 Motorcycles, Bicycles and Parts
3760 Guided Missiles, Space Vehicles, Parts
3790 Miscellaneous Transportation Equipment
3800 Measuring, Analyzing & Controlling Instruments. Photographic, Medical & Optical Goods, Watches and Clocks
3910 Jewelry, Silverware and Plated Ware
3930 Musical Instruments
3940 Toys and Sporting Goods
3950 Pens, Pencils, Office & Art Supplies
3960 Costume Jewelry and Notions
3990 Miscellaneous Manufacturers

E: TRANSPORTATION AND PUBLIC UTILITIES
4000 Railroad Transportation
4110 Local and Suburban Transportation
4120 Taxicabs
4130 Intercity and Rural Bus Transportation
4140 Bus Charter Service
4150 School Buses
4170 Bus Terminal and Service Facilities
4210 Trucking & Courier Services, Ex. Air
4220 Public Warehousing and Storage
4230 Trucking Terminal Facilities
4300 U.S. Postal Service
4400 Water Transportation
4500 Transportation By Air
4600 Pipelines, Except Natural Gas
4700 Transportation Services
4810 Telephone Communications
4820 Telegraph & Other Communications
4830 Radio and Television Broadcasting
4840 Cable and Other Pay TV Services
4890 Communications Services, NEC
4900 Electric, Gas and Sanitary Services

DIVISION F: WHOLESALE TRADE
5010 Motor Vehicles, Parts & Supplies
5020 Furniture & Home furnishings
5030 Lumber & Construction Materials
5040 Professional & Commercial Equipment
5050 Metals & Minerals, Except Petroleum
5060 Electrical Goods
5070 Hardware, Plumbing & Heating Equipment
5080 Machinery, Equipment & Supplies
5090 Miscellaneous Durable Goods
5110 Paper and Paper Products
5120 Drugs, Proprietaries & Sundries
5130 Apparel, Piece Goods & Notions
5140 Groceries & Related Products
5150 Farm-Product Raw Materials
5160 Chemicals & Allied Products
5170 Petroleum & Petroleum Products
5180 Beer, Wine & Distilled Beverages
5190 Misc. Nondurable Goods

DIVISION G: RETAIL TRADE
5200 Building Materials & Garden Supplies
5300 General Merchandise Stores
5400 Food Stores
5510 New & Used Car Dealers
5520 Used Car Dealers
5530 Auto & Home Supply Stores
5540 Gasoline Service Stations
5550 Boat Dealers
5560 Recreational Vehicle Dealers
5570 Motorcycle Dealers
5590 Automotive Dealers NEC
5600 Apparel & Accessory Stores
5700 Furniture & Home furnishing Stores
5800 Eating & Drinking Places
5910 Drug Stores & Proprietary Stores
5920 Liquor Stores
5930 Used Merchandise Stores
5940 Miscellaneous Shopping Goods Stores
5960 Nonstore Retailers
5980 Fuel Dealers
5990 Retail Stores, NEC

DIVISION H: FINANCE, INSURANCE AND REAL ESTATE
6000 Depository Institutions
6100 Nondepository Institutions
6200 Security & Commodity Brokers
6300 Insurance Carriers
6400 Insurance Agents, Brokers, & Service
6500 Real Estate
6710 Holding Offices
6720 Investment Offices
6730 Trusts
6790 Miscellaneous Investing

DIVISION I: SERVICES
7000 Hotels & Motels. Rooming & Boarding Houses. Camps & Recreational Vehicle Parks
7210 Laundry, Cleaning & Garment Services
7220 Beauty Shops
7240 Barber Shops
7250 Shoe Repair & Shoeshine Parlors
7260 Funeral Service & Crematories
7290 Miscellaneous Personal Services
7310 Advertising Services
7320 Credit Reporting & Collection
7330 Mailing, Reproduction & Stenographic
7340 Services to Buildings
7350 Misc. Equipment Rental & Leasing
7360 Personnel Supply Services
7370 Computer & Data Processing Services
7380 Miscellaneous Business Services
7500 Auto Repair, Services, & Parking
7620 Electrical Repair Shops
7630 Watch, Clock & Jewelry Repair
7640 Reupholstery & Furniture Repair
7690 Miscellaneous Repair Shops
7810 Motion Picture Production & Services
7820 Motion Picture Distribution & Services
7830 Motion Picture Theaters
7840 Video Tape Rental
7910 Dance Studios, Schools & Halls
7920 Producers, Orchestras, Entertainers
7930 Bowling Centers
7940 Commercial Sports
7990 Misc. Amusement, Recreation Services. Golf courses, Physical Fitness Facilities, Amusement Parks, Gaming Casinos. Amusement & Recreation NEC
8010 Medical Doctor Offices & Clinics
8020 Dentist Offices & Clinics
8030 Osteopathic Physicians Offices
8040 Other Health Practitioners Offices
8050 Nursing & Personal Care Facilities
8060 Hospitals
8070 Medical & Dental Laboratories
8080 Home Health Care Services
8090 Health & Allied Services NEC
8110 Legal Services
8210 Elementary & Secondary Schools
8220 Colleges & Universities
8230 Libraries
8240 Vocational Schools
8290 Schools & Educational Services NEC
8320 Individual & Family Services
8330 Job Training & Related Services
8350 Child Day Care Services
8360 Residential Care
8390 Social Services NEC
8410 Museums & Art Galleries
8420 Botanical & Zoological Gardens
8600 Membership Organizations: Business, Professional, Labor, Civic and Social, Political, Religious
8710 Engineering & Architectural Services
8720 Accounting, Auditing & Bookkeeping
8730 Research & Testing Services
8740 Management & Public Relations
8810 Private Households
8990 Services NEC

DIVISION J: PUBLIC ADMINISTRATION
9110 Executive Offices, Legislative Bodies, General Government NEC
9200 Courts, Police Protection, Legal Counsel & Prosecution, Correctional Institutions, Fire Protection, Public Order & Safety
9300 Finance, Taxation & Monetary Policy
9400 Administration of Education Programs, Public Health, Social & Manpower, Veterans' Affairs
9510 Environmental Quality
9530 Housing & Urban Development
9600 Administration of General Economic Programs. Regulation and Administration of Transportation, Utilities, Agricultural Marketing, Commercial Sectors. Space Research & Technology.
9710 National Security
9720 International Security

DIVISION K: NONCLASSIFIABLE ESTABLISHMENTS
9900 Nonclassifiable establishments including individual borrowers

An interesting factor in the job market is the variance that exists in wages for relatively the same job. Some deciding factors for establishing wages include the industry, geographic location, labor supply, and employer. The table in Figure 3.2 shows industry variances.

1992 GROSS AVERAGE WEEKLY EARNINGS AND HOURS WORKED

	$ Earnings	Hours
All Manufacturing	469.45	41.0
Petroleum & allied products	782.71	43.8
Motor vehicles & equipment	649.99	42.4
Tobacco manufacturers	644.23	38.6
Transportation equipment	633.69	41.8
Printing & publishing	447.68	38.1
Food & kindred products	413.71	40.6
Lumber & wood products	382.86	40.6
Apparel & other textile products	258.54	37.2
Nonmanufacturing Industries		
Bituminous coal & lignite mining	763.40	44.0
Electric, gas, sanitary services	674.17	41.9
Metal mining	652.94	42.9
Telephone communications	623.61	41.0
Nonmetallic metals	550.92	44.9
General building contracting	502.13	37.5
Radio & TV broadcasting	479.21	34.7
Wholesale trade	435.48	38.2
Local & suburban transportation	403.97	38.4
Laundry & dry cleaning plants	243.78	34.0
Hotels, tourist courts, motels	228.54	30.8
Retail trade	205.63	28.8

Source: *The 1994 Information Please Almanac* (Boston, MA: Houghton Mifflin Company, 1993), pp. 57–58.

Figure 3-2   Average Weekly Earnings, reprinted by permission of Houghton Mifflin Co.

Wages are mentioned here to increase your awareness of wage scales in different industries and companies.

To assist in your decision, it is important that you know what wage you need to live on. When deciding what salary you need, it's necessary to prepare a budget. Only by doing this will you understand what salary is necessary to support you. If the salary offered by a company is too low, you have several decisions to make: (1) try negotiating a higher offer, (2) reject the offer and keep looking, or (3) find ways to supplement your income until the wage can be raised to support you.

As you make decisions about your next job, consider the industrial wage variances. If you wish to reconsider your industrial classification, record the new classification in the space that follows and write your reasons for making the change.

You can learn your financial requirements by completing Form 39, Budget Work Sheet. The work sheet is only a rough listing of budgetary needs. Add categories where necessary. If you have major additions, use a columnar pad and create your own budget form. A master form is located in the Forms section of your notebook.

Step 1
Compute your monthly and yearly expenses.

For some items it will be easier to list them as a monthly item then multiply by twelve to arrive at the yearly total.

For other items, it will be easier to record the yearly cost and then divide by twelve to arrive at the monthly cost.

Step 2
Compute your taxes. You can use a current pay stub for an estimate, acquire the actual tax rates from your payroll department, or use an estimate. If you use an estimate of 30 percent tax burden, divide your net total before taxes by .70, or 70 percent.

Step 3
Total your budget requirements, and compute your hourly requirements.

Step 4
File this form in the FINANCIAL MANAGEMENT section of your notebook.

For more serious budgeters, you will be encouraged in Unit 3, "Market," to develop a full financial plan for the job hunt. This will include preparing a projected cash flow statement, a statement of assets and liabilities, a listing of income and expenses, and a list of all your job search expenses. But for now, complete a budget work sheet so you can establish an acceptable base wage.

BUDGET WORK SHEET	Date: March 1	
Expenses	Month	Year
Housing	$ 495	$ 5,940
Utilities (Phone, Electricity, Gas, Water, Garbage)	125	1,500
Furnishings Maintenance and Upkeep	10	120
Groceries	390	4,680
Clothing and Upkeep	50	600
Personal (Health and Beauty Aids)	25	300
Transportation (Gas, Oil, Maintenance)	125	1,500
Insurance: Life *Currently paid by employer		•
Insurance: Medical, Dental, and Vision *Currently paid by employer		•
Insurance: Long-Term Disability *Currently paid by employer		•
Insurance: Automobile	50	600
Insurance: Property/Household	70	840
Insurance: Personal Liability (Included in household insurance)		–
Insurance: Other		–
Savings and Other Investments	100	1,200
Retirement (Employer contributes 6% of gross wages to retirement)	50	600
Recreation and Entertainment	50	600
Education	25	300
Contributions and Gifts	100	1,200
Dues, Subscriptions, and Memberships	5	60
Loans and Interest Payments	235	2,820
Licenses and Fees	10	120
Property Taxes	100	1,200
Net before Payroll Taxes	2,015	24,180
Federal Income Taxes		
State Income Taxes		
Social Security Taxes (FICA)	864	10,368
FUTA Taxes		
Workers' Compensation Taxes		
State Unemployment Taxes (SUI)		
Total Budget Requirements	2,879	34,548
Rate per Hour (Divide year total by 2,080 hours)		$16.61/hour

© 1995 Harris Espérance Incorporated   Form 39/95

Figure 3-3   FORM 39, Budget Work Sheet

To get a handle on what it is that you really want in a job, let's review by pulling it together. Fill in all the following blanks.

Exercise 3-1

A job description from the DOT that fits me is:

Exercise 3-2

The worker functions I enjoy most are:

Data	People	Things

Exercise 3-3

The occupational category (from the Occupational Outlook Handbook) I like the most is:

Exercise 3-4

The skills I enjoy most from my data file are:

Data	People	Things

Exercise 3-5
A career path for my next job is:

	→		→		→		→	

Exercise 3-6
A description of the best employer environment is:

Exercise 3-7
The company size and geographic location best for me is:

Exercise 3-8
The company culture and management style best for me is:

Exercise 3-9
The standard industrial classification that fits me best is:

Exercise 3-10
The required wage necessary for me to live is:

JOB DESCRIPTIONS THAT FIT MY NEEDS

Find job descriptions from the DOT or other places that fit your criteria. Then fill in the form to find the job that fits you best.

Occupational Category:	Occupational Division:
Five ideal job titles that fit me are:	
The skills I most want to use in my next job are:	
Five organizations that fit me are:	

My geographic choice is:	The best size of organization is:

The management style and culture is:	
The ideal wage range and benefits package are:	

Most college campuses have a career library. A typical library contains thousands of college catalogs on microfiche and a collection of books, pamphlets, and computer software containing job descriptions, employment outlook information, education and training requirements, and salary trends. You are encouraged to take advantage of this informative resource. Examples of computerized programs available in Oregon are described here. Your state has similar programs.

THE CAREER INFORMATION SYSTEM (CIS)

This program provides the most current information on jobs in Oregon. It is designed to help you with career and educational planning and decision making.

CIS covers 268 occupational categories or about 95 percent of the employment found in the state of Oregon, as well as the major kinds of work found elsewhere in the country.

These programs are funded by the Oregon Department of Education. For more information contact:

Oregon Career Information Center
1787 Agate Street
Eugene, OR 97403
(503) 346-3872
Your state offers a similar program.

THE MICRO-SKILLS PROGRAM

The MICRO-SKILLS program can be used in conjunction with the CIS program. It helps you analyze seventy-two specific skills.

Skill Categories:

Self-management	Situational	Detail	Movement
Operational	Numerical	Communication	Conceptual
Judgment	Reasoning	Interpersonal	Leadership

By using this program, you will learn:

1. Which skills you enjoy most and want to use in your work.
2. Which occupations use the skills you enjoy using.
3. Your Holland personality code, as related to your satisfying skills.
4. Which CIS clusters best match your skills.
5. Which specific skills may cause you to be uncomfortable in an occupation you are now considering.
6. New information about several occupations.

Your library offers similar programs. Check it out.

THE SIGI PLUS PROGRAM

SIGI PLUS, pronounced "siggy plus," is a computerized program that can help you plan your career. It was developed by a team of researchers and specialists at the Educational Testing Service, SIGI PLUS (System of Interactive Guidance and Information PLUS). This program combines the capabilities of the computer with researched information about occupations, values, interests, skills, education programs, and more. SIGI PLUS covers the major aspects of career decision making and planning through nine separate but interrelated sections. These sections include:

1. INTRODUCTION—An overview.
   - See clearly what's in the whole system.
   - Decide which sections apply to you.
   - Request more details about each section before you choose.
   - Get a recommended pathway through the system.
2. SELF-ASSESSMENT—What do I want? What am I good at?
   - Look at work-related values and decide what's most important to you.
   - Choose the main interest fields you want to use at work.
   - Look at various activities and decide which ones you like and can do well.
3. SEARCH—What occupations might I like?
   - Choose features you want in your work.
   - Choose features you want to avoid in your work.
   - Receive a list of occupations that match what you asked for.
4. INFORMATION—What occupations might I like?
   - See what skills each occupation requires.
   - Look at possibilities for advancement in the field.
   - Find out the potential income.
   - Find out the national employment outlook in the field.
   - Find out the education requirements.
5. SKILLS—Can I do what's required?
   - See specific skills required for any occupation in SIGI PLUS.
   - Rate yourself on these skills.
   - See how job skills are applied in a chosen field.
6. PREPARING—Can I do what's required?
   - See typical preparation paths for any occupation in SIGI PLUS.
   - See the typical training or college education needed.
   - Consider four important factors related to preparing: finding time, finding money, handling the difficulty, and staying motivated.
   - Estimate your likelihood of completing preparation.
7. COPING—Can I do what's required?
   - Find out how to get practical help with issues related to preparing for a career.
   - Get suggestions about how to handle worries common to adults in a college or training situation, such as time management, fitting in, and competing.
8. DECIDING—What's right for me?

- What are the rewards? Will I enjoy this occupation?
- What are my chances? Can I get in?
- All things considered, would this be a good choice for me?

9. NEXT STEPS
   - Get more education or training.
   - Develop new skills.
   - Prove you can do the work.
   - Build a network of contacts.
   - Write a resume.
   - Overcome obstacles.

Explore your local library and discover the wealth of information and programs available to you.

CHART THE FUTURE
Goal Setting for Life

CHAPTER

4

We should all be concerned about the future because we will spend the rest of our lives there.

—Charles Franklin Kettering, *Seed for Thought*

From where I live I can see mountains in the distance. Sometimes they are bathed in sunshine and appear clean and sparkling; sometimes they are blanketed by clouds and appear dark and forbidding. I learned about goals from these mountains. Mountains, like goals, are distant, sometimes visible, sometimes invisible, and always a challenge to surmount. Goals are the mountains of life.

When setting a goal, you need to paint a mental picture of yourself reaching that goal. It's your mountain; it's where you want to be. As you travel toward your goal or mountain, it may disappear. Clouds may cover it, or a tree may temporarily block the view. It's still there—you just can't see it. The closer you get, the less you see the whole mountain and the steeper the climb becomes. You may need to reassure yourself by pausing to look back at how far you've come already.

I have also learned that as I travel the road to my mountain, I often encounter unexpected turns and detours. The road is under construction; a bridge is washed out; a fallen tree blocks the road. But as long as I know where I'm headed, I can detour around the obstacles, change my course, or reset my schedule. Some of the changes present unexpected benefits and pleasant surprises—new places and new faces. Eventually I arrive at my destination because I kept my focus on my goal and persevered in my efforts to reach that goal.

Goal setting is very similar to planning a trip to a mountain destination. From your starting point the mountain looks a certain way, but it changes as you get closer. It's possible for it to change so much that you decide to alter your plans. If that happens, don't feel defeated. If you hadn't begun the journey, you wouldn't have realized the truth and you would have maintained dreams of a false mountain, a false hope.

Now how do you choose your life goals—your mountains? You decide how you want to live your life and how much time and effort you are willing to commit to acquiring the knowledge and skills necessary to achieve those goals.

The future holds exciting promises for all who chart their

tomorrows realistically and pursue their goals with thoughtful determination—for those who act on their plans.

Opportunities you have never dreamed of await you. Set your sights high, plan your journey carefully, and tap into your potential to make it happen. Begin today. Chart the future you desire!

REVIEW YOUR LIFELINE

Before you begin the exercises in this chapter, consider three things: (1) how long you really have to accomplish your dreams and career, (2) a decision-making model, and (3) some guidelines to use when setting goals and making decisions. Let's begin with a review of the "rest" of your life.

Einstein was seventy-one when he started work on atomic nuclear fission. Grandma Moses was in her nineties when she began painting. Colonel Sanders was over sixty-five when he began his restaurant chains. Sophocles was ninety when he wrote one of his last tragedies, the Oedipus trilogy. You still have time to do the things you really want to do.

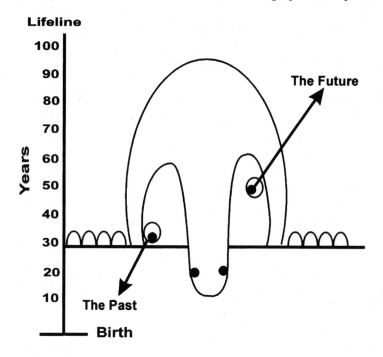

Where are you on the lifeline?
How much time do you really have?

Your FUTURE depends on where you're looking.
Are you looking up to the future or down at the past.?

The people who 45 years ago survived to age 65 had a life expectancy for a few months only. Today the 65 year old, man or woman, can expect 13 or 14 more years. . . . And most people who reach age 65 in developed countries today are physically and mentally "middle-aged" and able to function normally.

—Peter Drucker, *Managing in Turbulent Times*

A GOAL-SETTING AND DECISION-MAKING MODEL

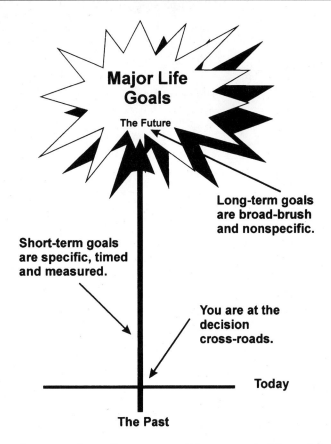

Major life goals cover these four areas: (1) personal, (2) social, (3) professional, and (4) financial. They are long-term, broad-brushed, and nonspecific. Major life goals provide the general direction for your life. They are the basis for setting all short-term goals and for making all decisions.

Short-term goals are specific, timed, and measurable. Short-term goals fit into the overall long-term goals for your life. They complement each other and take you closer to your long-term goals.

When you stand at a decision crossroad, the point between the past and the future, ask yourself this question before proceeding: Does this goal take me closer to my major life goals? If you answer is "closer to," continue on. If your answer is "farther from," rethink your decision. Asking yourself this question and responding with a "closer to" will keep you on target with your goals.

Before making decisions, ask yourself, "Does this decision move me closer to or farther from my major life goals?"

GUIDELINES FOR GOAL SETTING AND DECISION MAKING

Effective goals focus on results, not activities.

For effective goal setting and decision making, examine all four life zones. Then ask yourself these questions for each goal and each decision.

The Four Life Zones

1. Is this really **my** goal? Does this goal truly **fit** my interests, skills, and abilities?
2. Is this goal in **balance and harmony** with my life's other major goals?
3. Is this goal for **pleasure** (short-term) or for **happiness** (long-term)?
4. Is this goal **fair and equitable** (morally right) to all concerned?
5. Does this goal take my **closer to** or **farther from** my major long-term life goals?
6. Can I truly see myself reaching this goal? Is it **realistic**? Can I really believe in this goal? Is it really attainable and not just wishful thinking?
7. Is this goal **flexible**? Am I able to change direction when life and circumstances change?
8. Will I **review** this goal periodically? Yearly? Monthly? Weekly? Daily? Will I alter the goal to fit new situations?
9. Can I **emotionally commit** to start and persevere until this goal is reached?
10. Can I and will I set **priorities and time frames** for this goal? If not, is it really a goal?

You may choose to substitute the word *decision* for *goal*.

Conflicts often arise between goals. To avoid major setbacks, it is advisable to establish a set of priorities from which to operate. One way to establish priorities is to review life roles. There are many roles in life. Your roles may be father, husband, college student, church member, and employee. Oops! Don't forget that you are, above all, an individual.

Step 1
List the roles you have in your life.

Step 2
Prioritize each role according to its importance in your life.

Step 3
List your major long-term life goal for each role. Before writing these, you may want to review the guidelines for goal setting and decision making on the previous page.

Step 4
File this exercise behind the *Life Management* section in the *Companion Planner*.

Priority:	Role:	Major Goal:
2	Husband	To be a kind, supportive spouse and a good listener
3	Father	To always have time for my kids
4	Employee	To provide quality work
8	Church member	To always walk my talk
11	Political activist	To ensure a strong, fair government
9	Community volunteer	To help those in need
5	Son	To be the best son a mother and father ever wanted
6	Brother	To be supportive
7	Uncle	To help and listen when needed
12	Carpenter (hobby)	To build beautiful art pieces
13	Stamp collector (hobby)	To develop a world class collection
1	Person/myself	To be true to myself
10	Photographer (hobby)	To be creative and artistic

- Review your roles frequently to ensure that you don't get overly involved in one or two areas to the exclusion of other roles that are equally or more important.

- Adapt and revise your roles and goals to fit new and changing situations.

- Commit to doing the important activities and projects first. This allows you to manage life instead of managing crises.

- Use a priority listing when conflicts arise between goals. For example, working overtime versus taking care of personal needs. Choosing the goal with the higher priority may resolve the conflict.

To ensure balance and compatibility, I've created four life zones:

- Zone 1 is your personal area.
- Zone 2 is the social area.
- Zone 3 is your professional area.
- Zone 4 is the financial area.

STEP 1: WRITE GOALS FOR EACH ZONE

The Four Life Zones

**Create balance and harmony . . .
Look at the big picture.**

By examining each zone, you can set goals that will provide a positive base from which to plan your life. Focus on each zone. Identify what you want to accomplish in each area. Keep in mind that goals serve you best when they are compatible and mutually supportive of each other.

Ask yourself these questions for each of the areas of your life:

- What do I want PERSONALLY? Physically? Mentally? Spiritually? Emotionally?

- What do I want SOCIALLY? Family and friends? Personal relationships? Community, professional, political, or religious involvement?

- What do I want PROFESSIONALLY? What job do I want? What are the education requirements? What type of employer fits me? How much do I want to earn? What geographic area do I want? How far from home do I want to travel?

- What do I want FINANCIALLY? What does financial independence mean to me? How much available cash would make me comfortable? Which investments are important and necessary? What personal assets define success for me?

If you need motivation to write financial goals, consider this 1980 study conducted by the Department of Health, Education and Welfare. According to the study, for every 100 people born 65 years ago, the following situation exists for them today:

- 29 are dead.

- 13 have incomes under $3,500, which is far below poverty level.

- 55 have annual incomes between $3,500 and $20,000, with a median income of $4,700.

- 3 have annual incomes over $20,000, with only one being well-to-do.

Why do so many citizens of the world's richest nation live in poverty? Maybe they just failed to plan. Maybe there was never a convenient time for them to plan, to manage the money they had, or to save for retirement. They didn't plan on failing; they just failed to plan. If you want to retire with an adequate income, begin planning your financial goals today.

Ask yourself these questions:

- Can I believe in my goals?

- Are these goals really mine, the things I want?

- Are my goals in balance and harmony with each other?

- Are all goals viewed in the positive—what I want, not what I don't want?

- Does each goal take me closer to my long-term life goals? If not, why not?

- Can I morally and emotionally commit to these goals?

STEP 2: WRITE AFFIRMATIONS

Once you have established your long-term goals, it's not enough just to write them down. You need to visualize your goals as having already been accomplished. Then you need to put power behind them by writing affirmations. After specifying each goal, review it, and then write a positive sentence capturing what it is you want to achieve. Write your affirmations to cover all the life zones: personal, social, professional, and financial. Here are some guidelines for writing affirmations.

Affirmations must be:

- Mutually supportive and compatible with your major life goals.

- In balance and harmony with your major life objectives.

- In agreement with your personal life values.

- Written and personal. They are for you; not someone else. It's your goal, your dream. For example, write, "I enjoy writing every day. Writing is fun for me."

- Written in the first person. They usually begin with the pronoun I: "I weigh 138 pounds."

- Written in the present tense. See yourself as already having achieved your goal. For

GOALS Date:	___ LONG-TERM ___ SHORT-TERM Page 1 of 2	
Personal	**Goals**	**Affirmations**
Physical Weight Pulse Blood Pressure Cholesterol Level Personal Appearance Other	Weigh 138 pounds. Get cholesterol to 198. Improve personal appearance; have it professional and understated.	I'm physically, mentally, and spiritually fit. I eat only healthy foods. I enjoy exercising daily.
Mental Education Self-Improvement Technical Skills Special Knowledges Other	Become more computer literate. Improve speaking and presentation abilities. Obtain a bachelor's degree in psychology, then a Ph.D. Learn more about diet and nutrition so I can be healthier.	I celebrate today by being my best. I weigh 138 pounds. I always take time to play and rest.
Spiritual and Emotional Personal Values Stable Emotions: joy, sorrow, fear, hate, love Wholeness Balance Integrity Other	Be at peace with my past, with myself. Always be enthusiastic. Always be in balance with my personal values. Set the best example possible for others.	
Social	**Goals**	**Affirmations**
Personal Relationships Spouse or Partner Significant Other Family Friends Neighbors Other	Stay happily married. Be a supportive, loving parent. Be an understanding friend and family member. Be a helpful neighbor.	I am happy. I am a loving, caring person. I listen intently to others. I enjoy serving my community.
Professional Relationships Work Business Professional Organizations Other	Be a dedicated worker. Be totally trustworthy. Maintain confidentialities. Stay excited and enthusiastic about my work. Be an active club member.	I volunteer gladly. I make wise decisions. I am environmentally smart. I support my environment.
Community Relationships Religious Political Community Social Other	Become more globally conscious, locally active. Become more environmentally aware. Become less wasteful; be a wise steward of resources.	I live and walk my values. I think globally, act locally.

© 1995 Harris Espérance Incorporated   Form 37-1/95

Figure 4-1   FORM 37, Goals, Page 1

example, "I am a certified public accountant," or "I am a college graduate."

- Written in the **positive**. Concentrate on what you want, not what you don't want. Leave out all the negatives, the nots, the don'ts, and the can'ts. Write only the positive. For example, write, "I only eat healthy foods," instead of "I don't eat junk food."

- **Penned**. Your affirmations must be written down to be effective. Writing clarifies and confirms your thinking.

- **Spoken**. Speak your affirmations often. Repeat them to yourself several times every day. This helps to instill them in your mind and in your actions.

Consider these questions:

- Are my affirmations mutually supportive and compatible with my major life goals?

- Are my affirmations in balance and harmony with my major life objectives?

- Are my affirmations in agreement with my personal values—what I really believe, not what I think I should believe?

- Is each affirmation personal? Is it my affirmation, not someone else's?

- Is each affirmation written in the first person? Have I used the pronouns *I*, *my*, and *mine*?

- Is each affirmation written in the present tense? Have I visualized it as already being achieved?

File Form 37, Goals, in the LIFE MANAGEMENT section of the *Companion Planner*.

GOALS Date:	Goals	__ LONG-TERM __ SHORT-TERM Page 2 of 2
Professional	**Goals**	**Affirmations**
Job Job Title Position Job Description	Store manager of large metro jewelry store.	I am a jewelry store manager. I am a professional certifild jeweler. I provide quality service to all my clients. I listen intently to all my employees. I enjoy working every day. I love my job.
Education Credentials Degree(s) License(s) Other	Certified professional jeweler.	
Employer Size Type Description	Work for super-large international jewelry company (retail, wholesale, and manufacturer)	
Geographic Location Distance from Home	Want to work in Pacific Northwest. Will travel 25 miles one way to work.	
Financial	**Goals**	**Affirmations**
Liquid Assets Cash Money Market Funds Savings Bonds Annuities Life Insurance Cash Value	Have sufficient liquid assets to allow me to live one year without working. Have cash reserves for all emergencies. Have sufficient insurance to cover all possibilities.	I am financially independent. I am self-supporting. I invest wisely. I review my finances monthly. I review and revise my financial plans annually. I enjoy building my financial future.
Nonmarketable Investments Real Estate IRAs Keoghs Business Interests Other	Make wise and stable investments. Possess safe and large retirement funds. Have adequate college funds for the children.	
Marketable Investments Stocks Bonds Mutual Funds Corporate Bonds Other	Make wise and stable investments. Possess a large, growing investment portfolio.	
Personal Assets Home Automobiles Other Vehicles Home Furnishings Jewelry, Furs Other Collectibles	Own a 4,000-square-foot home in the country. Have a vacation cabin in the woods. Drive modern and efficient car and pickup. Own valuable pieces of art.	

© 1995 Harris Espérance Incorporated   Form 37-2/95

Figure 4-2 FORM 37, Goals, Page 2

Life without endeavor is like entering a jewel-mine and coming out with empty hands.
—Japanese proverb

Goals and affirmations should reflect your deepest values. They should be in harmony with nature (the natural rules of life) and reflect your individualism (uniqueness).

Use the "Powerful Ps" in writing your affirmations.

- **P**en each one; in other words, write it down.
- Make each one **P**ersonal.
- Write each one in the **P**resent tense.
- Concentrate on the **P**ositive trait you want.
- To maintain balance, write affirmations for each life zone.

Following are some more examples of affirmations.

Personal:

- Water is my drink of choice.
- I enjoy exercising daily.
- Walking is fun for me.
- I keep up with the local and national news.
- I read twelve new books every year.
- I read inspirational writings daily.
- I listen to inspirational tapes weekly.
- I celebrate today by doing my best.
- I take quiet time for myself every day.
- I see new opportunities for improvement every day.

Social:

- I am a loving wife and mother.
- I am a supportive family member.
- I play with my kids every day.
- I enjoy listening to others.
- I give sincere compliments.
- I take time to play every day.
- I enjoy serving my community.
- I find opportunities to improve our schools.
- I encourage others daily with positive comments.

Professional:

- I am a successful writer.
- I am the company's top salesperson.
- I clean off my desk each night.
- I keep only necessary items on my desk.
- I always find ways to improve my work.
- I have professional goals, and I act on them.
- I improve my skills every day.
- I always do my best.
- I enjoy my work every day.
- I see great opportunities in my job.

Financial:

- I am financially independent.
- I always pay myself first.
- I balance my checkbook monthly.
- I enjoy seeing my finances grow.
- Saving money is easy for me.
- I invest wisely.
- I always save 10 percent of my earnings.
- Investing wisely is fun for me.
- Planning my financial future is exciting to me.

What do you want to do? What do you need? Only you can decide.

After all the exercises and planning, it's time to choose your job objective—the job you should apply for next. In other words, if you were to lose your job today and go job hunting, what job should you apply for? This objective should mesh with your long-term career objectives. It should be the first (next) step in your chosen career/life path.

STEP I: DECIDE THE MAJOR ISSUES OF YOUR NEXT JOB

Decide what you really need (your "must have" list) before you go job hunting. Then decide what else you would like to have. Use the list below to help you determine your needs. Put a check mark by the factors that are most important to you. Six to ten factors should be sufficient for the analysis.

☑ Initial Salary	☐ Paid Vacation
☑ Commission	☐ Paid Holidays
☐ Bonus/Stock Bonus	☐ Paid Sick Leave
☐ Profit Sharing	☐ Pension/Retirement
☐ Travel/Per Diem	☐ Severance Pay/Policy
☐ Automobile	☐ Size of Organization
☐ Number of Bosses	☐ Degree of Privacy
☐ Publication Rights	☐ Purchasing Discounts
☐ Clothing Allowance	☐ Promotion Potential
☐ Medical Insurance	☐ Education Allowance
☐ Dental Insurance	☐ Training Allowance
☐ Vision Insurance	☐ Relocation Allowance
☐ Life Insurance	☐ Moving Refund
☐ Long-Term Disability	☐ Travel Requirements
☐ Geographic Location	☐ Independence
☐ Private Office	☐ Overtime
☐ Patent Rights	☐
☐ Job Security	☐

Make a chart like the one shown below. Separating your needs into the two categories allows you to determine what is really important to you. File this page with your Form 13, Job Objective, in the RESUMES section of the *Companion Planner.*

JOB REQUIREMENTS

What I Really Need	What I'd Like To Have
1. Medical insurance	1. Three weeks' paid vacation first year
2. Base salary of $28,000	2. Paid holidays
3. Retirement plan	3. Paid sick leave
4. Automobile + travel reimbursement	4. Only one boss
5. Paid relocation	5. Lots of independence (freedom to create)
6.	6.

STEP 2: COMPLETE FORM 13, JOB OBJECTIVE

Choose work that is in harmony with your values.

Now let's get even more specific. To create a clear picture of what you want, the employer, and geographic location, complete Form 13, Job Objective.

Be very specific here. Know your job objective.

- Employer ads are best to use. They provide a broader picture of job and personal requirements. Find several ads to achieve a better idea.

- If you are unsuccessful in finding an ad, use a job description from the DOT. Using the combination of an ad and DOT description may also be helpful.

JOB OBJECTIVE

Job Title

Medical Secretary

Help Wanted Ad or DOT Description

MEDICAL SECRETARY
IDAHO HEALTH SCIENCES UNIVERSITY
Cheerful, conscientious, full-time Medical Secretary to coordinate patient appointments and provide general secretarial support for the Audiology/Vestibular Services. Required skills and abilities include: strength in patient and public relations, typing and transcription 60+ wpm, use of WordPerfect 6.1 windows, Lotus 123, spreadsheets. Ability to work accurately under pressure while committed to excellence in patient services. Send resume to: Recruitment, Otolaryngology, P. O. Box 853, Boise, ID 83703

Employer Key Requirements

Strength in patient and public relations
Typing and transcription 60 + wpm
WordPerfect 6.1 Windows
Lotus and spreadsheet programs
Work under pressure
Committed to excellence
Cheerful
Conscientious
Full-time

Employer Type/Description

Medical Science University — Major hospital — Large Medical Clinic

Geographic Location

Pacific Northwest — Willing to relocate

Offering - Level

Entry-level, full-time. Seeking career opportunity with advancement potential

Skills: Data-People-Things

Medical terminology
Listening, Sensing, Feeling
Patient and public relations
Computers: WordPerfect, Lotus, Spreadsheets
Telephone

Required Education/Experience

AS. Health Record Technology
Customer Service — 3 years
Extensive word processing
Shorthand

Job Objective

Medical Records... working full-time for a hospital, university or medical clinic in Pacific Northwest

© 1995 Harris Espérance Incorporated   Form - 13/95

Figure 4-3 FORM 13, Job Objective

- Record major requirements, including the personal qualities desired.
- Know where you want to work.
- Identify level and offering. For example, "entry-level accounting position," "mid-management," or "full-time career opportunity."
- Compose a clearly stated job objective using as few words as possible. This information will be used in the job objective and personal sections of your resume.

File this form in the RESUMES section of your notebook.

STEP 3: WRITE A SPONTANEOUS, FREE-FLOWING DESCRIPTION OF YOUR NEXT JOB AND CAREER.

Soaring is an easier way to travel than climbing, but it's mighty hard to get off the ground.
—William Woolfolk

After you have written your description, ask yourself these questions:

- How does this job description fit with my long-term career objectives? If it doesn't fit my long-term objectives, why not?
- Does this "next" job objective take me closer to or father from my long-term career goal? If my answer does not take me closer, why not?
- How realistic is this "next" job? (Don't be afraid to reach, but use reason in your decision.) If you have never been in the field before and are straight out of school, don't expect to walk into a management position. If the goal is not within reason, why not? If the goal is within reason, go for it!

My ideal job is to work as the general manager of a resort or hotel, preferably the Riverhouse. The hotel has so much to offer in the way of challenges, and there is unlimited potential for changes I would like to see made. There could be extensive networking with other resort managers and unlimited opportunities to advance in the hospitality field.

There is a major problem at this time with employee satisfaction in this industry. Many employees feel used and unappreciated. My first goal would be to make employees feel appreciated and useful. I truly love the business and want to make a positive impact.

Figure 4-4 Spontaneous Writing. Courtesy of a student

The rung of a ladder was never meant to rest upon, but only to hold a person's foot long enough to enable him to put the other somewhat higher.
—Author Unknown

Draw a career ladder and fill in the rungs.

If you want to be in a certain place in ten years, you need to make some decisions now. Create a plan to take you from where you are to where you want to go. This plan isn't cast in cement, but it will supply you with the first steps. A career ladder will help you to visualize the way.

- Picture yourself climbing this ladder. The bottom rung is where you are now; the top rung is your ten-year goal. Each rung represents one year.

- Fill in the major steps needed to reach the tenth rung. Use your imagination. Don't worry about how you will achieve the goal, just establish time-measured steps (rungs).

- File your career ladder behind the CAREER MANAGEMENT section in the *Companion Planner*.

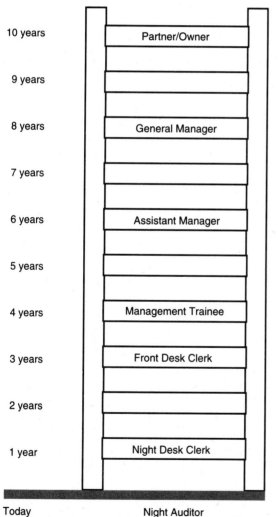

10 years — Partner/Owner

9 years

8 years — General Manager

7 years

6 years — Assistant Manager

5 years

4 years — Management Trainee

3 years — Front Desk Clerk

2 years

1 year — Night Desk Clerk

Today — Night Auditor

Draw your ladder, and climb to your highest rung.

Figure 4-5   Career Ladder

PACKAGE

Those who reach greatness on earth reach it through concentration.
—Upanishads

Creation and **expression**—capturing your true essence in person, on paper, and through others—are the goals of "Package." Once creation and expression are achieved, excitement and momentum for the job search can be sustained.

"Package" is an activity of imagination and ingenuity. In the beginning, you artistically capture yourself on paper by writing a resume that reveals your best essence. Next, you actively recruit others into your job-hunting program by building a supportive group of references. Then you create and use innovative letters to actively involve and broaden your network of contacts. Finally, you professionally express yourself through attire and personal presentation.

The exercises in this unit are designed to maximize your creative and expressive abilities. As you complete each chapter, you build self-confidence and courage. You find yourself manifested on paper and personally revealed in a way that fully captures your true and best self. At the end of this process, you feel confident and are motivated to call employers and seek your fortunes.

In Chapter 5, "Weave a Magic Carpet—The Resume-Writing Process," you weave words onto the page, capturing your best nature on paper. Seeing your true, best self on paper produces a catalyst for your whole job hunt. It's like a magic carpet that takes you wherever you want to go. *Package* your resume with focus and character, for it takes you right into employers' offices.

In Chapter 6, "Secure Quality References—A 'No Surprise' Support System," you select people who will support and help you the most in your job hunt. Your references are your mainstay. They will be there to encourage and direct you. By choosing references who believe in you, you will always have someone to turn to during times of discouragement. *Package* your references to secure the support you deserve and need.

In Chapter 7, "Master Job Applications—The Employer Screening Process," you learn to complete job applications with facts from your life—facts that depict your most appropriate skills, abilities, and experiences for the job. *Package* job applications so that you look your best on the employer's form.

> Most of us make two basic errors with respect to intelligence: we underestimate our own brain power, and we overestimate the other fellow's brain power.
> —David J. Schwartz, Ph.D.

In Chapter 8, "Write Power Letters—The Great Door Openers," you package a source of power, a force that works miracles. Through letters, you build a support network and develop job leads. Power letters introduce you to strangers, rebuild relationships, and bridge the gaps of time with old friends. Letters save money and time. They are the pipeline to better and more meaningful jobs and relationships. *Package* power letters and open the many doors to job leads and opportunity.

In Chapter 9, "Create a Confident You—The Finished Product," you package your personal outer being—your visual resume. This package includes your attire, briefcase, portfolio, and communication skills. The confidently packaged you complements all the other packages you have worked so hard to develop. The finished product is the final touch to *Package*.

Now it is time to move from the fancifulness of "Discover" into the reality and hard work of "Package." The work may be demanding at first, but the revelations and rewards are worth the effort. Create magic words on paper, fashion a self-made style, and build your self-confidence and courage through "Package."

WEAVE A MAGIC CARPET
The Resume-Writing Process

CHAPTER

5

Our thoughts are among the few things we can leave behind us in permanent form and I am anxious to begin writing.

—Elizabeth Forsythe Hailey

Like a magic carpet, a well-written resume takes you where you want to go—right into the interviewer's office. When I first met Cheryl, she had been unemployed for over a year. She had been fired from her last job. Her self-confidence had long disappeared, and she felt defeated. After reviewing her resume and a sample job application, it was no wonder. Everything spoke of failure. Red flags waved vigorously on both papers. No wonder she couldn't find work.

However, when Cheryl captured her best self on paper, her whole outlook changed. She moved from fear to confidence. It was truly magic. Within days of moving to a small community, she was back to work. She had received several job offers; then she accepted a full-time and a part-time job.

I often work with men and women who have been fired. They are angry, fearful, and afraid of being hurt again. They are afraid to apply for work knowing they might be rejected one more time. But I have found over and over again that when they capture their best and most relevant skills for their career direction, self-confidence and self-esteem return.

A well-written resume won't get you a job, but it will give you confidence and get you interviews with employers. That's what you're after, the opportunity to present yourself in person. There's no other piece of paper more important to you in the job hunt than a good resume.

How do you write an effective resume that opens doors? You write and rewrite until it's right. Read on for more specific information. It's time to weave your own magic carpet.

USING THE RESUME SECTION OF THE *COMPANION PLANNER*

We are all apprentices in a craft where no one becomes a master.
—Ernest Hemingway

The RESUME section of the *Companion Planner* contains the following forms and documents:

- Current Resume
  File a copy of your current resume here. Keep the original in a file folder so it remains clean and unmarked for future photocopying.

- Form 13: Job Objective
  File this form on top. When writing your resume and during the job search process, you need to be able to review your objective easily. Reviewing the job objective keeps you focused and on track and allows alterations to your resume if circumstances warrant.

- Form 14: Personal Checklist
  Complete this form prior to writing a resume draft. Write a positive response for each section. File the form with your final resume. This form should also be reviewed when completing job applications.

- Form 15 or 16: Resume Draft
  File a copy of your resume draft with your final resume. Keep the resume draft until you have completed the job-hunt process.

  When drafting your resume, review each response on form 14, Personal Checklist, and decide whether to include the information in your resume. There are no set rules on what information to put in a resume. If the information supports your job objective, include it. If it detracts, eliminate it.

  Including personal information on a resume is a matter of individual choice. It can add a personal touch that so often is missing in the job hunt process. For example, a recent "Help Wanted" advertisement listed these physical demands: "Position requires bending and lifting up to 25 pounds." Listing "Physically fit, lift weights regularly" may be appropriate to include in the "Personal" section if it is a true representation of you.

- Old Resume(s)
  Keep copies of all your resumes. They're helpful to refer to when preparing a new resume.

  File old resumes with the most current one on top. Put a date on each resume; the top or bottom right-corner is a good place for the date.

  You may find it helpful to add dividers to segregate the different types of resumes or time periods.

WRITE IT YOURSELF

Robert Half, author of *The Robert Half Way to Get Hired in Today's Job Market*, writes:

> I have other reasons, apart from money, for steering you away from the professional resume writing services. For one thing, professionally written resumes often have an assembly-line look. I can usually spot them at a glance, and so can any experienced hiring executive. Some personnel directors as a matter of policy automatically eliminate from consideration resumes that look to have been professionally done.
>
> But there's an even more important reason for working on your resume yourself. Doing so forces you to examine yourself, helps to give you a sense of just what you have to offer a prospective employer. It prepares you, in other words, for many of the situations you're going to run into when you go to interviews. Putting together your own resume helps you to appreciate aspects about yourself, or your job background, that you may not have been aware of before. You get to know the product better. You become a better salesperson.

Use your data file. Pull out all your relative experiences and use them.

TELL THE TRUTH

While it's important not to undersell yourself, it is equally important not to exaggerate or misrepresent your abilities, education, work history, or credentials. Lies and exaggerations have a way of coming back to haunt you at unexpected times.

MAKE IT READER-FRIENDLY

It's important to get your readers to like you. You can do this by:

- Writing clearly, colorfully, and concisely.
- Writing in a positive way and eliminating unnecessary words.
- Targeting a specific audience; for example, the wood products industry.
- Including only the necessary and appropriate data to portray your best self.
- Using strong active verbs and precise nouns.
- Using testimonials to build credibility.
- Creating illustrations relevant to your message. Generic comments or images are meaningless.

MAKE IT EASY TO READ

- Vast gray expanses of copy are unreadable.
- Use lots of white space.
- Top, bottom, and side margins should each be 1 inch.
- A minimum margin of 3/4 inch is permissible, if necessary.
- Write short paragraphs and sentences. Use headers or marginal comments.

FIELD-TEST YOUR RESUME

Try out your resume on others who will give you an objective and honest opinion—in other words, people who don't know you well. Allow them thirty to sixty seconds reading time. Then ask for a description of your background based on the reading. If your resume is fuzzy to these readers, go back and revise it until a clear, sharp image comes across at first glance.

STUDY OTHER RESUME SAMPLES

There are several examples in this chapter. For additional examples, read *Getting Hired* by Edward J. Rogers.

Choose a format that meets your needs. The four most commonly used resume formats are: historical, functional, achievement, and combination. Two other formats less commonly used are the creative and letter formats. We'll examine all formats except the letter format.

STEP 1: STUDY THE HISTORICAL RESUME FORMAT

This format features the employment history in a chronological order, with the most recent position listed first.

Advantages:

Most familiar to employer.

Easiest to prepare.

Provides excellent format for steady employment and increased responsibilities.

Disadvantages:

Easily reveals gaps in employment.

Duplicates information on job applications.

May over-emphasize job skills, narrow industry experience, or numerous job changes.

DAVID KIRK

3987 Silvas Road   Richmond, California 94807   (415) 555-2385

EMPLOYMENT OBJECTIVE
Restaurant Management. . . Assistant Manager or Trainee

EDUCATION
Associate of Science. Hotel and Restaurant Management.
Central Oregon Community College. Bend, Oregon 97701. 1993.
Personally financed college education by working in field. GPA 3.65.

Churchill High School. Eugene, OR. Graduated 1989. GPA 3.57.

EMPLOYMENT HISTORY
Waiter (6/90 to present)   **Assistant Waiter** (8/89 to 5/90)   (1989 to Present)
The Riverhouse Restaurant. Bend, OR. (503) 555-8810
Management and Supervision . . . Supervised and coordinated activities of dining room.
Planned details for banquets, receptions, and other social functions. Hired, trained, and
supervised dining room employees and banquet staffs in fine dining service. Directed setting up
of tables and decorations.

Tableside and Beverage Service . . . Carved and served dinners on chafing dishes at tableside
including Steak Diane, Rack of Lamb, and Chateaubriand. Setup and prepared Caesar and
Wilted Spinach salads. Flamed desserts and drinks including Bananas' Foster, Cherries Jubilee,
and Coffee Royales. Discussed wines with patrons and assisted in making appropriate selections.
Presented and opened wines.

Waiting Service . . . Served meals in formal and informal settings. Presented verbal and printed
menus. Recommended dinner courses, appropriate wines, and desserts. Answered questions
regarding food preparations.

Deli Counter Sales and Food Preparer. Boxer and Shelf Stocker.   (1987 to 1989)
Albertson's Food Center. Eugene, OR. (503) 555-0526

PERSONAL
Born 1971, U.S. Citizen. Willing to work varied work schedule. Excellent health.
Motivated and budget-minded. Desire relocation to continue education. Punctual.
Computer literate–use word processing, data base, and spreadsheet programs.

Figure 5-1   Historical Resume. Courtesy of a student

STEP 2: EXAMINE A FUNCTIONAL RESUME FORMAT

A functional format

- Organizes experience by skills or functions.

- Leaves out employment history.

- Usually lists highest skill or most applicable skill first.

- Eliminates job titles.

- Provides an excellent format for career changers, individuals with many job changes, late starters, homemakers in transition, and inexperienced workers.

___ CHERYL TURNER ___

Post Office Box 17 | Boise, Idaho 83704 | (208) 555-1005

Career Objective	General office employment . . . where a pleasant personality and excellent clerical and secretarial skills are required.
Office and Clerical Skills	Processed payroll, accounts payable, accounts receivables, and bank deposits for two checking and two savings accounts. Ordered and maintained a running inventory of all office supplies. Operated IBM computer terminal, 10-key calculator, and various copy machines. Obtained information for reports, and completed them prior to deadlines. Assumed the responsibility for typing these reports instead of handwriting them as previously done. Two supervisors remarked that they were done in a professional manner and easy to read. Made adjustments to daily correction of computer print-out edits.
Written Communication Skills	Created and typed letters pertaining to insurance coverage and claims, collection on past-due accounts, merchandise claims, and orders and inquiries of stock availability. The letters addressed large companies as well as individual customers. Also, typed loan papers that contained important financial information.
Innovative Ideas	Discussed with supervisor the advantages of installing com-lines on the telephones and designating one person to answer the phones, for which I volunteered. These two changes reduced the level of noise, added privacy, and created a more workable atmosphere. Reorganized the files of current policies, freight bills, and material orders. Developed a system for dead files. Created and typed my own resume.
Credit and Collections	Processed loan applications, which consisted of calling employers and other creditors for ratings and references. Called and visited customers regarding past-due accounts. Often complimented for ability to work with clients on verbal commitments.
Community and School Involvement	Central Oregon Timber Carnival Princess. Appeared in numerous parades. Represented Central Oregon Timber Carnival Association in statewide timber conventions. Co-captain and assistant advisor for high school Drill Team. High school journalism typist for two years.
Personal	Excellent health. Willing to travel or relocate. Single. No dependents. Enjoy meeting people and going to new and different places. Like to be assigned responsibilities requiring creative thinking. Looking for advancement opportunities.

Advantages:

Stresses marketable experiences and skills.

Camouflages spotty employment record or demotions.

Allows emphasis on professional growth.

Allows positions or experiences not related to current career objective to be played down or eliminated.

Disadvantages:

May create suspicion among employers.

Lacks employment history, which employers like to see.

Is more difficult to write.

May be longer than other formats.

Figure 5-2   Functional Resume. Courtesy of a client

STEP 3: ANALYZE THE ACHIEVEMENT RESUME FORMAT

The achievement format

- Highlights outstanding achievements regardless of positions, employers, or dates.

- Leaves out employment history.

- Eliminates job titles.

- Usually lists highest or most applicable achievement first.

- Provides an excellent format for applicants with minimal or no job experience, career changers, homemakers in transition, retirees returning to work, military and government personnel entering private industry, and late starters.

Advantages:

Stresses achievements.

Demonstrates ability to get things done.

Features accomplishments that support the job objective.

Stresses achievements that transfer from one job to another and from one industry to another.

Disadvantages:

May be unfamiliar to employers and create suspicion.

Lacks employment history, which employers like to see.

Is more difficult to write.

May be longer than other formats.

ROBERT JACKSON

1769 Powers Creek Loop	Silverton, Oregon 97381	(503) 555-9845

Employment Goal
Summer employment in lumber mill . . .where excellent physical condition and a good work attitude are required.

Education
Sophomore honors student at Willamette University. Psychology major. 3.957 GPA. Studied in Japan on primarily self-financed exchange program. Pending summer earnings, will study in Tokyo next year. Graduated first in high school class with a 4.00 GPA. (1990)

Lumber Mill and Slash Piling Experience
Improved working conditions and safety in two major production sheds by meticulously keeping them clear of all scraps and debris. By own initiative, improved stockyard efficiency by reorganizing and/or discarding several years' accumulation of unattended stock and debris. Upon leaving for a higher paid position, head sawyer argued for my promotion, but company policy would not allow it. Another sawyer said, "I hate to see you go. This is the cleanest this place has been in a long time." (1991)

Piled and trimmed slash for logging operation. Coworkers commended my work as "state fair" quality. Supervisor asked me to work the following summer. (1990)

Bought and Remodeled Old House
As partner with brother, age 18, bought and completely remodeled an old house: added 500 square feet and replaced all roofing, siding, flooring, wiring, plumbing, sheetrock, and windows. Added new sidewalk and lawn. All financial planning and work, except sheetrocking, was done by us. Received many compliments on quality of work. One carpenter said, "When you first got this place, I thought it would be a real [mess] when you finished, but now I'm really impressed." Sold house for profit. (1989–1990)

Retail Sales and Painting
Sought for work by manager of furniture store and by commercial painter. Thirty days after employment, received a promotion at store and a 25% raise with painter. (1989)

School and Community Activities
Organized two dance-a-thons for high school choir. Each raised nearly $4,500. Over a period of six years, sold $5,000 of magazine subscriptions for Prineville Music Boosters. Top salesman in Boosters' history. Wrote and circulated a petition for a stop sign on an unsafe corner. After some debate, city council approved installation. Organized fund-raising responsible for construction of bicentennial amphitheater in City Park.

Other Activities
Cross-country: 4 letters, team captain, most inspirational. Track: 3 letters. High school choir: publicity manager and vice president. Honor Society: president. Chosen counselor for Japanese exchange students, Willamette University. Placed first in local, district, and state Elks' Scholarship Leadership competition.

Personal
Eagle Scout. Appreciate challenges. 6'3". 175 pounds. Weight lifter. Runner. Active outdoors enthusiast.

Figure 5-3 Achievement Resume. Courtesy of a student

STEP 4: EVALUATE THE COMBINATION RESUME FORMAT

This format provides the employer with your employment history; however, it emphasizes skills and achievements rather than where and when you worked. The combination format

- Combines the functional or achievement format with the historical format.

- Lists employment history in a separate section, usually toward the end of the resume.

FRANCES GNOSE

896 NE Studio Road   Bend, OR 97701   (503) 555-3832

Career Objective

Real Estate Sales in Central Oregon for a growing, progressive organization.

Sales and Marketing Experience

Supervisor of Marketing Operations
Scheduled and coordinated work flow between Marketing, Manufacturing, Product Service, and Accounting departments. Supervised 7 contract administrators. Recruited, hired, and trained professional and technical staffs. Conducted employee performance reviews and made salary recommendations. Wrote and implemented standard office procedures.

Redesigned computerized order entry system. Evaluated department requirements for needs assessment. Simplified program to make it user-friendly. Expanded functions to include billing. Wrote training manual. Developed and conducted training program. Trained administrators in 12 districts across the United States. Staff comments included: "Can't believe it was done so quickly," and "These changes should have been made years ago."

Managed department financial reports, budget forecasts, and purchasing. Administered payroll, confidential personnel records, accounts payable, electronic mail, voice mail, and travel arrangements. Promoted to supervisor within 6 months.

Furniture Sales and Interior Design
Established and managed furniture and interior decorating business. Within 10 years, expanded to 2 locations with annual sales of $500,000. Purchased merchandise in domestic and European markets. Negotiated contractual leases for retail and warehouse operations. Hired, trained, and supervised staff of 10. Created and executed sales promotions and advertising campaigns. Approved customer credit limits. Created open-to-buy budgets. Established merchandise pricing policies. Worked with import and export brokers.

Air Freight Sales Support Representative
Administrative coordinator for the Sales Manager with annual sales volume of $8 million. Liaison between customers and sales staff in fast-paced environment. Prepared business proposals, sales analysis, and statistical reports. Processed payroll. Purchased office supplies and equipment. Created and implemented freight air bill distribution program.

Figure 5-4   Combination Resume, Page 1. Courtesy of a client

Advantages:

Allows emphasis on most relevant skills and abilities.

Satisfies employer's desire to know employment history.

Deemphasizes employment history, career changes, demotions, or narrow industry or government experience.

Disadvantages:

Is more difficult to prepare than historical resume.

May be longer and more difficult to read.

Although this resume is two pages, combination resumes can be written on only one page. The main advantage of using two pages is the deemphasizing of your employment history. The first page shows only skills and achievements relevant to the job objective. These experiences are prioritized according to the highest and most germane.

Notice the basic parts of this resume and the priority arrangement of each:

1. Identification
2. Job objective
3. Functional and achievement narratives
4. Other experiences
5. Education
6. Employment history

The parts and the arrangement you choose are a matter of personal judgment, job criteria, format used, and your particular background.

FRANCES GNOSE

Page 2

Other Experience

College Instructor
Taught credit and noncredit courses for Office Administration, Business, and Community Education departments. Classes included: Office Management, Beginning and Advanced WordPerfect 5.1, Getting Hired, and Career Change.

Comments from student evaluations include: "Wonderful class! I really learned a lot about communication and management"; "She teaches with excitement and enthusiasm"; and "Excellent speaking and lecturing. She keeps it interesting and fun to learn the subject."

Vocational Secretary
Assisted the Regional Vocational Coordinator for 3 counties in central Oregon. Organized meetings, workshops, and in-service activities. Made arrangements for facilities, meals, registration, and transportation. Compiled grant applications for technology vocational programs. Used WordPerfect 5.1, PlanPerfect, Byline, Nutshell, and Twin programs.

Education

Oregon Real Estate Sales License: Oregon Examination May 23, 1992.
Bachelor of Science: Psychology. Washington State University, Pullman, WA.
Masters Program: Social Work. Smith College, Northampton, MA.
Computer Training: WordPerfect 5.1, Novell Network, Lotus 1-2-3, Wangwriter.

Employment History

1990-92 **Instructor**. Central Oregon Community College. Bend, OR.
1991-92 **Sales Representative and Designer**. Interiors International. Bend, OR.
1989-91 **Secretary**. Deschutes County Education Service District. Bend, OR.
1987-89 **Supervisor Marketing Operations**. Anacomp, Inc. San Diego, CA.
1985-87 **Sales Support Representative**. Emery Worldwide. San Diego, CA.
1971-81 **Managing Owner**. Scandinavian Interiors. Eugene, OR.

Figure 5-5 Combination Resume, Page 2. Courtesy of a client

STEP 5: CONSIDER THE CREATIVE RESUME FORMAT

This format provides a job hunter with lots of flexibility and the employer with a document that may demonstrate the creator's ability. The creative format

- May be a sales brochure, an audiotape, a videotape, a postcard, or other forms less standard than the prior examples.

- Often provides a pictorial representation of the applicant.

- May provide a visual presentation of the actual skills and abilities of the applicant.

- Provides an excellent format for consultants, artists, sales representatives, independent contractors, and individuals who need to get their foot in the door. Establishing yourself as an independent business contractor provides the employer the opportunity to hire you on a contract basis without the employer/employee obligations. This can lead to full-time, permanent employment.

The following example is a tri-fold 8 1/2-inch brochure. It serves as a handout and a convenient mailer.

Why Fran Gnose?

Qualifications

LICENSE AND MEMBERSHIPS
- ▲ Oregon State Real Estate License
- ▲ Multiple Listing Service
- ▲ Oregon State Association of Realtors
- ▲ National Association of Realtors

EDUCATION
- ▲ Bachelor of Science
   Psychology and English
   Washington State University
   Pullman, WA
- ▲ Masters Program: Social Work
   Smith College, Northhampton, MA

PAST EXPERIENCE
- ▲ College Instructor
   Central Oregon Community College
- ▲ Marketing Operations Supervisor
   Anacomp, Inc. San Diego, CA
- ▲ Interior Design and Furniture Sales
   Owner/Manager Scandinavian Interiors
   Eugene and Salem, OR

MY PERSONAL PLEDGE TO YOU...
I pledge to keep you informed during the buying and selling of your property. Continuous communication is a must. I'll keep you informed.

It's my job.

COLDWELL BANKER
MORRIS REAL ESTATE
209 N.E. GREENWOOD
BEND, OR 97701

Your Real Estate PROFESSIONAL

Fran Gnose
Sales Associate

Coldwell Banker Morris Real Estate
209 N.E. Greenwood • Bend, OR 97701

(503) 382-4123 office
385-3253 FAX • 389-8808 home

Figure 5-6 Creative Resume, Page 1. Courtesy of a client

Advantages:

- Provides flexibility in approaching employers.
- Makes an excellent mailer or handout.
- Can be used by sales representatives, advertising/marketing independents, graphic artists, consultants, entrepreneurs, part-time applicants, and handicapped or disabled persons.

Disadvantages:

- Is the most difficult format to prepare.
- May cost more to prepare than other formats.
- May require hiring a professional to create the resume.
- Needs to be professionally printed on quality paper.

Why Coldwell Banker Morris Real Estate?

- ▲ America's Premier Real Estate Company
  **Residential • Commercial
  Ranches • Land • Lots**
- ▲ Member of the Sears Financial Network
- ▲ Multiple Listing Service
- ▲ Nationwide Relocation and Referral Service
- ▲ #1 Home Sellers In Bend
- ▲ Easy to Find

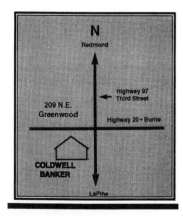

For The SELLER

To PRICE your property, I will:

- ▲ Provide a Comparative Market Analysis of similar properties in your area that have recently sold and are currently for sale.

To MARKET your property, I will:

- ▲ Submit listing to Multiple Listing Service
- ▲ Advertise in appropriate media
- ▲ Provide a **Coldwell Banker** "For Sale" sign
- ▲ Show property to qualified buyers
- ▲ Counsel buyers with financial alternatives

To keep you INFORMED, I will:

- ▲ Provide notification of property showings
- ▲ Explain the selling process
- ▲ Provide copies of signed documents
- ▲ Present all offers promptly
- ▲ Accompany you to settlement

For The BUYER

To HELP with your purchase... I will:

- ▲ Discuss your needs, style preferences, location, and price
- ▲ Provide listings of suitable properties
- ▲ Provide details on taxes, zoning, and local ordinances
- ▲ Provide community services information

To provide you COUNSEL, I will:

- ▲ Explain mortgage application procedures
- ▲ Accompany you to a lender
- ▲ Provide copies of signed documents
- ▲ Accompany you to the closing

For RELOCATION

To FIND you a new home, I will:

- ▲ Refer you to a **Coldwell Banker** relocation representative
- ▲ Coordinate sale and purchase of your property

Figure 5-7 Creative Resume, Page 2. Courtesy of a client

An Artist's Approach

Artistic people have a great opportunity to display their work by creating a visual resume. In the following example, Jennifer used a postcard to announce her intentions, followed up with a phone call to make an appointment, and then left her resume with the gallery when she went to visit. The postcard created a positive impression because of its unusual format and dramatic color. What do you think?

Cezanne, Renoir, Monet ...
They all had to start somewhere.

Figure 5-8 Creative Resume, A Postcard, Front.
Courtesy of a student

Hi, my name is Jennifer Dunn and I'm looking for a start in the exciting world of art.

I've been drawing and sketching for about a year and have taken classes at Central Oregon Community College. I possess a love of art as well as a strong desire to learn and grow. I am willing to volunteer my time in your gallery in order to gain experience.

I will give you a call next week to set up an appointment. I have a portfolio available and look forward to hearing your ideas and comments. Sincerely,

Jennifer Dunn, 764 South Third
Chicago, IL 60628 (312) 555-5486

Ms. Mary Larson
Blue Sky Gallery & Custom Framing
147 NW Minnesota
Franklin Park, IL 60131

Figure 5-9 Creative Resume, A Postcard, Back.
Courtesy of a student

Cezanne, Renoir, Monet ...
They all had to start somewhere.

Experience
- *I have drawn and sketched using charcoal, ink, conte, pencil, and oil pastels.*

- *I have studied both still life and figure as well as some wildlife and animals.*

- *I have studied works of the masters and through class work have done critiques and discussed them.*

Personal
- *I am enthusiastic and willing to learn.*

- *I am looking for a guiding hand in the art community and for a chance to study art more thoroughly. I have a positive attitude and a dedicated spirit. You will find that I am easy to get along with and that I attack tasks with optimism, excitement, and determination.*

Jennifer Dunn
764 South Third
Chicago, IL 60628
(312) 555-5486

Figure 5-10 Creative Resume. Courtesy of a student

A Video Approach

Robert Crest's career objective was video production and promotions. To demonstrate his abilities, Robert decided to create a video resume to go with his written resume. If you choose to do a video, take note of the guidelines that follow.

ROBERT CREST

2161 NE Greenwood   San Jose, CA 95112   (408) 555-3890

CAREER OBJECTIVE

Video Production and Promotions...Working for an innovative video production company.
Seeking challenge, variety, and part-time work in central Oregon.

VIDEO EXPERIENCE

Produced four promotional videos for Mt. Hood Summer Ski Camps. Filmed the first video in 1987 after Mr. Scott suggested making a film of the camp's summer activity program. What started out as just an idea has progressed yearly into a profit-making endeavor. In 1989, 20 videos were sold. In 1990, that number jumped to 110. The 1991 figures are exceeding prior totals despite 35% fewer campers than in 1990.

Produced, edited, and wrote promotional video for Wenatchee Valley College's Ski Area Management and Ski Instruction degree programs. Wrote script, filmed the programs in action, edited the raw footage, and dubbed in music and narration. This video is currently being used by WVC to provide new students information about the programs available and to attract future students.

Produced a creative video on "Coping with Stress" at Central Oregon Community College. Interviewed and filmed students, instructors, employees, and athletes. Edited films, selected sequences and interview portions, and dubbed in script and music. Earned an A for project and received many compliments from fellow students and participants.

Videotaped local ski race series and produced highlight video at season's end for Sno-Motion Video Services.

WORK EXPERIENCE

Sold skiing equipment and sports gear for **Fastgear Sports Outlet**, Government Camp, OR (87-91)
Provided ski instruction and coaching for students and faculty at **Mission Ridge Ski Area**, WA (87)
Supervised 22 workers in the Competition Services Department, **Squaw Valley Ski Corp.**, ID (85-86)

EDUCATION

Associate of Science. Marketing and Management. Central Oregon Community College, Bend, OR
Will Graduate with honors June 1991. Current GPA 3.56.
Associate of Science. Ski Resort Management. Wenatchee Valley College. Wenatchee, WA
Graduated with honors in 1986. GPA 3.86.

PERSONAL

Desire employment in video productions while completing bachelor's degree in Video Production.
Born 1965. Single. Willing to work varied hours. Available for travel and relocation.
Perfect college attendance. Punctual. Love getting paid to video!

Keep the length at five to seven minutes. Smile often. Think of the camera as your friend and talk to it, maintaining good eye contact.

Pay attention to

- Appearance.
- Posture.
- Attire.
- Mannerisms.
- Voice tone and pitch.
- Body language.
- The setting.
- The lighting.

The video should

- Highlight two or three of your most impressive achievements.
- Be benefit oriented—packed with "what you can do for them."
- Be positive, light, and entertaining.
- Leave the viewer with a good feeling.

Figure 5-11 Creative Resume, Courtesy of a student

If the video doesn't show you in the best light, don't use it. Stick with your written resume.

A cover letter and a written resume should accompany your video presentation. The employer still wants a written document.

The information you include on your resume depends upon the picture you desire to create. The order or placement will vary with your format choice, work and life experiences, and personal taste. A listing of the major parts to consider follows.

IDENTIFICATION

Your name, address, and a daytime phone number are required. It is advisable to write out your name and not use initials for your first name. For example, A. G. Ames should be written as Alice G. Ames.

The placement and layout of your identification depends upon your personal taste. If your resume is two or more pages, be sure that your name is at the top of each page. If the pages get separated, they can be easily rejoined.

JOB OBJECTIVE

If you choose to include an objective, it is necessary to include a functional description or job title.

Because the objective is generally the first thing read on a resume, its importance cannot be ignored. Your objective should relate to your immediate goal.

Many applicants decide to eliminate the job objective unless they are applying for a specific position. Experts disagree widely on whether or not to include it. You decide.

Job objectives should be short, specific, and clear. They should be general enough to allow consideration of several related jobs at more than one level or department within a company. Read the following examples.

Michael D. Wooldridge

79 Mountain High Road   Denver, CO 80239   (303) 555-2533

Career Objective
   Computer Aided Drafting and Design Operator specializing in mechanical design

Education
      CADD Certification. Central Oregon Community College. Bend, OR
         Certification to be completed June, 1993. GPA 3.5
         Associate of Science degree to be completed by 1994
      Burns High School Graduate with 3 years of drafting

AutoCADD Experience
      Operated computer aided design system and peripheral equipment to design, resize, and modify detailed mechanical drawings used in manufacture, assembly, installation, and repair.

      Examined electronic schematics and supporting documents received from design engineering departments to verify specifications such as dimensions and tolerances.

      Computed drafting specifications to determine configuration dimensions using computers, calculators, and conversion charts. Prepared final detail drawings of components and equipment.

      Located files relating to specified design projection database library and loaded program into computer. Entered commands for resizing specification. Conferred with engineers to determine design modifications. Produced graphic representation of design for review and approval.

Millwright Assistant
      Assisted in building, installing, dismantling, and moving machinery, equipment, and buildings according to layout plans, blueprints, and other drawings. Constructed foundations for machines. Aligned machines and equipment. Read blueprints and schematic drawings to determine work procedures. Used hoists, lift trucks, micrometers, squares, rules, plumb bobs, and power tools.

Figure 5-12   Resume for a CADD Operator, Page I

- **Medical Records** . . . working for a hospital or large medical clinic in central Oregon offering a full-time career opportunity.

- **Public Relations and Promotions** . . . working with an organization where a positive public image and excellent media skills are imperative.

- **Administrative Management** . . . focusing on special projects, program development, and community relations.

- **Sales and Customer Service** . . . where personal effort and quality customer service are important.

- **Summer Employment in a Lumber Mill** . . . where excellent physical condition and a good work attitude are required.

- **General Office Accounting Clerk** . . . part-time position where excellent clerical and secretarial skills and a pleasant personality are required. Desire weekend work and flexible hours.

EDUCATION—DEGREES, LICENSES, PROFESSIONAL CERTIFICATIONS

It is necessary to specify your diploma or credential, your specialization, and the name, city, and state of the school you attended. It is optional to include the school's zip code and phone number, the year graduated, GPA, awards, scholarships, and relevant courses.

Education is generally placed immediately after the job objective if it is the next most important qualification you have. Sometimes work experience and skills are more important. For example, a person who has fifteen years' experience in accounting would probably list education later unless the position required specific educational credentials, such as an accounting degree. To be given a top billing, your education credentials should be exactly the education required by the employer.

When you only have a high school education, you can place it under the personal data if you feel that it's relatively unimportant but nonetheless needs to be mentioned. The older you are, the less important high school becomes.

Always list your highest and most relevant educational credential first; for example:

- PhD. Curriculum and Instruction. University of Oregon. Eugene, OR. (1994)

- M.S. Early Childhood Education. Western Oregon State College. LaGrande, OR. (1990)

- B.S. Psychology major, English minor. Portland State University. Portland, OR. Graduated Cum Laude. (1988)

- A.S. Health Record Technology. Central Oregon Community College. Bend, OR. GPA 3.52. (1987)

- Bend High School graduate. Bend, OR. Class valedictorian. (1986)

EXPERIENCE NARRATIVES

These are functional and/or achievement descriptions of work and life experiences you have had that are relative to the job objective.

Experience, commonly known as "what you do," sells. Experience should take up more space on your resume than anything else. Stress the skills and accomplishments that relate directly to the job you want.

When you are ready to write your experience narratives, review your data file, Exercise 1-3, "Twenty-Five Things I Love to Do," Exercise 1-4, "Twelve Things I'm Good At," and Exercise 1-6, "My Five Greatest Achievements" from Chapter 1. Note the experiences and achievements that are relative to your job objective, and include them on the resume.

Experience comes from all areas of your life: paid employment, school, hobbies, volunteer work, club memberships. You may even have many relevant skills from home activities, such as carpentry, landscaping, cooking, sewing, and child care. Because of the volume of pertinent experience you may have, be very selective. If you possess a skill and it is relevant to the job, no mater where you learned it, include it on the resume. Select the highest levels of skills and accomplishments that fit the job criteria.

Michael D. Wooldridge

Page 2

Equipment Operation

Operated computerized and manual trimsaws, resaws, and bandsaws. Trimmed and sorted lumber to grade. Trained and evaluated new operators on computerized system. Qualified boiler operator for a 4-boiler powerhouse. Trained new boiler operators in boiler operations.

Supervised crew in repairing boiler inner walls and building scaffolding. Operated heavy equipment: 966 cat, D-8 cat, coal and chip dozer, dump trucks, forklifts, and lumber carriers.

Auto Body Repair

Repaired, welded, and painted damaged cars, buses, and trucks. Examined damage and estimated repair cost. Removed upholstery, accessories, and trim electrical and hydraulic equipment to gain access to body and fenders.

Operated oxygen/acetylene welder. Welded and repaired broken or cracked metal parts, filled holes, and built up metal parts as specified by layout, welding diagrams, or work orders.

Used cutting torches, welders, hoists, jacks, sanders, and paint guns. Filed, ground, sanded, and refinished repaired surfaces.

Employment History

1981-91	**DAW Forest Products Company.** Bend, OR 97701	(503) 555-2511
	Trimsaw operator. Boiler operator. Millwright helper.	
1973-80	**Edward Hines Lumber Company.** Burns, OR 97720 (Closed)	
	Trimsaw operator. Chain puller. Clean-up. Boiler Operator.	
1968-73	**Burns Ford.** Burns, OR 97720 (Closed)	
	Apprentice autobody repairer and detailer.	

Personal

Seeking part-time employment in CADD operation while completing degree. Willing to work varied hours and days. Excellent attendance and safety records. Enjoy designing and building decks and awnings.

Figure 5-13 A Resume for CADD Operator, Page 2

EMPLOYMENT HISTORY

It is necessary to list employment dates (generally just the years), job title, and the company's name, city, and state. It is optional to include the mailing address, phone number, and supervisor's name with courtesy and job title.

The resume format decides the placement of this information. If you have chosen a functional or an achievement resume format, employment history will not be included at all.

The amount of detail and arrangement is decided by each applicant's situation and needs. Present your employment history in the best light. Consider presenting as much information as space allows and providing easy access for reference verification.

Make the employer's job easy; it's usually beneficial.

Following are examples of how some applicants handled their employment history.

1982 to 1984 **Boxer and Shelf Stocker,**
Albertson's Food Center. Eugene, OR.

- Please call Mr. Lonnie R. Hayes, Store Manager, at 555-5261 for employment verification and for a personal reference.
- Boxed groceries and delivered them to customer cars. Checked incoming orders, verifying items received with invoice. Stocked shelves with product.
- Received many compliments from customers.

For long-term employment with one employer with numerous promotions and location changes:

1975-89 Georgia-Pacific Corporation
    1986-89   **Divisional Office Manager and Accountant**
               McAdam New Brunswick, Canada
    1980-86   **Timber Department Accounting Supervisor**
               Eugene, Oregon
    1975-86   **Plant Accountant, Secretary, Accounting Clerk**
               Springfield, Oregon

Fired? Here's an example of how one person handled the reference issue. Wanting to be sure that potential employers contacted a specific person within the company, the applicant listed the name of a prearranged reference.

Director of Personnel - 1987 to 1995
Alcore Lumber Company, Aberdeen, WA

- Please fell free to contact Ms. Leona Kenning, V-P of Human Resources, for employment verification and for a personal reference at (206) 555-5555, extension 4569
- Administered all industrial relations for plant of 230 hourly employees. Duties included employee training, affirmative action, union grievances, contract negotiations, workers' compensation, employee benefits, safety, environmental control, company newsletter, payroll. Supervised staff of three.

Numerous job changes and time gaps in employment should be and can be downplayed on your resume. These include

- Having large time gaps between jobs.
- Possessing numerous jobs with different companies over a short period of time.
- Being fired or terminated for any reason.
- Being demoted or taking a cut in salary.
- Working in unrelated positions and those below your capabilities.

If any of these situations exist for you, they can often be mentioned briefly or not at all. The following examples show how to handle these difficult situations.

1986 to 1990	Sales positions in real estate, home furnishing, jewelry, and clothing.
1979 to 1984	General office positions, including Accounting Clerk, Secretary, and Payroll Data Entry Clerk.
1981 to 1983	Gas Station Attendant, Waiter, Sales Clerk, Ski Instructor, Rafting Guide.

OTHER ACTIVITIES

These activities may include memberships in professional, political, or community organizations; publications you've written; awards or special recognitions received; CPR and first aid training; licenses; and other technical skills not previously mentioned. You may include unusual experiences or any other relevant information not listed elsewhere, such as hobbies.

When listing an organization you have been actively involved with, include

- dates of membership
- name and location of organization
- offices held
- any special accomplishments
- short explanation of the organization's purpose for clarification.

When listing publications, include

- dates of publication
- publication name
- publisher
- awards or recognitions
- any other details that add to your overall picture.

PERSONAL

Information in the personal section is optional. It may include working hours, desired location, travel, relocation, reason for change, health, age, gender, marital status, citizenship, personal characteristics, or any other relevant information not listed elsewhere.

Personal data depicts self-confidence and candidness—traits employers appreciate. Don't permit misrepresentation by omission. Silence often makes the loudest sound and is prone to misinterpretation.

There are no ironclad rules on what must be included on a resume or a job application. The primary objective is to convincingly sell what you can do. If you do this first, then age, marital status, or sex will not be a major issue. Include information that supports your cause; eliminate data that hurts your cause. There are no rules; if it sells, use it.

Use Form 14, the personal checklist, to cover all items that can benefit you. This form should be filed behind the RESUMES divider of your notebook.

Review this form each time you write a resume or complete a job application. Revise answers when necessary.

Ensure that all answers reflect the positive. Choose only those items that are relevant to the employer for inclusion on your resume. Now let's look at each section individually.

Age

Age becomes a barrier when you believe it is one. Don't convey this to the employer by omission. This only draws attention to it. State age with only the year. Add supportive comments to build a positive image. Examples include "Born 1986, ambitious and willing to learn," and "Born 1945. Mature, high energy, and excellent track record."

Marital Status

Marital status like age is one of those areas people have difficulty deciding whether or not to include. Including your marital status is a matter of choice. Will it be beneficial or detrimental? It's difficult to tell but consider the inclusion seriously.

PERSONAL CHECKLIST

Item	Comments	Item	Comments
Age Born in Kansas 1960.		**Citizenship** U.S. Citizen	
Marital Status Married, 2 children ages 8 and 10		**Sex** Female	
Health Physically fit Long-distance runner		**Travel** Willing to travel	
Working Hours Flexible		**Relocation** Will consider Topeka or Wichita areas	
Special Skills Computer literate WordPerfect 5.1 Lotus 1-2-3 MS-DOS, Dbase III software		**Hobbies** Writing children's stories Graphic design and layout	

Hiring Liability
Little experience in field - all volunteer work in marketing
Weight (20 pounds over)
Lack of a master's degree

Reason for Change
Seeking employment in field of education.
Graduating in spring.

Character Traits

Detail Minded. Enthusiastic. Artistic. Fast learner.
Work well with coworkers, employees, and clients.
Often complimented on listening skills.

© 1995 Harris Espérance Incorporated · Form 14/95

Figure 5-14 FORM 14, Personal Checklist

If your marital status is opposite of what you believe is best suited for the job or employer, add descriptive words to establish a more suitable tone. For example, Rhonda wrote, "Mother of two active grade-schoolers. Supportive supervision always available while attending evening meetings or traveling." These comments addressed the job requirements and eliminated the employer's objections to hiring a woman with small children.

Suitable descriptions for divorced or separated individuals include

- Single, no dependents.

- Family man.

- Single parent of two preschoolers. Quality child care available for extra hours and during school breaks, illnesses.

Gender

Identify gender only if it provides you with a hiring edge. Because it is advisable not to use initials in place of your name, first names generally inform the employer of your sex. This isn't always the case, however, as the name *Terry* could be a male or a female.

Because of stereotypes, job titles can also identify gender. *Electrician* typifies a male, while *nurse* typifies a female. If stereotyping creates an advantage for you, use it.

Health

Your health doesn't have to be mentioned, but leaving it out could cause questions. As long as you are able to perform the job without any health interference, write: "Health Excellent."

If you are uncomfortable with this statement, there are other ways of creating a strong, healthy image, particularly if you are physically active. Statements such as "Avid outdoor sports enthusiast—golfer, skier, and swimmer"; "Exercise regularly, enjoy hiking and biking"; and "Physically fit, trim and slim" would be appropriate.

Working Hours

Demonstrate your flexibility and willingness to do whatever the job requires. Possible comments include "Willing to work all shifts and days," and "Available for night meetings, out-of-town travel, and irregular hours."

Travel

Some organizations are large and may be interested in whether or not you would be willing to travel, even if the job you are applying for may not require it. Employers look for future potential each time they hire a new employee. So consider placing this information in the personal section on your resume. Here are two examples: "Willing to travel," and "Love to travel. Enjoy exploring different places and meeting new people."

Relocation

Relocation may be a factor with large companies. One short statement such as "Willing to relocate" will supply the necessary information.

If you are planning on moving to a new area, you may write: "Relocating to Phoenix area in June," or "Desire relocation to Seattle metropolitan area."

Special Skills and Hobbies

Stop, reread your resume. Are there any skills you have left out? List them here so you won't forget to consider including them on your resume. Some important skills may include first aid and CPR certification, public speaking, and calligraphy.

Hobbies can also be important. They may provide a common interest with the interviewer. Your hobby may also be a special skill, not part of the formal job, that an employer would like to have available on the staff. Some examples are photography, cake decorating, and writing.

Hiring Liabilities

This subject is included on this form for your reflection, not for the employer's information. An employer may have preconceived reasons for not hiring certain people, or your background may provide some questionable areas. Here is a place for you to identify any hiring liabilities. Then you can develop a plan for handling or removing them.

Hiring liabilities may include too many jobs, little or no experience, age (too young, too old), gender (job usually goes to males), education (no degree), personal appearance (physical handicap, weight), small children, marital status, discharge from last job, industrial injury, prison record.

Reason for Change

Employers are interested in why you want to change jobs. Consider your reasons and identify a positive reason the employer would enjoy knowing. Find a reason that makes an employer want to hire you. For example, "Seeking advancement opportunities."

In Chapter 6 on references you'll find detailed information on how to handle this question. Remember, there are many reasons why one leaves a job. The first reason that pops into your head often is not the only reason or the right one to provide to an employer. Search your mind for a good, positive answer, one that puts you in a good light.

Character Traits

You're looking for specific traits that fit the job objective. Different jobs require specific personalities and character traits. There are general traits and qualities employers want. For instance, being "detail minded" or "budget conscious" is beneficial for an accounting position. "Meeting and beating deadlines" is another good example. Here are some others to consider: "Good sense of humor," "Perfect attendance and safety record," "High energy level—enthusiastic," and "Excellent driver's record."

Summary Thoughts

As you can see, this form is a catchall. It forces you to stop and think if there are any messages left to be told to an employer.

- Put in one-liners that sell expertise, qualities, personal characteristics.

- Put in one-liners that provide the employer with answers no one else thinks to include.

- Put in one-liners that answer the employer's unasked questions.

Personal information helps employers like you and assists them in their hiring decision. Fill this section with "sizzle and sale" instead of "fizzle and fail." It's the last place to shine on your resume.

The deepest principle in human nature is the craving to be appreciated.
—William James

The employer's needs should always be considered when writing a resume. Employers want answers to these six questions:

1. Can you do the job?
2. Will you do the job?
3. How will you fit in?
4. How long will you stay?
5. Why are you looking now?
6. How much will you cost?

When you supply satisfactory answers to the first five questions, you are likely to get an interview. The last question is best answered at the interview. To tailor your resume to fit a potential employer's needs, ask yourself these questions:

1. What are the job requirements and personal qualities needed for this job?
2. What experiences do I have that best match these requirements and qualities?
3. How can I best capture the employer's attention in thirty seconds or less?

TAILORED RESUME FOR AN ELECTRICAL SUPERVISOR

A typical advertisement follows. Read the ad and identify the job requirements and personal qualities the employer wants. Record these requirements, listing the highest priority items first.

HELP WANTED   **210**

ELECTRICAL SUPERVISOR
Split shift. Opening at modern wood products complex. Must have state journeymen's license. Programmable controller and solid-state drive experience desirable. Excellent physical condition required. Must not be afraid of heights. Must enjoy working in cold weather. Excellent opportunity for multitalented person. Send resume giving work history and salary requirements.

EMPLOYER'S PRIORITY OF NEEDS AND BUZZWORDS

1. _____
2. _____
3. . _____
4. . _____
5. . _____
6. . _____
7. . _____
8. . _____
9. . _____
10. . _____

Notice how John Keneday's resume matches the employer's requirements in the advertisement on the prior page. John matched the employer's needs to his experiences. He divided his experience into functional areas of interest to the employer. He supported each area with strong skills statements. Then he ranked each group and each sentence within each group so the most relevant information was listed first.

JOHN KENEDAY

311 East Canyon Road   Cleveland, Ohio 44135   (216) 555-7172

Career Objective
Electrical Supervisor . . . for a modern lumber products complex desiring a multi-talented person.

Licenses and Education
Licensed State Supervisor and Manufacturing Plant Journeyman Electrician. Licensed State Millwright. Former Navy Nuclear Power School Instructor. Completed 4 years Boiler 2nd (E5) rating. Completed training in Gas and Arc Welding, Basic Fire Fighting, Supervisory Training, plus more.

Training and Supervision
Trained and schooled in supervision. Taught state electrical apprenticeship program for local community college. Qualified nuclear reactor mechanic, operator, and operator trainer.

Supervised production, maintenance, and construction personnel. Full responsibility for mill operations including sawmill, boilers, dry kilns, and planers.

Programmable Controllers
Researched, installed, and operated various programmable controllers and solid-state drives. Trained operators and maintenance personnel on equipment. Designed electrical power systems for production increases.

Employment History
92 to   OHIO LUMBER. New London, OH 44851. Phone (419) 555-9295
present   Sawmill Superintendent (86-present). Chief Engineer (82-86).

88-92   K-P INC. Cleveland, OH 44982. Phone (216) 555-9876
        Electrician Helper. Resaw and Tenoner Operator.

78-88   UNITED STATES NAVY.
        Instructor, Nuclear Reactor Operator, Mechanic.

Personal
Seeking long-term career opportunity in Alaska. Excellent physical condition. Unafraid of heights. Winter enthusiast on and off the job. Enjoy traveling. Willing to work flexible hours and schedules. Married. Born 1960.

Figure 5-15   Tailored Resume

- The job objective matches the advertisement.

- Licenses exceed the requirements.

- Experience meets the employer's requests.

- Work history is provided as requested.

- Personal data covers some of the other job requirements.

- Salary requirements are not covered on the resume. They will be addressed in the cover letter.

Would you have done it any differently? If so, how?

When writing your resume, identify the employer's job requirements. Look for the "must have's" and the "required's." If you're not sure what these are, get the employer's job description, ask someone who has this type of job, find advertisements in newspapers for this job, or put yourself into the employer's shoes.

If you fail to communicate that you have what the employer requires, you will most likely never get an interview. It is your responsibility to communicate your skills, abilities, education, and personal characteristics.

TAILORED RESUME FOR FINANCIAL MANAGEMENT POSITION

HELP WANTED 210

ASSISTANT FINANCE DIRECTOR Must have strong technical accounting skills in accounts receivable, accounts payable, trial balance, general ledger, cash receipts, cash disbursements, utility billing, and LID billing. EDP experience desirable, preferably IBM System 34. Good communications skills required. Minimum education requirements include a degree with minimum of 9 hours of accounting; or any equivalent combination of experience and training that indicates an ability to perform duties.

List the employer's hierarchy of needs:

_____

_____

_____

_____

_____

_____

_____

_____

_____

_____

_____

_____

_____

_____

_____ JEANNE STAPPLES _____

5989 Shellborne Street, Philadelphia, PA 19111   (215) 555-2224

CAREER OBJECTIVE
Financial Management . . . working for an organization that needs a team member with strong technical accounting, communication, and data processing skills.

ACCOUNTING
Prepared monthly, quarterly, and annual operating and capital expenditure budgets. Monitored capital investments and reinvestment programs. Analyzed monthly operating results relative to annual and quarterly budgets. Prepared trial balances, balance sheets, income and operating statements, profit and loss statements. Maintained general ledgers, and cost accounts, and prepared journal vouchers. Processed computerized payroll and all related tax reports. Recorded, posted, and balanced cash receipts. Reconciled bank statements.

Verified credit applications. Authorized credit extensions. Approved and established credit lines. Developed and implemented new credit policies. Personal collection efforts decreased delinquent debts 60% and increased cash flow 63% in two years. Worked with attorneys on legal collection matters. Filed liens and lien notices.

Managed and maintained accounts receivable for over 3,700 accounts with average active monthly balances of $400,000. Converted accounts receivable to in-house computerized system that handled all billings. Developed format for aged receivables, identification of COD accounts, account classification listings, and maintenance of current status on active accounts.

Approved, checked, and audited cash disbursements for equipment, supplies, and services. Monitored contracts and agreements for compliance. Established and maintained internal controls for accounts payable, ensuring proper protection of company assets.

COMMUNICATIONS
Published numerous business and organizational newsletters, developing logos and format. Wrote many feature articles presenting positive image of organization, emphasizing recognition and accomplishment, and informing readers of changes and upcoming events. Publications created involvement.

Wrote news releases. Planned special promotions for newspapers, TV, and radio broadcasts. Familiar with printing processes, typography, photography, paper, and inks, plus layout of brochures and pamphlets. Wrote employee policies and procedures, legal and financial documents, and data processing parameters.

Extensive speaking experience in business, education, and community. Company representative for various civic and educational organizations. Developed and conducted management workshops.

DATA PROCESSING
Diversified data processing background through work experience and formal education (Hewlett/Packard, IBM, Integrated Business Computers, Burroughs). Specified computer parameters for accounts receivable, accounts payable, payroll, and inventory control. Prepared cost/equipment evaluation for conversion to word processing.

Selected and implemented word processing system. Developed community contact program for potential new customers.

Figure 5-16   Tailored Resume, Page 1. Courtesy of a client

- Does this resume match the employer's needs listed in the advertisement?
- Is every item in the employer's ad covered by the resume?
  Strong accounting skills?
  Communication skills?
  Data processing experience?
  Education?

_____ **JEANNE STAPPLES** _____

Page 2

OTHER
Wrote and implemented an approved IRS pension plan. Negotiated new employee benefit programs, including health, dental, disability, and life insurance coverage.

Interviewed, selected, and hired employees. Supervised staffs. Conducted orientation and training. Evaluated employee performances. Established cross-training programs. Developed and implemented procedures decreasing work duplications by improving paper flow of accounting office.

Organized annual conferences with full responsibility for all meeting and social details. Edited board and committee official minutes. Prepared agendas. Established and maintained file systems. Processed and monitored insurance claims. Maintained hourly and salaried personnel records.

COMMUNITY/PROFESSIONAL ASSOCIATIONS
National Association of Credit Management of Oregon. Member.
Professional Secretaries International. Oregon Division Board Director and immediate past President.

Oregon Business Education Council. Administrative Management Society. Lane Community College Office Careers Advisory Committee. Lane Community College Vocational Advisory Committee. Past member.

EDUCATION
Bachelor of Arts. Business Education major. Accounting, Math, History, and English minors.
Colorado State University. Ft. Collins, Colorado. 1972.

Updated education at University of Oregon. Courses in upper level math, computer technology, word processing, and personnel administration procedures. 1978-1989.

EMPLOYMENT
1992-1994 **Credit Manager and Accounting Office Manager.**
          Avery Lumber Company. 1143 Court Street. Eugene, Oregon. (503) 555-6123
1986-1992 **Office Manager and Executive Administrative Assistant.**
          Douglas Fir Timber Assn. P.O. Box 16. Eugene, Oregon. (503) 555-5709
1978-1986 **Executive Secretary to General Manager.**
          Atlantic-Pacific Corp. 79 Hill Road. Eugene, Oregon. (503) 555-7625
1975-1978 **Administrative Assistant to Professor of Soil Mechanics.**
          University of Michigan. Ann Arbor, Michigan. (313) 555-9301
1973-1975 **Secretary, Quality Control Department.**
          General Motors Corp. Flint, Michigan. (612) 555-3201
1972-1973 **Secretary: Titan Missiles, Material Department Manager. Top secret clearance.**
          Martin Marietta Corp. Denver, Colorado. (303) 555-5601

PERSONAL
Good sense of humor. High level of energy and enthusiasm. Willing to travel. High adaptability to change. Operate well under pressure. Like assignments to challenging opportunities requiring creative solutions.

Figure 5-17 Tailored Resume, Page 2. Courtesy of a client

- Did Jeanne order her resume according to the employer's hierarchy of needs?
- Would you have listed the groups differently? If so, how?
- Are the job requirements in the resume ranked according to the employer's priorities? If not, can you explain why?

Form 16, Combination Resume Draft, is used as an example because many people use this format rather than the historical format (Form 15). The combination format works for writing achievement, functional or historical resumes. Even if you chose to eliminate employment data on your resume, fill it in on the draft resume. It's good to have the details. The difference between the forms is in the employment history section.

COMBINATION RESUME DRAFT

This form is designed to help you write your resume. It consists of several pages, but your final resume should be no more than two typewritten pages.

Identification

NAME	Candy Hudson

MAILING ADDRESS	1445 Eagle Crest Road, Bend OR 97702

DAYTIME PHONE NUMBER(S)	
Home (503) 555-7039	Daytime Message (503) 555-6508

Job Objective

JOB TITLE (General Description of Work Area)
Accounting or Data Entry Position

TYPE OF BUSINESS
Insurance or Medical Records Offices

GEOGRAPHIC AREA
Central Oregon

OFFERING   Full-time employment with advancement and growth opportunities

Education

DIPLOMA/CREDENTIAL	
Associate of Science	High School Diploma
MAJOR/SPECIALIZATION	
Business Administration Accounting	College Prep Courses
SCHOOL/MAILING ADDRESS/CITY/STATE/ZIP/PHONE/FAX	
Central Oregon Community College 2600 NW College Way Bend OR 97701-5998 (503) 555-7700 (800) 555-3041 OR only	Bend Senior High School 230 NE 6th Bend OR 97701 (503) 555-6290
YEAR GRADUATED	
June 6, 1992	June 8, 1990
GPA/AWARDS/SCHOLARSHIPS GPA 3.78 Honor Student Worked while going to school	FBLA 88-90 Nat'l. Honor Society 87-90 GPA 3.97 1990 OR Scholar Ranked 9th out of 234 students

RELEVANT COURSES		
Applied Accounting 1, 2, 3	Electronic Spreadsheets	Business Data Processing
Fund and Cost Accounting	Systems Analysis	Database Management
	International Business	Business Economics

© 1995 Harris Espérance Incorporated   Form 16/95

Figure 5-18   Combination Resume Draft, Page 1. Courtesy of a student

STEP 1: COMPLETE PAGE 1

Identification

Write in your full name. Avoid using just initials for your first name. List a daytime phone number that will be answered.

Job Objective

Review Form 13, Job Objective from Chapter 4. Include all relevant details from that form.

Education

Review your EDUCATION section in your data file. Don't forget the important details. List them on the form.

If you are in your early twenties, it may be appropriate to list your high school information. Just divide your education section in half, as in the example, and fill in the data.

Fill in all the details. You can edit out the items that don't fit. It's best to start with more than you need than to not have sufficient information to fill the page.

STEP 2: COMPLETE PAGE 2

Review your data file for relevant skills and achievements. If you did a good job putting together your data file in Chapter 2, the work for writing these narratives should already be done.

Functional and Achievement Narratives

Write detailed information for each functional or achievement narrative. Be as specific as possible.

Copy narratives from your data file. Choose narratives that support your career objective. Use as many examples as possible. At this stage of writing, it is important to have an excess of information. You should select a minimum of three categories.

Place the most relevant functional skill or achievement first.

List each supporting statement in order of the highest level or most relevant skill or statement.

Fill in all the narratives. You can combine categories and edit later.

Functional/Achievement Narrative #1

Accounting:
- Prepared end-of-night detail transaction reports.
- Verified and balanced totals transferred from cash register tapes onto daily report sheet against cash and charges-on-hand.
- Computed dinner tickets from waitresses' brief-hand slips for an average of 200 diners per night.
- Collected cash and charges.
- Made change and operated electronic data capture VISA machine.

Functional/Achievement Narrative #2

Supervisory:
- Trained 5 new employees to cashier.

Functional/Achievement Narrative #3

Computers:
- Operated IBM and Mac PCS using Appleworks, WP 5.1, Lotus 1-2-3, and several database programs.

Functional/Achievement Narrative #4

Office Machines:
- Accurately type 35-40 wpm.
- Operate 10-key add by touch, averaging 180 dpm.

Functional/Achievement Narrative #5

© 1995 Harris Espérance Incorporated   Form 16/95

Figure 5-19 Combination Resume Draft, Page 2. Courtesy of a student

STEP 3: COMPLETE PAGE 3

Employment History

Review the EMPLOYERS section in your data file for the details. Put it all in at this time. That includes the full dates (month, day, year) and full names of key personnel.

Employment History (Current or Most Recent Employer)
DATES   9/10/90 to present
JOB TITLE   Dinner cashier
EMPLOYER NAME/MAILING ADDRESS/CITY/STATE/ZIP Pine Tavern Restaurant Foot of NW Oregon Street, Bend OR 97701
PHONE NUMBER/FAX NUMBER   (503) 555-5581   FAX 555-8805
SUPERVISOR/COURTESY TITLE/JOB TITLE/DEPARTMENT Ms. Shirley Henderson, Manager
FOR EMPLOYMENT VERIFICATION PLEASE CALL/FAX/WRITE Ms. Shirley Henderson, Manager
FOR PERSONAL REFERENCE PLEASE CALL/FAX/WRITE Ms. Shirley Henderson, Manger   Mr. Leon Orion, Owner Ms. Sally Eisler, Coworker

Employment History (Next Employer)
DATES   07/01/90 to 09/07/90
JOB TITLE   Cashier/Server
EMPLOYER NAME/MAILING ADDRESS/CITY/STATE/ZIP Bachelor View Dairy Queen   61337 So Highway 97, Bend OR 97754
PHONE NUMBER/FAX NUMBER (503) 555-6880, 555-9419
SUPERVISOR/COURTESY TITLE/JOB TITLE/DEPARTMENT Mrs. Betty Gillespie, Manager
FOR EMPLOYMENT VERIFICATION PLEASE CALL/FAX/WRITE Mrs. Betty Gillespie, Manager
FOR PERSONAL REFERENCE PLEASE CALL/FAX/WRITE Mrs. Betty Gillespie, Manager, and Ms. Janice Evans, Coworker

Employment History (Next Employer)
DATES
JOB TITLE
EMPLOYER NAME/MAILING ADDRESS/CITY/STATE/ZIP
PHONE NUMBER/FAX NUMBER
SUPERVISOR/COURTESY TITLE/JOB TITLE/DEPARTMENT
FOR EMPLOYMENT VERIFICATION PLEASE CALL/FAX/WRITE
FOR PERSONAL REFERENCE PLEASE CALL/FAX/WRITE

© 1995 Harris Espérance Incorporated   Form 16/95

Figure 5-20   Combination Resume Draft, Page 3. Courtesy of a student

Cover a minimum of ten years. It's a matter of choice, space, and relevancy as to whether you list employers beyond the ten-year criterion.

Use as many pages as necessary. Just be sure that you include all employers for the period you are covering.

When you type your final resume, you can group short-term employment. Refer back to the Employment History portion of Exercise 5-2, page 114, for ideas.

STEP 4: FILL IN PAGE 4

Other

Review your data file, especially the OTHER ACTIVITIES section, so you don't forget to list key information.

Other
PROFESSIONAL AFFILIATIONS Toastmasters - Member, Secretary/Treasurer 1994
COMMUNITY ACTIVITIES Volunteer at local library
PUBLICATIONS High school journalist - wrote for newspaper and annual
LANGUAGES 1 year of Spanish - not very fluent
LICENSES/CPR/FIRST AID/AGE/GENDER/MARITAL STATUS/CITIZENSHIP
OTHER

Personal
WORKING HOURS/DESIRED LOCATION/RELOCATION Willing to work evenings and weekends. Would consider relocating.
TECHNICAL SKILLS/LICENSES AND SKILLS NOT MENTIONED ELSEWHERE/HOBBIES Oregon driver's license - perfect record - no citations
REASON FOR CHANGE Graduating from college - ready and anxious to go to work full-time.
PERSONAL CHARACTERISTICS/HEALTH Excellent health. Enjoy music, math, and computers. Dependable and organized. Detail oriented. Avid reader and writer. Outdoor enthusiast.
AGE/GENDER/MARITAL STATUS/CITIZENSHIP Born 1972, young, ambitious, and enthusiastic.
OTHER Love working with people.

© 1995 Harris Espérance Incorporated   Form 16/95

Figure 5-21   Combination Resume Draft, Page 4. Courtesy of a student

Do not be concerned about including too much information. The editing will happen as you type and lay out the resume. Right now you want to list important data so if you need an extra line to balance out the appearance of your resume, you will have plenty to choose from.

Personal

Review Form 14, Personal Checklist, from Exercise 5-2, page 119. Make sure you list relevant information not listed elsewhere. Put in some "sizzle." It's your last place to shine. Tell the employer something he or she really wants to learn.

STEP 1: TYPE OR COMPUTER PROCESS RESUME

If you use a computer, save your resume on a disk.

Select an attractive business typeface (font).

Use all the space available. The writing should be well balanced on the page. One-page resumes are generally the best, but if you use two pages, each page should be filled and balanced.

CANDY HUDSON

1445 Eagle Crest Road	Home (503) 555-3826
Bend, Oregon 97702	Days (503) 555-3826

CAREER OBJECTIVE
Accounting or Data Entry position in an insurance agency working full-time with advancement opportunities.

EDUCATION
Associate of Science degree with a Business major to be completed June 1992.
Central Oregon Community College. Bend, Oregon.
Education funded by COCC Honor Scholarship.

Bend Senior High School Graduate. June 1990. GPA 3.96.
Ranked 9th out of 234 students.
Awards: 1990 Oregon Scholar. Member of National Honor Society 1987-90.
Member of Future Business Leaders of America 1989-90.

ACCOUNTING AND SUPERVISORY SKILLS
Trained 5 new employees to cashier. Prepared end-of-night detail transaction reports. Verified and balanced totals transferred from register tape onto daily report sheet against cash and charges-on-hand. Computed dinner tickets from waitresses' brief-hand slips for an average of 200 diners per night. Collected cash and charges, made change, and operated electronic data capture VISA machine.

COMPUTER AND OFFICE MACHINES
Operated IBM and MacIntosh personal computers using AppleWorks, WordPerfect 5.1, Lotus 1-2-3, and database programs. Accurately type 35-40 words per minute. Operate 10-key calculator by touch, averaging 180 digits per minute.

EMPLOYMENT HISTORY

Dinner Cashier   **Pine Tavern Restaurant**. Bend, Oregon.
09/90 to present   Phone (503) 555-5581.

Cashier/Server   **Bachelor View Dairy Queen**. Bend, Oregon.
07/90 to 09/90   Phone (503) 555-6880.

PERSONAL
Born 1972, young and enthusiastic. Excellent health. Avid reader and writer. Enjoy music, math, and computers. Dependable and organized. Detail oriented. Oregon driver's license with perfect driving record.

Figure 5-22   Combination Resume. Courtesy of a student

- Make it easy to read. Use 1-inch margins on the sides, top, and bottom. Use lots of white space. Break up the grey with headlines or marginal comments. Use bold lettering, all caps, or underlining to highlight important information.

- Left-justify (ragged right edge) the copy. When you full-justify, the words are often spaced unevenly, which makes reading more difficult.

- Proofread, proofread, proofread. Read your resume word for word backwards.

STEP 2: FIELD-TEST

Have a qualified friend review your resume. Revise if necessary.

STEP 3: SELECT PAPER AND PRINT

Choose 8 1/2-by-11-inch high-quality 20-pound bond paper. Use white, off-white, ivory, tan, or grey paper. Buy a full box or ream of paper and matching envelopes from your local office supply store, stationery store, or printer. Check the quality of the copier before printing. Copies must be clean and unmarked.

As you evaluate the following resume examples, try to put yourself in the employer's shoes. Employers look for quality applicants with specific job-related skills. See what types of personal qualities and related job skills you can identify in each of the following resumes.

STEP 1: EXAMINE HISTORICAL RESUMES

NANCY MILLER

906300 Scenic Drive   Prineville OR 97754   (503) 555-4479

EMPLOYMENT OBJECTIVE
Accounting Office Staff Person . . . where a pleasant personality and accurate accounting and secretarial skills are required.

EDUCATION
Associate of Applied Science. Business Administrant and Accounting specialization   (1995)
     Central Oregon Community College. Bend, OR   (503) 555-7700 or (800) 555-3041
Crook County High School graduate. Prineville, OR   (503) 555-5661   (1993)

EMPLOYMENT HISTORY
File Clerk   (January 93 to present)
     Les Schwab Tires. Main Office, P.O. Box 667, Prineville, OR 97754   (503) 555-4136

Organization and Filing . . . Organized the filing of sales tax, accounts payable, and microfiche. Organized filing system for various reports, including trial balances, warehouse computations, general journals, and interest computations. Filed journal entries and profit and loss statements once a month by store number.

Accounting . . . Completed account analysis for selected accounts, including manager draws, licenses, dues and subscriptions, legal fees, and moving expenses. Monthly reconciled various accounts through the trial balance. Completed and performed maintenance on the out-of-balance report between the general ledger 2000 and account analysis.

Computers . . . Five years of computer experience with WordPerfect 5.1, Lotus 1-2-3, Excel, and DOS. Use Excel spreadsheets to update the rent income account every month. Use WordPerfect to write letters and to create filing system forms.

File Clerk   (January 92-January 93)
     Crook County Court. 300 East Third Street, Prineville, OR 97754   (503) 555-6555

Transcription . . . Transcribed manual minutes into Commissioner's Journal using both a computer and typewriter. Transcribed minutes from taped meetings using a transcribing machine with WordPerfect for distribution throughout courthouse.

Computers . . . Used WordPerfect on various tasks for the County Judge. Tasks included preparing letters to be sent to various government agencies, preparing spreadsheets for court cases such as land foreclosures, and preparing public notices to be sent to local paper for printing.

PERSONAL
Willing to work flexible hours. Excellent health. Very motivated and punctual.
Lots of computer experience with WordPerfect 5.1, Excel, Lotus 1-2-3, and DOS.

Figure 5-23   Historical Resume. Courtesy of a student

Qualities Employers Want

Reliability
Dependability
Punctuality
Timeliness
Team player
Independence
Adaptability
Flexibility
Commitment
Foresight
Going-the-extra-mile
Enthusiasm
Energy

Skills Employers Want

Computer
Communication
Leadership
Decision-making
Analytical
Evaluation
Budget management
Supervision

Qualities Found:

_____

_____

_____

_____

Historical Resume Sample Using the Data File

This is Form 9 from Sherry's data file. Notice how easily she was able to select relative experiences from her mill manufacturing job. Do you think Sherry chose skills that would be of interest to an employer hiring for an accounting position?

Read Sherry's job description; then record all transferable accounting skills.

Accounting Skills

_____

_____

_____

_____

_____

_____

_____

_____

_____

_____

DESCRIPTION BY JOB TITLE

Employer No. 6	Employer Name	Bend Millwork Company	503-555-1444
		62845 Boyd Acres Road Bend OR 97701	

Job Title	Hire Date	Beg. Wage	Supervisor
Board Patcher	09/25/79	$6.00/hour	Mr. Tom Adams

Job Title	Term. Date	End. Wage	Supervisor
Shipping Tally	06/30/94	$10.14/hour	Mr. Leon Savage

Job Description (Functional/achievement Narrative)
- **Shipping Tally:** Verified and maintained records of incoming and outgoing shipments. Compared identifying information, counted and measured items, and verified against bills of lading, invoices, and orders.
- **Production Tally:** Compiled and recorded production data from customer orders, work tickets, and product specifications. Calculated quantities of items produced, materials used, amount of waste, and frequency of defects.
- **Inventory Control:** Processed data using computer, and reconciled with actual physical inventory. Solved inventory problems through troubleshooting, using computer-generated information and hand-recorded documentation.
- **Freight:** Used knowledge of shipping procedures and transportation routes and rates to find the "best way" to ship.
- **Supervised:** Often in light of Supervisor's absence in the Shipping Department. Oversaw a crew of 3 people.
- **Volunteered:** In various offices throughout company. Acquired knowledge in many departments, such as invoicing, AR & AP, Cost Accounting, and Scheduling. Acquired computer and clerical skills.

Quotable Quotes/Special Recognitions/Awards
- Was often told of my amazing ability to learn quickly with a high degree of accuracy, very dependable.

Licenses
- None

What I Liked Best about this Job
- The knowledge I gained through working in the various offices throughout the company, and the experience of using different computer programs in each of those departments.

What I Liked Least about this Job
- The lack of communication between management and employees—I worked hard to ensure that the communications flowed.

Job Description Summary
- Kept accurate production and shipping records. Tracked production and shipment of products using customer orders, product specifications, and computers.

© 1995 Harris Espérance Incorporated   Form 9/95

Figure 5-24   Form 9 from Date File. Courtesy of a student

Remember to think: Divide—Support—Rank.

- Divide the job into functional areas or achievements
- Support each function or achievement with support statements.
- Then rank (prioritize) each functional or achievement group and each statement within each group.

Do Sherry's education and skill narratives support her job objective? Is she qualified for consideration?

What qualities do you find in this applicant's resume? List them on the blank lines.

Qualities Found:

_____

_____

_____

_____

_____

_____

Accounting Skills Found:

_____

_____

_____

_____

SHERRY ALEXANDER

735 Bear Creek Road   Bend, OR 97701   (503) 555-3832

CAREER OBJECTIVE
Accounting position, working for a large veterinary hospital or clinic that needs a team member with a positive attitude.

EDUCATION
Associate of Applied Science in Business Administration specializing in Accounting. (1995)
    Central Oregon Community College. Bend, OR 97701   (503) 555-7700   GPA 3.88

CLERICAL EXPERIENCE AND TRAINING
Office Skills . . . acquired 10 years experience in technical environment.
    Operated computers, printers, calculators, multi-line phones, and copy and fax machines.
    Type 60-65 wpm accurately. Operate 10-key calculator by touch, averaging 255 dpm.
    High degree of mathematical aptitude.
Computer Skills . . . operated personal computers, IBM and MacIntosh Networks.
    Used DOS, Windows, WordPerfect, Lotus, database programs, and other business software.
    Operated laser, ink-jet, and dot matrix printers.

EMPLOYMENT HISTORY
79-94   **Technical Support Production/Shipping Tally**. Moulder Tally, Feeder, Board Patcher.
    Bend Millwork Company. 62845 Boyd Acres Road, Bend, OR 97701 (503) 555-1444
    For employment verification please call Ms. Anne Gibson, Personnel Director.
    For personal reference please call Mr. Leon Oats, former Supervisor.

Volunteered . . . in several offices throughout the company. Acquired knowledge in many departments:
    Cost Accounting, Invoicing, Accounts Receivable, Accounts Payable, Scheduling, Traffic, Customer
    Service, and Sales.
Shipping Tally . . . verified and maintained records of incoming and outgoing shipments.
    Compared identifying information, counted and measured items, and verified against bills of lading,
    invoices, and purchase and sales orders.
Inventory Control . . . processed data using computer, and reconciled with actual physical inventory.
    Solved inventory problems through troubleshooting, using computer-generated data and hand-
    recorded documentation.
Freight . . . used knowledge of shipping procedures, transportation routes, and rates to find the "best
    way" to send shipments.
Supervised . . . often, a crew of 3, in light of Manager's absence in the Shipping Department.

PERSONAL
Love animals. Raise and train burros for packing, pets, and fun. Willing to work varied schedule.
    No dependents. Available to travel. Enjoy math and computers. Fast, efficient, and thorough.
    Exceptional memory. Cheerful and dependable.

Figure 5-25   Historical Resume. Courtesy of a student

Examine another historical resume sample.

Notice how Francis handled her work experience block? She included detailed information for reference checking. She made it easy for an employer to verify her claims. Even for the company that is no longer in business, she provided a name with a current phone number. How do think an employer views this type of information and effort? Are you willing to go to this much work to help an employer?

What qualities do you find in this applicant's resume? List them on the blank lines.

Qualities Found:

_____

_____

_____

_____

_____

_____

_____

_____

_____

Francis Beauvais

(503) 555-3894   161 Cedar Road   Bend OR 97702

Short-Term Career Objective
Data Processing and Accounting . . . Part-time employment through the Cooperative Work Experience program for credit through Central Oregon Community College.

Available: Monday, Wednesday, and Friday afternoons and evenings
                   Thursday 2 p.m. through evening, and all hours on weekends

Education
Candidate for the **Associate of Applied Science** degree specializing in **Information Systems Analysis** and **Accounting**. Expected graduation 1995. Central Oregon Community College. Bend, OR
Completed one year in Liberal Arts at Northwest Christian College. Eugene, OR
General Secretarial Certificate from Coleman College. San Diego, CA

Work Experience
1991-present - **Full-Charge Bookkeeper**. Rotz's Maintenance Service. Bend, OR
        For reference please call Mr. Chris Yardley, Business Manager, at 555-5739.
        Maintain full set of books on IBM PC using MS-DOS, First Choice, and Lotus 1-2-3.

1988-1991 - **Circulation Department Data Processor**. Good Family Magazine. Sisters, OR
        For reference please call Ms. Linda Dixon, former Office Manager, at 555-7175.
        Entered data using Hewlett Packard PC with WordPerfect 6.0. Transmitted data by modem.

1985-1987 - **Accounting and Data Processing Clerk**. Mountain View Hospital. Madras, OR
        For reference please call Mr. Frank Krueger, Financial Controller, at 555-3882.
        Used IBM PC with Tallgrass hard disk and modem to enter and transmit data. Used DOS, PAS, and Lotus 1-2-3 software. Brought current accounts receivable and billings that were three years in arrears. Maintained accounts and billing in current status.

1984-1985 - **Computer Operator**. Dynatron, Inc. Bend, OR (now out of business)
        For reference please call Mr. Tom Richesin, former Business Manager, at 555-2299.
        Brought forward production reports that were four months in arrears to current. Maintained current status. Complimented on the quick and accurate job.

Long-Term Career Objective
Plan on continuing education to earn a bachelor's degree in Accounting and then sitting for the Certified Public Accountant's examination. Will be enrolling in the off-campus degree program with Linfield College.

Personal
Single, no children. Nonsmoker who enjoys singing with the community choir and the Sweet Adelines. Enjoy central Oregon and all its outside activities. Avid skier.

Figure 5-26   Historical Resume. Courtesy of a student

STEP 2: ANALYZE FUNCTIONAL RESUMES

The *Dictionary of Occupational Titles* can be used in writing resumes. The following DOT descriptions were used in writing this resume:

301.474-010 HOUSE WORKER, GENERAL (domestic ser.) alternate titles: housekeeper, home	301.677-010 CHILD MONITOR (domestic ser.) alternate titles: nurse, children's	305.281-010 COOK (domestic ser.)
Performs any combination of following duties to maintain private home clean and orderly, to cook and serve meals, and to render personal services to family members: Plans meals and purchases foodstuffs and household supplies. Prepares and cooks vegetables, meats, and other foods according to employer's instructions or following own methods. Serves meals and refreshments. Washes dishes and cleans silverware. Oversees activities of children, assisting them in dressing and bathing. Cleans furnishings, floors, and windows, using vacuum cleaner, mops, broom, cloths, and cleaning solutions. Changes linens and makes beds. Washes linens and other garments by hand or machine, and mends and irons clothing, linens, and other household articles, using hand iron or electric ironer. Answers telephone and doorbell. Feeds pets.	Performs any combination of following duties to attend children in private home: Observes and monitors play activities or amuses children by reading to or playing games with them. Prepares and serves meals or formulas. Sterilizes bottles and other equipment used for feeding infants. Dresses or assists children to dress and bathe. Accompanies children on walks or other outings. Washes and irons clothing. Keeps children's quarters clean and tidy. Cleans other parts of home. May be designated Nurse, Infants' (domestic ser.) when in charge of infants. May be designated Baby Sitter (domestic ser.) when employed on daily or hourly basis.	Plans menus and cooks meals, in private home, according to recipes or tastes of employer: Peels, washes, trims, and prepares vegetables and meats for cooking. Cooks vegetables and bakes breads and pastries. Boils, broils, fries, and roasts meats. Plans menus and orders foodstuffs. Cleans kitchen and cooking utensils. May serve meals. May perform seasonal cooking duties, such as preserving and canning fruits and vegetables, and making jellies. May prepare fancy dishes and pastries. May prepare food for special diets. May work closely with persons performing household or nursing duties. May specialize in preparing and serving dinner for employed, retired, or other persons and be designated Family-Dinner Service Specialist (domestic ser.).

LUCY MADISON

8939 James Street	Reading, PA 19603	(215) 555-4333

EMPLOYMENT OBJECTIVE
Commercial or Domestic Housekeeper

HOUSEKEEPING EXPERIENCE

1985-95: Self-employed as a domestic housekeeper. Supported family of five. Worked continuously for six clients over ten years.

Housekeeping: Cleaned furnishings, floors, and windows, using vacuum cleaners, rug shampooers, mops, brooms, cloths, and cleaning solutions. Changed linens and made beds. Washed, mended, and ironed linens and other garments by hand or machine. Washed dishes and cleaned silverware. Answered telephone and doorbell. Fed pets and watered plants.

Cooking: Planned menus and cooked meals according to recipes or tastes of employer, observing diet restrictions. Prepared meats and vegetables for cooking. Cooked, boiled, broiled, fried, and roasted meats and vegetables. Baked breads and pastries. Created hors d'oeuvres and salads. Performed seasonal cooking, including preserving and canning fruits, vegetables, jams, and jellies. Ordered and shopped for household groceries and cleaning supplies. Meal preparation specialities include Mexican, Chinese, and Italian.

Child Care: Monitored activities of children. Assisted children in schoolwork. Amused children by reading to or playing games with them. Prepared and served meals and formulas. Sterilized bottles and other equipment used for feeding infants. Dressed and assisted children in dressing and bathing. Accompanied children on walks and other outings.

PERSONAL
U.S. citizen, born 1953. No dependents. Trustworthy.
Excellent physical health.
Quality references available.

Notice how Lucy used these descriptions to write her work experiences.

Compare the DOT descriptions with her experience narratives.

As you study the resume example, notice how the experience narratives support her job objective.

Pay attention to the personal qualities that become apparent when you read the resume. Is this person someone you would want to work for you? Why?

What personal qualities and characteristics make you want to hire Lucy? Record your answers below.

_____

_____

_____

_____

_____

Figure 5-27   Functional Resume

Let's analyze another functional resume. This time we have the advertisement Terry used when she wrote her resume.

HELP WANTED   PERSONNEL, SAFETY, AND PURCHASING DIRECTOR

Responsible for all phases of Industrial Relations and Purchasing. Successful candidate must possess strong administration and communication skills. Salary commensurate with experience. Please submit resume and salary needs. Women and minorities encouraged to apply.

Read the ad and list the employer's hierarchy of needs.

TERRY S. MORELAND
7712 South Heather Drive Tempe, Arizona 85285   (602) 555-5502

GOAL
Long-term career opportunity utilizing administration and communication skills to increase productivity, safety awareness, and job satisfaction. Emphasis on team and individual employee efforts.

INDUSTRIAL RELATIONS
Wrote and established county personnel policies. Troubleshooter. Intermediary for grievances to avoid formal hearings. Developed employment application to ensure compliance with federal/state laws on Equal Opportunity, Affirmative Action, and Protected Classes.
Monitored State Accident Insurance program. Interacted with current state staff. Motivated early return of injured workers to sometimes modified positions, thereby reducing employer costs and psychological effects of injury to the worker.

Managed Comprehensive Employment and Training Act participants in coordination with central Arizona on Intergovernmental Council. Recruited, selected, trained staff members. Urged personnel toward continuing education, goal setting, and teamwork approach.

Researched, evaluated, and presented benefit programs to county court, including medical, dental, vision, and deferred compensation programs. Maintained department records of sick leave, vacation, disciplinary action, injuries, and unauthorized absences.

Evaluated positions throughout county for cost effectiveness and need, allowing cutbacks through attrition rather than layoffs.

COMMUNICATION SKILLS
Adult education instructor for community college. Developed ten-week course. Motivated, encouraged, and aided participants to reach out, learn, and participate. Excellent evaluation from students.

Experienced in one-on-one interviewing as well as group leadership. Conducted tours for all ages with historical presentations. Former correspondent for *News Register* newspaper. Speakers' Bureau presenter for KICK Radio "Backtalk" program. Speaker for company meetings and community organizations.

Designed and presented concise written and oral reports for county on status of lands, roads, laws, benefits, and proposed ordinances.

1. _____
   _____

2. _____
   _____

3. _____
   _____

4. _____
   _____

5. _____
   _____

6. _____
   _____

Would you organize this resume differently. How?

Notice that there is no employment history on this resume. Why do you suppose it was omitted?

Figure 5-28   Functional Resume, Page 1. Courtesy of a client

Remember to think: Divide—Support—Rank.

- Divide the job into functional areas or achievements.

- Support each function or achievement with support statements.

- Rank (prioritize) each functional or achievement group and each statement within each group.

In the advertisement, what does "salary commensurate with experience" mean? How would you handle such a statement?

What personal qualities do you find in this resume? List them on the blank lines.

Personal Qualities:

_____

_____

_____

_____

_____

_____

_____

_____

TERRY S. MORELAND
Page 2

ADMINISTRATION
Managed federal/state grants, including airport development grant of $500,000. Prepared final audit documentation for Arizona Aeronautics Division and Federal Aviation Administration, Region 10. Received letter of commendation from Seattle Regional Office.

Headed report team for Arizona judicial systems analysis of courts takeover. Represented county position in special session of the Arizona legislature.

Prepared bid specifications for heavy equipment to office machines. Evaluated proposed purchases. Planned public auction of surplus equipment--sold everything advertised, exceeding anticipated revenue.

Interacted with work crews on daily basis. First woman ever invited to participate in Road Department Christmas party and retirement functions.

Liaison to state health division. Served as county registrar of vital statistics. Received certificate of appreciation for exceptional dedication. Competent, knowledgeable, and experienced in grant writing and management, budgetary processes, and cost controls.

CIVIC PARTICIPATION
American Society of Safety Engineers. Member. Past President.
National Personnel Managers Association. Member. Program Coordinator.
Central Arizona Employers/Medical Co-Op Council. Member. Organizer.
Eastern Arizona Health Systems Agency Council. Member and Officer.
Tempe Toastmasters Club. Member. 88-94 State Toastmaster of the Year.

EDUCATION
University of Arizona. B.S. in Management. Graduated Cum laude. 1976.

OTHER PERTINENT DATA
Enjoy music, sports, and poetry (dubbed county "Poet Laureate").
High energy level. Abundance of enthusiasm.
Available for night meetings, travel, and public speaking.
Born 1948. Married. Son in high school.

Figure 5-29 Functional Resume, Page 2. Courtesy of a client

STEP 3: STUDY COMBINATION RESUMES

When Michele wrote her resume, she took it to a former teacher and asked for an opinion. The teacher said, "I really think you should use a more standard format." Michele gave serious thought to these comments but decided to test her resume in the real world. So off she went. One interviewer said to her, "You know, Michele, usually I fall asleep reading resumes. But your resume was different. I felt that I really got to know you." She got the job.

While others can provide valuable input, what you choose to put in your resume is really your choice.

MICHELE LEATHERS

2232 N.W. Columbia Avenue   Portland, OR 97210   (503) 555-3512

Career Objective
Public Relations and Promotions . . . working with an organization where a positive public image and excellent media skills are imperative.

Education
Bachelor of Science. Broadcasting and Television Production. University of Wyoming (89).

Visual Communications
In 1988, narrated video recruiting tape for the University of Wyoming women's basketball team. Assisted in script creation and advised on production. Received many compliments from viewers. Typical comments: "Great presence on camera," and "Her voice, the accent, and tone are what we in the general public have learned to expect from the electronic media." Tape still being used for recruiting.

Hosted a University of Wyoming television production for the 1989 NCAA ski championships in Jackson Hole, Wyoming. Conducted live interviews of skiers and organizational sponsors. Updated competition results daily on live broadcasts.

Guest and impromptu speaker at many community organizations (Kiwanis, Lions, school career days). Asked to return several times. Anchored weather and sports sections of student television news broadcasts.

Audio Communications
Interviewed many times by television, radio, and newspaper reporters. Diplomatically answered questions on sensitive and controversial issues and successfully maintained integrity of self and organization represented.
Recorded county campaign advertisement and sports announcements for radio.

Written Communications
Wrote press releases, television and radio announcements, and newspaper feature articles. Revised employee, safety, and general information manuals for Adelaide Brighton Cement Company, Adelaide, South Australia.

Sales and Promotions
Recruited Division 1 players for Australia and Wyoming basketball teams.
Sold and promoted memberships for Hyatt Regency Adelaide through international telemarketing.
Ranked in top 20% of sales representatives.

Personal Work Ethics and Characteristics (Quotes from reference letters)
Dave Arnold, Dave Arnold Productions, wrote: "In my 13 years in business, no one has been more professional and pleasant to work with. She is always early to work, late to leave, and as relentless during a show as she was as a player."

Maggie McDonald, Executive Director of High Country Athletic Conference, wrote: "You will find Michele very upbeat and excited about what she is doing, and her enthusiasm permeates everyone with whom she comes into contact."

Figure 5-30   Combination Resume, Page 1. Courtesy of a client

What do you think of Michele's format and choice of categories?

Are the categories appropriate to her stated career objective?

Are the categories arranged in the order of relevance?

Are there too many categories? Could any of them be combined?

Is the resume too long? If yes, what would you eliminate?

Notice the use of testimonials on Michele's resume. These were quotes from personal reference letters.

Notice how Michele handled her employment history. Can you figure out another way to clearly state her work record?

There's no one right way to record your employment record; you need to lay it out in a manner that will represent you best.

What personal qualities do you find in this resume? List them on the blank lines.

Personal Qualities:

_____

_____

_____

_____

_____

_____

_____

_____

_____

_____

_____

_____

MICHELE LEATHERS

Page 2

Television Equipment Operations
Floor director for the television productions of the Cowboys' coaches shows (the Voice of the Wyoming Cowboys) for two years.
Set up and operated dollies, camera mounting heads, and related equipment for network broadcasting.
Covered football and basketball games. Assisted camera operators in acquiring the "perfect" shot.

International Professional Basketball Experience
Played starting forward for the West Adelaide Bearcats, South Australia.
Averaged 22 points per game in local competition and 17 points per game in National League. Leading offensive rebounder in South Australia (90-91).
Played starting strong forward and center for Sporting Luxembourg. Voted Player of the Year.
Averaged 29 points per game. Team won Luxembourg country championship (87-88).

Special Achievements and Awards
Achieved all-time career leading rebounder and scorer for U of W.
Nominated for **Kodiak All-American Basketball Team**.
Selected four times for the **High Country Athletic All-Conference First Team**.
Chosen twice for a **Converse All-American College Basketball Team**.
Received a **NCAA Sixth Year Grant** to complete college education.
Awarded **UW Full-Ride Athletic Scholarship** for entire collegiate career (83).
Voted **Most Valuable Player** at Oregon State AAA High School Basketball Championship playoffs (83).
Received Oregon State AAA High School Basketball **Player of the Year** (83).

Employment History
    Adelaide, South Australia
        90-91   Basketball Player. West Adelaide Bearcats.
        91   Promotional Sales Representative. Hyatt Regency.
        90   Special Project. Adelaide Brighton Cement Company.
        90   Receptionist/Clerical. Kelly Temporary Agency.
    Laramie, Wyoming
        88-89   Floor Director for all TV sports shows and Assistant Secretary for all nonrevenue sports. University of Wyoming.
        88-89   Operations Assistant. CBS and ESPN Television Networks.
    Luxembourg, Luxembourg
        87-88   Basketball Player. Sporting Luxembourg.
    Prineville, Oregon (summers)
        86-91   Grocery Checker. Scotty's Thriftway.
        82-86   Lifeguard and Water Safety Instructor. City of Prineville.

Personal
Seeking full-time career position in the Pacific Northwest.
Excellent health. Single, no dependents. Available for travel.
Willing to work varied hours and shifts. Always meet or beat deadlines.
Enjoy working with the media and diverse social and economic groups.

Figure 5-31   Combination Resume, Page 2. Courtesy of a client

Did Linda address the interests of the employers? If yes, what makes you believe this? If no, what should she have addressed?

Are the categories listed in a logical order? Would you have listed them differently? In what way? Why?

Record your answers on the blank lines.

Linda Kuulei

699 West Second Street
Reno, NV 89431

Home (702) 555-5270
Work (702) 555-9571

Objective
- ▸ **Oregon High Desert Conservation Director** . . . working to enhance our environment through education, research, restoration, and conservation.

Education
- ▸ Master of Science, Botany and Paleoecology. University of Washington. 1989.
- ▸ Bachelor of Arts, Botany. University of Hawaii. 1981.

Managed Conservation, Restoration, and Natural Resource Programs
- ▸ Developed and implemented rare plant and plant community monitoring program, the largest rare plant program within the National Forest System. Wrote and administered plant inventory and monitoring contracts. Coordinated and prepared annual and out-year budget planning.

- ▸ Prepared and implemented habitat protection and conservation strategies. Developed standards and guides for Land Management Plans for threatened, endangered, and sensitive species. Conducted plant inventory, monitoring, association mapping, habitat characterization, restoration, and rehabilitation of native ecosystems.

- ▸ Hired and supervised permanent and seasonal employees. Promoted equal opportunity employment. Conducted new employee orientation and training. Performed employee performance evaluations. Fostered employee development to meet work standards through education, mentoring, and disciplinary procedures.

Established Partnership Projects
- ▸ Built cooperative partnerships with diverse community and watershed interests as Forest Service Community Representative for Crooked River Watershed Cooperative Education Project. Activities include curriculum development, class instruction, and field trips.

- ▸ Initiated programs to meet shared native plant management goals on National Forest System lands with state and federal agencies, private conservation organizations, and local business community. As Research Natural Area Coordinator, identified potential areas meeting state heritage goals on National Forest System lands using Oregon Natural Heritage Plan.

- ▸ Identified and enlisted partners for cost share projects as State President of the Native Plant Society of Oregon.

Figure 5-32 Achievement Resume, Page 1. Courtesy of a client

What personal qualities do you find in this resume? List them on the blank lines.

Personal Qualities:

_____

_____

_____

_____

_____

_____

_____

_____

_____

_____

_____

_____

Linda Kuulei

Page 2

Teaching, Training, and Facilitating
- Developed and taught Conservation/Environmental educational curriculum for K-12. Presented Wildflower, Native Vegetation, and Environmental Education programs for Crook County School District. Used storytelling skills to present environmental education for all ages.

- Conducted training sessions in Total Quality Management (TQM), Conservation Strategy Development and Implementation, Inventory and Monitoring of Rare Plants, Program Development and Management, and Plant Identification.

- Facilitated community meetings, team-building sessions, and staff meetings. Taught university laboratory classes in biology, botany, and mycology. Member of national training cadre for BLM. Conducted public education to promote the Northwest Wine Industry.

Grant Writing and Published Works
- Wrote and received grants for the U.S. Forest Service, the Native Plant Society of Oregon, and the Universities of Washington, Nevada, and Hawaii.

- Wrote technical environmental documents for the NEPA process. Created brochures, reports, marketing, and educational materials.

- Published technical reports and journal articles for the Bulletin of Native Plant Society of Oregon, the National Park Service, *Quaternary Research*, the *Journal of the Hawaiian Botanical Society*, and the Universities of Hawaii and Nevada.

Professional and Community Activities
- Society for Conservation Biology
- Natural Areas Association
- Society for Ecological Restoration
- Nevada and California Native Plant Society
- Committee for Schools

Certificates of Merit and Cash Awards
- 1993 - Establishment of Willows Federal Daycare Facility
- 1992 - Report writing of Ecosystem Restoration Opportunities Report
- 1990 - Development of rare plant program

Figure 5-33 Achievement Resume, Page 2. Courtesy of a client

What personal qualities do you find in this resume? List them here.

_____

_____

_____

_____

DEE BERMAN

WILL

Continue courteous, honest and efficient services;

Provide a balance between getting the job done with limited resources, while providing quality service to the people of Crook County;

Protect the integrity of the election process

DEE BERMAN

✗ **Proven Ability**
✗ **Quality Leadership**
✗ **Dependable**

Endorsed and supported by elected officials, county employees, and Crook County Citizens.

WE SUPPORT DEE BERMAN:

Lela Bonny	Dr. Evan Jones
Dr. Denison Thomas	Barbara Boyd
Vera Schnoor	Mary Thurman
Joan M. Gerke	Lindy Simmons
Ken Smith	Gary Stephens
Mike Warren	Jan Jones
Debbie Layton	Todd Vallie
Gene Wheeler	Joe Nelson
Sandra Wilson	George Wittmer

Printed by Country Printing

COMMITTEE TO ELECT DEE BERMAN
JACQUE WHEELER, TREASURER
475 S. Belknap
Prineville, OR 97754

THIRD-CLASS
U.S. POSTAGE PAID
Prineville, OR 97754
Permit No. 63

ELECT DEE BERMAN CROOK COUNTY CLERK

Figure 5-34 Creative Resume, Page I. Courtesy of a client

What differences do you notice in this resume compared to the more conventional resumes?

_____

_____

_____

_____

DEE BERMAN
UNDERSTANDS CROOK COUNTY

Dee's great-grandparents homesteaded in Crook County in 1910. Her parents are Floyd and Evelyn Rachor. Dee is a graduate of Crook County Schools. Dee and her husband Don have three children: Bobbie, Lanny and Casey, and four granddaughters.

DEE BERMAN
IS QUALIFIED

"Dee has worked for me in the Crook County Finance office for three years. She's a model employee and cheerfully takes on new tasks and handles problems in my absence with great skill. She's been an asset to the county by filling in for County administrative assistants during their absences."

Mike Pawley, County Finance Director (90-94)

DEE BERMAN
ENDORSED BY DELLA HARRISON

"Dee's dedication, integrity and experience makes her the most qualified candidate for the job of Crook County Clerk. Her knowledge of county government is an asset to us all. It is with confidence that I urge you to elect Dee Berman as your County Clerk."

Della Harrison, County Clerk (86-94)

DEE BERMAN
IS EXPERIENCED

91-94 Crook County Finance Clerk
84-93 Local Business Owner
        Independent Meat Market
        Makin' Bacon & More
90-91 Museum Research Librarian
77-84 Bookkeeper
69-70 Legal Secretary

DEE BERMAN FOR CLERK

DEE BERMAN
DEDICATED AND PROFICIENT

"I had the opportunity to observe Dee's performance and work with her for approximately three years at the Courthouse. She is highly skilled, intelligent, loyal, completely honest, industrious and consistently pleasant."

Dick Hoppes, County Judge (77-92)

DEE BERMAN
COMMUNITY INVOLVEMENT

Active community
volunteer since 1981

Chairman
Prineville Legislative
Committee

President elect of
Prineville Kiwanis Club

Board of Directors
Crook County
Historical Society

Chairman
Oregon Trail
Celebration Committee

Past President
Prineville Camp Fire
Association

Paid for by the Committee to
Elect Dee Berman
Jacque Wheeler, Treasurer
475 South Belknap
Prineville, OR 97754

Figure 5-35 Creative Resume, Page 2. Courtesy of a client

This combination resume is different in tone than most resumes. Most resumes eliminate the personal pronoun *I*, because it is already assumed you are writing about yourself. Ryan chose to use *I* in his resume. What do you think? What personal qualities does Ryan display through his writing? Would you want to interview him if you were looking for an office machine technician? Why? What is it about Ryan that you like or dislike?

What skills and personal qualities do you find on Ryan's resume? List them here.

Ryan Smith

HCR 11 Box 59   Fairbanks, AK 99707   (907) 555-5752

Job Objective
Looking for **Office Machine Technician** position in a modern, growing business with the opportunity for advancement. Would prefer to be located in central or eastern Oregon.

Education
I am currently enrolled in the **Office Machine Technology** (OMT) program at Central Oregon Community College in Bend, Oregon. This is a modern, industry-based program that stresses service, management, customer relations, and communication skills. I will graduate with an OMT certificate in June 1996 and with an Associate of Applied Science degree in June 1997.

Work Ethic/Attitude
While growing up, I spent most of my spare time working on the family ranch. Having pride in one's work, following instructions, and getting the job done right the first time were stressed. Along with the attention to detail and responsibility I learned in the service, this instilled in me a strong work ethic and a can-do attitude.

Management/Supervision
While in the service, I supervised up to 50 men, providing security for vital areas. I supervised 12 men full-time and was held accountable for them both on and off duty. I was picked from a 300-man guard force to coordinate with the Guard Office to set up security for another base. I followed this through by training and troubleshooting the new guard force.

While working as a lumber grader at the mill, I was expected to stay within a 10% margin of error with little or no supervision. Most of the time I was under 5%.

Technical/Mechanical
I have always enjoyed electrical/mechanical tinkering and have successfully completed many projects through self-teaching. Upon completing the OMT program, I will be a fast-learning technician strong in these areas: electrical/mechanical, customer relations, and service management.

Employment History
1987-93 **Chain-Puller**, Lumber Grader
    Big Timber Lumber Company, West Highway, John Day, OR 97845   Phone: (503) 555-1054
    For employment verification please call Ms. Julie Erickson, Personnel Manager
    For personal reference please call Mr. Harry Danielson, Quality Control Supervisor
1986-87 **Knot-Bumper, Skidder-Operator**
    Ponderosa Logging, Prairie City, OR 97869   Phone: (503) 555-8203
    For employment verification and personal reference please call Mr. James Owens, Owner
1979-83 **Marine Security Guard**
    U.S. Marines, NSB, Bremerton, WA 98315   Phone: (206) 555-6323

Personal
I changed occupations to get into something with a better future. I am honest, hardworking, and fairly flexible in hours. My wife and I prefer a rural, country setting for raising our three boys.
Computer literate. Comfortable in DOS and Window environments. Proficient in word processing, spreadsheets, and database programs. Excellent driving record. Willing to work flexible hours and schedules.

Figure 5-36 Combination Resume. Courtesy of a student

SECURE QUALITY REFERENCES
A "No Surprise" Support System

CHAPTER

6

You will find it a very good practice always to verify your references, sir.
—Martin Joseph Routh

I distinctly remember John during the interview. When asked for references, he handed me a list, then proceeded to tell me what each was likely to say about him. He included a well-balanced picture—the good and the bad.

For example, he said, "When you call Mr. Reeves, he will say that I sometimes get too involved in the employee's side of an issue." He went on to explain why this was true and then provided interesting and detailed examples of potential reference comment.

What I found most amazing was that when I called each reference, they told me exactly what I had been told by John. Each reference provided an informative and helpful description of John. Each told me about his strengths and weaknesses, his skills and potentials.

I came away with a strong sense that John knew his abilities and what he could do. I found congruence in John's interview and the reference comments and felt that I knew who John really was.

Knowing what your references will say about you increases your self-confidence in the interview and increases your credibility with potential employers. In this chapter you will find out how to build a "no surprise" support system and how to create the needed rapport with all your references, even the "not-so-good" ones.

The following forms and documents are kept in the REFERENCES section:

- **Form 17: Reference list**
  Use this form to list all your potential references. This includes all individuals who may be contacted by a potential employer. Contact everyone you list, recording the date and results of the call.

- **Form 18: Employment Verification Request**
  File this completed form with the appropriate Employer Record in the EMPLOYER section of your *Companion Planner*.

- **Form 19: Education Verification and Transcript Request**
  File this information in the EDUCATION section with the applicable school.

- **Form 20: Personal Reference Request**
  File this form with all information from your personal reference. Include form 22, Reference Contact Record and letters of reference. You will probably choose to make a separate divider for each individual reference you use.

- **Form 21: Authorization to Release Information**
  If you use this form, file a copy with the appropriate employer or personal reference so you know that you have provided the release.

- **Form 22: Reference Contact Record**
  Use this form to record your telephone conversation with your reference. Keep an accurate and detailed account of the call. If necessary, use the back of the form or an extra page.

- **Form 23: Draft Reference List and the formal Reference List**
  Type your personal list of references. Keep the original in a file folder and a copy here.

- **Reference Letters**
  File a copy of each reference letter behind form 26, Reference Record. File a copy of reference letters from employers with form 8, Employer Record. Original reference letters should be kept in file folders labeled with the person's name; this keeps each document fresh and clean. Make photocopies when you are in the job-hunt/interviewing process.

- **Telephone Scripts and/or Clusters**
  These scripts may be filed with the individual employer or reference record. Keep generic telephone scripts and the list of Frequently Asked Questions in this section. You may have scripts for conversations with receptionists, the personnel department, former employers, and bosses. The degree of detail and types of scripting will vary with your personal experience.

- **Individual Reference Dividers**
  You may find it useful to make individual dividers for each reference. This keeps the information on each person separate and easy to find.

WHAT DO POTENTIAL EMPLOYERS LOOK FOR?

Congruency, that's what employers look for.

Employers want to find a common thread emerging from all your references. Your personality, skills, and abilities need to blend into a congruent picture.

Employers want to discover your abilities, potentials, and personal qualities. The following questions provide a basis of what employers want to know:

1. Can you do the job? Your experience level, skills, education, learning ability, and accomplishments provide them with clues.
2. Will you do the job? Your motivations, interests, and attitudes tell the story here.
3. How will you fit in? How you get along with others and your age, sex, personality, ethnic background, and education level may be factors. Who you associate with may also shed light on this area.
4. How long will you stay? Your prior employment history may provide correct or incorrect answers. Your short-term and long-term goals also contribute information to the employer.
5. How much will you cost? Past earnings often provide clues to this question. Geographic location, industry classification, and labor supply also play a role.
6. Why are you looking now? This question is tricky. Employers realize that some job applicants are looking for work because of problems in their existing job. The so-called personality conflict surfaces often. Whatever your reason for looking for a job, be sure you provide a positive motive.

When employers find positive answers to these six questions, they are apt to be interested in you. It is up to you to present the positive answers they want to hear. How do you do this? You select a career objective that's congruent with your interests and abilities. You create a well-written resume that represents you properly. Then you secure references that will work for you.

NO SURPRISES EVER

References are people who can speak knowledgeably about your work performance, abilities, and attitudes. What do you suppose a potential employer would think if your reference said, "Carole, who?" This situation could prove embarrassing for you, maybe even fatal in regards to your getting the job. Credibility is easily destroyed when a reference responds in such a manner. Don't let it happen to you. Prepare each reference for that reference check call.

References must be informed ahead of time. This enables them to discuss you intelligently. Uninformed references can undermine your chances of getting the job.

You will want to know what each reference will say about you—the good, the bad, and the in-between. Ask each reference to describe your strengths and weaknesses. Asking references to identify your weaknesses

Carole, who?

may make them uncomfortable. If this happens, rephrase your request to sound more positive; for example, "In what areas could I make improvements?" Well-balanced responses from references increase your credibility.

References should never be surprised that you have used their names. Always get their permission. After receiving permission from your references, send each one a thank-you letter. Enclose your latest resume. This enables them to discuss you intelligently and to assist you in the job hunt.

References are too valuable to waste. They can't be of help if you fail to alert them of what you're doing. Keep in touch. Let them know what's happening.

Manage the flow of information from your references. Make references work for *you* rather than for the employer.

WHO ARE YOUR REFERENCES?

References are people who can speak knowledgeably about your work performance, abilities, and attitudes. Each of you has many qualified references. Each reference should be able to discuss how you perform on the job and your work-related skills and attitudes. References fall into three groups: (1) employers, (2) business associates involved with your employment, and (3) other associates. Let's look at each group and discover the wealth of references available to you.

EMPLOYERS

When thinking about who your references are, begin with your employment history. This is where employers begin checking first. Include at least one contact person from each employer listed on your job application or resume. It's advisable to cover all employers from the past fifteen years.

Consider these possible references from your workplace(s):

1. Your immediate supervisor
2. Other department heads or the operations manager
3. Your peers or subordinates
4. The personnel manager
5. The company president or a vice president
6. Board members

Current Employer

Potential employers will not contact your current employer unless you give them permission. They're sensitive to your need for confidentiality. So, if your current employer is unaware of your job search, don't worry. Employers will respect a "no contact" request. However, if you can provide a contact person from this employer, it will be appreciated. This person should be able to speak knowledgeably about your work and maintain confidentiality.

Sometimes current employers who are aware of your desires will cooperate fully in your quest. If this is the case, ask for their help and keep them informed. Often they can provide job leads and valuable advice. Enlist them in your search. It can pay off.

Past Employers

It is common practice for a potential employer to verify employment records with all prior employers in the past ten years. Some may go back even further. Therefore, make sure you have a current telephone number and the name of a contact person for each employer. If the company is no longer in business, locate someone that you worked with and provide a name and daytime phone number.

Making it easy for a potential employer to verify your work record may put you ahead of other job hunters. Employers will notice your effort and may reward you with a job offer. Do the necessary footwork and provide current contact information. It will be appreciated.

BUSINESS ASSOCIATES

There are many other valuable references available from the workplace and community. Try to select individuals who can speak knowledgeably about how you perform on the job. These references can provide a different and interesting picture of you.

Consider these possible references:

1. Customers or clients
2. Sales representatives or insurance agents serving your employer
3. Auditors—independent and government
4. Other government officials, such as the safety inspector from OSHA
5. Vendors selling to your company
6. Company or outside attorneys
7. Bank representatives

Employers automatically suspect references of bias. So choose them very carefully. Select references an employer will feel confident about. With so many possible references to choose from, why list your mother, father, sister, brother or friend? Choose someone who has worked or viewed your work.

While you may not have exposure to all of these potential references, there are probably several that you could list. Business associates may become some of your best sources for references other than your immediate supervisor. If you've established a good reputation with a business associate, consider listing him or her.

OTHER ASSOCIATES

If you have never worked and therefore have no references to list from the employment environment, there are still many viable references out there. Consider listing some of the following people:

1. A person from a professional business organization
2. A member from a volunteer community activity
3. An associate from a political, religious, or social organization
4. Your personal physician, lawyer, or insurance representative
5. A teacher
6. Any community leader

A SEVEN-STEP REFERENCE APPROACH

The following seven-step approach will show you the proper procedure for selecting references that will work for you. This approach is explained in the exercises that follow.

1. Make a reference list.
2. Verify employer records.
3. Obtain written verifications.
4. Call personal references.
5. Obtain quality reference letters.
6. Formalize the reference list.
7. Do your follow-up.

A FINAL THOUGHT

References are too important to leave to chance. Take the time to inform all of them. Make an additional effort and get a reference letter. We will proceed by examining each step individually.

Provide variety—the broader, the better. Choose people who can speak specifically about your skills and character traits relative to the job for which you are applying—people who can speak knowledgeably and favorably about you—people who know you and your abilities.

Record all potential references on Form 17, Reference List.

STEP 1: LIST ALL EMPLOYERS FOR THE PAST FIFTEEN YEARS

REFERENCE LIST
Page __1__ of __6__

Name of Reference Company Affiliation	Phone Numbers	Result of Call			
		Date	Call Back	Will Return Call	See Record
1. Mr. Rod Arrons, Store Manager. Ericson's Sentry Market Current Employer	Work 555-6291				
2. Mr. Ben Williams, Retired Ericson's Sentry Market Former Supervisor	Home 555-9233				
3. Mr. Gene Anderson, President Ms. Sara Joseph, Manager Ace Air Electronics, Past Employer	Work 555-9354				
4. Mrs. Elaine Olson, Personnel Manager Western Temporary Services Past Employer	Work 555-9424				
5. Mr. Alex Randall, Controller Former Supervisor Norpac Foods	Work 555-7895				
6. Mr. Amos Ritter, Comptroller and Supervisor Tektronix, Inc.	Work 555-9231				
7. Mrs. Beverly Stillman, Freelance Consultant Community Volunteer United Appeal/COBRA	Home 555-5589				
8. Mr. Ray Dorman, Sales Representative Dechutes Pine Ltd. Family Resources Committee Member	Work 555-6805 Home 555-2238				
9. Ms. Emily Erickson, Partner Shelby, Rice & Erickson, C.P.A.'s Former State Tax Auditor for the State of Oregon	Work (209) 555-7300				
10. Mr. Albert Wise FARMER'S INSURANCE, Agent Former customer at Ericson's and current insurance agent	Work 447-7603 Home 475-0318				

© 1995 Harris Espérance Incorporated   Form F17/95

Figure 6-1   FORM 17, Reference List

List at least one person from each employer on your job application. The person can be anyone in the company. The higher the title, the more influential, the better. Your immediate supervisor is recommended. The company president, your supervisor's boss, the personnel manager, other department heads, former supervisors, peers, and subordinates are other choices.

STEP 2: LIST BUSINESS ASSOCIATES

Include customers, clients, patients, auditors, bankers, attorneys, and sales and service personnel.

STEP 3: LIST OTHER ASSOCIATES

Others may include community leaders, professional and community club members, your doctors, attorney or insurance agents, real estate professionals, and teachers.

The purposes of this exercise are to

1. Verify your employment records. If an employer finds discrepancies between what you list on an application and what is in your resume, your credibility and honesty become an issue. You can't afford to let this happen.
2. Identify the person or persons who will provide employment reference checks.
3. Find out how the reference checks will be handled and what will be said. You need to know what will be said about you and your employment record.

Think accessibility, believability, and congruency. That's what employers need.

All employers and personal references that a potential employer might call should be contacted by you first. Accuracy and congruency of information is vital to your job search; so cover all bases. Here are three reasons for calling each reference:

1. To make sure the reference remembers you
2. To make sure you have not been confused with someone else
3. To verify that the reference is aware of all the skills you've acquired

Protect yourself by calling each reference before you begin your job search. The steps you'll want to take are explained as follows.

STEP 1: KNOW THE QUESTIONS POTENTIAL EMPLOYERS WANT TO ASK

Listed below are the question a potential employer would like to ask your past employers. It is important for you to know how each question will be answered. When calling to verify employment records, find out the answers to these questions. You should query each person involved in providing reference information. Your aim is congruency in the reporting.

1. What dates did _____(name)_____ work for you? the company?
2. What positions (job titles) did he hold?
3. What did she get paid?
4. How was his attendance? Any major illnesses, injuries, or absences?
5. What kind of safety record did she have? Any loss-time accidents/illnesses?
6. Why did he leave this job? Describe the circumstances. Was he fired?
7. Would you rehire her?
8. Please describe the duties performed and any significant accomplishments.
9. What are his major strengths?
10. What are her major weaknesses?
11. Did he meet deadlines?
12. How did she get along with superiors, peers, customers, clients, etc.?

13. How was his work attitude? or What kind of employee was he?
14. Do you know anything that would disqualify her for this job?
15. Who else in the company can provide additional information?
16. Why is he looking now?

By knowing the answers to these questions, you can direct potential employers to references who will provide complete and accurate information.

STEP 2: SCRIPT YOUR CONVERSATION

You may be uncomfortable calling an employer. One way to ease this nervousness is to script your call. Scripting gets the facts, keeps you on target, and alleviates nervousness. Scripting builds confidence and saves time. It guarantees accurate information. Use the questions in Step 1 as a guide when preparing your script.

Script #1: Conversation with Receptionist

- Identify yourself.

- Keep conversation specific and businesslike. Know why you're calling.

- Request the individual's name and job and courtesy titles.

- Close on a friendly note.

Opening statement:
- Hello, this is ___(your first and last names)___.
- Hello, I need to speak with someone in charge of reference checks. Would you please tell me this person's name and job title? Does she prefer Ms. or Mrs.?

Body statements:
- I need to verify my employment records. With whom should I speak?
- Who most likely will provide employment and reference verification?

Closing statement:

Thank you. I appreciate your help.

Script #2: Conversation with Person in Charge of Reference Checks

- Identify yourself.

- State your reason for calling.

- Find out if it's a convenient time to talk.

- Include questions from Step 1.

- Ask general questions if needed.

- Thank the person. Express sincere gratitude.

Opening statement:

Hello, this is ___(your first and last names)___.

Body statements:

I will be looking for work soon; therefore, I need to verify my employment records. I have several questions to ask. Is this a good time for you? (If no, set a time to call back. If yes, continue the conversation.)

My records indicate that I was hired on ___(date)___ as a ___(beginning job title)___ at ___($ amount)___ per hour/month/year. Does this agree with your records?

I also show that I was promoted to ___(job title)___ on ___(date)___, earning ___($ amount)___. Is this correct?

What will you say about my work, attendance, and safety records?

What do the records say about why I left, and would the company rehire me?

What else might you be able to tell an employer about me?

Closing statement:

Thank you ___(Mr./Ms./Mrs. name)___. You've been very helpful, and I appreciate your time. Good-bye.

Script #3: Conversation with Former Boss

Problems can arise when bosses don't remember you or get you mixed up with another employee. For example, when Mary, a former student, called her former boss, she learned that he didn't really remember her. What's more, he was confusing her with someone else, who was a marginal employee. Imagine what would have happened if Mary had left the reference call to the employer. Because of her call, she received an excellent referral.

Begin your call with a friendly opening.

Be as brief as possible. You're talking to busy people.

In closing ask for referrals and permission to use the person's name as a reference.

End on a friendly note. Always thank the person for his or her help and time.

Opening statement:

Hello ___(name of former boss)___, this is ___(your first and last names)___. I'll be applying for work soon and would like to review my work record and performance with you. Do you have a few minutes to answer some questions? (If no, set another time to call. If yes, continue the conversation.)

Body statements:

I show that I worked for you between ___(dates)___ as ___(job title)___. I was making ___($ amount per hour/month/year)___. Does this agree with your records? Your position at that time was ___(supervisor's job title)___, is that correct?

Would you please describe my job duties? How was my work performance, attitude, attendance, and safety?

If you were asked to describe my strengths and weakness, what would you say? (If the person has difficulty addressing your weaknesses, rephrase the question, and ask him or her to describe areas in which you needed to make improvements.)

After he or she has answered the question concerning your weaknesses, you may want to respond with the following: "Thanks. I'm glad you shared that with me. I will be sure to work on that right away."

Would you now describe why I left and describe to me the circumstances behind my leaving? Would you or the company rehire me?

How did I meet deadlines and goals? Please describe how I worked under pressure.

Would you describe how I got along with ___(superiors, peers, subordinates, clients, patients, customers)___?

Do you know of anything that would disqualify me for a job in ___(describe job areas you are applying for)___?

Who else in the company would you recommend to provide additional information?

Closing statements:

___(Mr./Ms./Mrs. reference's name)___, I really appreciate all your comments. They have been very helpful to me. Do you know anyone who could use a person with my skills? Could you recommend three people that I could contact?

(Get permission to list the person as a personal reference.) May I list you as a personal reference? If yes, say, "Thanks a lot. I'll send you a copy of my resume and keep you informed." If no, say, "That's okay, I understand."

Thanks for all your help. Good-bye.

Script #4: Conversation with an Unfriendly Boss

Begin in a businesslike manner, and use a friendly tone of voice. Make requests, not demands.

- Check to see if it's a convenient time to talk.

- Ask for help. You want to learn from this experience and go on to better things.

- Find out how the reference check will be handled.

- Ask who will provide the information.

- Learn what will be said about you.

- Don't ask for a reference letter at this point. You will draft one later.

- Try to agree on a nonconfrontational reason for the termination.

Opening statement:

Hello ___(name of former boss)___, this is ___(your first and last names)___. I'll be job hunting soon, and I need your help. I know we parted under unfriendly terms, but I would like to try mending our relationship. I have several questions to ask. Is this a good time for you? (If no, set another time to call. If yes, continue the conversation.)

Body statements:

I want to learn from my termination and to understand where I went wrong. At the time it happened, I wasn't in any mood for learning and would like to apologize for my behavior. I'm looking for ways to improve, so I won't make the same mistake again. Will you help me? Thanks.

Thanks. Here's what I would like to know:

(Now use one of the previous scripts as a guide. Cover all the questions.)

(Be sure to cover the reason for termination. Try to agree on a term other than "fired." You may want to try this question concerning the reason for your termination:)

Would it be permissible to list the reason for termination as a layoff or a department reorganization?

Fired? Turn Adversaries Into Allies

Being fired, a fate viewed worse than death by many. Will it happen to you? Here's something to consider: The higher you go in management, the greater the chance you will be dismissed. Do you remember when Lee Iacocca was fired from Ford Motor Company? Just read the news, and it seems to happen to the best of the best. I know many people (friends, family members, students, and clients) who have been fired. Your only real security rests with your ability to accept the situation, learn from the experience, and go on with a positive attitude.

Firing an employee is a messy business that nobody relishes. I know—I've had to do it. It means that both parties failed. The situation is painful for everyone involved. So generally, you can get help from your former employer. The following paragraphs outline some actions you can take.

- Arrange a meeting to find out where you went wrong. Stress the fact you want honest answers, no matter how critical those answers are. State you want to learn from this experience so you won't make the same mistake again. This is no time to make your boss feel guilty. Make requests, not demands. Don't argue. Get the facts and learn from them.

- During this meeting, ask your former boss specifically what will be said in a reference check. Get the positive and the negative sides. Have your boss identify your strengths and weaknesses. Come to a thorough understanding of what will be said. It is extremely important to become comfortable with the facts of your termination. You must begin viewing it as a positive learning experience, one which helped you grow.

- Next, share this growth experience with potential employers. When you relate this experience, many interviewers will identify with you. They may not admit it, but it is likely that they, too, have been terminated at some stage in their career.

- In an interview, relate how you came to grips with the reality of being fired and how you turned the experience into a positive lesson. Tell the interviewer what the employer will say about you. Specifically, tell the interviewer how your boss views your strengths and your weaknesses. In telling an interviewer, in optimistic, straightforward language, what you have learned from being fired and what the employer will say about you (the positive and the negative), you create a beneficial atmosphere. A potential employer will confirm your comments while reference checking. This confirmation creates a favorable environment and enables the interviewer to develop a positive impression of you because of your honesty.

In summary, come to grips with the facts. Accept the reality of being fired. Meet with your former employer and learn what will be said about you. Turn the firing into a positive learning experience. Share this experience with potential employers. Employers appreciate hiring employees who learn valuable lessons from devastating experiences.

STEP 3: CLUSTER THE CALL

Because using a script is not the easiest thing to do, here's a tip to make scripting more effective—try clustering. The script gives you the words; the cluster provides the flexibility and serves as a guide. Because conversations don't flow in a straight line, using a pictorial cluster of what you want to say will help. A cluster gives you a representation of the conversation and allows the conversation to flow naturally.

Clustering is a tool used for effective expression; it is a pictorial outline of your thoughts. It's a technique developed by Gabriele Lusser Rico, author of *Writing the Natural Way*. It's a method that increases natural expression by tapping into the creative side of your brain. I've adapted its use here to help you express yourself more effectively. Clustering—bringing wholeness to your writing and thinking. It develops your own "voice," that manner of expression unique to you.

Clustering is similar to brainstorming, in that you never cast out thoughts or ideas when they come to you. No matter how crazy the idea may seem, you just record it. Following are the general principles of clustering:

> To create a cluster, you begin with a nucleus word, circled, on a fresh page. [For the purpose of this exercise, you will put the person's name you want to call in the circle.] Now you simply let go and begin to flow with any current of connections that come into your head. Write these down rapidly, each in its own circle, radiating outward from the center in any direction they want to go. Connect each new word or phrase with a line to the preceding circle. When something new and different strikes you, begin again at the central nucleus and radiate outward until those associations are exhausted.

> As you cluster, you may experience a sense of randomness or, if you are somewhat skeptical, an uneasy sense that it isn't leading anywhere. That is your logical Sign mind wanting to get into the act to let you know how foolish you are being by not setting thoughts down in logical sequences. Trust this natural process, though. We all cluster mentally throughout our lives without knowing it; we have simply never made these clusterings visible on paper.

> Since you are not responsible for any particular order of ideas or any special information, your initial anxiety will

soon disappear and in its place will be a certain playfulness. Continue to cluster, drawing lines and even arrows to associations that seem to go together, but don't dwell on what goes where. Let each association find its own place. If you momentarily run out of associations, doodle a bit by filling in arrows or making lines darker. This relaxed receptivity to ideas usually generates another spurt of associations until at some point you experience a sudden sense of what you are going to write (say) about. At that point, simply stop clustering. . . .

(Gabriele Lusser Rico, *Writing the Natural Way*)

Figure 6-2 shows a sample cluster that I used when I was calling a former employer.

Cluster for two to three minutes. When no more thoughts come, relax. Review your cluster. When you've covered all the bases, you're ready to make your phone call.

Clustering is an easy way to script your conversation. As you talk to your party, you can make notes on your cluster. When the conversation is almost over, you can say, "Let's see, have I covered all of my questions?" Then you can quickly check all the circles and comments to verify that all questions have been asked and answered. Cluster your conversation with each employer like the example in Figure 6-2.

Remember, it is unfair to expect good references from people who

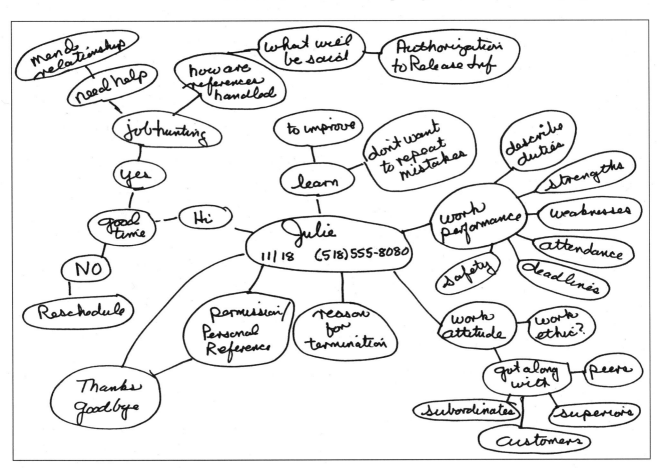

Figure 6-2 Cluster a Script

do not know what you are doing. Therefore, call each employer and each person that may be contacted during your job search. This means all employers and immediate supervisors for the past ten years. Besides, one of them may offer you a job or know of the perfect job for you. Call all your references before you begin your official job search.

STEP 4: CALL THE EMPLOYER

Use the telephone. It's the quickest and most efficient method to get information. Use the following tips when calling an employer:

- Keep your conversation businesslike. Be diplomatic. This is no time for arguments.

- Use your phone cluster or script. Get all the information. At the end of the conversation, quickly review your cluster to ensure that you have covered all the important areas.

- Make detailed notes. Don't be concerned with their appearance. Get all the details. You will be transferring these notes to Form 22, Reference Record, later.

- As much as possible, keep the conversation short.

- Contact all persons cited on the job application, your cover letter, or resume. Mention that you are job hunting. Often, these people can provide you with leads. Inform references and all other persons contacted of the type of job you are looking for and the employers you plan on contacting.

- Ask references for advice and help. Ask them

  1. To identify your strengths (areas in which you excel).
  2. To identify weaknesses (areas in which you need improvement).
  3. If they know of any openings that might be of interest to you.
  4. If they can refer you to someone who could help you.

STEP 5: MAKE A RECORD USING FORM 22, REFERENCE RECORD

Making and keeping accurate records are important functions in the job-hunting process. If you don't write it down and file it in a convenient place, it's soon lost or confused with another person or record. Take the time to record the information in detail. It pays off in the long run. Record all other pertinent comments on Form 22, Reference Record. Make a complete record of the conversation, using the guidelines that follow.

- Get the full name and correct spelling.

- Ask for thier courtesy title preference; for example, Ms., Mrs., Mr., Dr., Judge.

- Record the date of the call.

REFERENCE CONTACT RECORD

Full Name Gene Anderson	Courtesy Title Mr.	Date 09/02/XX
Job Title President	Type/Length of Relationship (Year) Former boss (1991)	
Employer, Address, Phone Number ACE Air Electronics 2303 Highway 126 Prineville, OR 97754 (503) 555-4476 FAX (503) 555-2981	Secretary Mrs. Carol Boeskey	
Home Address, Phone Number 135 Crest View Drive Prineville, OR 97754 (503) 555-9988	Other Important Names Ms. Sara Joseph, Personnel Manager Mr. Terry Vargas, Vice President	

CONVERSATION NOTES

Strengths	Weaknesses (Improvement Needed)
Handled over-100-employee payroll and personnel records with accuracy. Maintained confidentiality. Met all deadlines and goals. Satisfactory attendance.	Attitude—very stubborn (resisted following orders). He said we had a personality conflict and that he never liked me from the very first day (his wife had hired me; I don't know if this had any bearing on the matter or not).

Other Comments

Worked well with coworkers, employees, and clients.
Agreed on termination language: Termination due to company reorganization.

Referrals (Courtesy Title, Name, Phone, Company, Relationship)

None—suggested that all potential employers be referred to Ms. Sara Joseph, Personnel Manager.

© 1995 Harris Espérance Incorporated   Form 22/95

Figure 6-3   FORM 22, Reference Record

- To record the type of relationship, use such terms as Employer, Supervisor, Business Associate, Customer, Client.

- Record the length of relationship by year.

- Get the name of the secretary or receptionist. Make friends. Secretaries and receptionists can become valued allies.

- Jot down other names for future referral. Remembering names is an important skill.

- Record the employer, address, and phone number, as well as the official job title, of your reference. This information changes often; so keep it up-to-date.

- Keep the home address and phone number of key references. This helps to maintain contact.

- Listen for key words or phrases, such as energetic, cost-conscious, articulate, stubborn, moody.

- Always ask for referrals. Find out their courtesy title, the correct spelling of their name, their job title, their employer name and phone number, and the type of relationship.

STEP 6: PROVIDE FORM 21, AUTHORIZATION TO RELEASE INFORMATION

Sometimes past employers are reluctant to supply adequate information to an inquiring employer. If you find this to be the case, provide your former employer with an authorization to release information, such as Form 21. This allows the employer to answer all questions without being concerned about potential lawsuits. It also allows the potential employer to verify your information in detail.

AUTHORIZATION TO RELEASE INFORMATION

I have authorized potential employers to conduct a complete investigation of my prior employment record for the past _____ years. I understand that this investigation will include a reference check with some or all of my prior employers and personal references, as well as an effort to verify the fact that I have provided complete and accurate information.

Therefore, I authorize _____
and any of its representatives to provide any and all information concerning my previous employment and any pertinent information that you may have, personal or otherwise. This information may include, but is not limited to, the following:

1. The fact of my past employment
2. Dates of employment
3. Job titles and positions held
4. Salary information
5. Description of all duties and responsibilities
6. Reasons for and circumstances surrounding my separation of employment
7. Questions concerning attendance, safety, health, attitude, etc.
8. Additional names to provide further information, if requested
9. Any and all information concerning my previous employment

I agree to hold harmless and to waive any claims I may have against any and all of my former employers, whether or not identified above, for any loss or injury I may sustain as a result of any disclosure made in accordance with this release.

This authorization shall remain in effect until notified in writing of cancellation.

This authorization was granted and signed on _____

by: _____

© 1995 Harris Espérance Incorporated   Form 21/95

Figure 6-4 FORM 21, Authorization to Release Information

This is a voluntary act, but it is one that can help potential employers a lot. Consider the benefits; then act accordingly.

If this form is too broad for you, rewrite it to fit your needs. Remember, you do not have to send a release. But it makes an employer more comfortable and more willing to share the good things about you with a potential employer. It may allow your prospective employer to receive glowing reports on your work performance.

Employer records must be verified, and a company representative should be quizzed as to how the reference check will be handled and what will be said. In the long run, you will be glad you put forth the effort to do this work.

There may be times when it's necessary to write an employer, a school, or a personal reference to get a written verification. The following pages provide examples of a cover letter and an employment verification request form. Use Form 18 whenever you want a written employment verification.

STEP 1: COMPLETE FORM 18, EMPLOYMENT VERIFICATION REQUEST

EMPLOYMENT VERIFICATION REQUEST

To:
Mr. Joe Salinez, Operations Manager
Western Wood Manufacturing
P O Box 7984
Minneapolis, MN 55440
(612) 555-9274

From:
Harriett McGuire
6872 Alabama Road
Wichita, KS 67217
(316) 555-0853

I will be looking for employment soon and would like to verify my employment records. Since it is imperative that employers verify applicant claims, I have authorized potential employers to conduct a complete investigation of my prior employment. I understand that this investigation will include an employment and personal reference check, as well as an effort to verify the fact that I have provided complete and accurate information.

Therefore, I authorize the above company and any of its representatives to provide any and all information concerning my previous employment. I release the above company and any of its representatives from any and all potential claims for damages whatsoever that may result from their actions and comments in responding to a reference request.

Name while in your employ: Harriett Fanijello
Social Security Number: 999-23-7398

I've recapped my records below to the best of my ability and memory. Please verify the accuracy by initialing, if correct, or by crossing out the information and supplying the correct information.

Question	My Record	Verification/Comments
Original Hire Date	October 20, 1979	
Last Day Worked	May 30, 1983	
Official Termination Date (if this date varies from last day worked, please record reason)	June 30, 1983 Accum. vacation	
Beginning Salary	$18,000/year	
Beginning Job Title	Personnel Director	
Beginning Supervisor	Mr. Joe Salinez	
Ending Salary	$27,500/year	
Ending Job Title	Personnel Director	
Ending Supervisor	Mr. Joe Salinez	

Description of Duties
Administered all company industrial relations, health and welfare, employee benefits, union negotiations, and grievances. Wrote affirmative action plan and monitored for compliance. Established company policy and adherence thereof of hiring and termination processes, and worker safety. Wrote company advertising and maintained a high-quality community image. Supervised payroll.

© 1995 Harris Espérance Incorporated   Form 18/95

Figure 6-5 FORM 18, Employment Verification, Page 1

Complete the form in detail. Be as specific as you can.

Name Change:
Be sure to list the name you used while in this company's employ.

Official Termination Date:
Many times the last day you worked is not your official termination date. You may have had vacation pay coming, and the company may have recorded your termination date to include those extra days. There are other reasons why your last day worked may not be the official date of termination. Check the dates so your records will agree with the employer's.

Description of Duties:
If you don't have sufficient room to describe your job duties, write them on another page. Be very specific. Include a complete description.

Leave the second page blank for the employer to complete. It's always good to get the employer's viewpoint of your work performance. If the employer chooses not to complete this portion, do not be concerned. At least you will have written confirmation of the hiring and termination dates, job titles, wages, and duties.

Be sure to date and sign the form. An employer won't release any information if it's not signed and dated.

It would be appreciated if you would provide me with a rating and comments in the following areas:	Below Avg.	Avg.	Above Avg.	Comments
Attendance				
Attitude				
Work Ethic				
Safety Attitude				
Reliability				
Flexibility				
Quality of Work				
Personal Initiative				
Cooperation				
Quantity of Work				

I would also appreciate it if you could take the time to comment on the following areas:

What are my greatest strengths/attributes?

What are my weakest points? (Areas needing improvement)

Would you rehire? ☐ Yes ☐ No Why?

Additional Comments

Completed by _____ Date _____
Name and Title

This authorization shall remain in effect until notified in writing of cancellation and was granted and signed on _May 30, 19XX_ by: _Harriet McGuire_

Please sign and return this form in the enclosed stamped, self-addressed envelope. Thank you.

© 1995 Harris Espérance Incorporated   Form 18/95

Figure 6-6   FORM 18, Employment Verification, Page 2

VERIFY EDUCATION RECORDS

Personal experience taught me this one. When I called to verify my college records, my records weren't there. I had changed my name and when the college updated their records, they inadvertently misspelled my name. So if a potential employer had called, they would have found no record. What do you suppose that employer might have thought?

- Call the schools you attended and verify your records.

- If you want written verifications , use Form 19, Education Verification and Transcript Request.

Take the time to check your education records. Then you will know that all your impotant education records are in order.

STEP 2: WRITE A COVER LETTER

Keep your letter simple, short, and business related. However, if you know the person well, you may want to make it friendlier and more personal.

- Date the letter.
- List the items you are sending in a separate paragraph.
- If the person you are writing to will also serve as a personal reference, enclose the Personal Reference Request form and adjust the body of your letter to cover this request.
- Enclose a self-addressed, stamped envelope.
- Always thank the person for his or her help.
- Sign the letter.
- Be sure to include all enclosures. Put in same order as listed in your letter.

STEP 3: MAIL LETTER AND ENCLOSURES

Sometimes I've had students do all the work but never take the time to mail the letter and enclosures. It may be that they fear the response that might come back. But rest assured that this extra effort to verify your work history and to obtain written verification will be very valuable in the job hunt, especially as the years go by.

STEP 4: SEND A THANK-YOU LETTER AND ENCLOSE RESUME

When you receive the verification back, send a thank-you note and enclose your resume. Thank-you's are always appropriate and by sending your resume, references will be even more prepared to speak favorably about you.

Harriett McGuire

| 6672 Alabama Road | Wichita, KS 67217 | (316) 555-4279 |

September 1, 19XX

Mr. Joe Salinez
Operations Manager
Western Wood Manufacturing
P.O. Box 7984
Minneapolis, MN 55440

Dear Mr. Salinez:

I'll be looking for work when I complete school in June and would like to verify my employment records with you before I approach employers. Enclosed are the following documents:

- **Employment Verification Request:** I've put together the information to the best of my ability and hope that it's sufficiently accurate for you to support. If there are discrepancies or recommendations, please note them on the enclosed form.
- **Personal Reference Request:** Since you were my immediate supervisor, it would be helpful to know what you will say about me--the good and the bad. So, if you could take a few moments to respond to the enclosed form, it will be greatly appreciated. I encourage you to be open and honest, especially in areas where your comments may be unfavorable. Honest answers can help me learn to improve. Thanks.
- **Authorization to Release Information:** I've written and signed this form to release you from any potential harm. I believe that it's imperative that potential employers are provided with complete, accurate information. I do this freely and release you completely.
- **Resume Draft:** I've enclosed a copy of my resume and ask that you review it for accuracy. If you find any information that doesn't appear correct, please make notes and recommendations. It's important to have your support of the statements in my resume.

I've enclosed a self-addressed envelope for your response. Please call if you have any questions. I can be reached at the above number between 8 and 11 each weekday morning.

Joe, thanks for taking the time to complete these forms. Your comments are appreciated, and I look forward to hearing from you. I will keep you informed as to what's happening during my job search. Thanks again.

Sincerely,

Harriet McGuire

Harriett McGuire

Enclosures

Figure 6-7 Cover Letter

There's no better contact for finding a job than your personal references. Because they already think highly of you, they'll help you in your search. They know people. They can provide advice and possible job leads. They may even have a job for you. The last time I was job hunting, a personal reference offered me a job.

- Use your references wisely and effectively.

- Call them before you begin to look for a job.

- Let them know the type of job you're looking for and ask for help.

- Find out what each reference will say about you. Ask specifically about your strengths and weaknesses. Get a broad and honest picture.

- Ask permission to use the reference's name.

PERSONAL REFERENCE REQUEST

REQUESTED FROM:	REQUESTED FOR:

1. DESCRIBE MY STRENGTHS.

2. DESCRIBE AREAS OF WEAKNESS (AREAS NEEDING IMPROVEMENTS).

3. DESCRIBE HOW I MET DEADLINES.

4. DESCRIBE HOW I GOT ALONG WITH OTHERS (SUPERIORS, PEERS, SUBORDINATES, VENDORS, CUSTOMERS, ETC.).

5. DESCRIBE MY WORK ATTITUDE.

6. DESCRIBE OUR RELATIONSHIP.

7. HOW LONG HAVE YOU KNOWN ME?

8. IF YOU LEARNED SOMETHING SPECIAL FROM ME, PLEASE DESCRIBE WHAT IT WAS.

9. ARE THERE ANY REASONS YOU CAN THINK OF THAT MIGHT DISQUALIFY ME FOR THIS POSITION? IF YES, EXPLAIN.

10. WHO ELSE WOULD YOU RECOMMEND TO PROVIDE FURTHER INFORMATION ABOUT ME?

11. EXPLAIN WHY YOU BELIEVE I'M SEEKING A JOB CHANGE NOW.

12. OTHER COMMENTS

SIGNED: NAME AND TITLE   DATE:

© 1995 Harris Espérance Incorporated   Form 20/R95

Figure 6-8   FORM 20, Personal Reference Request

- Use Form 20, Personal Reference Request, to guide your conversation.

STEP 1: CREATE A CLUSTER OR A SCRIPT

Review Form 20, Personal Reference Request, for the type of questions to ask. Then create a cluster or a script for your conversation. Include personal comments, such as inquiring about children, spouse, or other special interests.

STEP 2: CALL THE REFERENCE

During the call, make notes on your cluster or script.

STEP 3: MAKE A RECORD

Use Form 20 to record responses in detail. Then file your cluster and Form 20 in the REFERENCES section of your notebook.

You may choose to make dividers for each reference.

STEP 4: MAIL A THANK-YOU LETTER AND ENCLOSE RESUME

References are not always available by phone, so sometimes you may need to write your reference. Enclose Form 20, Personal Reference Request, Form 21, Authorization to Release Information, and a stamped, self-addressed return envelope with your letter.

STEP 1: WRITE A LETTER

If your personal reference is a personal friend, your tone can be very friendly, like the example in Figure 6-9. Otherwise, keep your letter more businesslike.

STEP 2: PREPARE ENCLOSURES

Steven Henderson

222 Hill Road   Baton Rouge, LA 70821   (504) 555-9836

September 8, 19XX

Mrs. Rita Sanchez
875 New Castle Drive
Dudley, North Carolina 28333

Dear Rita:

How are you? What have you been doing since retiring? Becoming a stand-up comic or what? It's been a long time since we've seen each other or even talked. You've been missed. Chris is in his third year of college and looking forward to graduate school. He's maintained a 3.5+ GPA. Carole is now the Director of Young Life and loving it also.

As you can see, life is great for me, but I want to make a career change. I've decided to make a move into the sales field, which I have always loved. So I would like to ask you to be a personal reference for me. I'm sending a Personal Reference Request form to save you time. If you could just fill in the blanks and mail it back to me, I would greatly appreciate it.

I've enclosed a signed Authorization to Release Information form. This way you can really be honest and open with all potential employers. Seems like there's so much fear of lawsuits these days. I know that you're not worried about such an event happening between us, but I just wanted you to be as comfortable as possible.

Also enclosed is my resume. If you have any suggestions on how I can improve it, there's still time, and I would appreciate your input.

If you have any questions, call, write, or even come visit. I would enjoy seeing you again.

Best regards,

Steven

Steven

Enclosures: Personal Reference Request Form
              Authorization to Release Information Form
              Resume
              Self-addressed, stamped envelope

Figure 6-9   Cover Letter for Personal Reference Request

Generally, you will enclose the following items:

- Form 20, Personal Reference Request
- Form 21, Authorization to Release Information
- Stamped, self-addressed envelope
- Copy of latest resume

STEP 3: MAIL THE LETTER

You've done all the work, now send it. Don't get cold feet.

STEP 4: SEND A THANK-YOU LETTER

When you receive your request back, send a thank-you note. Common courtesy goes a long way in life and in a job hunt. Don't overlook this step. You will also be able to update your reference on the progress of your job search. Your references will appreciate knowing what's happening.

If you didn't mail a copy of your resume with the first letter, be sure to enclose one now.

A friend of mine was fired from her job recently. Her boss wanted to assist her with finding a new job, so he decided to write her a reference letter. I know he had good intentions, but the letter was so ambiguous, actually rather damaging, that it was useless to my friend. There was no way she could have presented it to a prospective employer. It created too many questions. You can prevent this from happening to you by drafting the reference letter yourself.

Draft your own reference letter? This may sound strange, but it's the only way you can guarantee that the letter will say what needs to be said.

All too often reference letters are meaningless and include unflattering statements. How do you draft your own reference letters? Follow these simple steps.

STEP 1: CREATE A CLUSTER OR A SCRIPT

Use the "questions employers want to ask," which are listed on pages 152 & 153, as a guide in creating your cluster or script. Michelle wrote the script in Figure 6-10.

STEP 2: CALL THE REFERENCE

Follow your cluster or script, keeping detailed notes. When Michelle called Pat, he suggested that she come in to see him. When she met with him, she gave Pat the script and he filled in the blanks.

STEP 3: MAKE A RECORD OF THE CALL

Your record will depend on how you completed the call. Use Form 22, Reference Record; Form 20, Personal Reference Request, and/or notes from your script or cluster. Just make sure you have a complete, detailed record.

REFERENCE SCRIPT FOR Pat, Skipper's Seafood owner

Hi Pat,

This summer I will be looking for a job dealing with my field of study, CADD operator. Do you have a few minutes to go over my work record here at Skipper's? Thank you. If you don't, when would be a good day and time to come talk to you? *Monday, May 10 at 4:50 pm.*

- I show that I was hired *May 7, 1988* in the position of *Cashier/Waitress*.
  Your position at that time was *Owner of Skipper's*. Is this correct? *yes.*
- I show that I started at *$3.35* per hour and that I received a raise to *$5.00?* per hour on *?*. Does this agree with your records? *yes.*

What would you say to a prospective employer to the following questions:
- How was Michelle's attendance and safety record?

  Excellent

- What would the company say for the reason I left Skipper's?

  For a better-paying job with more opportunity for advancement

- Would Skipper's hire Michelle back?

  Yes

- Please describe duties performed and significant accomplishments.

  Cashiering — cash control, suggestive selling at the order station. Performed as "Skipper the Parrot" at fund-raising events. Service permit.

- If you were asked to describe my strength's and weaknesses (improvements I need to work on), what would you say....?

  Strengths — quick learner, good personality with customers, takes the initiative.
  Weaknesses — not many. Maybe enjoys gossip more than she should. Michelle is critical of others' poor performance.

  - Thank you for letting me know, this is very helpful. I will be sure to improve on my weaknesses.

- How was I in meeting deadlines and establishing goals?

  Excellent

- How did I get along with others (superiors, peers, subordinates, customers, vendors, etc.)?

  Very well

Figure 6-10 Reference Script. Courtesy of a student

MICHELLE LARSON

21444 Bear Creek Road   Bend, OR 97701   (503) 555-1866

May 17, 19XX

Mr. Pat Chevez
Skipper's Seafood'N Chowder
1091 SE 3rd Street
Bend, OR 97702

Dear Pat:

Thank you for taking the time to fill out the questions on May 10 concerning my work record with you. I appreciate your comments, which were very informative and helpful. I have learned a great deal from them.

My job hunt has presented me with one more thing to ask your help on . . . a letter of reference.

Based on the way you answered the questions, I have taken the liberty of drafting a reference letter that you may change as you desire. I have enclosed a copy of the questions you answered to refresh your memory of what you wrote. Please provide the letter on your company's letterhead.

I greatly appreciate your assistance and have enclosed my current resume for your information. If you have any questions or comments on either the letter or resume, please let me know.

Enclosed for your convenience is a stamped, self-addressed envelope. Thank you.

Sincerely,

Michelle

Michelle

Enclosures

Figure 6-11 Cover Letter for Reference Request. Courtesy of a student

Make your own personal stationery by using the header format from your resume.

Date the letter.

Include a formal inside address.

Request a reference letter; ask that the final reference letter be written on company stationery.

Invite former associates to review and edit the draft.

Enclose your resume, and ask for recommendations.

Enclose a stamped, self-addressed envelope.

SAMPLE DRAFT REFERENCE LETTER
To Be Written on Company Stationery

Date

TO WHOM IT MAY CONCERN:

Ms. Michelle Larson was employed by Skipper's Seafood'N Chowder Restaurant from May 1988 to November 1990.

She was responsible for cashiering, which involved cash control and suggestive selling at the order station. She also performed as "Skipper the Parrot" at fund-raising events. She received her liquor license in 1988.

Michelle got along well with her coworkers and customers. She was a good, dependable worker, someone who helped improve our team by setting a good example.

If you have any questions, myself or Jon Flegel will gladly provide you with further details of Michelle's work performance. Please feel free to call either of us at 555-7851.

Sincerely,

Pat Chevez

Mr. Pat Chevez, Owner
Skipper's Seafood'N Chowder

Figure 6-12 Draft Reference Letter. Courtesy of a student

STEP 5: WRITE A DRAFT REFERENCE LETTER

Date the letter.

Keep your statements work related.

Include only the positive statements made during your conversation.

Cover these points:

- Type of relationship
- Length of relationship
- Dates of employment
- Job position(s)
- Strengths
- Achievements and results

STEP 6: MAIL THE LETTER WITH ITS ENCLOSURES

It may seem ridiculous to list this as a step, but often students do the work, then fail to follow through. Having quality reference letters is important in an effective job hunt. Sometimes a letter can take the place of an actual reference check.

STEP 7: SEND A THANK-YOU LETTER

After Michelle received her reference letter back from her boss, she wrote the thank-you letter illustrated in Figure 6-13.

Notice the comment about her resume and the fact that she revised it and sent a new copy to Pat.

SOME FINAL THOUGHTS

Keep letters short and businesslike—one page only.

Date and sign all letters.

If you used a script during your conversation, you may choose to enclose the scripted questions with the answers. Elicit the reference's assistance in supporting your responses.

Enclose a copy of your final resume. This provides references with the up-to-date information they need in order to respond intelligently during reference checks.

MICHELLE LARSON

21444 Bear Creek Road   Bend, OR 97701   (503) 555-1973

May 24, 19XX

Mr. Pat Chevez, Owner
Skipper's Seafood'N Chowder
1091 SE 3rd Street
Bend, OR 97702

Dear Pat:

Thank you for the reference letter and the valuable comments concerning my resume. Based on these comments, I made some changes and have enclosed the revised resume.

I appreciate your help. If you have any questions or further comments, please let me know. I'll keep you informed as to when a potential employer may call. Thank you again.

Sincerely,

Michelle Larson

Michelle Larson

Enclosure: Revised resume

Figure 6-13 Thank-You Letter to Reference. Courtesy of a student

MORE SAMPLES

A Cover Letter
This cover letter and reference draft were used by Karen to get a reference letter from a boss who had fired her. Karen used her reference phone record as the basis for her letter.

Consider these points when writing your cover letter:

- Keep the letter short and friendly.
- Thank the reference for talking with you.
- Request a reference letter.
- Recap the comments made during your call or visit.
- Mention the draft reference letter and the fact that the reference may change it in any manner whatsoever.
- Request that the reference letter be retyped on company stationery.
- Enclose your current resume and ask for comments.
- Again, be sure to thank the reference.
- Close on a positive note.

KAREN L. SIMPSON

829 SW Deschutes   Redmond, OR 97756   (503) 555-6397

September 12, 19xx

Mr. Gene Anderson, President
Ace Air Electronics
2303 Highway 126
Prineville, OR 97754

Dear Gene:

Thank you for taking the time to talk with me on September 2nd. I appreciated your comments, which were very informative and helpful. I have learned a great deal from them.

My job hunt has presented me with one more challenge--a need for reference letters. I would like to ask you for your help and consideration. Would you write a reference letter for me?

To recap our call, you stated that my work was satisfactory on all payroll tasks and monthly bank reports. Also, you said that I met goals and deadlines, adapted easily to the computer, and worked well with coworkers, employees, and clients.

Based on these comments, I have taken the liberty of drafting a reference letter for you. Please feel free to change this draft in any way you desire. Please provide the letter on your company's letterhead.

I greatly appreciate your assistance and have enclosed my current resume. If you have any questions, comments, or suggestions on the reference letter or resume, please let me know. The best time to call me at home is in the mornings before noon.

Gene, thanks again for your help. I wish you every success in your business, and I'm glad that we have come to this better understanding.

Best regards,

Karen L. Simpson
Karen L. Simpson

Enclosures: Draft reference letter
           Resume
           Self-addressed, stamped envelope

Figure 6-14   Request for Reference Letter

```
┌─────────────────────────────────────────────┐
│        Sample Draft Reference Letter          │
│        To be written on company stationery.   │
└─────────────────────────────────────────────┘

Date

TO WHOM IT MAY CONCERN:

Ms. Karen Simpson was employed by Ace Air Electronics from
December 1987 until May 1988.

She was responsible for our bimonthly computerized payroll and
manual monthly bank statements. She handled in excess of 100
employee payroll and personnel records with accuracy and
confidentiality. She verified payroll hours and pay rates to insure
accuracy.

Karen got along well with her coworkers, employees, and our clients.
She met all deadlines and company goals. Her work and attendance
were satisfactory.

If you have any questions, Ms. Sara Joseph will gladly provide you
with further details of Karen's performance. Please feel free to call
her at 555-5897.

Sincerely,
```

Figure 6-15   Draft Reference Letter

```
                    KAREN L. SIMPSON

829 SW Deschutes        Redmond, OR 97756        (503) 555-4863
────────────────────────────────────────────────────────────────

September 23, 19XX

Mr. Gene Anderson, President
Ace Air Electronics
2303 Highway 126
Prineville, OR 97754

Dear Gene:

Thanks for the reference letter and the valuable comments concerning
my resume. Based on your suggestions, I made some changes and
have enclosed the revised resume.

I truly appreciate your help. If you have any questions or further
comments, please let me know. I'm sure we'll both feel good when
I'm once again gainfully employed. Work has always been a satisfier
for me.

I'll keep you informed as to when a potential employer may call. I'll
be sure to direct employers to call Sara.

Best regards,

Karen L. Simpson
Karen L. Simpson

Enclosure:  Revised resume
```

Figure 6-16   Thank-You Letter to Reference

A Draft Reference Letter

Keep the letter factual. Follow closely the comments made by your reference. Use the reference's words. Use exact quotes whenever possible.

Cover these points:

- Type of relationship
- Length of relationship
- Dates of employment
- Work performance
- Strengths
- How you get along with others
- Specific achievements
- Attitude
- Related personal characteristics
- Reason for leaving if not controversial

The Thank-You Letter

After receiving the reference letter, send another letter thanking the reference.

Another Thank-You Example

Alice Bailey called Ms. Williams to find out what would be said about her and her work. Alice already had a satisfactory reference letter from Ms. Williams but wanted to inform her of potential reference check calls. She wanted Ms. Williams to be properly prepared for all reference checks. The first part of that preparation includes the phone call; the second part includes the thank-you letter, which encloses her latest resume.

ALICE BAILEY
Post Office Box 89
Madras, OR 97741
(503) 555-1742

April 21, 19XX

Ms. Jennifer Williams, Manager
Central Oregon Housing Administration
2445 Southwest Canal Boulevard
Redmond, OR 97756

Dear Ms. Williams:

Thank you for the advice yesterday. It was helpful to hear your views on my strengths and weaknesses. I was glad to learn that I need to smile more often--I'm already smiling more!

I appreciated your comments about my being "a person that doesn't intimidate, but inspires--an executive who relates to the experiences and frustrations of the people she serves."

I've enclosed a copy of my resume. It outlines my latest business experiences and major accomplishments. These experiences are relative to the administrative management position I'm seeking. If you have any suggestions concerning my resume, they would be appreciated.

Again, thanks for your willingness to be a reference. I look forward to talking with you soon. I'll keep in touch to let you know what's happening.

Best regards,

Alice Bailey
Alice Bailey

Enclosure: Resume

P.S. If you hear of anyone who may need someone of my qualifications, please let me know or pass on my resume. Thanks.

Figure 6-17 Thank-You Letter to Reference

Remember to do the following:

- Say thanks.
- Refer to specific comments that were meaningful and helpful to you.
- Mention your current job objective. This will remind your reference of your employment goal.
- Enclose your current resume.
- Tell the reference you will keep him or her informed.
- Write a postscript. These comments receive high readership. Save postscripts for important statements.

Access is the key to effective reference listing. Create a reference list to fit your situation and to meet the needs of the employer. Provide potential employers with the detailed information necessary to verify employment, education, and personal references. Make it easy for the employer to contact all parties.

STEP 1: CHOOSE REFERENCES CAREFULLY

Use Form 23, Draft Reference List, to help you cover all the necessary details

DRAFT REFERENCE LIST

For Employment Verification please call, write, or FAX

CONTACT PERSON/TITLE/DEPARTMENT
Ms. Sally M. Phillips, Director of Human Relations

COMPANY NAME/ADDRESS/PHONE/FAX
Greater Horizons, 8732 Sunrise Blvd. Potomac MD 20851
Phone 301-555-8865   FAX 301-555-7681

CONTACT PERSON/TITLE/DEPARTMENT
Mr. Robert Samson, General Manager/Owner

COMPANY NAME/ADDRESS/PHONE/FAX
Northwest Travel, 545 SE Burnside Portland, OR 97201 (503)555-9721 FAX (503) 555-1183
*Records are filed under Georgia Anderson

For Education Verification, please call, write or FAX

CONTACT PERSON/TITLE/DEPARTMENT
Mr. Ronald Benson, Director of Admissions & Records

SCHOOL NAME/ADDRESS/PHONE/FAX
Linfield College 900 South Baker McMinnville OR 97128 (503) 555-4121 FAX (503) 555-2215
*Records are filed under Georgia Anderson

For Personal References, please call write or FAX:

NAME/JOB TITLE	DAYTIME PHONE NUMBER	KNOW SINCE
Mr. Raymond James, Controller	(301) 555-8865	1991

MAILING ADDRESS (COMPANY OR HOME) CITY, ZIP
Greater Horizons 8732 Sunrise Blvd. Potomac, MD 20851   FAX(301) 555-7681

RELATIONSHIP/COMMENTS
Former Supervisor

NAME/JOB TITLE	DAYTIME PHONE NUMBER	KNOW SINCE
Mrs. Alice Paisley, Acct Supervisor	(503) 555-9712	1987

MAILING ADDRESS (COMPANY OR HOME) CITY, ZIP
Northwest Travel 545 SE Burnside Portland OR 97201   FAX (503) 555-1183

RELATIONSHIP/COMMENTS
Former Accounting Supervisor

NAME/JOB TITLE	DAYTIME PHONE NUMBER	KNOW SINCE
Mr. Randal Severance, Auditor	(301) 555-5234	1992

MAILING ADDRESS (COMPANY OR HOME) CITY, ZIP
Arthur Anderson & Company 658 Center Potomac, MD 20851   FAX (301) 555-6656

RELATIONSHIP/COMMENTS
Independent auditor who audited my department books and critiqued my work performance.

© 1995 Harris Espérance Incorporated   Form 23/95

Figure 6-18 FORM 23, Draft Reference List

Employment Verification
Include this information if it is not clearly stated on your resume.

If you worked under a different name, provide the name here.

Education Verification
Provide this information if you believe your education credentials will need to be verified.

If your records are under a different name, mention the name under which the file is maintained.

Personal References
List at least four references; six would be even better. This provides for greater variety.

If your references are employed, list their employer's name, address, and phone and FAX numbers. Otherwise, list their home address and phone number. Always provide daytime phone numbers, and identify the length and type of relationship.

STEP 2: TYPE OR WORD PROCESS REFERENCE LIST

Generally, references are not listed on your resume, but on a separate page. Therefore, list personal references separately. Consider the following points when formalizing your reference list:

■ Provide the list only when requested, after an employer shows genuine interest in hiring you.

■ Use your resume heading format for your reference page. A daytime phone number should be provided for each reference.

Think: Accessibility
■ Consider adding your Social Security number. This allows verification of individual files in case there's a duplication or confusion over a name.

■ Include employment, education, and personal sections if appropriate for your situation.

■ If you have had a name change, provide the name under which the records are maintained.

■ For employment verification include the name of the person to contact. Provide a courtesy and job title, full name, and department.

■ For personal references include the type and length of relationship. If the reference is retired, state that information and provide a home telephone number. For example, "Mr. James Runyon, Retired (Former Comptroller and Supervisor at AvCo)." You may include a short sentence describing your personal relationship; this personalizes your reference list and can add to the overall impact.

■ Provide a variety of references. Choose them from various aspects of your life: work, professional organizations, volunteer community activities. Include past and current employers or supervisors, customers, clients, business associates, community leaders.

Georgia Simmons
Social Security Number 999-34-6309

Post Office Box 893   Potomac, MD 20854   301-555-6247

For **Employment Verification**, please call, write, or FAX:

▸ Ms. Sally M. Phillips, Director of Human Relations   Phone 301-555-8865
   Greater Horizons, 8732 Sunrise Blvd., Potomac, MD 20851   FAX 301-555-7681

▸ Mr. Robert Samson, General Manager/Owner   Phone 503-555-9721
   Northwest Travel, 545 SE Burnside, Portland, OR 97201   FAX 503-555-1183
   *Records are filed under Georgia Anderson.

For **Education Verification** please call, write, or FAX:

▸ Mr. Ronald Benson, Director of Admissions and Records   Phone 503-555-4121
   Linfield College, 900 South Baker, McMinnville, OR 97128   FAX 503-555-2215
   *Records are filed under the name of Georgia Anderson.

For **Personal References** please call, write, or FAX:

▸ Mr. Raymond James, Controller   Phone 301-555-8865
   Greater Horizons, 8732 Sunrise Blvd., Potomac, MD 20851   FAX 301-555-7681
   Relationship: Former Supervisor   Known since 1991

▸ Mrs. Alice Paisley, Accounting Supervisor   Phone 503-555-9721
   Northwest Travel, 545 SE Burnside, Portland, OR 97201   FAX 503-555-1183
   Relationship: Former Supervisor   Known since 1987

▸ Mr. Randal Severance, Auditor   Phone 301-555-5234
   Arthur Anderson & Company, 658 Main, Potomac, MD 20851   FAX 301-555-6656
   Relationship: Independent auditor at Greater Horizons   Known since 1992
   Mr. Severance audited my department's books and critiqued my work.

▸ Ms. Jennifer Eisler, Junior Accountant   Phone 503-555-9721
   Northwest Travel, 545 SE Burnside, Portland, OR 97201   FAX 503-555-1183
   Relationship: Subordinate   Known since 1987

Figure 6-19   Reference List

ANOTHER EXAMPLE

Think: Accessibility. Employers need quick access to all your references.

Linda included this reference list with her resume. It was actually page 4. Why four pages? Well, the first two pages were her resume, and the third page was an extensive list of her employment history. This was what was appropriate for her situation and the audience she was addressing. You, too, may find that you will need to bend or break the general rules if it makes sense to do so.

Read Linda's reference list and notice the:

- Variety of references. Linda's experience is varied. Each can provide a different picture of Linda.

- Courtesy titles are given.

- A personal note is provided on each reference to give the employer an understanding of the relationship.

- Bullets are used, which continues the pattern established on the resume. Parallel construction creates a unified appearance.

Linda Kuulei

Page 4

References

▸ Dr. Christopher Tennent, National Rare Plant Program   (202) 555-0850
  Wildlife, Fisheries and Rare Plant Staff, Washington Office
  USDA FS, POB 96090, Washington, DC 20090-6090

  I've known Dr. Tennent since 1990 and have served in his position as acting
  Program Director in 1991, 1992, and 1994.

▸ Mr. James Krueger, Oregon Natural Heritage Program Director   (503) 555-5078
  The Nature Conservancy, 1205 NW 25th Street, Portland, OR 97210

  I have worked with Mr. Krueger since 1990 on partnerships for conducting rare
  plant inventory and monitoring.

▸ Mr. Dave Hubble, Director of Natural Resources   (503) 555-9658
  A.G. Crook Company, 1800 NW 169th Place, Beaverton, OR 97006

  Mr. Hubble was my immediate supervisor at the Forest Service from 1991
  through 1993.

▸ Ms. Cheryl McCarthy, Bureau of Land Management   (503) 555-7050
  Oregon State Office, Post Office Box 2965, Portland, OR 97208

  I worked with Ms. McCarthy on joint BLM/USFS projects for the rare plant
  protection, inventory, and monitoring programs. We also taught together.

▸ Dr. Stuart Gannon, East-Side Conservation Committee Chair   (503) 555-6981
  6398 High Banks Road, Bend, OR 97710

  I worked with Dr. Gannon as a forest service botanist and as the NPSO
  President on partnership projects for the USFS/NPSO.

▸ Mr. David A. Nixon, Bring Back the Natives Coordinator   (503) 555-FISH
  Trout Unlimited, 6322 NW Atkinson Avenue, Redmond, OR 97756

  I've been working with Mr. Nixon on the Crooked River Watershed Cooperative
  Education Project since 1991.

Figure 6-20   Reference List. Courtesy of a client

AN EXCEPTION TO THE RULE

Generally, references are listed on a separate page and are not part of your resume. But, as you saw in the preceding example, there are times when this rule needs to be broken. Coral found this when she applied for a job where the hiring decision would be made quickly from the submitted resumes. She knew it was important for the employer to have her references. Since there was ample space on her resume, she included references on her resume. Following is a copy of her resume.

Coral Lundquist

86329 Crest View Drive   Prineville, OR 97754   (503) 555-4762

CAREER OBJECTIVE

Seeking summer employme
skills are essential and use

PUBLIC RELATIONS AND

Interact with public on a d
services. Generated public
computerized flyers for pro
Central Oregon Community

Processed routine correspon
reports, and other documen
possible. Created and proce

Balanced and reconciled ban
and cash receipts. Monitore
placing orders as needed. Pr

Prepared calendars for meet
and collected tuition and fe
organize and develop term s
programs.

EMPLOYMENT HISTORY

1989 to present	**Secretary** . C Prineville Ce Warm Spring
1987-1989	**Custodian.** Supervisor:
1981-1986	**Secretary a** Supervisors:
1975-1977 1970-1974 1967-1970	**Professional Return Depa Part-time wor** Secretary, Sa Grocery and

Coral Lundquist

Page 2

EDUCATION

1993   Certificate of Completion for More for Less: Time Management workshop
        Certificate of Completion for Self-Esteem and Peak Performance workshop

1992   Certificate of Completion for Office Skills Update workshop

1969   Graduated Baker High School, Baker City, OR
        Educational Focus: Secretarial skills for education and business related fields

PERSONAL REFERENCES

Ms. Jane DeJarnett	Program Analysis Officer Ochoco National Forest Service, Prineville, OR	503-555-9596
Ms. Susan O'Dell	Prineville Community Education Director Central Oregon Community College, Prineville OR	503-555-4418
Mr. Gene Lupinacci	Warm Springs Community Education Director Central Oregon Community College, Warm Springs, OR	503-555-2136
Mr. Anthony Riley	Principal Madras Elementary School, Madras, OR	503-555-3520
Mrs. Alice Pena	ABE/GED Instructor, Prineville Center Central Oregon Community College, Prineville, OR	503-555-4028
Mr. Pat Ambers	COIC/COCC Instructor Central Oregon Intergovernmental Council, Prineville, OR	503-555-4418

PERSONAL

Take pride in being trustworthy, dependable, efficient, flexible, and creative.
Entrusted with confidential information. Excellent organizational skills.
Ability to learn and adapt to new situations quickly.
Available from June 14 through August 10, 1993.

Figure 6-21   Resume with References. Courtesy of a client

Here's the advertisement that Coral answered.

---

61 - HELP WANTED
CHAMBER OF COMMERCE MANAGER needed immediately.
Temporary, full-time position (2 to 3 months). Oversee chamber
activities and volunteer staff. Public relations and communication skills
essential. Salary commensurate with skill level. Mail letter and resume
by May 25 to: Selection Committee, P.O. Box 580, Prineville, OR 97754

- What do you think of her resume?

- Did she include items of importance for the selection committee?

- Did she provide all necessary information?

Coral got the job and received many compliments on her thorough resume.

FINAL THOUGHTS

Choose each reference carefully. References are valuable allies. But don't abuse them; their time is precious. Providing references to prospective employers before there's a genuine interest in hiring you creates undue work for references. Provide references only when asked.

- Notify references when a reference check seems likely.

- Tell them the job title and its requirements.

- Highlight the key points of your interview.

- Tell them about the company and the interviewer.

- Ask them for advice on how to improve your interviewing skills.

- Ask for suggestions on follow-up techniques.

- Keep in touch, but don't become a nuisance. Use good judgment.

Manage the flow of information from your references to potential employers. This will make references work for you, rather than for the employer.

MASTER JOB APPLICATIONS
The Employer Screening Process

. . . the competition you need to be most concerned about comes from within.
—Dorothy Leeds, *Marketing Yourself*

Having read thousands of job applications, I am always amazed by the lack of awareness many job applicants display. One particular applicant, Steve, comes to mind. Steve had applied for a job he really didn't want. Everything on the application spoke of "noninterest." In answer to why he left the last three employers, Steve wrote **FIRED** in huge capital letters. What would your reaction be to such a message?

I had the opportunity many months later to counsel Steve. When I asked him about that particular job application and why he had bothered to apply, he said, "What made you think I really didn't want that job?" I explained that the application made a very negative impression because of his answers and manner of writing. I went on to explain that applications are specifically designed to help the employer screen out applicants and often applicants help in this process.

Job applications are designed to make applicants look their worst. The questions are selected and phrased to elicit information uniformly. In this chapter you will learn the intricacies of the job application process and how to make it work for you and the employer.

USING THE JOB APPLICATION SECTION OF THE *COMPANION PLANNER*

Having copies of completed job applications makes the task of completing another employer's application form easier, even if it is in a different format. The form and documents listed below should be maintained in this section.

- Form 24: Job Application
  Complete form 24, Job Application, and file it here. This form contains most of the information you'll need to complete other job applications.

  Carry a copy of the completed form with you when applying for work. Even when the employer's form is different, you will have most of the information requested on a different application.

- Job Applications during a Job Hunt
  During the job hunt, make copies of all job applications, if possible. File these applications in the *MARKET* section of your notebook behind the Employer Record divider. When the job hunt is over, you can file the copies in this section.

- Other Applications
  File any job applications that you have here. Having a variety of formats conditions you for the various applications you will complete.

If possible, photocopy all job applications you complete during the job hunt. File each application under the Employer Record section of your notebook. When the job hunt is over, file the applications in this section. These examples will be helpful for the next job hunt. Don't throw them away; having a variety of application formats prepares you for the various applications you will encounter during a job search.

APPLICATION TIPS

Be prepared before arriving at an employer's office. Pack a briefcase with your data file, a dictionary, two pencils with erasers, two erasable black ink pens, extra resumes, scratch paper, and reference letters. Be prepared to be interviewed on the spot. Follow these tips in completing job applications.

1. **Study the application thoroughly.** Read and follow the directions on the application. If you choose to disregard the directions, do so for a good reason. For example, you may list volunteer work in the space for employment because it explains what you were doing between jobs.
2. **Complete a trial run,** if possible. Plan your answers on an extra application form or sheet of paper before completing the final application. Use your data file and a dictionary. Use the action word format when writing experience: Action word + object + comments and results. Check your data file for examples.
3. **Use an erasable black ink pen.** Visit your local stationery store and find a high-quality pen with erasable ink. Make sure the ink doesn't smudge. The erasable ink allows you to correct mistakes

with ease. Carry a minimum of two pens just in case one stops writing.

4. **Tell the truth.** Don't undersell; don't oversell. Avoid exaggerations and misrepresentations; they can come back to haunt you at inopportune times. Lying on a job application is grounds for termination, even after many years of employment.

5. **Spell and use words correctly.** Check your grammar and punctuation. Carry a dictionary with you.

6. **Avoid abbreviations.** They are shortcuts that can be easily misinterpreted. You may know what an abbreviation means, but the reader may not know the correct meaning. For example, NRA may stand for the National Rifle Association or the National Ranchers Association. Abbreviations cause readers extra work, something they don't need.

7. **Answer all questions completely.** Fill in every blank. When you leave a question unanswered, the employer does not know why. You may have intentionally left the question blank or you may have accidentally missed the question. Whatever the employer's conclusion, it won't help you. It only tells him or her that you are either careless or have something to hide. Silence, the unanswered question, often shouts for attention. Fill in the blank in the most positive manner possible. If necessary, write "N/A" (not applicable) or place a dash in the space.

8. **Use all the space** to plug your abilities. Include only appropriate data that portrays an active, effective employee. Include memberships in professional and community organizations. Even hobbies and special interests can be listed. Listing activities besides work history provides the employer with a broader view of you as a person. But do not list too many activities; the employer wants to be assured that you have time to work.

9. **Never write "See resume" on the application.** You're being lazy and creating extra work and frustration for the employer. The words "See resume" on an application are not appreciated and viewed with disdain.

10. When asked for "position desired," **choose an appropriate job title** for your experience and educational level; for example, entry-level accounting, upper management, data entry.

11. **Write "Open," "Negotiable," or "Prevailing wage"** when asked for "salary wanted."

12. **Eliminate religious references** unless they are relevant to the employer or job. Use generic terms.

13. **Review Form 14, Personal Checklist,** to see if there is anything else you want to say on the job application. Messages such as "Excellent attendance record," or "Always meets or beats deadlines" are valuable. Do not forget them.

14. **Sign and date** the application.

15. Always **attach your resume.**

Completing job applications is one of the most important jobs you have during the job hunt. It's important because your next job depends on it! Applications are designed to aid employers in their hiring decision. The format is devised to quickly obtain information in a uniform manner, making it easy to compare applicants.

Neatness counts; it shows you care.

Study each job application carefully before beginning to write. Use an erasable black ink pen. Pencil or blue ink reproduces poorly.

Form 24, Job Application, in your notebook was designed to stimulate your thought as to the answers you would supply on job applications. The application covers many of the situations you will encounter when completing applications during your job search. Review the following steps, and learn ways to improve your job application.

STEP I: COMPLETE THE GENERAL INFORMATION ON PAGE I

JOB APPLICATION

NOTICE TO JOB APPLICANT

Please read the following information carefully. Follow all instructions. Read the policies on Hiring, Physical Information, and Criminal Convictions before completing application. Complete application in your own handwriting using a black ink pen. Complete all sections and questions IF they are relevant to the position you are seeking. Enclose a resume, if available.

NAME	Roger A. McEntire	
ADDRESS	8041 South 38th Street	

CITY	STATE	ZIP
Springfield	OR	97478

HOME TELEPHONE	OFFICE TELEPHONE	MESSAGE TELEPHONE
(503) 555-7474	N/A	N/A

POSITION(S) APPLYING FOR (EXAMPLE: CLERICAL, COMMON LABOR, MILLWRIGHT)
Millwork, Warehousing, or Delivery Driver

ARE YOU BONDABLE? YES _x_ NO___
HAVE YOU EVER BEEN CONVICTED OF ANY FELONY VIOLATION?
YES_ NO_x_

SALARY EXPECTED:
Prevailing Wage

I DESIRE FULL-TIME WORK ___   I DESIRE PART-TIME WORK _x_
I AM WILLING TO WORK: WEEKENDS YES_x_ NO__   HOLIDAYS YES _x_ NO__
I AM WILLING TO WORK: DAYS_x_ SWING_x_ GRAVEYARD_x_ ROTATION _x_

I CAN BEGIN WORK ON:
Current employer notification of two weeks requested

HIRING POLICY
It is our policy to hire the most qualified person for the job and to hire and promote without regard to race, color, sex, national origin, religion, age (18-70), or mental or physical handicap unrelated to job performance.

PHYSICAL INFORMATION
Some of our jobs have specific physical requirements or limitations. If you are applying for such a position, our personnel staff will ask you about limitations or disabilities that would be dangerous to you or your coworkers if you were to fill this particular position. Such questions must be related to your potential performance on the job for which you are applying.

CRIMINAL CONVICTIONS
Some jobs may not be held by persons convicted of certain crimes. If you are applying for such a position, you will be asked if you have been convicted of a crime that would disqualify you for that particular job. The existence of a criminal record, per se, is not an automatic bar to employment. You may not be asked if you have ever been arrested or held for a crime for which you were not convicted.

© 1995 Harris Espérance Incorporated   Form 24/95

Figure 7-1   FORM 24, Job Application, Page I. Courtesy of a client

Name and Address
Write your name and address carefully. Make sure it's legible. Spell out your name; avoid using initials.

Telephone Numbers
Provide a daytime phone number that will be answered. Answering machines are acceptable. Be sure the phone number is legible.

Position(s)
Choose a job title compatible with your skills, experience level, and education. Then support your desire with appropriate experiences.

Bondable?
This question is usually asked when money is involved. If you have no problems in this area, you can safely say yes. If you're not sure, you can still say yes. It's when you know that you are not bondable that you need to say no. Then reconsider the types of jobs you are applying for, and apply only for those that do not require a bond.

Salary Expected
Avoid writing a specific figure here. Write "Open," "Prevailing wage," or "Negotiable." If forced to state a wage, use a range, such as $8 to $10, $28,000 to $32,000, or mid-forties.

Working Hours

Build flexibility into your answers relating to work hours. Don't eliminate yourself from the hiring process because you don't want to work the graveyard shift. Working hours are often negotiable. Get the interview first, then negotiate.

Starting Date

If you are currently employed, it is usually wise to write something like "Employer notification of two weeks requested" in this spot. This is considered common courtesy, and employers will appreciate your thoughtfulness. If you're unemployed, writing "Immediately," or "At completion of school term" with the date is appropriate.

Criminal Record

Study the small print on applications concerning this area. Some jobs require this information; read the job requirements. Depending on your record, there may be certain jobs you should not apply for. For example, if you were convicted of embezzlement, you will not be considered for jobs involving money. Or if you have a drunk-driving conviction, applying for a school bus driver position will be a waste of your time. Find jobs that are not connected with the area of your conviction. Employers do hire applicants with criminal records. Being open and honest is the best policy. One alternative is to write "N/A" if you cannot check "No."

STEP 2: COMPLETE THE EMPLOYMENT SUMMARY ON PAGE 2

You probably won't find another application like this one, but this summary should supply you with all the basic information needed when completing most job applications. Complete it in detail. Use your data file information to fill it out accurately. If you do not have the information, locate it now.

Always read and follow the directions. Not following the directions is one thing that can screen out an applicant. It raises the question, If he/she cannot follow these simple directions, what will he or she do on the job? You can imagine how this scenario might affect the employer's decision.

However, problems can arise in following the directions. Your answers may not fit the application's format. When this happens, you will need to use sound judgment in how you respond to the questions. Remember, job applications are generic and designed for the majority of situations. If you find that your information doesn't fit the form, then use your best judgment to handle the situation.

In the example (Figure 7-2), the applicant added an explanation for an unusual situation concerning his hire and termination dates. As you can see, work history is not always easy to record on an employer's application form. Know the details of your work history, and be prepared to make sound judgment calls when completing applications.

My recommendation for this applicant would be to trim down the information. List Morgan's official employment dates and the temporary jobs; then drop the last two employers. This satisfies the employer's requests: a minimum of fifteen years and all employment during those years. There is no need to explain the additional employers. If questions on work history arise, they can be handled during the interview. Now let's look a little closer at the challenges this form presents.

Dates/Years of Employment

Complete the dates in the format requested. If you have done a thorough job with your data file, this will not be a problem. But you will notice in the example that Roger provided not only the month and year but also the actual day. This is a judgment call. Generally, providing the day will not create a major problem for the employer.

The application requests a listing of all employers for a minimum of fifteen years. If you're young and don't have fifteen years of work experience, just list what you have. If you are older, you have two options: (1) include only the last fifteen years, or (2) include as many years as you wish as long as you cover the "minimum" of fifteen years. Leaving out experiences of over fifteen years may result in an impression of your being younger than you are. This may work to your advantage, but it also could eliminate some of your valuable expertise. This is where judgment plays a part. Check the rest of the application to see if you have revealed your true age elsewhere.

Gaps in Employment

Note the reasons for any gaps in employment. Employers want to know what you have been doing. Everyone who has been unemployed was busy doing something. If you were self-employed or in school, put that down. If you volunteered at the hospital, list that. If you worked part-time, list these jobs. See Exercise 7-2 for further information.

Job Titles

If you know your official job title, use it. Otherwise, use a generic title. For example, Roger could have used mill worker for his job title. Sometimes the official title doesn't do justice to the job you performed, and you may want to consider changing it. For example, you could change Senior Accountant to Accounting Supervisor. Be sure your employer will support the change.

Wages

It's important to have complete and accurate wage information. That's why you want to keep good records of your employment history. Question marks and empty spaces do not convey a positive message. Many applicants leave blank spots in the wage question, but you do not have to be one of them. Begin today to keep good employment records; then you will always be able to fill in this information accurately.

EMPLOYMENT SUMMARY (Cover a minimum of 15 years.) Please answer all questions completely.
Begin with your current or most recent employer and list all employers for a minimum of 15 years. Include all paid employment: outside employers, military service, and self-employment. Full-time volunteer work may be included. Do not omit any employers. Ask for a supplemental page, if needed, to complete 15 years of experience.

No.	Dates Month and Year	Employer City, State	Job Titles Beginning and Ending	Wages Beginning and Ending
Sample	07/89-11/90	St. Charles Hospital Bend, OR 97701	B-Accounts Rec. Clerk E-Payroll Clerk	B-$1,500/mo. E-$1,700/mo.
1	02/18/70- 05/27/94*	Morgan Manufacturing Springfield, OR 97477	B-Rail/Style Grader E-Rail Repair Person	B-$3.89/hour E-$9.35/hour
2	01/92-03/92	Staff Management Eugene, OR 97401	B-Mill Laborer E-Mill Laborer	B-$6.00/hour E-$6.50/hour
3	10/91-01/92	Able Temporary Eugene, OR 97201	B-Sticker Layer E-Sticker Layer	B-$6.00/hour E-$6.50/hour
4	06/91-10/91	Babyland Diaper Portland, OR 97701	B-Delivery Driver E-Delivery Driver	B-$0.29/drop E-$0.35/drop
5	5/67-7/88*	Morgan Door/Nicolai Springfield, OR 97477	B-Rail/Style Grader E-Door Inspector	B-$2.95/hour E-$10.35/hour
6	66-67	Agripac Inc. Eugene, OR 97401	B-Labeler E-Warehouse	B-$2.35/hour E-$2.55/hour
7	65-66	Mark's Big M Springfield, OR 97477	B-Boxer E-Shelf Stocker	Minimum wage
8				
9	* Please note that employment with Morgan actually began May 1967 and was basically continuous until the plant was closed. The company's dates were adjusted to reflect a 60-plant closure notification and a union dispute. If you have any questions, please call Ms. Donna Zabrinski at 800-555-6823 for employment verification.			
10				
11				
12				
13				
14				
15				

© 1995 Harris Espérance Incorporated   Form 24/95

Figure 7-2   FORM 24, Job Application, Page 2. Courtesy of a client

STEP 3: COMPLETE THE EDUCATION AND JOB TRAINING ON PAGE 3

High School

Complete all information requested. If room is available and it's to your advantage, you may choose to include the following:

- Year graduated
- Telephone number
- GPA if above 3.0
- Class rank
- Relevant courses
- Scholarships
- Honors and awards
- Extracurricular activities (including employment after school, sports, school clubs, and volunteer activities)

College

Generally, you will provide the following information:

- School name
- City and state
- Type of degree
- Major and minor

If space is available, you may choose to include the following:

- Year graduated
- Telephone and FAX numbers
- GPA if above 3.0
- Relevant courses
- Scholarships
- Honors and awards
- Extracurricular activities (including employment after school, sports, school clubs, and volunteer activities)

Other Schooling

Include all other formal schooling: business, trade, vocational, and military, as well as in-house training.

Other Training

Do not forget valuable skills; these could include computer expertise (hardware and software), first aid and CPR,

EDUCATION AND JOB TRAINING

HIGH SCHOOL Springfield High School		TELEPHONE 503-555-6881
CITY, STATE, ZIP Springfield, OR 97754	SCHOLARSHIPS/AWARDS None	GRADUATED Yes
Course of Study General Studies		
EXTRACURRICULAR ACTIVITIES Part-time jobs after school	% OF SCHOOL EXPENSES EARNED 50%	GRADE POINT AVG. 3.1
COLLEGE Lane Community College		TELEPHONE 503-555-4501
CITY, STATE, ZIP Eugene, OR 97403	SCHOLARSHIPS/AWARDS None	GRADUATED No
DEGREE: MAJOR, MINOR, SPECIALIZATION Classes in computers, accounting, and business relations		
EXTRACURRICULAR ACTIVITIES Worked full-time	% OF SCHOOL EXPENSES EARNED 100%	GRADE POINT AVG. 3.17

OTHER SCHOOLING: TRADE, BUSINESS, VOCATIONAL, CORRESPONDENCE, MILITARY

Community education classes in photography, skiing, and weight lifting

OTHER TRAINING, LICENSES, CERTIFICATES, ON-THE-JOB, SPECIAL SKILLS (NOT MENTIONED ELSEWHERE)

CPR Yes   FIRST AID Yes   DRIVER'S/CHAUFFEUR'S LICENSE # 76890246   STATE OR

© 1995 Harris Espérance Incorporated   Form 24/95

Figure 7-3   FORM 24, Job Application, Page 3. Courtesy of a client

Never write "See resume" on a job application.

writing, public speaking, photography, drafting, or drawing. Skills and hobbies are of interest to an employer. Do not underestimate the value of your personal skills. One applicant told me that he once got a job because he listed being a certified scuba diver. Although that skill had nothing to do with the job qualifications, the department supervisor was also a scuba diver.

STEP 4: FILL IN THE EMPLOYER DETAIL ON PAGES 4 AND 5

Spell and use words correctly. Avoid abbreviations. Answer all questions completely. Fill in all the blanks. Tell the truth—do not exaggerate or undervalue your abilities. Follow the employer's format.

Military service and self-employment may be placed in this section. Under some instances, you may want to list schooling, volunteer work, domestic duties, or imprisonment. For more details involving difficult questions, see Exercise 7-2.

EMPLOYER DETAIL

Select the 4 most recent or relevant employers and complete the following. Please answer all questions.

No. 1 Employer - Most Recent or Relevant   **TELEPHONE**
Morgan Manufacturing (formerly Nicolai Door and Clear Fir Sales)
ADDRESS   995 South A Street, Springfield, OR 97477 (Plant Closed)   503-555-1971

HIRE DATE 05/26/67   **WAGE** $2.95   **PER** hr.   **SUPERVISOR** Mr. Jim Ivey

JOB TITLE Rail and Style Grader   **DEPARTMENT** Cutting

TERMINATION DATE 05/27/94 **WAGE** $9.35 **PER** hr. **SUPERVISOR** Mr. Al O'Hara

JOB TITLE Rail Repair Person   **DEPARTMENT** Machine and Assembly

DUTIES
- Rail Repair (92-94). Door Inspector (86-88 and 80-82). Patio Door Assembler (82-86).
- Door Rail and Style Grader (67-80). Glazed doors.
- Operated forklifts, rabbs, ripsaws, shrink-wrap, and strapping machines.
- Shipped orders and received parts. Tallied inventory.
- Operated air tools, electric saws, and sanders.

INDICATE YOUR SUPERVISORY RESPONSIBILITY BY COMPLETING THE APPROPRIATE AREAS: Not Applicable
NUMBER OF EMPLOYEES SUPERVISED ___ **HIRED OR RECOMMENDED HIRING** ___ **OTHER** _____
ASSIGNED AND REVIEWED WORK ___ **RATED WORK PERFORMANCE** ___ **HANDLED DISCIPLINARY PROBLEMS** ___

REASON FOR LEAVING Plant closure

MAY WE CONTACT THIS EMPLOYER?   Ms. Kathi Hernandez, Corporate Personnel Director
NO ___ **YES** x **WHO AND HOW?**   1-800-555-1463 ext. 488 Morgan Manufacturing, Oshkosh, WI

No. 4 Employer - Next Most Recent or Relevant   **TELEPHONE**
Babyland Diaper Service
ADDRESS   5224 NE 42nd Street, Portland, OR 97701   503-555-2229

HIRE DATE 06/01/91   **WAGE** $0.29   **PER** drop   **SUPERVISOR** Mr. John Simon
JOB TITLE Delivery Truck Driver   **DEPARTMENT** Deliveries

TERMINATION DATE 10/21/91 **WAGE** $0.35 **PER** drop **SUPERVISOR** Mr. John Simon
JOB TITLE Delivery Truck Driver   **DEPARTMENT** Deliveries

DUTIES
- Loaded truck according to route requirements. Delivered and picked up diapers.
- Collected monthly payments and solicited new customers. Received many compliments from customers.

INDICATE YOUR RESPONSIBILITY BY COMPLETING THE APPROPRIATE AREAS: Not Applicable
NUMBER OF EMPLOYEES SUPERVISED ___ **HIRED OR RECOMMENDED HIRING** ___ **OTHER** _____
ASSIGNED AND REVIEWED WORK ___ **RATED WORK PERFORMANCE** ___ **HANDLED DISCIPLINARY PROBLEMS** ___

REASON FOR LEAVING Accepted work closer to home

MAY WE CONTACT THIS EMPLOYER?   Ms. Joni O'Flannery, Office Manager, or Mr. Sam Olson, Owner
NO ___ **YES** x **WHO AND HOW?**   503-555-2229   FAX 503-555-9985

© 1995 Harris Espérance Incorporated   Form 24/95

Figure 7-4 FORM 24, Job Application, Page 4. Courtesy of a client

---

No. (Number)
This refers to the number listed in the Employment Summary section, page 2 of the Job Application Form.

Telephone Numbers
Provide daytime phone numbers. Provide 800 numbers if available.

Names and Titles
Use job and courtesy titles with all names.

Dates
Use only years (for example, 89-91) for employment history, if application permits and if it serves your purpose.

Duties
Divide, support, and rank. Use action statements.

Supervisory Duties
Mark the appropriate boxes.

Reason for Leaving
Make sure it's positive. For suggestions, review Exercise 7-2.

Employer Contact
Mark "Yes" when asked if a former employer may be contacted. If you are currently working, it is permissible to mark "No" for this question. If the employer is no longer in business, supply a way for verifying your information

(for example, provide a name and home phone number of your former supervisor).

STEP 5: FINISH WITH REFERENCES AND OTHER COMMENTS ON PAGE 6

Provide complete and accurate information.

References
Spell all names correctly. Provide a job and courtesy title with every name.

Other Skills/Comments
Do not forget volunteer work or memberships in professional or community organizations.

Use all the space available to sell yourself. Review Form 14, Personal Checklist, for relevant comments to include here. Messages such as "Willing to work varied shifts and hours," or "Always meets or beats deadlines" are valuable. Do not forget your personal messages. These messages set you apart from the rest of the applicants.

Don't be afraid to state what you are looking for, for example, "Seeking a career opportunity in the Southeast."

Certification
Read the employer disclosures before signing. Sign and date the application; then hand the application to the employer with a smile.

If you mail the application to the employer, prepare your envelope with the same care and preparation that you used for the job application. Address the envelope to a specific person whenever possible. Use the correct courtesy and job titles. Avoid writing "To Whom It May Concern"; instead write "Dear Employer," "Dear Reviewer," or "Gentle Reader."

As you can see, judgment is a critical factor in completing a job application. Even the simple listing of your employment history may not be as easy as you would like to believe. Have the facts, consider the alternatives, and follow the directions as closely as possible. But by all means, tell the truth. Do not misrepresent or omit information that the employer requests. Omissions and/or lying can be cause for termination if discovered after hiring.

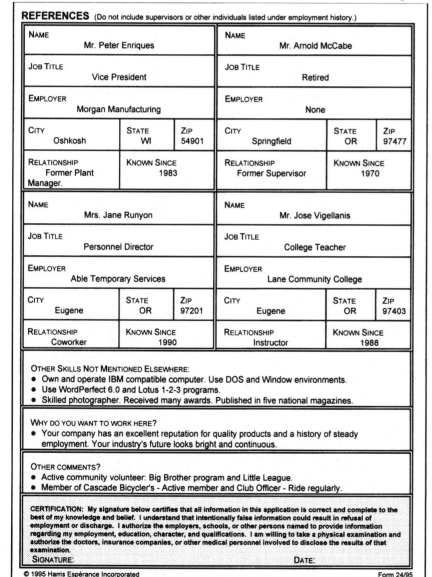

Figure 7-5 FORM 24, Job Application, Page 6. Courtesy of a client

Forewarned is forearmed.
—Miguel de Cervantes

There will probably be some sticky questions for you to handle during your job hunt and while completing job applications. Few applicants have unflawed records—there really are few, if any, "perfect" applicants and employees out there. Similarly, there are few "perfect" employers. Recognizing that you are not the only one who has to handle difficult situations may help. Employers do hire "imperfect" people with so-called flawed backgrounds. The secret is to turn adverse situations into positive life experiences.

Many difficult questions have been eliminated from employer applications due to regulations under the Civil Rights Act (1964–1991) and the Americans with Disabilities Act (ADA). Under these acts, it is illegal to discriminate against any employee because of sex, age, race, national origin, ethnic group, religion, color, family status, or physical or mental conditions. But not all employers abide by the law. This often happens out of ignorance to the law.

The problem for you is in deciding how to respond in a manner that will allow you to be considered for hiring, not whether or not the question is legal. Your goal in completing a job application is to get a job interview and/or a job offer. We will review a few of the areas that cause difficulties for many applicants, and explore ways to respond in a positive manner.

GAPS IN EMPLOYMENT

If gaps in employment shout at the employer, you may have a problem. Look for ways to explain these gaps in positive terms. If you went to school, stayed home to raise a family, volunteered at the library, spent a year traveling the world, whatever the case, mention it in a positive way. Fill in the gaps.

Other not-so-positive reasons can cause problems. One such experience may be a gap in employment due to a criminal conviction. If this is the case, read the section "Reason for Leaving" or "Criminal Record."

Many unemployed applicants can list self-employment, such as consulting, housekeeping, or selling.

What did you do during the time you were not working full-time? Research your activities for ways to fill any gaps in employment with a positive response.

CRIMINAL RECORD

I've found that openness and honesty are usually the best policy here. Employers hire people who have made mistakes and are ready to return to society in a productive way. Locate and find these employers. Often you can get help from your parole officer, a school, or a state placement advisor.

One student recently had this problem. He had been paroled from the state penitentiary after serving several years for a drug conviction. When he asked me how to handle this situation, I suggested that he list the state institution as an employer. Under duties, he listed the training and counseling he had received in prison and the fact that he had become an active leader in the drug rehabilitation program.

HEALTH

While it may be illegal for an employer to inquire directly about your health, you may be faced with indirect or direct questions concerning your health. Health-related problems are major concerns for employers. Absenteeism, medical insurance, and production losses are affected when a health problem surfaces. If your prior health has been poor, it does not necessarily mean that it will continue to affect you in the future; but employers tend to jump to this conclusion. Therefore, it's smart to be prepared to handle this sensitive subject.

Whenever possible, always write "Excellent health" if, in your opinion, your health will not interfere with your job duties. The key here is that your health, no matter what your medical situation may be, will not interfere with your work performance. If you believe this to be so, "Excellent health" is a reasonable response. Writing "Health good" leaves too much room for employer interpretation and often results in your being screened out of the hiring process.

Physical and/or Mental Limitations

Some limitations are difficult to hide, even during the application process. If you have a physical or mental limitation but still feel that you are qualified for the position, it may be best to tell the employer about your limitation and needs. Talk with a qualified counselor or job placement expert. Get expert advice; then proceed. Identify your need for reasonable accommodations and apply.

Employers must provide reasonable accommodations to the known physical or mental limitations of an otherwise qualified applicant or worker. The law prohibits discrimination in all employment practices, including job application procedures, hiring, firing, advancement, compensation, advertising, layoffs, leaves, fringe benefits, training, and all other employment activities.

If you feel you have been discriminated against because of a physical or mental limitation, there is recourse. But before proceeding down the path of lawsuits and threats, look closer at your qualifications, requests for accommodations, and presentation of your personal being. It is still your responsibility to present your qualifications in a manner that demonstrates the fact that you're capable of doing the job. Often an applicant is not chosen because of factors based on the job requirements. Take an active role in presenting your qualifications. An employer may not be familiar with new technologies and alternative methods of accomplishing the job. Help educate employers instead of condemning them. They have difficult jobs and want to hire qualified employees, regardless of limitations or disabilities.

ATTENDANCE/ABSENCES

While it may be inappropriate to ask questions concerning medical problems, employers may ask questions about your attendance. Employers want to know how dependable you are. If you're absent a lot, for whatever reasons, you may be screened out of the hiring process. Poor attendance often reveals problems with health, accidents, attitude, and/or work performance.

If you have good attendance, state it. Perfect attendance is the answer employers hope to hear. But not all of us have this kind of record. Writing "Excellent attendance" is a good response. Writing "Good attendance" may create many questions. Your interpretation of "Good" and "Excellent" can be explained in the interview.

If you are asked for the number of days you have missed in the past year, and if you were absent recently, you could respond with a general comment like, "I've had an excellent attendance record. Over the past three years I've missed only ten days." This will answer the question truthfully and eliminate the absences in the current year.

If you have a poor attendance record and there's no positive way to explain it, you may have to confess and promise to do better. If you live up to your promise, the situation will correct itself in the future.

UNEMPLOYMENT COMPENSATION

This is money you received from the state employment service while you were unemployed and qualified to draw it. The employer looks for people who have abused this program, because providing unemployment benefits can cost employers large sums of money.

If you have received unemployment compensation, you must respond yes. You may want to explain if there is room on the application but watch how you word your explanation. There are some suggestions that may be helpful under the section "Reason for Leaving."

Questions concerning unemployment compensation are disappearing from many job applications, but be prepared to respond in a positive way if asked.

WORKER'S COMPENSATION

This question concerns the money you received while off work due to an industrial accident, injury, or illness. If you have received compensation, you must respond with yes; and if there is room, you may choose to provide details. Bear in mind that it is not what you say but how you say it. Make sure your explanation leaves the employer with the impression that you returned to work as quickly as possible. Many employers prefer to screen out an applicant who has drawn worker's compensation. Employers fear the applicant may be prone to accidents, injuries, or illnesses, and/or is just lazy and looking for ways to be paid for not working.

There are alternatives to answering this question. You can leave the space blank, write in "N/A" (not applicable), or draw a line in the space. However, any of these responses can create major questions in the employer's mind. Sometimes silence speaks louder than words. The employer's interpretation of the blank may be worse than the facts.

Few applications address this issue today, but you should be prepared to handle it if asked.

REASON FOR LEAVING

This question is loaded. It's the one area I've found that applicants really mess up on. Answers such as "Couldn't get along with the grumpy old boss," "Personality conflict," "Fired," or "Standing made my legs hurt" all create negative reactions. It just leaves the employer prone to screen you out. So what can you write?

Avoid negative statements about your employer or yourself. If there were problems, learn from the experience. Then phrase your response in a way that is not negative. Avoid criticizing your prior employer; instead, find ways to compliment. Never write "Fired"; instead write "Laid off" or "Terminated." Whatever the reason for being fired, the real issue is, Have you resolved the problem so it won't happen again? If so, let the employer know. For example, you may have missed too much work because of car problems. Let the employer know that this situation has been resolved and will no longer create problems.

Current Employer

Even if you are employed, this question needs to be answered. Respond as if the question read, "Why do you want to leave your job?"

There will be many honest reasons you may think of for wanting to change jobs. Look at all of the answers, and select a response that is positive and one an employer wants to hear. Your first knee-jerk response is probably not the best answer. Viable reasons may include your seeking the following:

- Full-time permanent employment
- Advancement opportunities
- Employment in your field of training
- More responsibilities
- Higher wages
- Part-time work while attending college

The reasons can be many; the answer must be one an employer would accept and understand.

POSITION WANTED

Always choose a position and level that is compatible with your work experience and education. Many young and/or inexperienced students write "Manager" or "Management" when asked for "position applying for." If you don't have management experience and your application and resume do not support the request for "Manager," do not expect to be selected for an interview. A better choice would be to write "Management Trainee" or "Entry-level management."

WORK SCHEDULE

It is important for you to be able to work the schedules required by the employer. If there are certain days, hours, or holidays that you will not or cannot work, be sure to apply at companies that offer the schedules that meet your needs. For example, do not apply at an employer whose hours require you to work Sundays, if this is a day you will not work. There are many employers who are closed on Sundays. Find the employers that offer the type of work you do and the schedule you require; then apply there.

SUFFICIENT SPACE FOR ANSWERS

Many applications provide limited space for answers. This is why it's important to study the application and job opening announcement before completing an application. Your answers must be adjusted to fit the space. Completing a trial application ahead of time is smart. Having scratch paper available on which to write the answers provides you with a visual concept of the space. Attaching a well-written, targeted resume generally alleviates the problem.

This application is the most popular application in the country. It belongs to the federal government, our country's largest employer.

STEP 1: READ THE INSTRUCTION PAGE THOROUGHLY

- **Read the application and job announcement carefully.** It is detailed, and you'll want to do it right.

- **Organize all information and documents in the order listed on the job announcement.** Include all requested information.

- **Include all jobs held during the last ten years.** Consider summarizing employment history for jobs beyond the ten-year requirement or for seasonal or part-time work. See the Continuation Sheet example in Figure 7-9.

- **Type or computer process the application.** If you can do a neat and accurate job, do it yourself. Otherwise, hire a professional.

- Be neat and thorough. It's your first impression. Make it count. You will not get a second chance for this opening. Spend the time to do it right because the competition is tough.

Standard Form 171 — **Application for Federal Employment**

Read The Following Instructions Carefully Before You Complete This Application

- **DO NOT SUBMIT A RESUME INSTEAD OF THIS APPLICATION.**
- **TYPE OR PRINT CLEARLY IN DARK INK.**
- IF YOU NEED MORE SPACE for an answer, use a sheet of paper the same size as this page. On **each** sheet write your name, Social Security Number, the announcement number or job title, and the item number. Attach all additional forms and sheets to this application at the top of page 3.
- If you do not answer **all** questions fully and correctly, you may delay the review of your application and lose job opportunities.
- Unless you are asked for additional material in the announcement or qualification information, **do not** attach any materials, such as: official position descriptions, performance evaluations, letters of recommendation, certificates of training, publications, etc. Any materials you attach which were not asked for may be removed from your application and will **not** be returned to you.
- We suggest that you keep a copy of this application for your use. If you plan to make copies of your application, we suggest you leave items **1, 48 and 49** blank. Complete these blank items each time you apply. **YOU MUST SIGN AND DATE, IN INK, EACH COPY YOU SUBMIT.**
- To apply for a specific Federal civil service examination (whether or not a written test is required) or a specific vacancy in an Federal agency:
  — Read the announcement and other materials provided.
  — Make sure that your work experience and/or education meet the qualification requirements described.
  — Make sure the announcement is open for the job and location you are interested in. Announcements may be closed to receipt of applications for some types of jobs, grades, or geographic locations.
  — Make sure that you are allowed to apply. Some jobs are limited to veterans, or to people who work for the Federal Government or have worked for the Federal Government in the past.
  — Follow any directions on "How to Apply". If a written test is required, bring any material you are instructed to bring to the test session. For example, you may be instructed to "Bring a completed SF 171 to the test." If a written test is not required, mail this application and all other forms required by the announcement to the address specified in the announcement.

Work Experience (*Item 24*)

- Carefully complete each experience block you need to describe your work experience. Unless you qualify based on education alone, your rating will depend on your description of previous jobs. Do not leave out any jobs you held during the last ten years.
- Under **Description of Work**, write a clear and brief, but **complete** description of your major duties and responsibilities for each job. Include any supervisory duties, special assignments, and your accomplishments in the job. We may verify your description with your former employers.
- If you had a major change of duties or responsibilities while you worked for the same employer, describe each major change as a separate job.

Veteran Preference in Hiring (*Item 22*)

- **DO NOT LEAVE Item 22 BLANK.** If you do **not** claim veteran preference, place an "X" in the box next to "NO PREFERENCE".
- You **cannot** receive veteran preference if you are retired or plan to retire at or above the rank of major or lieutenant commander, **unless** you are disabled or retired from the active military Reserve.
- To receive veteran preference your separation from active duty must have been under honorable conditions. This includes honorable and general discharges. A clemency discharge does not meet the requirements of the Veteran Preference Act.
- Active duty for training in the military Reserve and National Guard programs is not considered active duty for purposes of veteran preference.
- To qualify for preference you must meet ONE of the following conditions:
  1. Served on active duty anytime between December 7, 1941, and July 1, 1955; (If you were a Reservist called to active duty between February 1, 1955 and July 1, 1955, you must meet condition 2, below.)
  or
  2. Served on active duty any part of which was between July 2, 1955 and October 14, 1976 or a Reservist called to active duty between February 1, 1955 and October 14, 1976 **and** who served for more than 180 days;
  or
  3. Entered on active duty between October 15, 1976 and September 7, 1980 or a Reservist who entered on active duty between October 15, 1976 and October 13, 1982 **and** received a Campaign Badge or Expeditionary Medal **or** are a disabled veteran;
  or
  4. Enlisted in the Armed Forces after September 7, 1980 or entered active duty other than by enlistment on or after October 14, 1982 **and:**
     a. completed 24 months of continuous active duty or the full period called or ordered to active duty, or were discharged under 10 U.S.C. 1171 or for hardship under 10 U.S.C. 1173 **and** received or were entitled to receive a Campaign Badge or Expeditionary Medal; **or**
     b. are a disabled veteran.
- If you meet one of the four conditions above, you qualify for 5-point preference. If you want to claim 5-point preference **and** do not meet the requirements for 10-point preference, discussed below, place an "X" in the box next to "5-POINT PREFERENCE".
- If you think you qualify for 10-Point Preference, review the requirements described in the Standard Form (SF) 15, Application for 10-Point Veteran Preference. The SF 15 is available from any Federal Job Information Center. The 10-point preference groups are:
  — Non-Compensably Disabled or Purple Heart Recipient.
  — Compensably Disabled (less than 30%).
  — Compensably Disabled (30% or more).
  — Spouse, Widow(er) or Mother of a deceased or disabled veteran.
- If you claim 10-point preference, place an "X" in the box next to the group that applies to you. To receive 10-point preference you must attach a completed SF 15 to this application together with the proof requested in the SF 15.

Privacy Act and Public Burden Statements

The Office of Personnel Management is authorized to rate applicants for Federal jobs under sections 1302, 3301, and 3304 of title 5 of the U.S. Code. Section 1104 of title 5 allows the Office of Personnel Management to authorize other Federal agencies to rate applicants for Federal jobs. We need the information you put on this form and associated application forms to see how well your education and work skills qualify you for a Federal job. We also need information on matters such as citizenship and military service to see whether you are affected by laws which follow in deciding who may be employed by the Federal Government.

We must have your Social Security Number (SSN) to keep your records straight because other people may have the same name and birth date. The SSN has been used to keep records since 1943, when Executive Order 9397 asked agencies to do so. The Office of Personnel Management may also use your SSN to make requests for information about you from employers, schools, banks, and others who know you, but only as allowed by law or Presidential directive. The information we collect by using your SSN will be used for employment purposes and also may be used for studies, statistics, and computer matching to benefit and payment files.

Information we have about you may also be given to Federal, State, and local agencies for checking on law violations or for other lawful purposes. We may send your name and address to State and local Government agencies, Congressional and other public offices, and public international organizations, if they request names of people to consider for employment. We may also notify your school placement office if you are selected for a Federal job.

Giving us your SSN or any of the other information is voluntary. However, we cannot process your application, which is the first step toward getting a job, if you do not give us the information we request. Incomplete addresses and ZIP Codes will also slow processing.

Public burden reporting for this collection of information is estimated to vary from 20 to 360 minutes with an average of 50 minutes per response, including time for reviewing instructions, searching existing data sources, gathering the data needed, and completing and reviewing the collection of information. Send comments regarding the burden estimate or any other aspect of the collection of information, including suggestions for reducing this burden to Reports and Forms Management Officer, U.S. Office of Personnel Management, 1900 E Street, N.W., Room 6410, Washington, D.C. 20415; and to the Office of Management and Budget, Paperwork Reduction Project (3206-0012), Washington, D.C. 20503.

DETACH THIS PAGE—NOTE SF 171-A ON BACK

Figure 7-6 Application for Federal Employment, Standard Form 171

STEP 2: COMPLETE PAGE I OF THE FEDERAL EMPLOYMENT APPLICATION—SF 171

Make it easy for reviewers to ascertain your qualifications. Be as concise as possible.

General Information

Item 1: Know the job you want. Be specific. Give the job title and announcement number.

Items 2 through 10: These items are self-explanatory.

Availability

Item 11: Understand the parameters of your current employment and the resignation procedures. Generally, when employed, request a minimum notification period of two weeks.

Item 12: The job announcement will provide this information. If uncertain, write "Prevailing wage."

Items 13 and 14: Be flexible here. Show a willingness to work whatever the job requires.

Items 15 and 16: Answer these truthfully; but be as flexible as possible.

Military Service and Veteran Preference

Items 17 through 22: Reread the instructions carefully. Answer the questions completely and accurately.

Application for Federal Employment—SF 171
Read the instructions before you complete this application. *Type or print clearly in dark ink.*

Form Approved
OMB No. 3206-0012

GENERAL INFORMATION

1 What kind of job are you applying for? *Give title and announcement no. (if any)*

Range Conservationist OSO-90-71

2 Social Security Number
999-83-7732

3 Sex
[X] Male [ ] Female

4 Birth date *(Month, Day, Year)*
07/31/60

5 Birthplace *(City and State or Country)*
Boise, ID U.S.A.

6 Name *(Last, First, Middle)*
Henry, James Frederick
Mailing address *(include apartment number, if any)*
P.O. Box 73 (Residence 34 Railroad Blvd.)

City — Salem
State — OR ZIP Code — 97306

7 Other names ever used *(e.g., maiden name, nickname, etc.)*
N/A

8 Home Phone
Area Code 503 Number 555-8380

9 Work Phone
Area Code 503 Number 555-3909 Extension 1237

10 Were you ever employed as a civilian by the Federal Government? If "NO", go to Item 11. If "YES", mark each type of job you held with an "X".
[X] Temporary [ ] Career-Conditional [X] Career [ ] Excepted
What is your **highest** grade, classification series and job title?
GS-454-9 Range Conservationist
Dates at **highest** grade. FROM 03/01/90 TO Present

AVAILABILITY

11 When can you start work? *(Month and Year)*
01/9X

12 What is the **lowest** pay will you accept? (You will not be considered for jobs which pay less than you indicate.)
Pay $ _____ per _____ OR Grade 9

13 In what geographic area(s) are you willing to work?
Continental United States

14 Are you willing to work:

	YES	NO
A. 40 hours per week *(full-time)*?	X	
B. 25-32 hours per week *(part-time)*?		X
C. 17-24 hours per week *(part-time)*?		X
D. 16 or fewer hours per week *(part-time)*?		X
E. An intermittent job *(on-call/seasonal)*?		X
F. Weekends, shifts, or rotating shifts?	X	

15 Are you willing to take a temporary job lasting:

	YES	NO
A. 5 to 12 months *(sometimes longer)*?		X
B. 1 to 4 months?		X
C. Less than 1 month?		X

16 Are you willing to travel away from home for:

	YES	NO
A. 1 to 5 nights each month?	X	
B. 6 to 10 nights each month?	X	
C. 11 or more nights each month?	X	

MILITARY SERVICE AND VETERAN PREFERENCE

17 Have you served in the United States Military Service? *If your only active duty was training in the Reserves or National Guard, answer "NO".* If "NO", go to item 22.

YES	NO
	X

18 Did you or will you retire at or above the rank of major or lieutenant commander?

	X

THE FEDERAL GOVERNMENT IS AN EQUAL OPPORTUNITY EMPLOYER
PREVIOUS EDITION USABLE UNTIL 12-31-90

Page 1

FOR USE OF EXAMINING OFFICE ONLY

Date entered register

Form reviewed:
Form approved:

Option	Grade	Earned Rating	Veteran Preference	Augmented Rating
			[ ] No Preference Claimed	
			[ ] 5 Points *(Tentative)*	
			[ ] 10 Pts. *(30% Or More Comp. Dis.)*	
			[ ] 10 Pts *(Less Than 30% Comp. Dis.)*	
			[ ] Other 10 Points	

Initials and Date

| [ ] Disallowed | [ ] Being Investigated |

FOR USE OF APPOINTING OFFICE ONLY
Preference has been verified through proof that the separation was under honorable conditions, and other proof as required.

[ ] 5-Point [ ] 10-Point–30% or More Compensable Disability [ ] 10-Point–Less Than 30% Compensable Disability [ ] 10-Point–Other

Signature and Title

Agency _____ Date _____

MILITARY SERVICE AND VETERAN PREFERENCE *(Cont.)*

19 Were you discharged from the military service under honorable conditions? *(If your discharge was changed to "honorable" or "general" by a Discharge Review Board, answer "YES". If you received a clemency discharge, answer "NO".)* If "NO", provide below the date and type of discharge you received.

YES	NO

Discharge Date *(Month, Day, Year)*	Type of Discharge
10/15/83	Honorable

20 List the dates *(Month, Day, Year)*, and branch for all **active duty** military service.

From	To	Branch of Service
10/15/79	10/15/83	U.S. Navy

21 If all your active military duty was after October 14, 1976, list the full names and dates of all campaign badges or expeditionary medals you received or were entitled to receive.
N/A

22 **Read the instructions** that came with this form **before completing this item.** When you have determined your eligibility for veteran preference from the instructions, place an "X" in the box next to your veteran preference claim.

[X] NO PREFERENCE
[ ] 5-POINT PREFERENCE -- You must show proof when you are hired.

[ ] 10-POINT PREFERENCE -- If you claim 10-point preference, place an "X" in the box below next to the basis for your claim. **To receive 10-point preference you must also complete a Standard Form 15, Application for 10-Point Veteran Preference, which is available from any Federal Job Information Center. ATTACH THE COMPLETED SF 15 AND REQUESTED PROOF TO THIS APPLICATION.**

[ ] Non-compensable disabled or Purple Heart recipient.
[ ] Compensably disabled, less than 30 percent.
[ ] Spouse, widow(er), or mother of a deceased or disabled veteran.
[ ] Compensably disabled, 30 percent or more.

NSN 7540-00-935-7150 171-110

Standard Form 171 (Rev. 6-88)
U.S. Office of Personnel Management
FPM Chapter 295

Figure 7-7 Application for Federal Employment, Page 1

STEP 3: COMPLETE THE WORK EXPERIENCE ON PAGE 2

By dividing each job into parts, you can use headers to make the reading and comprehension easier. Then support each header with experience statements. Be sure you rank each header and each skill statement. Read the instructions carefully.

Always remember to divide, support, and rank your job descriptions.

- Cover ten years of employment. Do not leave out any jobs.

- Employment includes volunteer work and military service.

- Keep your current employer (listed in block A) preferably to one page, two pages maximum.

- If you were unemployed for more than three months, describe where you were and what you were doing.

- Use courtesy titles with names.

Headers
Break up job descriptions with headers, buzzwords, or job titles.

Bullets
Use bullets; they make your writing easier to read and to comprehend.

Unnecessary Phrases
Do not use phrases such as "Duties included" or "Responsible for." Instead, begin job descriptions with action verbs, such as "Wrote," "Scheduled," "Measured," or "Managed." The skill is in the verb.

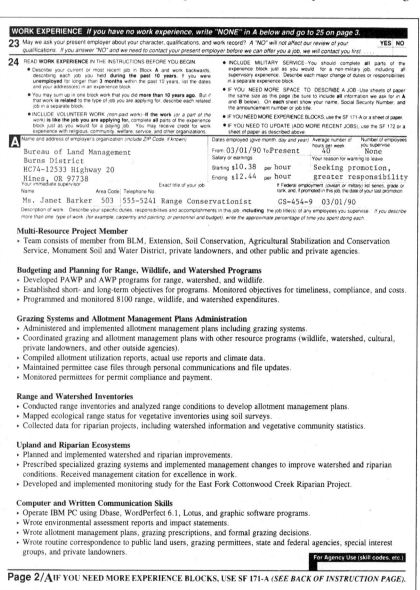

Figure 7-8 Application for Federal Employment, Page 2

STEP 4: COMPLETE ANY ADDITIONAL WORK EXPERIENCE BLOCKS

Use Standard Form 171-A, Continuation Sheet, for additional employers. This helps reviewers keep track of the employer and the page number. These numbers will be used as reference numbers when you answer the Evaluation Criteria questions.

Bullets

- The "experts" believe bullets make reading and comprehending detailed information easier.
- Bullets force you to split dense text into shorter chunks.
- Bullets decrease reading time by an estimated 30 percent.
- Bullets decrease errors in writing an estimated 55 percent.

Page Numbering

Number all pages using a numbering system like the following:

> Page 2/A 1 of 2
>
> Page 2/B and C
>
> Page 2/D and E
>
> Page 2-Summary of Employment History, Employers A-K.

In this way the reviewer knows which employment blocks these pages refer to.

The number is placed at the bottom of each page, similar to the placement of the application page numbers.

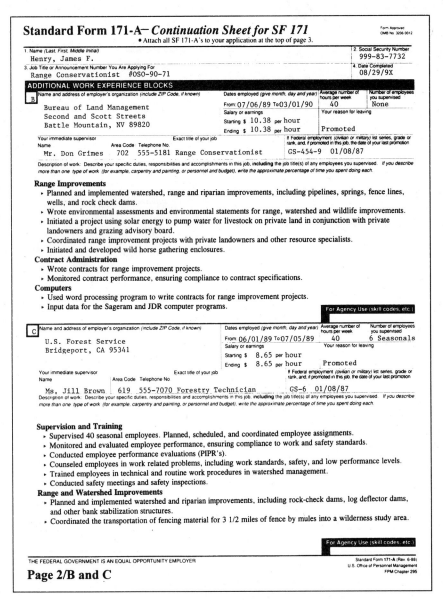

Figure 7-9   Application for Federal Employment, Continuation Sheet

Make a Summary of Work Experience Blocks

If you have extensive work experience and/or many employers you may have several of these pages. There are several ways that you can handle the challenge of many employers. The form below is a recap of employment that one client used.

If you choose to recap your employment history on this page, include all the basic information:

- Dates employed
- Employer name
- Job title
- Starting wage
- Ending wage
- Supervisor's name
- Reason for leaving

Page Numbering

Many of my clients have chosen to number the Continuation Sheets as "Page 2/C-D." In this way the reviewer knows that these pages refer to employment blocks C and D. This number is placed at the bottom of each page, similar to the placement of the application page numbers.

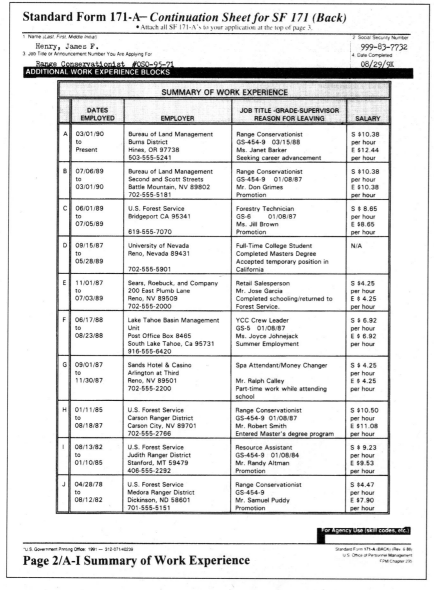

Standard Form 171-A– *Continuation Sheet for SF 171 (Back)*
• Attach all SF 171-A's to your application at the top of page 3.

1 Name *(Last, First, Middle Initial)*	2 Social Security Number
Henry, James F.	999-83-7732

3 Job Title or Announcement Number You Are Applying For	4 Date Completed
Range Conservationist #OSO-95-71	08/29/9X

ADDITIONAL WORK EXPERIENCE BLOCKS

SUMMARY OF WORK EXPERIENCE

	DATES EMPLOYED	EMPLOYER	JOB TITLE -GRADE-SUPERVISOR REASON FOR LEAVING	SALARY
A	03/01/90 to Present	Bureau of Land Management Burns District Hines, OR 97738 503-555-5241	Range Conservationist GS-454-9 03/15/88 Ms. Janet Barker Seeking career advancement	S $10.38 per hour E $12.44 per hour
B	07/06/89 to 03/01/90	Bureau of Land Management Second and Scott Streets Battle Mountain, NV 89802 702-555-5181	Range Conservationist GS-454-9 01/08/87 Mr. Don Grimes Promotion	S $10.38 per hour E $10.38 per hour
C	06/01/89 to 07/05/89	U.S. Forest Service Bridgeport CA 95341 619-555-7070	Forestry Technician GS-6 01/08/87 Ms. Jill Brown Promotion	S $ 8.65 per hour E $8.65 per hour
D	09/15/87 to 05/28/89	University of Nevada Reno, Nevada 89431 702-555-5901	Full-Time College Student Completed Masters Degree Accepted temporary position in California	N/A
E	11/01/87 to 07/03/89	Sears, Roebuck, and Company 200 East Plumb Lane Reno, NV 89509 702-555-2000	Retail Salesperson Mr. Jose Garcia Completed schooling/returned to Forest Service.	S $4.25 per hour E $ 4.25 per hour
F	06/17/88 to 08/23/88	Lake Tahoe Basin Management Unit Post Office Box 8465 South Lake Tahoe, Ca 95731 916-555-6420	YCC Crew Leader GS-5 01/08/87 Ms. Joyce Johnejack Summer Employment	S $ 6.92 per hour E $ 6.92 per hour
G	09/01/87 to 11/30/87	Sands Hotel & Casino Arlington at Third Reno, NV 89501 702-555-2200	Spa Attendant/Money Changer Mr. Ralph Calley Part-time work while attending school	S $ 4.25 per hour E $ 4.25 per hour
H	01/11/85 to 08/18/87	U.S. Forest Service Carson Ranger District Carson City, NV 89701 702-555-2766	Range Conservationist GS-454-9 01/08/87 Mr. Robert Smith Entered Master's degree program	S $10.50 per hour E $11.08 per hour
I	08/13/82 to 01/10/85	U.S. Forest Service Judith Ranger District Stanford, MT 59479 406-555-2292	Resource Assistant GS-454-9 01/08/84 Mr. Randy Altman Promotion	S $ 9.23 per hour E $9.53 per hour
J	04/28/78 to 08/12/82	U.S. Forest Service Medora Ranger District Dickinson, ND 58601 701-555-5151	Range Conservationist GS-454-9 Mr. Samuel Puddy Promotion	S $4.47 per hour E $7.90 per hour

For Agency Use (skill codes, etc.)

*U.S. Government Printing Office: 1991 — 312-071/40239

Standard Form 171-A (BACK) (Rev. 6-88)
U.S. Office of Personnel Management
FPM Chapter 295

Page 2/A-I Summary of Work Experience

Figure 7-10   Application for Federal Employment, Continuation Sheet

STEP 5: COMPLETE EDUCATION, SPECIAL SKILLS, AND REFERENCES ON PAGE 3

Education

If there isn't room for a complete answer, make a separate page. Then write "See page 5," or whatever number it happens to be, on the application.

Special Skills, Accomplishments, and Awards

Be sure to include your first aid and CPR training.

Don't forget your driver's license.

Make a separate listing and attach it to the application if there is not sufficient room. Number the page, and write "See page 6," or whatever number, on the application.

References

Select people who are not related to you and who are not supervisors listed under item 24.

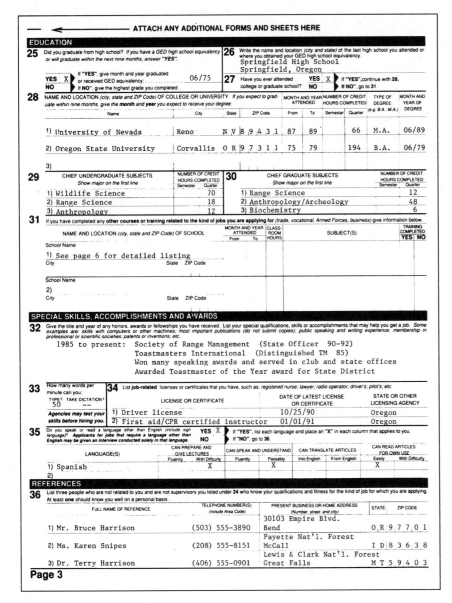

Figure 7-11 Application for Federal Employment, Page 3

STEP 6: COMPLETE BACKGROUND INFORMATION AND SIGNATURE BLOCK ON PAGE 4

Background Information

Read this section carefully, and follow all the directions. Answer all questions honestly. Misrepresentations have a habit of coming back to haunt you at inopportune times.

Need More Space?

If you need more space for your answers, use another sheet of paper. Be sure to head the page with your name, Social Security number, the announcement number or job title, and the item number. It is helpful to write "See page 7" in the item number needing further explanation. Then place the page number at the bottom of the extra page so that it's similar to the page numbers on the application form.

Signature, Certification, and Release of Information

Again, read before you sign. Know what you are doing and why. Your application will not be processed or accepted without the necessary signature and date. Sign and date the application.

BACKGROUND INFORMATION--*You must answer each question in this section before we can process your application.*

		YES	NO
37	Are you a citizen of the United States? *(In most cases you must be a U.S. citizen to be hired. You will be required to submit proof of identity and citizenship at the time you are hired.)* If "**NO**", give the country or countries you are a citizen of:	X	

NOTE: It is important that you give complete and truthful answers to **questions 38 through 44.** If you answer "**YES**" to any of them, provide your explanation(s) in **Item 45.** Include convictions resulting from a plea of nolo contendere *(no contest)*. Omit: 1) traffic fines of $100.00 or less; 2) any violation of law committed before your 16th birthday; 3) any violation of law committed before your 18th birthday, if finally decided in juvenile court or under a Youth Offender law; 4) any conviction set aside under the Federal Youth Corrections Act or similar State law; 5) any conviction whose record was expunged under Federal or State law. We will consider the date, facts, and circumstances of each event you list. In most cases you can still be considered for Federal jobs. However, **if you fail to tell the truth or fail to list all relevant** events or circumstances, this may be grounds for not hiring you, for firing you after you begin work, or for criminal prosecution (18 USC 1001).

		YES	NO
38	During the last **10 years**, were you **fired from any job** for any reason, did you **quit after being told that you would be fired**, or did you leave by mutual agreement because of specific problems?		X
39	Have you **ever** been convicted of, or forfeited collateral for **any felony violation**? *(Generally, a felony is defined as any violation of law punishable by imprisonment of longer than one year, except for violations called misdemeanors under State law which are punishable by imprisonment of two years or less.)*		X
40	Have you **ever** been convicted of, or forfeited collateral for **any firearms or explosives violation**?		X
41	Are you **now** under charges for **any violation of law**?		X
42	During the **last 10 years** have you forfeited collateral, been convicted, been imprisoned, been on probation, or been on parole? Do **not** include violations reported in 39, 40, or 41, above.		X
43	Have you **ever** been convicted by a military **court-martial**? If no military service, answer "**NO**".		X
44	Are you **delinquent** on any Federal debt? *(Include delinquencies arising from Federal taxes, loans, overpayment of benefits, and other debts to the U.S. Government **plus** defaults on Federally guaranteed or insured loans such as student and home mortgage loans.)*		X

45 If "**YES**" in: **38** - Explain for each job the problem(s) and your reason(s) for leaving. Give the employer's name and address.
 39 through 43 - Explain each violation. Give place of occurrence and name/address of police or court involved.
 44 - Explain the type, length and amount of the delinquency or default, and steps you are taking to correct errors or repay the debt. Give any identification number associated with the debt and the address of the Federal agency involved.
 NOTE: If you need more space, use a sheet of paper, and include the item number.

Item No.	Date (Mo./Yr.)	Explanation	Mailing Address
		N/A	Name of Employer, Police, Court, or Federal Agency
			City / State / ZIP Code
			Name of Employer, Police, Court, or Federal Agency
			City / State / ZIP Code

		YES	NO
46	Do you receive, or have you ever applied for retirement pay, pension, or other pay based on military, Federal civilian, or District of Columbia Government service?		X
47	Do any of your relatives work for the United States Government or the United States Armed Forces? Include: *father; mother; husband; wife; son; daughter; brother; sister; uncle; aunt; first cousin; nephew; niece; father-in-law; mother-in-law; son-in-law; daughter-in-law; brother-in-law; sister-in-law; stepfather; stepmother; stepson; stepdaughter; stepbrother; stepsister; half brother; and half sister.* If "**YES**", provide details below. If you need more space, use a sheet of paper.		X

Name	Relationship	Department, Agency or Branch of Armed Forces
N/A		

SIGNATURE, CERTIFICATION, AND RELEASE OF INFORMATION

YOU MUST SIGN THIS APPLICATION. **Read the following carefully before you sign.**
- A false statement on any part of your application may be grounds for not hiring you, or for firing you after you begin work. Also, you may be punished by fine or imprisonment (U.S. Code, title 18, section 1001).
- If you are a male born after December 31, 1959 you must be registered with the Selective Service System or have a valid exemption in order to be eligible for Federal employment. You will be required to certify as to your status at the time of appointment.
- **I understand** that any information I give may be investigated as allowed by law or Presidential order.
- **I consent** to the release of information about my ability and fitness for Federal employment by *employers, schools, law enforcement agencies and other individuals and organizations,* **to** *investigators, personnel staffing specialists, and other authorized employees of the Federal Government.*
- **I certify** that, to the best of my knowledge and belief, **all** of my statements are true, correct, complete, and made in good faith.

48 SIGNATURE *(Sign each application in dark ink)*	**49** DATE SIGNED *(Month, day, year)*
James F. Henry	August 29, 199X

Page 4

☆ U.S. GOVERNMENT PRINTING OFFICE: 1992 312-071/50114

Figure 7-12 Application for Federal Employment, Page 4

Divide—Support—Rank, the formula for writing understandable KSAs.

You may be required to complete a set of questions known as Evaluation Criteria or KSAs (Knowledge, Skills, and Abilities). These are specific job-related questions that applicants must answer when applying for many federal government jobs.

By dividing each question into parts, you can use headers to make the reading and comprehension easier. Then support each header with experience statements. Be sure you rank each header and each skill statement. Some guidelines to help you follow.

- Head each page with your name, announcement number, and position title.

- Read each KSA carefully. Break each question into parts, and label each part.

- Make it easy for the reviewers. Consider supplying a reference number for each KSA category. This number should identify the page, employer block, and/or item number.

FINAL THOUGHTS

As you can see, completing a job application takes skill, time, and judgment. You will want to put in the effort to do an exceptional job; otherwise, you are likely to be screened out of the process. Job applications often get no more than a quick scan, sixty seconds or less. If your application fails the first review, it is likely that you will not be considered again. You get one chance, don't blow it.

KSA NARRATIVE STATEMENT

Raymond F. Jackson   Social Security Number 999-69-8239
Announcement: MSO-88-41   Position: Supervisory Natural Resource Specialist

---

KSA (1) Knowledge of land use and natural resource programs to direct a multi-resource staff to accomplish multiple use management objectives in range, wildlife, soils, watershed, and engineering programs.

Range Management Eleven years of solid experience as range conservationist and two years of graduate study. (See SF171, pages 2A, 2B, 2C, and 3–Education)
▸ Advised Area Manager on budget and staffing requirements, progress, problems, and need for changes in program emphasis.
▸ Directed and performed full range of administrative and technical functions of range management program.
▸ Used a balanced approach to range management that accommodated other resources and accomplished other resource objectives.
▸ Made management adjustments when allotment evaluations indicated resource objectives were not being met.
▸ Reviewed other professionals' work to ensure consistency and adherence to range policy guidelines.
▸ Stayed current with new developments in the field through active participation in the Society for Range Management.

Soils and Watershed (See SF171, page 2B)
▸ Made budget and program recommendations to Area Manager.
▸ Advised District Soil Scientist of resource area watershed requirements for AWP.
▸ Prescribed specialized grazing systems and made management changes to improve rip-rap along stream banks; prescribed burns.
▸ Initiated studies to monitor and document changes in upland watersheds, riparian zones, and stream quality.
▸ Completed watershed rehabilitation training that included mining reclamation.
▸ Mapped ecological range sites for vegetative inventory by using soil surveys.

Wildlife B.S. Wildlife Management, Montana State University, 1983. (See SF171, page 3)
▸ Prepared budgets and program recommendations to Area Managers and District Biologist.
▸ Conducted studies to monitor habitat quality and inventory wildlife.
▸ Planned prescribed burns for antelope and sage grouse habitat improvement, changes to fences for wildlife passage, and water guzzler developments; assisted with bass and trout reintroduction.
▸ Monitored 30 black-tailed prairie dog towns for behavior interactions, expansion rates, and impact on vegetation. Searched for evidence of the black-footed ferret.

Horse Management Program
▸ Planned and coordinated roundup of wild and feral horses on grazing allotments.
▸ Arranged horse care with veterinarians.
▸ Accomplished rider. Rode horses to inspect livestock and vegetation.

KSA Page 1 of 4

Figure 7-13   KSA Sample

WRITE POWER LETTERS
The Great Door Openers

Every writer, by the way he uses the language, reveals something of his spirit, his habits, his capacities, his biases.

— E.B. White, *The Elements of Style*

Over the years, I've learned that many job hunters, myself included, have a horrible time writing letters. Most of us dislike writing so much that we avoid it like the plague or we spend hours agonizing in the process. So if you're worried about writing, you are not alone.

Writing is unlike talking. When you talk, you can see or hear if the person understands you. If you notice that your message isn't clear, you can restate it or ask the person to tell you what he or she didn't understand. You have a second, even a third, opportunity to make sure your message is understood. But when you write, you have to get the message correct the first time. You may not have a second chance.

The letters you write during the job hunt become some of the most important letters you will ever write. If you write an imaginative, well-thought-out letter, it's apt to be read and seriously considered. This chapter will help you brush up on your writing skills. Good writing takes time, thought, and imagination. Spend the time to do an excellent job of letter writing, and it will pay off.

USING THE LETTERS SECTION
OF THE *COMPANION PLANNER*

The LETTERS section of your *Companion Planner* will help you stay organized. It can even act as a lifesaver. You may choose to use the LETTERS section just for your "day letter file" or you may add a section for "sample" letters.

The Day Letter File

Suppose the letter you wrote to a key employer simply isn't filed where it's supposed to be. What do you do? You turn to your LETTERS section in the *Companion Planner,* which is where you keep copies of all the letters you write and receive. Here's how to use a day letter file:

- File copies of all the letters you write and receive during your job hunt in chronological order here.

- Put the most recent letter on top and the oldest letter on the bottom. These letters include personal notes to references and friends as well as formal letters to employers.

- Make a notation on the bottom of each letter of the actual location of the original letter.

Sample Letters File

You may elect to file samples of your best letters in this section. Samples may include cover letters, thank-you notes and letters, employment verification requests, personal reference requests, draft reference letters, follow-up letters, acceptance letters, and rejection letters.

LETTERS FOR THE JOB HUNT

What's in a letter? A letter is more than words on paper. It conveys sounds, feelings, and ideas. It may cast a magic spell or weave a mystery of intrigue. A letter is thought on paper, whether written with ease or blood and tears.

There are many types of letters. Some, like the reference request letters, have already been discussed. This chapter will concentrate on six commonly used letters:

An empty bag can not stand up right.
—Benjamin Franklin

1. Cover letter
2. Thank-You letter or letter of appreciation
3. Network letter
4. Acceptance letter
5. Rejection letter
6. Letter of resignation

When writing your letters, consider format and style. Format is the general plan or organization and arrangement of the letter. Style is your mode of expressing thought on paper, the written word. It is the identification of your personality. Style is the picture your words paint on paper.

Take time to write every letter with a personal touch. Write each word in your own voice, using the sounds and tones that speak your thoughts and feelings. Enhance your image with a personal letter, one that reveals your "best" spirit, habits, and capacities.

GUIDELINES FOR LETTER WRITING

1. **Write original letters.** Form letters are taboo. The key to originality is innovation. It gives you an edge over other writers. Original, innovative letters personalize your job hunt. It is your way to touch the employer in your unique way.

   Type or write each letter individually. Be professional. Be sure your spelling, grammar, and punctuation are correct. Get professional help if you need it.

2. **Address your letter to a specific person.** Use a courtesy title and job title, if appropriate, with the full name written out. Telephone each organization you plan to write and ask for the name, spelling, job title, courtesy title, and current mailing address. This may require extra time and money on your part, but it's imperative to address the right person and to spell his or her name correctly. Directories that provide you with the names of officers, owners, managers, etc., are often dated. Don't rely on this information. Your letter will probably end up in the wrong place, and all your efforts will be for nothing.

3. **Avoid sexist language in your greeting and throughout the letter.** "Gentlemen" or "Dear Sir" may be offensive to a reader. Many readers are not men, and even a first name doesn't always tell the correct sex. If you've done all your homework, you should have courtesy titles. Use them correctly.

   Try "Dear Reader," "Dear Employer," or "Gentle Reader," when responding to a blind ad (an advertisement where the employer's identity is withheld). "To Whom It May Concern" is cold and impersonal; select other expressions to greet your reader.

4. **Keep the letter short; limit it to one page.** Write three to five short paragraphs. Each paragraph should be at least two lines, but not more than eight lines. Keep sentences short (six to seventeen words). Write complete sentences, and eliminate all unnecessary words. Wordiness and flowery writing alienate the reader. The reader is busy and has far more important things to do than read a long-winded, self-serving letter from a job applicant.

   Saying too much or too little is suicide. Two lines may not be enough; two pages or three-hundred-word paragraphs are too much.

5. **Check language, grammar, spelling, and abbreviations. Use everyday English.** Avoid nonconversational expressions. "Enclosed herewith, please find my resume," is windy, pretentious, and poor phrasing. Just write "Enclosed is my resume." Eliminate the long, windy phrases. For example, write "I can" instead of "I am in a position to."

   Use positive expressions. Write "Please call" instead of "Don't hesitate to call." Replace "You won't be sorry" with "You'll be glad." Avoid sentences using negatives (nots and nevers). Avoid statements that alienate the reader. A statement such as "I trust you to keep this in the strictest of confidence" reeks with latent hostility.

Although you may not intend to sound hostile, those words can be interpreted by the reader in such a manner. Find ways to express your ideas in the affirmative.

Check the letter for correct grammar, spelling, word usage, and sentence structure. Word processing spell checkers and grammar programs do not catch everything. For instance, you may write a work correctly (Oops, I meant word, not work), but the program generally does not correct misusage.

Eliminate abbreviations. Abbreviations are shortcuts and can be misinterpreted. They are inconsiderate and easily misunderstood. Using them is a lazy person's way—and you don't want to appear lazy.

6. **Eliminate the almighty I.** It may be impossible to eliminate or rewrite all *I* sentences, but change as many as possible. Readers are interested in their desires and problems, not your whims. Write in terms of the employer's needs. The tone of the letter should reveal solutions to the employer's problem, not smack of egotism from what you want.

   Write your first draft using all the *I*'s you want. Don't even be concerned at this point with the number of *I*'s. After completing the letter, read each sentence and rearrange to eliminate as many *I*'s as possible.

7. **Write a postscript (P.S.).** This marketing technique gets attention and often receives action. The postscript is generally the very first paragraph read. This last thought should entice the reader to act. For example, "Please call our mutual friend Greg Jones. He knows my work and character."

8. **Type or word process your letters.** Handwriting is for personal letters, not business letters. Save fancy fonts and various type sizes for creative ventures. Business letters require conservative business fonts. During the job hunt, your letters are strictly business.

   Check the quality of your printer or typewriter ribbon before printing. The letter must be clean and unmarked.

9. **Use the same quality stationery you used for your resume.** Choose 8 $\frac{1}{2}$-by-11-inch high-quality 20-pound bond paper with matching envelopes. Select an ivory, off-white, buff, tan, or grey color. The linen texture adds a quality touch. Avoid parchments and onion skin papers.

   Use the same heading you used for your resume. This should include your name, address, and a daytime telephone number. Your name should be spelled out. Using initials, rather than spelling out your first name, projects coldness and leaves the reader wondering. Sometimes this is unavoidable, but generally that is not the case. Use a street address instead of a post office box number, if possible. Boxes appear transitory. Provide a daytime telephone number where you can be reached or where a message can be left. An employer must be able to reach you or leave a message during business hours (generally eight in the morning until five at night).

10. **Date and sign your letter.** Write out the date; for example, April 3, 1996. Writing 4/3/96 is a shortcut and should be avoided. Failing to sign your letter may be a small detail, but it could be fatal. It's a sign of failing to pay attention to the details.

11. **Prepare your envelope with care.** Use the same care you used for your resume and cover letter. Write out the person's full name and use courtesy and job titles. Write the complete address, including the zip code. Verify all spellings. Use correct postage; have it weighed, if necessary. Mail it yourself; do not rely on someone else to do it for you.

BASIC PARTS OF A LETTER

. . . neither boy nor angel knows how hard it is to write.

— **Richard Bach,**
Running from Safety

Below is a list of the basic parts of a letter. See if you can identify each part in the sample letter shown in Figure 8-1.

- Personal Identification
- Date
- Inside Address
- Salutation

- Opening Paragraph
- Body Paragraphs
- Closing Paragraph
- Complimentary Closing
- Signature
- Typed Name
- Enclosures
- cc—The "cc" means carbon copy. In other words, you are mailing copies to another party or parties. (Always mail a copy of your letter to anyone mentioned in the letter.)
- P.S.—The "P.S." stands for postscript. It is a marketing technique that receives high readership and response. It's worth putting a key point in this area.

Cornelius Anderson

204 Country Loop   Office 804-555-2648
Emporia, Virginia 23847   Home 804-555-8714

August 24, 19xx

Mr. Fredrico Martinez
Executive Vice President
Argonaut Insurance Company
675 North First Street
San Jose, California 95113

Dear Mr. Martinez:

I will be in the San Francisco area September 6 through 12 and would like to set up an appointment with you to discuss the safety consultant opening.

Enclosed are examples of my safety achievements to assist you in your evaluation of my safety capability:
- Employee Handbook that I wrote and published in-house. Please note the safety sections on pages 10 and 11.
- Supervision Manual that I created for management. Pages 17 through 28 address the company's safety policy.
- Safety Inspection Walk-Thru dated January 9, 19xx (all items on this list, plus several other improvements, have been completed).

Having produced major safety changes and improvements in an industry that resists change gives me an understanding of the challenges faced by the people I would be supervising. My personnel, safety, and supervisory experience provide a strong base of skills that should satisfy your needs.

Mr. Martinez, I'm looking forward to talking and meeting with you. Trusting that the enclosed documents increase your interest in my application, I'll give you a call a week before coming to San Francisco to set a time for our meeting. I can be reached during the day at my office or at home after seven. I'm known to work late in order to visit the evening shifts.

Sincerely,

Cornelius Anderson

Cornelius Anderson

Enclosures

cc: Ms. Tatiana Anglen

P.S.   Please feel free to call our mutual friend, Tatiana Anglen. She knows my work and can confirm my credentials. Thank you.

Figure 8-1   Job-Hunting Letter—A Follow-Up

She'll wish there were more, and that's the great art o' letter writing.
—Charles Dickens

A cover letter is used **every time** you mail your resume to an employer, reference, business associate, or friend. It introduces you, explains the purpose of your writing, and highlights your capabilities. We'll concentrate on a cover letter going to an employer. Here are some guidelines to follow.

- Attach an original letter to every resume you mail. Type each letter individually.

- Address each letter to a specific individual. Use the correct courtesy and job titles. Take care to spell the name correctly.

- Establish a bond with the reader in the first paragraph. This can be done by explaining why you are applying or why you are interested in the job or company, or even by expressing thanks for the opportunity to apply.

- Share your accomplishments. Then support claims with evidence.

- Keep the letter short—short words, short sentences, short paragraphs.

- Postscripts receive attention and often get a response. Use one.

- Date and sign every letter.

- Mail copies of the letter to everyone mentioned.

Cornelius Anderson

204 Country Loop
Emporia, Virginia 23847

Office 804-555-2648
Home 804-555-8714

July 15, 19XX

Mr. Fredrico Martinez
Executive Vice President
Argonaut Insurance Company
675 North First Street
San Jose, California 95113

Dear Mr. Martinez:

I have great appreciation for the difficulty you are experiencing in hiring a safety consultant. Three months into the looking process tells me you are looking for a highly qualified producer. That makes this opportunity even more interesting for me. I have enclosed my resume for your review and feel that you will find it most interesting.

Currently I am working for a small manufacturing company. I've had the opportunity to establish the safety and personnel programs from scratch. I've found that the ability to change attitudes is one of my best assets. For example, when I first started, the production superintendent remarked, "What do you want me to do, slow down production for safety?" He was serious. One year later, he cannot do enough to promote safety because the new program has increased production, cut costs, and improved worker morale.

Before accepting this position, I worked for a large manufacturing corporation employing over 40,000 people. During my time there I was employed by the controller's department. This experience taught me to talk dollars and cents to management. I have found that this background is priceless in talking to management. When money talks, management listens. I can prepare cost/benefit analyses to promote safety. I can develop budgets that work. And I can monitor and evaluate costs effectively.

Mr. Martinez, I'm excited about this opportunity and trust that my experience will meet your requirements. I look forward to hearing from you.

Sincerely,

Cornelius Anderson
Cornelius Anderson

Enclosure: Resume

P.S.   I'm planning a vacation in your area soon; perhaps we can get together then. I'll give you a call next week to let you know my travel plans.

Figure 8-2 Cover Letter

A COVER LETTER WITH EXCITEMENT

Good letters take time, thought, and imagination.

Here are some ideas to consider when writing your cover letter.

- The mast head will vary in style and appearance. Your personal taste and available space dictate.
- Be sure to date every letter.
- Always address letters to a specific person. Use a courtesy title and a job title. Generally, titles can be obtained with a quick phone call to the employer.
- Write a positive, friendly letter. Appeal to the needs and interests of the employer.
- A reference line (RE:) allows you to get the message across immediately as to the purpose of your letter. The reader doesn't have to wade through a lot of words to know why you are writing.

- Expressing emotions must be genuine and part of your personality. Don't try to sound enthusiastic if that's not your natural way of expression.
- In the postscript, Terry says she'll call the employer. If you choose to use this approach, be sure you follow through and do what you say. It's suicide to do otherwise.
- Keep each letter short. If you can't write well on one page, two pages won't make it better.
- Type the letter so it is well balanced on the page. This creates a positive image and a professional appearance.
- Use a businesslike type style, nothing fancy. Avoid the script font.

TERRY S. MORELAND
7712 South Heather Drive Tempe, Arizona 85285   (602) 555-5502

                                                        July 8, 19xx

Ms. Joanne Libbey
Human Resource Manger
TEMPE LUMBER COMPANY
2256 Industrial Way
Tempe, Arizona 85285

RE: Personnel, Safety, and Purchasing Director Opening

Dear Ms. Libbey:

Seldom does a person see an employment advertisement and say to herself: "That's it! The job I've been waiting for. Perfect!" Well, that's what happened when I read your advertisement. The opportunity to share my qualifications and experience with you and to meet your expectations and requirements is exciting.

Having worked on projects affecting Tempe Lumber Company, including your road status off Wolf Creek and Snow Mountain, I am aware of many of your special concerns. Knowing your ability to remain viable in recessionary periods and your desire for expansion, this opportunity presents the "chance of a lifetime" for me.

I look forward to meeting and working with you. Enclosed is the resume you requested. Thank you for this terrific opportunity.

                                        Yours truly,

                                        Terry S. Moreland
                                        Terry S. Moreland

Enclosure: Resume

P.S. I'll be in Phoenix next week to receive the Toastmaster of the Year award for our district. That will make it hard for you to reach me, so I'll take the liberty of calling you next week.

Figure 8-3   Cover Letter. Courtesy of a client

AN ALL-BUSINESS COVER LETTER

Below are some additional points to consider when writing a cover letter.

A letter reflects your personality; make sure it's yours, not someone else's.

- A return address includes your name, mailing address, and a daytime phone number. If you have a FAX or voice mail number, include it.

- Use a courtesy title with each name.

- Avoid large expanses of grey. Use spaces between paragraphs to improve the readability.

- Use bullets to set off lists of skills or achievements.

Charles W. Sporre
89 Maple Drive
Augusta, Georgia 30903

Home Phone and FAX (404) 555-8891
Office Phone (404) 555-7124

April 23, 19xx

Ms. Amanda Wright, Corporate Comptroller
City Construction Company
3096 Gay Street
Manchester, New Hampshire 03103

Dear Ms. Wright:

The minute I read your job announcement, my heart started pounding. It was exactly what I've been looking for. Your job requirements and my experience, education, and career goals are a perfect match. Enclosed is my resume and references as requested.

Considered to be a take-charge person able to cope with a wide variety of challenges, I would like to share with you some of my achievements:

> ▸ Developed and implemented cost and management accounting systems by designing computer programs to oversee accounting policies and practices. These programs decreased accounting errors by 30% and cut costs by an estimated 15%.

> ▸ Increased profitability through closer attention to management requirements, the supervision of staff, and the institution of cost-control computer programs.

> ▸ Developed a high-quality staff with high morale and energy using the team management style.

By far the greatest satisfaction in my work comes from selecting, training, and motivating personnel. I have learned that remarkable results are produced when an energetic drive is coupled with management's concerns for results and the needs of the employees. I believe these qualities can be used effectively in your company.

I've researched your company. The closer I look, the more excited I get. I trust that after you research my credentials, accomplishments, and references, you will agree with my findings — that we are a great match.

If, after your review, you also conclude that you are indeed interested in what I can bring to your company, please call. I can be easily reached through my answering service and voice mail. I'm looking forward to hearing from you soon. Thank you for your consideration.

Yours truly,

Charles W. Sporre

Charles W. Sporre

Enclosure

Figure 8-4 Cover Letter

A COVER LETTER FOR A FEDERAL JOB OPENING

Create a bond between writer and reader. Avoid flattery; it always shows. Notice how Alex addressed his reason for wanting to make a change. He wants to return to his home state. Besides, it's smart to provide an answer for the question, Why are you looking now?

Sharing reasons for making a job, career, or location change is a personal matter. Writing about family matters is also a personal matter and another story. However, doing so often works to the advantage of the applicant, especially when there's a major change in location or careers. Employers want to be assured that this decision is well thought out. They can't afford to make mistakes.

Alex R. Bentley
43981 Spring Road
Amarillo, TX 79101
(806) 555-8732

August 21, 19XX

Fish and Wildlife Service
Refuges and Wildlife
Bismarck Habitat and Population Evaluation Team
Bismarck, North Dakota

RE: Vacancy Announcement FWS6-94-35

Dear Reviewers:

Enclosed please find my application package for the above vacancy announcement. I am applying for this position for career advancement and to return to my native home state. Being a native of North Dakota and living there as well as in Wisconsin for twenty-one years, my family is familiar with the Midwest climate and geography. We thrived there before and look forward to returning. Being closer to family and friends is another reason I am applying for this position.

I have been permanently employed by the federal government for the past four years. My education, previous experience, and career goals have been oriented toward wildlife biology with an emphasis in avian biology. I accepted my current position as a Range Conservationist with the Bureau of Land Management as a means to achieve this goal. The position you offer is in line with my long-term career objectives.

This career move is fully supported by my family. My wife, Sue, is also employed by the BLM. While a dual career move would be the ideal situation for us, Sue's qualifications allow her to easily obtain employment in many fields and industries. She's looking forward to the opportunities that await her in North Dakota. Our son, Josh, is about to enter high school and would like to attend a larger school than he is in currently. A larger community would offer several advantages for Josh both socially and academically. He's an excellent student and athlete and will be an asset to any school. Our family would welcome a permanent position that allows our son to finish high school in one location.

I am excited about this opportunity and look forward to hearing from you. Thank you for your kind consideration.

Sincerely,

Alex R. Bentley

Alex R. Bentley

Enclosures

Figure 8-5   Cover Letter for a Federal Position

A LETTER OF THANKS AFTER AN INTERVIEW

JoAnne Timmons

144 James Street   Bend, OR 97701   (503) 555-3897

May 8, 19XX

Mr. Gary Wright, Vice President
Research and Marketing
SUNNY VALE REALTY
Post Office Box 555
Sisters, Oregon 97759

Dear Mr. Wright:

Thanks for a most informative and enjoyable interview. You stimulated my interest in your organization and in this position. I'm sure I can do the job.

Reflecting back, I would like to assure you that I have the time and the experience in both sales and layout to complete the *Showcase of Homes* booklet by your deadline of June 15. As we discussed, the format is laid out, and some pages will not require major changes. Often, repeat advertisements do not change a great deal either. With this in mind, I hope you will seriously consider my application.

I have also called several advertisers and filled both issues of the *Broadside*, so my obligations to the college paper have been fulfilled. I am taking three finals this week and will take my last final on Saturday. This frees my time to work for you full-time beginning on May 15.

Thank you again for your thoughtful consideration. Mr. Wright, I really would enjoy working with your firm and look forward to hearing your decision.

Best regards,

JoAnne Timmons

JoAnne Timmons

Figure 8-6   A Thank-You Letter

After an interview, take a few minutes to review what took place. Jot down your thoughts, and make some notes. (You'll learn more about evaluating an interview in Chapter 13.)

Later that evening, draft a thank-you letter. Then set it aside, and get a good night's rest. Edit and revise the letter the next day. If necessary, take another day or two for rewriting. Just be sure to mail it within three days.

A HANDWRITTEN THANK-YOU NOTE

January 31, 19xx

Dear Roberto,

Just a note of thanks for all your encouraging words. It helps so much to have someone like you believe in me during a time when things are hard. I really appreciate your positive support.

I also appreciated the constructive suggestions you made about my resume. I'm in the process of making the revisions and will mail you a copy as soon as it's completed.

I'll keep in touch and let you know what happens with Desert Inns.

As always, your grateful friend
Lupe

Figure 8-7   Thank-You Note

Handwritten notes are used to say thanks for small favors. You'll use a lot of these.

Select a conservative card. A plain ivory thank-you note works well.

Keep in mind, however, that notes are for friendships, and letters are for business.

Be sure your handwriting is legible.

A CREATIVE THANK-YOU AFTER CALLING AN EMPLOYER

Alice learned too late about this job opening. But she decided to take action and send her resume off anyway. She sends a thank-you letter for the help and time given her.

This is an approach you can use with an employer after finding out there are no job openings. You can still send a resume. Write a letter to the party that gave you all the information, thanking him or her for the help. The more people that are involved in your job search, the more eyes and ears there are working for you. And this is a good way to get employers involved.

This letter was written on 8 ½-by-14-inch stationery. The top part was folded back, and the resume was tucked behind it. The letter was then folded in three, which put the "Thank You" on top of the three-fold letter.

Making a thank-you letter like the example is a matter of choice; saying thanks is not. It's a must.

Thank You

- -

ALICE BAILEY

Post Office Box 89   Home (503) 555-4759
Madras, OR 97741   Voice Mail (503) 555-9821

September 10, 19xx

Ms. Susan Nakamura
Central Oregon Battering and Rape Alliance
Post Office Box 1411
Sisters, OR 97759

Dear Ms. Nakamura:

Thank you for all your time yesterday. It was most helpful to me, even though I missed the deadline for applying for the Executive Manager position. I understand the necessity of following set procedures.

In case your selection process fails to find a suitable candidate for the position, I've taken the liberty of enclosing my resume. My experience and education match your requirements. COBRA needs an executive who relates to the experiences and frustrations of the people it serves . . . a person who doesn't intimidate, but inspires. That's me; I've been there on all sides.

I wish you every success in hiring the best candidate. If I can be of any help to you, please call. Thanks again for your interest.

Best regards,

Alice Bailey

Alice Bailey

Enclosure: Resume

P.S. If you hear of a position for me, please give me a call or feel free to forward my resume.

Figure 8-8   Thank-You Letter

Few worthwhile things are ever accomplished alone.

Use a network letter to enlist friends, business associates, and acquaintances in your job hunt. The more eyes and ears you have job hunting for you, the quicker a job will be found. Contact your friends and even strangers, and ask them for advice and ideas. Most people will gladly share. Don't be embarrassed about using friends. Most relish giving advice; and if, for some reason, they do not, there is nothing requiring them to help. You never know who will know about that perfect job opportunity.

Your business associates, friends, and acquaintances do not have to live where you're moving. They can be anywhere in the world. The world is a small place, and someone living in Missouri may know just the right person in Montgomery, Alabama, the city to which you're relocating. You will never know who might know about that perfect job opportunity.

Joy Powell
4518 NE Eighth Street
Denver CO 80239
(303) 555-4746

June 12, 19XX

Dear Cindy,

Bryce and I are moving back to Grant County in July. We're both excited about the move because it feels like coming home. Bryce has been retired for ten years and likes retirement. I tried retirement for a year after we left the Willamette Valley. Retirement didn't agree with me, so I went back to work. Although I've reached my "golden years," I plan to continue working. My health is excellent, I have an abundance of energy, and I thrive on doing good work for an appreciative employer.

Most of my experience is in banking, accounting, medical insurance billing, and human resource management; but I will consider other kinds of work. I'm always open to new challenges. I like being part of a team, but I also do a good solo act. Because I don't need a job for financial support, I can be flexible in terms of time and money.

If you know of any employers in John Day or Canyon City who may be looking for a skilled, dedicated employee with a proven track record, please call or write and give me their names and the titles of the jobs they have open or pending. If the jobs appear to be interesting, challenging, and rewarding, I can follow up with a telephone call and a letter.

Any advice or assistance you can give me will be greatly appreciated. Call me collect or write to me with your ideas for getting me back in the harness. I'm enclosing my updated resume, so you will know how I am presenting myself. Feel free to pass it on to anyone you think would be interested in seeing it.

Give my warmest regards to your family, especially Jeff. I'm excited about seeing his baby boy. It must be wonderful to live so near your grandchild. We have four grandchildren but don't see them very often. They all live far, far away.

Thank you, Cindy, for your help. I look forward to returning to John Day. I'll call you as soon as we are settled in, if not sooner.

Affectionately,

Joy

Enclosure

Figure 8-9 Network Letter to a Friend. Courtesy of a client

A NETWORK LETTER TO A FRIEND

This letter is more informal than a network letter to a business associate or an acquaintance. The tone you use will depend on the person to whom you are writing.

You'll still want to be sure the letter is well written, with complete sentences, accurate spelling, and correct grammar. You're making a professional impression; don't blow it, even with a personal friend.

Don't judge the value of any one person. The one friend or associate you feel will help will probably be the one that ignores you. The one you really didn't have any faith in may be just the one that comes through with great ideas and the right job lead. Just write the letters, and let nature take its course.

A NETWORK LETTER TO A BUSINESS ASSOCIATE

These letters work well for everyone and for all occasions. They work exceptionally well for people who have to conduct a job search campaign from a distance. If you're relocating or changing careers or jobs, write everyone you know a network letter.

Your business associates need not live where you plan to move. They can be anywhere in the world. It's a small world, and someone you write to in Hong Kong may know someone in Pierre, South Dakota—the place you're moving to.

You'll learn more about networking in Chapter 11.

Joy Powell
4518 NE Eighth Street
Denver CO 80239
(303) 555-4746

June 12, 19xx

Ms. Rhonda Raney, County Clerk
Grant County Courthouse
Canyon City, OR 97820

Dear Rhonda:

My husband and I will be moving back to Grant County in July. He has been retired for several years and likes retirement. Even though I have reached retirement age, I plan to continue working.

It is now more than twelve years since we worked together for the lumber company. Both of us have seen many changes during that time. It has given me pleasure to follow your success in your own business and now in public service.

You already know about my experience in accounting and banking. While living in the Willamette Valley, I had the opportunities to learn medical insurance billing and human resource management. When we returned to the East Side, I stayed in human resource management. That job was with a lumber company that went out of business. I know you understand the problems in the timber industry.

Even though I have many years of experience in several industries, I am always open to new challenges. My health is excellent, I have an abundance of energy, and I thrive on doing good work. I like being part of a team but also work well alone. Because I don't need a job for financial support, I am flexible in terms of time and money.

If you know of any employers in John Day or Canyon City who may be looking for a skilled, dedicated employee with a proven track record, please call me collect or send me their names and the titles of the positions they have open or pending. I will follow up directly with the ones that appear interesting, challenging, and rewarding. I am enclosing my updated resume. Please feel free to pass it on to anyone you think would be interested in seeing it.

Please give my warm regards to your brother, Richard. I always think of both of you on our common birthday.

Thank you for any assistance you can give me in my job search. I look forward to returning to John Day, and I will see you when I come to the courthouse to change my voter registration.

Best regards,

Joy
Joy Powell

Enclosure

Figure 8-10   Network Letter to a Business Associate. Courtesy of a client

It is good news, worth of all acceptation! and yet not too good to be true.

—Matthew Henry

Here are some reasons for writing an acceptance letter:

- It allows you to say thanks for the opportunity and to express your enthusiasm for the job and employer.

- It provides the opportunity to confirm your understanding of the terms of employment. Sometimes confusion occurs during the excitement of the job offer and acceptance. This is the time to get all the details verified.

- It provides written proof of verbal agreements. This can be critical if you negotiated an agreement different from the company's standard policy; for example, if it was agreed that you could take two weeks off in three months, even though no vacation time was due you.

Here are some points to remember when writing an acceptance letter.

- Begin with a short opening paragraph. Express your enthusiasm for joining the firm and thank the employer for the job.

- Spell out the terms of employment. Include all the terms agreed upon. This is especially important if there are terms that are different from the standard operating policies.

- Include a sentence to cover misunderstandings. This allows for face-saving by all parties.

- Restate your excitement for joining the company in the closing paragraph.

JoAnne Timmons

144 James Street   Bend, OR 97701   (503) 555-8396

May 15, 19xx

Ms. Ireneo Borja, Marketing Director
BUSINESS IDENTITY GRAPHICS
Water's Edge Business Center, Suite 203
3608 Juniper Street
Portland, OR 97201

Dear Ms. Borja:

Thank you for the great opportunity to work with you. I'm excited to be a part of your team and look forward to my first day. If I understood correctly all that we talked about, the terms of my employment are:

- Report to work on Thursday, June 1, 19xx, at 8:30 a.m.

- Salary is $28,000 annually with a 5% bonus override after $400,000 in sales.

- Salary review is in 3 months, then 6 months, then annually.

- Vacation allowance: 3 weeks after 1 year, 4 weeks after 3 years, 5 weeks after 10 years.

- Company-paid benefits include major medical, dental, vision, long-term disability, and $100,000 life insurance effective 30 days after first working day.

- Company-paid retirement with stock bonus options available after first full year of employment.

- Company car to be provided after first 30 days. Mileage allowance for personal car is $0.38/mile.

If there are discrepancies in my understanding, please call. Thanks again for this great opportunity. I'm looking forward to joining you next month.

Best regards,

JoAnne Timmons

JoAnne Timmons

Figure 8-11   Acceptance Letter

Beware of allowing a tactless word, a rebuttal, a rejection to obliterate the whole sky.

—Anïs Nin

Sometimes it is necessary to reject a job offer. You may find that the job is not right, that it doesn't meet your requirements, or that you have accepted another offer. Whatever the case may be, take the time to thank the employer for the offer.

If you need to reject an offer, handle it with care. It is a very small world, and you may be back at this employer's door again. Express your appreciation for the offer, then state your rejection. It isn't necessary to provide a reason or to expound on your reasons.

Consider these points when writing a letter of rejection:

- The first paragraph should express thanks for the job offer and then state your regrets of having to reject the offer.

- If appropriate, compliment the company on one aspect of its business (make sure it is a deserving aspect). The second paragraph can be used for this purpose. Try to sincerely praise the organization, staff, interviewer, or offer.

- Pure flattery can backfire. True praise will leave the door open for future opportunities.

- In the third and final paragraph you can restate your appreciation for the offer.

JoAnne Timmons

144 James Street   Bend, OR 97701   (503) 555-8396

May 8, 19xx

Ms. Phyliss LaMarche
LaMarche Communications Incorporated
753 Northwest Bond Street
Bend, Oregon 97701

Dear Ms. LaMarche:

Thank you for choosing me for your new Marketing Assistant. However, I regret that I will be unable to accept the offer at this time. Since the position is full-time and I still have one month before completing my degree, I feel that it's best for me to stay focused on my education. It would be difficult to give you the time and energy you deserve.

You have a fine organization and excellent people working for you. Ms. Mary Adams was exceptionally helpful. This has been a difficult decision, because I really would love to join your firm. Perhaps at another time.

Thanks again for the opportunity. I enjoyed meeting with you and learning about your company. I wish you and your company success. If I can be of any help to you in the future, please let me know.

Best regards,

Jo Anne Timmons

JoAnne Timmons

Figure 8-12   Rejection Letter

If you would not be forgotten,
As soon as you are dead and rotten,
Either write things worthy of reading
Or do things worth the writing.
    —Benjamin Franklin

Resigning is a rejection of sorts and must be handled tactfully. Resigning can be emotional, joyful, or sorrowful. It's a mixed bag to say the least.

Writing a resignation letter is your last opportunity to leave the company on a good note, no matter what the circumstances. Always leave an employer with dignity. Mend broken bridges, if necessary.

Your employer has provided you with a job for months, or possibly for many years. You've been paid for it, so it's fitting that you show your appreciation. Take the time to thank the employer for the job, to build good rapport, and to heal any wounds, if necessary.

Don't burn bridges; build and reinforce them. You never know, you may be back asking for help or a job in the future.

Lung Gui Fim
2211 Eleventh Avenue South 207
Manchester, New Hampshire 03103

June 30, 19xx

Mr. Robert Jamison, President
Acme Limited
Post Office Box 831
Manchester, New Hampshire 03105

Dear Mr. Jamison:

It is with regret that I submit my resignation as Vice President of Finance and Administration. I have accepted the position of Chief Executive Officer with Tomco Incorporated beginning September 1. My resignation is effective four weeks from today. If this creates any problems, I will gladly work through August 15 or discuss other alternatives.

It has been a pleasure to be associated with this organization and its people. I have enjoyed working with you. You have contributed immensely to my professional and personal growth. I will always be grateful for all that you have done.

It's with mixed emotions that I say "thanks" and "good-bye." I wish you continued success for your company. Thanks for everything and for the great opportunity to work for your company.

Sincerely,

Lung Gui Fim

Lung Gui Fim

Figure 8-13   Letter of Resignation

Read the letter aloud; the ear hears what the eye can't see.

Use the creative part of your brain to draft the letter. According to theory, your creative traits live in the right side of your brain. Your logical traits live in the left side of your brain and provide you with sequence and reason. Writing is an art, not a science. Draft your letter using your creativity. Don't fret about accuracy, errors, or spellings. Write the letter with feeling and let it flow; then rewrite it later. Just get a letter written; the hard work of editing comes later.

Set your letter aside before editing it. Writing is like making a decision—it's best to sleep on it, give it time to gel. Put it aside and do something else. It may be an hour or several days before you're ready to edit it. The amount of time is unimportant as long as you take some time between writing and editing.

Revise by ear; that is, read your letter aloud. Listen for the sounds, the movement of the words, the tone, and the structure. Hear your thoughts. Often you'll hear an attitude, word, or tone that needs to be changed because it doesn't sound right.

Ask yourself these questions:

Active voice: Have I written in the active voice? Have I built each sentence or idea around a specific action verb?

Short sentences: Have I kept my sentences short (six to seventeen words)? Long, rambling sentences are hard to read and even more difficult to understand. Have I cut out all unnecessary words and sentences?

Short paragraphs: Have I kept my paragraphs short (two to eight lines)? Paragraphs in job-hunting letters are usually shorter than those in literary writing. Ideally, each paragraph deals with one subject or a division of a lengthy subject.

One page: Have I kept my letter to one page? These are busy people; be considerate of their time. Besides, long-winded letters usually never get read. A lengthy letter is an immediate turnoff.

Short simple words: Have I used a one- or two-syllable word instead of a four- or five-syllable word? Consider substituting these words: *use* for *utilize, change* for *modification, quickly* for *expeditiously, later* for *subsequently, improve* for *ameliorate,* or *preventive* for *preventative.*

Nouns, adjectives, adverbs: Have I used a specific, tangible noun with each verb? Have I used a minimum number of modifiers? Does every word count? Have I used concrete, necessary adjectives and adverbs?

Editorialization: Have I stated fact, not opinion? Can I support each statement with an example?

I sentences: Have I eliminated as many *I*'s as possible? You want to write about what interests the employer, not about you and what you want.

Redundancies: Have I eliminated redundant usage? Here are a few examples:

Instead of	Write
General consensus of opinion	Consensus
Eliminate completely	Eliminate
Absolutely essential	Essential
Complete monopoly	Monopoly
Various and different	Different
Completely unanimous	Unanimous
May possibly	May
Advance warning	Warning
The current status	Status
Both the English and French translations	The English and French translations

Pretentious and nonconversational expressions: Have I avoided windy expressions and used everyday English? Here are some examples to consider:

> Apt words have power to suage the tumors of a troubled mind.
> **—Milton**

Instead of	Use
Please find enclosed, enclosed herewith	Enclosed, here
Attached hereto	Attached
Per annum	A year
The writer	I, me
Under separate cover	Separately
To date	Until now, as yet
Via, in due course	By, by first class, U.P.S.
At hand	Here
At all times	Always
Acknowledge receipt of	Thank you for
Advise	Tell, let know
Deem	Think
Per	By, through
In the manner of	Like
In the midst of	Among
Up to this writing	Until now
Is indicative of	Indicates
Whether or not	Whether
Am in a position	Can
Owing to the fact that	Because
In view of the fact that	Since
Meets with your approval	If satisfied, if you like
In the amount of	For
In regard to, in connection with, in accordance with,	About
In reference to, in re	About

Positive expression: Have I expressed myself in the affirmative, avoiding negative connotations and expressions? For example:

Instead of	Write
Problem	Challenge, opportunity
You won't be sorry	You'll be glad
If this information is not sufficient	If you would like further information
Do not hesitate to call/write	Please call/write
To avoid further delay	To hasten delivery

Correct word usage: Have I used the right word? The following words are often misused, confused, or abused. If you have used one of these words in your letter, make sure you have used the correct word for the meaning you intend.

Advice/advise	Discreet/discrete	Its/it's
Affect/effect	Disinterested/uninterested	Lay/lie
Allude/refer	Economic/economical	Lend/loan
Allusion/illusion	Eminent/imminent	Like/as
Alright/all right	Enthuse	Loose/lose
Alternate/alternative	Etc.	Meantime/meanwhile
Among/between	Farther/further	People/persons
Ante-/anti-	Fewer/less	Predominant/predominate
Bi-/semi-	Firstly/secondly	Principal/principle
Can/may	Flammable/inflammable	Regardless/irregardless
Capital/capitol	Foreword/forward	Shall/will
Chose/choose/chosen	Fortuitous/fortunate	Stationary/stationery
Complement/compliment	Good/well	That/which
Continually/continuous	Hopefully	Was/were
Council/counsel/consul	I/me/myself	Which/who
Different from/different than	Imply/infer	Who/whom
	Insure/ensure/assure	

Transitions: Does each sentence flow smoothly and logically after the sentence before? Does each paragraph also move logically and smoothly? Good use of transitional words is your key. Here are some helpful hints:

- However, still, yet, otherwise, in contrast, on the contrary—indicate change or contrast.

- Therefore, thus, consequently, accordingly, hence, for this reason—introduce conclusions.

- In the same way, likewise, similarly—introduce comparisons.

- For example, for instance, let's say, let us assume—precede illustrations.

- Obviously, fortunately, naturally—initiate opinions.

- In fact, in any event, indeed—signify intensification.

- Again, in other words, as you know, as I mentioned—indicate repetition.

- By the way—shows relative importance.

- Also, in addition, further, moreover—indicate additions.

- In summary, in brief, in conclusion, on the whole, in short—indicate a summary.

- For this reason, with this goal in mind—stipulate suitable action.

Readability: Have I made this letter enjoyable to read? Here are some suggestions for improving the readability of a letter:

- Use lots of white space.

- Left-justify. When you justify right margins, large gaps between words and/or letters are created. This makes it more difficult to read.

- Use a business style font that is large enough to read. Don't shrink the font to get all the information on one page; rework the letter and eliminate unnecessary words, sentences, etc.

- Use a laser printer, even if you have to borrow one or visit a friend.

- Get professional help if you need it.

- Eliminate the *I* word as much as possible.

THE AGONY AND ECSTASY OF JOB HUNTING

Life shrinks or expands in proportion to one's courage.

— Anaïs Nin

Job hunting is not easy. Job hunting can be an emotional roller coaster. Letters are more than mere records. They tell the story and capture the pain, the excitement, the highs, the lows. Here is part of Michele's story.

MICHELE LEATHERS

2232 N.W. Everett   Portland, OR 97210   (503) 555-3512

May 29, 19xx

Dear Maurice:

As promised, here is a copy of my resume. I have a really big favor to ask of you, though, before you begin distributing this copy. I don't feel prepared enough to just hand you a resume and let you distribute it yet. I would like my resume and myself to be perfect, and the only way I know how is to ask you to assist me in my efforts.

My resume is really a rough draft. I've worked hard on it, but I'm sure there are ways to make improvements. Any suggestions? I know you are a very busy man, but I would truly appreciate it if you could read over the resume and possibly give me some recommendations. I'll give them careful consideration.

Also, there is a "strengths and weaknesses" sheet. Could you answer the questions concerning my strengths and weaknesses? I know I will learn a lot about myself when you do. I value your opinion and encourage you to be open and honest, especially when it comes to my weaknesses.

I want to do my best before approaching your organization. All help will be much appreciated.

Thank you so much for your time.

Best regards,

Michele Leathers

Michele Leathers

Enclosed: Resume
          Personal reference
          Self-addressed stamped

Figure 8-14 Network Letter.
Courtesy of a client

Agony is waiting, hoping, losing, and hard work. It is doing what has to be done when it has to be done. Agony is planning, preparing, doing.

In the follow-up letter (Figure 8-14), Michele asks for help with her resume and for an evaluation of her strengths and weaknesses. Then she thanks Maurice for all his help.

MICHELE LEATHERS

2232 N.W. Everett   Portland, OR 97210   (503) 555-3512

May 29, 19xx

Dear Jody:

How are you doing, besides being extremely busy? First of all, I want to thank you for calling the other day and giving me the opportunity to get my foot in the door with the company. I haven't received a phone call though, so I think that one might have slipped through my fingers.

What I am really writing about is to ask yet another favor of you. I have enclosed a rough draft of my resume and wondered if you might take the time to read over it and give me some recommendations on it.

I'm staying with Mom and Dad and will be here for probably another month unless something jumps out and grabs me. Jody, I know you are busy, but I would really appreciate your input.

Thanks so much for all of your help,

Michele

Figure 8-15 Network Letter. Courtesy of a client

For the follow-up letter in Figure 8-15, Michele says thanks for a referral and then tells Jody the results of her call. Michele also asks for help with her resume.

For the network letter in Figure 8-16, Michele touches base with a former college professor, letting her know she is job hunting and catching Joyce up on the past and her plans. Again, she asks for advice on her resume.

MICHELE LEATHERS

2232 N.W. Everett   Portland, OR 97210   (503) 555-3512

May 29, 19xx

Hello, Joyce!

As you can see, I have returned to the states and am all in one piece. Barely. My knee rehab is going very well, and I have even begun running some. However, this is proving to be a very long process.

The reason I'm writing, besides simply to say hello, is to ask a very big favor of you. I have enclosed a copy of my rough draft resume. I would appreciate it if you could find the time to read it and give me some feedback as to improving it. I also want to know if I could use your name as a reference. I'd like to get a feel for what you might say my strengths and weaknesses would be. So, if you could take the time to fill out the personal reference request form, I'd be forever in your debt.

I have finally found some direction outside of hiking and basketball, just like you told me I would that day at the restaura~~nt in Laramie. My dream is to assist~~ and eventually work my way to the have a lot to learn and a long w that, but I must start somewhe greatly appreciated.

OK, enough of the busine Everything is fine here. It is nic great parents I have.

Oh yes, I have officially re bit. Basketball has been very g any of the time spent on the co

Please tell your family hel help, Joyce.

Love,
Michele

Figure 8-16 Network Letter.
Courtesy of a client

The network letter in Figure 8-17 touches base with a former college basketball coach . . . who better to help her get inside sports contacts? She asks Dave to review her resume and complete a personal reference request form. She tells him her plans for the future.

MICHELE LEATHERS

2232 N.W. Everett   Portland, OR 97210   (503) 555-3512

May 29, 19xx

Mr. Dave Arnold, President
DAVE ARNOLD PRODUCTIONS
University of Wyoming
Laramie, WY 82070

Dear Dave,

Hello there, do you remember me? How could you possibly forget, right? How have you been, Dave? Are you still doing the coaches' shows?

You are probably wondering, "Where has Michele been and what has she been doing?" Well, for the past two years I have been spending my time in Adelaide, South Australia. Since I've been down there, I have been hampered with nothing but injuries; from breaking my feet and having to be put back together to blowing my knee this past January and having to have an ACL reconstruction. Yes, Dave, I have decided to retire from the sport that has taken me so far.

I returned to the states a couple of weeks ago and have been working very hard to get my resume in order and begin the difficult job of looking for work. So I am writing not only to say hello but to ask a favor of you. I realize you are a very busy person and you probably thought you were rid of me with the last reference letter you wrote two years ago; but, Dave, I'm back!

If you have time, please review my resume. I would really appreciate it. I also would like to list you as a personal reference and need your permission to do so. Therefore, I have enclosed a personal reference request form. It will really help me to know what you will say about me to an employer. Would you please complete the form and return it to me in the enclosed envelope.

Dave, I'm sorry I haven't stayed in better touch with you since I've been "down under." I know that this is a lot to ask of you out of the blue, but I am trying to get a life outside of basketball started. I am focusing on public relations instead of television. My dream is to go to work for the Portland Trailblazers. I realize I have a lot of work to do before I can set my sights this high, but I'm hoping that with the help of you and Maggie, I'll be headed in the right direction soon.

Thank you so much for your time, and I truly hope to hear from you soon. Please tell everyone hello from me in the great "Cowboy Country."

Sincerely,
Michele Leathers

Figure 8-17 Network Letter. Courtesy of a client

May 24, 19xx

Dearest Cheryl,

I know we have a long way to go before I'll be the "perfect product," but you will never know how much your help and enthusiasm means. I'll do my best for you and I'll keep working hard. I'll get what I want with you by my side!

Thank you so much for everything! You mean the world to me, Cheryl!
Love,
Michele

In Figure 8-18, Michele writes a thank-you note to a friend. During the job hunt, your friends are invaluable. Stay close to those who support your goals and believe in you. Sometimes only a friend can keep you going.

Figure 8-18 Thank-You Note. Courtesy of a client

Here's another network letter (Figure 8-19). Reestablishing contact, touching base, keeping everyone informed, following up on referrals and leads, and saying thanks are all elements of a well-organized job hunt. It takes time to write letters, but it will pay off.

MICHELE LEATHERS

2232 N.W. Everett   Portland, OR 97210   (503) 555-3512

May 30, 19xx

Dear Ted,

How are you and your family doing? Well, I am doing just fine. I have returned to the states and am all in one piece, barely. I don't know if you have spoken to Dad or not, but I had a rather unfortunate accident in my first game this season and ended up tearing my knee up. Therefore, I've decided to hand over the basketball responsibilities to someone younger.

Besides writing to simply say hello, I am writing to ask a rather big favor of you. Enclosed is a rough draft of my resume. I wonder if you might take the time to look it over and possibly send me back some recommendations on improving it before I head out into the cruel world of job searching. I am emphasizing public relations because I have decided this would be more up my alley than sitting under hot lights and reading someone else's script.

I also wanted to know if I could use you as a personal reference. I have enclosed a personal reference request form. If you could possibly fill this out, it would be much appreciated.

It is nice to be home; every time I come back, I realize what great parents I have. For the first time in my life, however, Ted, my road is not perfectly paved, and I'm really having to work to achieve my goal. I guess I'm a little scared.

Well, I have some things I'd better be taking care of. Ted, please tell everyone hello for me, and I will be in touch. Take care. Thanks for all the help.

Love ya!
Michele

Figure 8-19 Network Letter. Courtesy of a client

Figure 8-20 shows another thank-you letter that Michele wrote after an interview.

MICHELE LEATHERS

2232 N.W. Everett   Portland, OR 97210   (503) 555-3512

June 7, 19xx

Mr. Samuel Goldstein, CLU, ChFc
President
Pacific Cascade Insurance Companies
1584 NE Yamhill, Suite 200
Portland, OR 97205

Dear Mr. Goldstein,

Just a short note to say thank you for the time you gave me on Wednesday. I also greatly appreciate all the company information you gave me.

I 've been reading the material and must admit that I don't understand a great deal of it. I find myself in unfamiliar territory, and this concerns me. However, with the advice you've given me, I get the feeling that almost everyone who has walked through your doors for the first time felt the same way I do. I do, however, have confidence in myself to learn anything I set my mind to.

Once again, thanks for yo
pleasure meeting you and

Sincerely,

Michele Leathers

Michele Leathers

Figure 8-20 Thank-You Letter.
Courtesy of a client

AGONY . . .

In the follow-up letter shown in Figure 8-21, Michele is touching base again. She has been through more agony and needs to share with a friend.

MICHELE LEATHERS

2232 N.W. Everett   Portland, OR 97210   (503) 555-3512

June 12, 19xx

Dear Joyce,

Thank you so much for your helpful comments on my resume and for your wonderful letter. I'm sorry about surprising you with my "knee news." I thought I had written you a letter right after it happened. Oops, I guess not. Well, during the first ten minutes of my first game, I went one way and my right knee went the other. I tore my anterior cruitate ligament in two and had to have reconstructive surgery. Like I said before, the rehab is going fine.

I have had my first interview with a life insurance company. It was really a good experience, but I don't think I would like the life of an insurance salesperson. However, I am not closing any doors. I am also meeting with some people from Nike next Tuesday and would not be disappointed at all if I could get a position there. I'm also making a few more contacts with the Trailblazer people. Dave called me the other night; he is a good friend of one of the assistant coaches for the Blazers, so he is helping me out on his end too.

I'm finding myself a little stressed out though, Joyce. I love being home and seeing Mom and Dad, but it is time to get going with a career. I just feel like I'm at a crossroads as to what to do. I need something to just fall out of the sky for me. Do you think there is a possibility of that, Joyce? Neither do I.

I suppose I will feel better when and if I begin getting some job offers. Then I can start planning more of a future. I really appreciated the compliments and comments about my resume. I have made the changes and had it laser printed, as you can tell by the enclosed copy.

Thanks, Joyce, for your help and support. It is greatly appreciated; you'll never know how much. I'll keep in touch, so you'll know what's happening.

Love,

Michele

Figure 8-21 Follow-Up Letter. Courtesy of a client

> August 7, 19xx
>
> Dearest Cheryl,
>
> How's my friend? Well, your little job hunter is hanging in there. I didn't get the Blazer job. But both interviewers called me to tell me how well I had done. The two guys who were in the finals had both worked for the Blazers for six years. And I was third. That still doesn't make me feel much better. However, both interviewers gave me a good recommendation for a future public relations job coming open in a few weeks. So I'm picking myself up off the floor and going to do my best to nab this next one.
>
> It's awfully hard, but I'm hanging in there, hoping something will come my way soon. Thanks again for all of your help and support.
>
> Love ya!
> Michele

Figure 8-22 **Personal Note.** Courtesy of a client

As evidenced by the personal note in Figure 8-22, Michele is still having a difficult job search. So she shares her troubles with another friend.

ECSTASY AT LAST!

Michele has finally gotten the job she wants. She shares her excitement with a friend (Figure 8-23).

Ecstasy. What is ecstasy? It is getting the right job with the right company, in the right location, for the right money!

What's in a letter? You tell me.

> October 15, 19xx
>
> Dearest Cheryl,
>
> Alas! Please observe my first business card! I just got them today, and you are the first to receive one.
>
> Work is great! I am attending a sales seminar tomorrow in downtown Portland. Should be good! I have started training people and making some good contacts. No sales as of yet, but it's only my second day. So I guess I can't complain. The hardest part is building my clientele, but I will in due time!
>
> Well, I just wanted to write a quick note to say hello. Take care. I look forward to seeing you soon!
>
> Love,
> Michele
>
> P.S. I get to have stationery with my own name on it. It's almost too good to be true.

Figure 8-23 **Personal Note.** Courtesy of a client

CHAPTER 9

CREATE A CONFIDENT YOU
The Finished Product

We are all apprentices in a craft where no one becomes a master.
—Ernest Hemingway

Just a few days ago, Sherrie called and asked what to wear to an interview. She was confused. The employees wore jeans and sweatshirts—should she dress like them? Should she wear informal attire for the interview? After we discussed the situation in depth, she decided to dress professionally. When she arrived at the interview, she found that the bosses had "dressed up" for the occasion. "Boy, was I glad I dressed up," she told me. "It gave me confidence and poise. I felt great." Sherrie got the job.

It's the small things that give you confidence. As I've watched students and clients prepare the written materials and practice their interviews, I've learned that personal appearance and little touches bring together the total look. In this chapter you will learn how to package a confident you.

FIRST IMPRESSIONS

You may never know when you made the all-important first impression on an employer. It may have been the first telephone call, the job application, the resume, or when you walked through the employer's door. Whenever that first impression took place, you can be assured that the first impression is a lasting impression.

FIRST JUDGMENT made within four seconds.
FINAL JUDGMENT made within 30 seconds.
OUTWARD APPEARANCE is 93 percent of impression.

Many applicants believe the first impression is made when they walk through the interviewer's doors. However, this may be far from the truth. The first impression begins with the first contact made with the company or the interviewer. For the interviewer, the first impression of you may happen when he or she first picks up your job application.

First impressions are made quickly. Whether we're talking job applications, personal visits, or telephone conversations, the first impression is based on outward appearance. Many first impressions are lasting, can be superficial, and may be totally incorrect.

OUTWARD APPEARANCES CREATE FIRST IMPRESSIONS

Your outward appearance is your visual resume.

Outward appearance (the clothes you wear, the smile on your face, the way you talk, the way you walk) makes up 93 percent of the first impression. Resumes, job applications, letters, and phone calls all possess qualities of outward appearances. The first impression happens fast. Therefore, it is critical to understand and control its impact.

55%	Physical impression (attire, posture, facial expressions, body language)
38	Voice and speech patterns (tone, rate, pitch)
93%	The outward appearance
7	The words you speak
100%	The total message

The first judgement is made in approximately four seconds, and the final judgement takes only about thirty seconds. As you can see, a job applicant could be rejected in only a few seconds based on superficial elements. Therefore, it is important to build rapport by making positive impressions. Avoid damage by eliminating negative impressions. Take the time to make a good, lasting impression. Remember, outward appearance makes up 93 percent of the first impression. We will now examine ways to control these first impressions.

CONTROL THE HOW, WHEN, AND WHERE OF FIRST IMPRESSIONS

You never get a second chance to make a first impression.

There are choices you can make concerning the how, when, and where to make that first impression. Let's examine five methods.

BY TELEPHONE

Use the telephone. It is the quickest and most efficient way to contact an employer. Prepare a script; know what you're going to say. Practice the conversation; then make the call. Be friendly and professional. Don't waste time chatting; the person on the other end has other things to do.

BY LETTER AND RESUME

Write a professional business letter, and attach your resume. Pay attention to all the details. Review the chapters on letter and resume writing. After a week or ten days, make a follow-up phone call. Build on the first positive impression by being prepared. Have your script or cluster ready for the conversation. Stick to business. Be friendly and professional.

ON A JOB APPLICATION

There may be no other way to create a first impression than by filling out a job application. If this is the case, study the application carefully and follow the employer's directions. If you choose to ignore the instructions on the application, do so by doing more than what's expected. Make sure the application is neat and clean. Write legibly. Spell and use words correctly. Provide complete information. Attach your resume. Make your application a positive experience for the employer to read.

BY REFERRAL

Ask a mutual friend to call an employer for you. This paves the way for you. Just recently I did this for a friend. The person I called telephoned my friend immediately. They got together and struck a deal. Both parties were comfortable with the transaction from the very beginning because there was a mutual friend running interference.

THROUGH PERSONAL MEETING

Dropping in unannounced works sometimes, but, generally, it's not a good idea. Running from employer to employer takes a tremendous amount of time and money. It's best to stay home, work the phones, write your letters, and wait for an appointment before visiting an employer uninvited. If you do decide to drop in unexpected, don't expect to receive the red-carpet treatment. Busy people can't always accommodate an unexpected visitor. Call or write and make an appointment first. It will be appreciated.

By choosing the time, place, and method of your first impression, you can control factors that might otherwise work against you. For example, an overweight job applicant made his first impression over the telephone and by letter. Because he had already made a strong positive impression, his physical appearance was not an issue at the interview. Another applicant was physically disabled; she decided to have a friend call an employer to recommend her for a job. This opened the door for her to meet with the employer. These methods worked for both job applicants. Besides opening doors, the applicants felt more confident.

Whenever possible, control the how, when, and where for each first impression. You want to establish a strong first impression; it has long-lasting effects. Let's examine further the effect of a first impression.

POSITIVE AND NEGATIVE IMPRESSIONS

Positive Impressions Create Rapport

What is rapport? Genie Z. Laborde, author of *Influencing with Integrity*, writes, "Rapport is like money, it increases in importance when you do not have it, and when you do have it, a lot of opportunities appear."

Rapport is a relationship marked by harmony, accord, and good chemistry. It is what you want to happen when you call an employer, complete a job application, write a resume, and land an interview. You want to create positive impressions and have these impressions continue and build with each contact. You want the positive impressions to continue long after the job hunt.

There are many ways to create rapport. Matching or mirroring the person's body language and speech patterns are two methods. For example, when a person speaks rapidly, adjust your speech rate to match. Dressing according to the company's culture is another way to create rapport. In Exercise 9-3, we'll look at some specific ways to build rapport by matching or mirroring another person.

Negative Impressions Require Damage Control

Negative impressions happen when you fail to create rapport. When you fail to meet employers' expectations, you enter a damage control phase.

Damage control means you're on the defensive, and this is not what you want to happen. Once you are in this position, you face an uphill battle. It's a struggle you can't afford. Damage control takes time and energy—time and energy that should be spent on other projects.

There are many ways to eliminate or at least reduce negative impressions. The limitations of this text don't allow for a full examination, but we will look at some basics to broaden your awareness of the importance of first impressions.

Now, let's examine some things that create the first impression and ways to control or improve these impressions, beginning with your outward appearance.

Before Leaving Home or After Eating Out . . .

Check yourself in the mirror before entering the employer's office. Check your hair, makeup, teeth, and attire. Make sure there's no food caught in your teeth, that your hair is neat and in place, and that there's no food on your tie or blouse. This last-minute check can eliminate a potentially embarrassing moment.

YOU TELL ON YOURSELF
You tell on yourself by the friends you seek,
By the very manner in which you speak,
By the way you employ your leisure time,
By the use you make of dollar and dime.

You tell what you are by the things you wear,
By the spirit in which your burdens bear,
By the kind of things at which you laugh,
By the records you play on your phonograph.

You tell what you are by the way you walk,
By the things of which you delight to talk,
By the manner in which you bear defeat,
By so simple a thing as how you eat.

By the books you choose from a well-filled shelf,
In these ways and more, you tell on yourself.
So there's really no particle of sense
In an effort to keep up false pretense.

You tell on yourself.

—Author Unknown

Because it is common for job applicants to have two or three interviews before being offered a job, it pays to prepare a minimum of three interview outfits. I've known cases where applicants were interviewed six and seven times. So get ready, you may need several outfits.

When choosing interview outfits, analyze the situation and possible interview settings. First and subsequent interviews may take place in the same office, but this is not always the case. Terry had her first interview at the office, the second interview was a trip through the mines, and the third interview took place at an elegant restaurant. Each interview required different clothing, not because she was meeting with the same people, but because the interviews involved varying activities.

When you know what you're going to wear, your time is free and your mind is at ease to concentrate on other important aspects of the job interview. Set your interview clothes aside. Then they're readily available when you need them. If an unexpected interview comes up, you can be ready in minutes.

Let's examine a conservative wardrobe for the standard first interview setting—the office interview.

The best advice I can give you about dressing is to buy and read *Dress for Success,* by John T. Molloy. Everything you ever needed to know about dressing professionally is in there. Buy it, read it, and follow it. Another good book to read is *Professional Presence,* by Susan Bixler. Following is a short summary of business attire for men.

The Suit

The suit is the most important garment you'll wear. Interviewers often judge your character, abilities, and income by your suit. Because a suit is the most expensive article in your wardrobe, take care and time to buy one that fits you and your needs.

A BUSINESSMAN'S WARDROBE

**Any man may be in good spirits and
good temper when he's well dressed.
—Charles Dickens**

Choose a wool or quality wool blend suit in a solid color. Blue or gray are your best choices. Select a plain, single-breasted style without fancy buttons, stitching, or other decorations. Be sure the suit fits properly. Pay special attention to sleeve and pant lengths.

Shirts and Ties

The white, long-sleeved dress shirt is still the best business shirt to wear for all occasions. Buy at least two. If you can afford it, also buy a solid blue or a pin-striped shirt. Buy tailored shirts with removable plastic collar stays. Polyester or cotton blend shirts hold up well and do not wrinkle. They are practical for everyday wear.

The tie may be a small item, but besides the suit, it is the most important item in your attire. The tie broadcasts your life status. Pay particular attention to its purchase. Choose a quality, solid-colored silk or a polyester silk look alike. Blue and red are basic colors. Texture, pattern, and color need to be coordinated with your shirt and suit. Besides a solid-colored tie, a blue tie with small white polka dots or a diagonally striped tie is a suitable selection. Avoid bow ties because interviewers would have a hard time taking you seriously.

When choosing colors for shirts and ties, remember that the shirt must be lighter than the suit and that the tie must be darker than the shirt. Two successful combinations for suit, shirt, and tie are (1) solid blue or grey suit, white shirt, small polka dot or striped tie, and (2) solid suit, pin-striped shirt, solid tie.

Shoes, Socks, Handkerchiefs, and T-Shirts

With a limited budget buy plain black lace or wing-tip dress shoes (black goes with everything). Shoes must be shined, clean, and in good repair. Buy black or dark blue over-the-calf dress socks and white hand-rolled cotton or linen handkerchiefs. Choose V-necked T-shirts so your T-shirt won't show if you wear an open-collared shirt.

Briefcase, Wallet, Coat, Umbrella, and Gloves

Your briefcase should be dark brown leather, plain, and functionable. Both the hip-pocket and secretary type wallet in rich dark brown leather are okay. The secretary type wallet fits inside the suit pocket and is an upper-middle class status symbol. Your wallet should never be stuffed. It should be well organized and contain appropriate credit cards. Select a quality beige raincoat with a black umbrella. According to John Molloy, "Beige raincoats are worn by members of the upper-middle classes and black rain-coats are worn by the lower-middle classes." Choose dark brown leather gloves.

Belts, Jewelry, and Pens

Choose a dark brown or black leather belt with a small traditional buckle. A thin, plain gold watch and wedding ring are the only acceptable jewelry for the job interview. Earrings, beads, chains, cuff links, fancy buckles, lapel pins, and tie bars and tacks should not be worn. Buy a quality thin gold or silver pen and pencil set. Having two pens is a good idea, or at least carry a spare ink cartridge with you. Erasable black ink is recommended.

Hair, Beards, Mustaches, and Grooming

Hair must be clean and well trimmed. It should be styled within the context of the employer's culture and position you are seeking. What really matters during the interview is that your haircut meet the expectations of the employer. Beards and mustaches almost always create negative impressions.

Bob told me this story about his interview:

> I'm so glad I paid attention to my attire and appearance. There were over 2,000 applicants and only 200 jobs. I wanted one of them. I dressed professionally even when I went to complete the application. I got out my suit, white shirt, tie, dark dress socks and shoes. I shaved off my beard and had my hair cut and styled. I looked so different; my wife didn't recognize me. Naturally, I felt good about myself. I got the interview and the job. I'm glad I learned the importance of wearing a suit for the job interview. It made a difference. On the job, I wear sweaters, jeans and tennis shoes, but I never would have gotten the job if it wasn't for the suit. The suit made the difference.

A PROFESSIONAL WOMAN'S WARDROBE

Style is the dress of thoughts.
—Philip Dormer Stanhope

Choosing attire for the job interview is one of the most important decisions you will make. If you are a professional woman, a skirted business suit is essential. This is appropriate for secretaries, clerical positions, sales jobs, and most other jobs. Now if you are applying for a job in a skilled trade, your attire may need adjustments. Common sense should play a major role in the selection of attire. Because dress is such an important part of getting a job, buy and read *The Woman's Dress for Success Book,* by John T. Molloy, or *Color Me Beautiful,* by Carole Jackson. You'll be glad you did.

A general rule of thumb for attire is to wear clothes comparable to others working in similar positions. Another general rule is to dress as if you were applying for a position one or two steps higher than the job you're interviewing for.

The Business Suit

Choose a solid-colored gray or medium blue skirted suit with a blazer-cut jacket. The jacket should be fingertip in length and loose enough to cover the contours of the bust. Wool, wool blends, and linen are the most suitable materials. Wool comes in a variety of weights, therefore allowing you to select one for all seasons.

Avoid high fashion and fads when purchasing your suit. Buy quality. The skirt should be a comfortable length, preferably to the knee. If you find yourself tugging at your skirt while sitting, it's too short.

The Blouse/Shirt

The best blouse is a tailored shirt with long sleeves and no ruffles or frills. Cotton, silk, or quality look-alikes are appropriate materials. The best and most versatile color is white.

Appropriate attire, style, and color create a picture of authority, presence, and trust. For example, a white blouse projects authority; a pale yellow blouse builds likability and credibility. A pale pink blouse is too soft for an interview and destroys authority. Study the effects of color and style; then match the appropriate style and color to your purpose and audience.

Shoes, Hosiery, Briefcase, Purse, and Wallet

Buy sensible low-heeled pumps, with quiet soles and heels, no open toes or heels. The best colors are blue, black, dark brown, or gray. Shoes should be polished, clean, and in good repair. Wear skin-colored pantyhose.

A dark brown leather briefcase is standard. If you can afford it, match your briefcase, shoes, and purse. This creates a visually attractive appearance. I prefer a soft-sided briefcase that sits on the floor. By sitting my briefcase on the floor next to me, I can easily retrieve documents without placing it on a desk or table.

There is a debate on whether you should carry a purse. I've found that it works nicely for me. I use a purse with a shoulder strap that matches my briefcase. By having my purse, I'm able to pull out my wallet, lipstick, or pen without having to open my briefcase. Your wallet should be dark brown or black leather with no designs or gadgets. Your purse and wallet should be organized so you don't have to fumble around for keys, credit cards, or pens. Keep your purse and wallet orderly. Get rid of all unnecessary items.

Jewels, Scarves, and Pens

Appearances to the mind are of four kinds. Things either are what they appear to be; or they neither are, nor appear to be; or they are, and do not appear to be; or they are not, and yet appear to be. Rightly to aim in all these cases is the wise man's task.

—Epictetus

When it comes to jewelry, keep it simple; less is better. Jewelry should be functional or give you presence. A small gold watch is really all you need. A wedding ring or a small, unpretentious ring is appropriate. Bracelets and dangling earrings are taboo. Earrings should be no larger than your eyes. If you have expensive jewelry, do not wear it on the first meeting. You don't want to evoke feelings of jealousy. Save the expensive jewelry for an elegant evening out.

Scarves add variety and color to an otherwise standard suit or dress. They are an inexpensive way to add zest to an outfit. The best styles are the ascot, a long tie that wraps around the neck, and a large square. The best patterns are solid colored, stripe, plaid, paisley, and polka-dot. Buy silk scarves or polyester scarves that look like silk. Avoid designer labels; they are overpriced and considered in poor taste. Also avoid a man's tie.

Buy a quality thin gold pen and pencil set. It should be comfortable in your hand. Try to find pens with erasable black ink. Always carry a spare pen or ink cartridge with you.

Coat, Gloves, and Umbrella

Because a coat broadcasts your socioeconomic level and is sometimes the only piece of attire showing, you should take special care in its selection. If you can only afford one coat, make it a quality beige raincoat. You can find some with zip-out linings that allow you to use the same coat for all seasons. The coat should completely cover your suit skirt or dress, (no hems showing, please). For a winter coat, buy a camel-colored wraparound. If you are overweight, select a single-breasted coat. Buy dark brown, black, or gray leather gloves. A quality umbrella has ten or more solid spokes and should be large enough to keep the rain off. A black or tan umbrella with no gaudy attachments is a good choice.

Hair, Makeup, and Grooming

Hair should be medium length (short but not masculine and no longer than shoulder length). It should be styled so you don't have to fiddle with it. Your hair can be wavy, but not too curly. Curly and long hair send the wrong messages; they're sexy, not professional.

Makeup should be subtle and understated. It should be used, but invisible. Avoid obvious eye shadow and eyeliner. Mascara takes special attention. Use the type that doesn't smear or run in rain or tears. Use lipstick that blends in, not stands out. Use perfume sparingly; if it can be noticed, it's too much.

Wendy wore business attire for her interviewer at Safeway. She was hired as a boxer. After she began working, her boss told her: "The real reason I hired you was because you dressed professionally for the interview."

There is much more that could be said about attire. We've just touched the basics here. Buy a couple of good books on the subject. Shop carefully. Buy quality. It's a wise investment. Expensive doesn't necessarily mean quality or correct style. If you err, be sure to err on the conservative side.

BRIEFCASE TIPS

A well-packed briefcase should contain the following:

1. Writing tools—a quality gold or silver pen and pencil set, which includes two erasable black ink pens and two pencils with erasers; and a notepad (scratch paper)
2. Activity planner—a calendar (showing year/month/week) and addresses and phone numbers
3. Pocket dictionary
4. Data file
5. Resume (ten copies)
6. Reference list (ten copies)
7. Three to five reference letters (five copies)
8. Company dossier
9. Portfolio (examples of your work, if appropriate)
10. List of questions to ask the employer

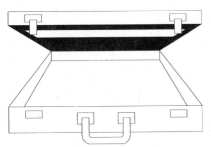

Miscellaneous Items

Optional items for your briefcase include breath mints, toothbrush, dental floss, quick shoe shine kit, and a small sewing kit. You may want to include office supplies, such as a stapler, rubber bands, and a staple remover.

For women, slip these additional items in your purse, if you choose to carry one (otherwise, carry them in your briefcase): tissues or a handkerchief, spare pantyhose, and a makeup kit.

PORTFOLIO POINTERS

It's quality rather than quantity that matters.
—Lucius Anaeus Seneca

A portfolio is a collection of your best works in a variety of areas. It is assembled to capture the best essence of your abilities and talents. It is presented to support claims of professional expertise. Your portfolio is a testament of your achievements and experience.

Who Needs A Portfolio?

Carpenters, bricklayers, writers, artists, and models all could use a portfolio of their work. And the list doesn't stop there. Anyone who feels that a physical presentation of his or her work would improve the chances of getting a job offer could benefit from using a portfolio.

As you prepare your portfolio, consider quality, variety, holders or folders, and testing.

Quality and Quantity

Quantity confuses; quality enlightens. Always choose quality over quantity. An interviewer doesn't have time to wade through dozens of samples. Select three to five styles, and provide one to five examples for each style. The portfolio should have at least three styles and no more than twelve examples. Each should be an example of your highest quality work. Keep your portfolio small. You can always provide additional samples later.

Variety

Variety is the spice of life. Select variety, not duplication. The key to a quality portfolio is diversification. Establish three to five varied examples for each category or style. Strive for variety of examples within each group. Concentrate on the employer's interest. Build your portfolio on the requirements of the job.

Holders, Folders, and More

Select a suitable holder, binder, or case to hold your portfolio. Put your portfolio in a quality case that suits the size and spirit of your work. Your examples will dictate the type of holder. The physical layout and order depend on the work.

If your work doesn't fit in a binder or folder, what do you do? Sam, a tile layer, took beautiful, colored pictures of his work and placed them in a three-ring notebook. Jennifer, a watercolor artist, included originals and photographs of her work. She selected an artist's portfolio case.

When purchasing a portfolio case, consider ease of transporting, carrying, displaying, and organizing. A loose-leaf, three-ring binder is one example of an inexpensive, flexible holder. It allows for flexibility, easy organization, and ease of carrying. This binder meets the needs of many job applicants. Artists have special cases for portfolios. Sample cases used by many salespeople is another alternative. If your examples are heavy and bulky, consider getting a case on wheels like the airline pull luggage.

For those with different needs, visit a large stationery store and ask to see portfolio and sample cases. Request a catalog to take home to study.

Testing

You will want to practice showing your portfolio before you start interviewing. Before starting the job hunt, practice showing your portfolio

to friends with a critical eye for detail. Choose those who will provide you with constructive evaluation and an honest assessment. Solicit comments for improvement in the selection of samples, on the holder, and on the presentation. Listen closely to their suggestions. Keep an open mind; then make changes if necessary.

Your portfolio tells as much about you as the work itself. You will use it as a backup for your claims, not as a sole demonstration of your work. Outstanding examples of your work provide an employer with concrete evidence of your capabilities. A portfolio can make or break you. Take time for quality; it pays.

NONVERBAL COMMUNICATIONS

A man's attire, and excessive laughter, and gait, show what he is.
—**The Apocrypha**

Nonverbal communication is considered the true expression of oneself, of one's emotions. It is your personal style for self-expression. It works at the unconscious level and involves all your senses: sight, hearing, touch, smell, feelings, and taste. In the business world, nonverbal communications are those things seen, heard, and felt.

Nonverbal communications encompass posture, touch, body movement, facial expressions, dress, and voice (tone, pitch, volume, and rate). These communications are your being. They form the nucleus of your true identity.

Research has determined that only about 7 percent of the impression you make on another person comes from the words you speak. This means that 93 percent of your total impact is based on nonverbal communications, or physical (55 percent) and voice (38 percent) factors.

Because nonverbal communications play a major role in creating an impression of who you are, let's look for the messages in the following examples.

What's In A Face?

If you were on the other side of this door, what message would you be feeling from the woman in the picture? Is she happy with you? Does she like you?

What message does the man's face tell you? Does he approve of you? Is he proud of what you've done?

What kind of face causes you to feel happy or liked? Demonstrate it.

What kind of face makes you feel inadequate? Make one.

What kind of face makes you feel trustworthy? Demonstrate it.

What are your impressions of each of these people? How do you feel about the attire each person is wearing? What about their facial expressions? the stance? hand gestures?

Put yourself in each person's position and feel the messages.

What's happening in this picture? Who's the boss? Is there a boss present? Who's in control?

Record your comments in the space below.

What does this person's attire tell you?

What does his facial expression reveal?

What nonverbal messages can you detect?

Record your responses in the space below.

What messages do you see in the picture below? Who is the boss? Who is the subordinate? Or are they equal in status?

Do you believe the two people have established rapport? What indicates to you that rapport is or is not established?

The face is the mirror of the mind, and eyes without speaking confess the secrets of the heart.
—St. Jerome

To build rapport, match or mirror the person's speech, breathing, and posture patterns. If the person speaks rapidly, you speak rapidly. If the person walks fast, you walk fast. If the person crosses legs, you cross yours.

It's important to remember that your goal in matching or mirroring another person is to build rapport, not to manipulate. Rapport is built on truth. It's used to improve communications. All parties involved should reach satisfying results. The encounter should be harmonious and mutually beneficial to everyone.

Listening is a major part of building rapport. Listen with your eyes and ears. Pay full attention to the other person's facial expressions, posture, voice tone, and gestures. Listening and watching closely will provide the clues you need to build and improve rapport.

Consider these factors when evaluating nonverbal communications:

- Facial expressions
- Gestures
- Attire
- Stance
- Posture
- Body movement
- Touch
- Emotion
- Voice quality, pitch, tone
- Spatial proximity
- Physical appearance

REPRESENTATIONAL STYLES

Improved communications builds rapport.

There is a concept concerning how people store and retrieve memories. It is called neuro/linguistic programming (known as NLP), and by understanding this theory, you can improve your communication skills and increase rapport. Even a little understanding will improve communications. Here's a quick lesson.

The three styles people use most are visual, auditory, or kinesthetic. Actually you use all three styles, but you will have a favorite style. It's like being right- or left-handed. You use both hands, but you prefer the left or the right. A summary of the three styles follows.

VISUAL	AUDITORY	KINESTHETIC
Selects pictures from memory. Breathes high in chest. Uses high-pitched voice, is slightly breathless. Has fast voice tempo. Often displays tension in neck and shoulders. Is deeply affected by color, order, chaos, sunsets, scenery. Likes lots of windows to look out of. Collects lots of internal (mental) pictures. Seldom gets lost; carries a mental map. Talks with lots of blank spaces. Has jerky conversation. Uses a preponderance of visual words: "I see," "Paint a picture," "Show me," "Here's a preview," "That clouds my thinking," "Let's focus on," "Please clarify," "That looks fishy."	Selects words from memory. Breathes in middle of chest. Is proud of voice (radio/TV announcer, singer, musician, speaker). Voice has a rhythm that is pleasing to the ear. Doesn't mind a room without windows. Often talks out loud to self. Engages in lots of internal dialogue. Has difficulty making decisions. Seldom trusts feelings. Enjoys reading aloud. Uses a preponderance of auditory words: "I hear you," "That rings a bell," "Stay tuned," "Let them voice their opinion," "That sounds fishy."	Stores memories by feelings. Breathes low down in the stomach. Leaves spaces in conversation, which allows time to check out feelings, to get in touch with what is going on. Likes or hates; feels warm, cold, or lukewarm about almost everything. Is often athletic; easily keeps physically fit; is "outdoorsy" type. Enjoys working with hands— building, fixing, making. Is great in bed, unless he or she gets carried away with his or her own responses and forgets partner. Uses a preponderance of feeling words: "Keep in touch," "I can't put my finger on it," "Hold on a minute," "I'm impressed," "That smells fishy."
WORDS	WORDS	WORDS

Bright	Draw	Glimpse	Paint	Accent	Compose	Ring	Sound	Carry	Impress	Rub	Stroke
Clear	Expose	Graphic	Picture	Amplify	Hear	Say	Tone	Grab	Irritate	Shock	Tap
Depict	Flash	Illustrate	See	Ask	Key	Shout	Tune	Feel	Handle	Stir	Throw
Discern	Focus	Outlook	Show	Click	Note	Sing	Voice	Finger	Move	Strike	Touch

HOW TO BUILD RAPPORT—MATCH WORDS

After identifying the style, begin using words that match the style. For example, if the person is kinesthetic, speak with a preponderance of feeling words; if the person is auditory, use auditory words; and if the person is visual, select visual words.

HOW TO IDENTIFY STYLE—WATCH EYE MOVEMENT

Watch the eye movements and listen to the words. One way to develop these skills is to watch and listen to people being interviewed on TV. Another way is to ask a person a question, one that needs thought and reflection. Questions like "Tell me about your childhood," or "What do you remember most about your mother?" work well.

VISUAL	AUDITORY	KINESTHETIC
EYE MOVEMENTS	EYE MOVEMENTS	EYE MOVEMENTS
Eyes Up Right	Eyes Level Right	Eyes Down Right
Eyes Up Left	Eyes Level Left	
Eyes Straight Ahead Defocused	Eyes Down Left	

Read over the styles and see if you can identify your favorite style. Can you identify the style your best friend uses? What style does your instructor favor?

I'm a visual person; my husband is an auditory person. We used to have difficulty communicating until we learned about representational styles. He would say, "Here are the directions to . . . ," and I would immediately say, "Draw me a map." After learning about the styles, we both have made adjustments to make sure that we are on the same communications channel. Try to match your style with the person you are talking with, and rapport will begin.

Neuro/linguistic programming can improve your communications. For further information, read *Influencing with Integrity,* by Genie Z. Laborde, or *Unlimited Power,* by Anthony Robbins.

PERSONALITY TYPES

Another exercise that can improve your ability to communicate more effectively deals with personality types. There are many such exercises around, and they all can help you improve your effectiveness with others. But this one in particular I have always enjoyed and appreciated.

Years ago I attended a workshop that had an exercise called "Personatypes." The presenters did not provide credit of origin, but I've never forgotten the impact this exercise had on me. It opened new ways to recognize why some people create frustration for me when talking or working with them. The key elements of the exercise follow. See if you can identify yourself in one of the categories; see if you can identify those around you.

As seen by others, are you a Choleric, Phlegmatic, Melancholic or Sanguine?

The Choleric is full of passion, knows what is right and wrong, is easily irritated and angered, and is often hot tempered and unforgiving.

The Melancholic tends to depress his or her feelings and may be abnormally introspective and sad. Depression is no stranger to the Melancholic.

The Phlegmatic is cool and collected, shows little emotion, and may appear to be dull or apathetic, showing indifference.

The Sanguine is generally confident, optimistic, cheerful, positive, and very hopeful. Often this type displays "magic" leadership ability because of his or her magnetic charm or appeal.

Personatype:	At Your Best:		At Your Worst:	
Choleric **The hard boiled indicator**	Courageous Decisive Determined Independent Optimistic	Practical Productive Self-confident Strong willed Visionary	Cold Crafty Cruel/Sarcastic Dominating Hostile/Angry	Insensitive Opinionated Proud Unforgiving Unsympathetic
Phlegmatic **A kindly monarch**	Calm/quiet Conservative Dependable Easygoing Dry sense of humor Reluctant leader	Efficient Likeable Organized Practical	Blasé Fearful Indecisive Indolent Self-protective	Selfish Stingy Stubborn Unmotivated
Melancholic **A Jekyll and Hyde**	Aesthetic Analytical Conscientious Gifted Idealistic	Loyal Perfectionist Sensitive Self-sacrificing	Critical Legalistic Moody Negative Prone to persecution	Revengeful Rigid Self-centered Touchy Unsociable
Sanguine **The democrat**	Carefree Charismatic Enthusiastic Friendly Generous	Outgoing Responsive Talkative Warm	Disorganized Egocentric Loud Obnoxious	Restless Undependable Undisciplined Unproductive Weak willed

Beside the personality traits in this list, each type has a preferred priority and pace. Have you ever worked with someone who was so fast paced that you thought you were going to go crazy? Or someone who was so involved with a person's private life that the job never got done? Well, chances are you are a slow-paced, task-oriented person. Understanding the other person's priority and pace allows you to adjust and build rapport. Here's how to do it.

Personatype	Priority	Pace	How to Build Rapport
CHOLERIC Dictator	Task	Fast	Ask questions. Keep relationships business oriented. Give recognition to ideas. Provide alternative plans. Be precise, organized, efficient. Speak fast. Give them projects they can do on their own. Act quickly on projects. Keep your feelings to yourself. Provide competition; they love it.
PHLEGMATIC Kindly monarch	Relationship	Slow	Support their feelings. Project interest in their personal life. Give "gut" level feedback. Be patient. Take time to make decisions. Avoid conflicts and controversy. Provide them with security. Make them feel they belong. Talk slowly. These people are good listeners and make excellent counselors, consensus builders.
MELANCHOLIC Jekyll and Hyde	Task	Slow	Support objectives with visuals. Be systematic. Be organized. Provide structured environments. Be cautious, so as to provide them time to verify facts and to make decisions. Give them problems to solve. Allow them to work alone. Give them lots of time to verify the facts. Speak slowly. Summarize projects in writing. These people are analytical and perfectionists.
SANGUINE Democrat	Relationship	Fast	Talk about dreams and ideas. Give them many projects. Provide lots of action. Be lively and entertaining. Get them involved. Support their ideas and dreams. Talk fast. Put them with a team and let them lead. These people are idea people, dreamers. They like to generalize and exaggerate; be open-minded.

A word of caution: Use these new understandings to build rapport, not to manipulate. Manipulation is the enemy of rapport. It will destroy credibility and opportunity. Rapport is built on trust and mutual understanding.

**You will be liked or disliked more on your mannerisms
and your attitude than on the way you dress.**
—John T. Molloy, *The Woman's Dress for Success Book*

S = SMILE

The smile on your face is worth more than the clothes on your back. A smile helps you walk faster, stand taller, and radiate confidence. It makes you feel and look good. Check your smile. Put it on before making a phone call, meeting a person, or writing a letter. It has a positive effect on all you do. Smile often; it makes you feel and look better.

H = HANDSHAKE

A firm, friendly handshake invites openness and trust. It manifests poise and determination. Practice shaking hands with friends who will tell you the true message of your handshake. Practice until you shake hands with warm enthusiasm and confidence. You'll be glad you did.

A = ATTIRE

Dress appropriately. Feel good in your clothes. They should flow with you; they should be a part of who you are. Your attire should be comfortable and similar to others in the same position. Dress for business, not for sport or evening affairs. If you must err, err on the conservative side.

G = GROOMING

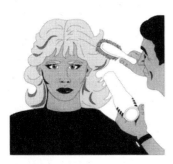

Use perfume and aftershave sparingly. Save the onions and garlic for another time. Leave the alcohol alone. And if you must smoke, be considerate of others. The smell of smoke goes with you, in your clothes and hair.

Shine your shoes. Make sure all hems and buttons are properly mended. Clean and press your clothes. Wash and style your hair. Use deodorant; this is a time of stress and high energy.

Between now and graduation, you should be planning your strategy for the job hunt. This should include assembling your interview attire. One way to ease the financial burden is to start early. Make a list of the items you'll need. Ask your family and friends to help you get ready. Post your list for all to see. When there is an occasion to celebrate and your family or friends want to give you a gift, have them choose an item from your list. Your friends and family will enjoy sharing in your success and will happily assist in such a good cause.

Here are some ideas for your list:

The Interview Outfit*:

Business suit
White blouse or shirt
Solid-colored shirts
Tie or scarf
Dress shoes
Dress socks/hosiery
Belt
Gloves
Umbrella
Raincoat
Jewelry
Wallet

Other Items:

Briefcase
Daily/weekly planner
Gold pen and pencil set
    with erasable black ink
Pocket dictionary
Notepad with cover
Portfolio case
Computer
Laser printer
Word processing software
Stationery with matching
    envelopes

Books for Your Bookshelf:

Dress for Success or
The Woman's Dress for Success Book, by John T. Molloy

Professional Presence, by Susan Bixler

Color Me Beautiful, by Carole Jackson

Seven Habits of Highly Effective People, by Stephen R. Covey (and tape)

*It is smart to have at least three outfits readily available for interviewing, because it is common to have two or more interviews with the same employer. Be prepared; plan ahead.

To save money, look for ways to change your appearance without changing the big items. For a man, change your tie or the color of your shirt. For a woman, wearing a different colored blouse or adding a scarf can make a major difference; you can also substitute your suit with a dress and blazer for the second or third interview.

PACKAGE A CONFIDENT YOU

In the job hunt, the packaging often plays as big a role as the content.

Employers have set expectations and biases when it comes to job applicants. These expectations concern matters such as what you wear and how you act before being hired as well as how you perform on the job. These expectations are the unwritten, informal rules of the workplace, or of the individual employer or person. You risk creating a negative impression when you violate the employer's concept of what is "right."

The rules are difficult to identify. Common sense and a keen eye and ear become essential in ferreting out the cultural norms in an individual job or for a particular employer. Adjusting your presentations to fit the environment is not manipulation. It is good sense. Your goal is not to decieve or mislead others intentionally regarding the sort of person you are. Your goal is to communicate effectively, to positively influence the employer so that your desirable traits are emphasized.

Effective use of nonverbal messages is your best vehicle to productive, constructive communication. Your message begins with the very first contact you have with the employer. The message flows in and through your job application, resume, references, and then your personal being. But it begins with that first impression.

Now that you understand the importance of all your packaging, it is time to begin learning how to market yourself. In the next unit, *Market*, you will learn the techniques to successfully acquire the job you want.

MARKET

There are costs and risks to a program of action, but they are far less than the long range risks and costs of comfortable inaction.
—John F. Kennedy

Implementation and **realization**—planning and executing the step-by-step job-hunting process—are the goals of "MARKET." Once achieved, you are on your way to the job and career you deserve. "MARKET" is an experience of action. It is filled with excitement, fears, and thrills. There are the ups of winning and the downs of rejection. There is agony, and there is ecstasy as you reach out to tap new resources for employment.

In the beginning, you create the plan that takes you into action. Then you work your plan until it is fulfilled. Because there are many unexpected twists in the job hunt, you can expect to review and revise your plan along the way. The number of changes is not important. What is important is having a plan and making it work. In the end, you will reach fulfillment and satisfaction.

As you complete each chapter in this unit, you will develop the skills and knowledge to implement and complete your action plan. Let us now examine each chapter for an overview.

In Chapter 10, "Develop a Master Plan—The Self-Paced Schedule," you examine your finances and prepare a plan of action. This plan identifies all the steps and time frames needed to bring your dreams into reality. The goal of a schedule is to provide you with a road map for action. Once you have the map, you are ready to put the plan into action by marketing.

In Chapter 11, "Land Interviews—A Marketing Game," you learn the secret to marketing and how to market your way into employers' offices for interviews. The marketing game includes three strategies: telemarketing, letter marketing, and group marketing. Each of these methods requires different skills. Each method provides varying ways to increase your job hunt network and to get interviews. The goal of marketing is to get interviews. Learn and use all three methods of marketing and get the interviews you want and need.

In Chapter 12, "Interview Like a Pro—Win-Win Encounters," you learn the steps to effective and successful interviewing. The goal of an interview is to get the job offer. When you have worked hard to get an interview, you want to do everything to get the offer. You can decide later if it is the right job for you.

In Chapter 13, "Complete the Cycle—The Follow-Up Process," you learn to do the little things that make a difference. You learn to examine each interview objectively and to follow up each interview with a thank-you letter and timely telephone calls. You also learn about wage negotiations, and how to accept or reject job offers. In Chapter 13, the goal is to get "Hired."

Now it is time to leave the safety of "PACKAGE" and move into the action of "MARKET."

DEVELOP A MASTER PLAN
The Self-Paced Schedule

Our plans miscarry because they have no aim. When a man does not know what harbor he is making for, no wind is the right wind.

—Seneca

Over the years, I've watched many people look for work. The ones that find what they want in a timely measure, no matter what their situation, are the ones that work at it full-time. I remember Jeanne, who had been fired from her job. The reasons why are not important. What is important is how she responded to being fired. Like most people, there was a time of anger, resentment, and confusion. But unlike many others in this situation, she put those feelings aside and proceeded to do what needed to be done to get another job.

Jeanne took the time to create a powerful, targeted resume. She used this resume as a tool to market herself. In just a few weeks she found openings, interviewed for numerous jobs, and acquired several offers to choose from. In no time at all, she was back at work and was making more money than before.

Why did Jeanne find work so quickly? Because she worked full-time at the job of job hunting. She pursued even when she was rejected. She kept going until she found what she wanted. She believed in herself. Jeanne had established goals. She planned on getting a job quickly and pursued her dream.

You, too, can shorten your job hunt time by setting specific goals and working at each of them. Let's examine some of the steps that need to be taken.

USING THE ACTION PLAN SECTION OF THE *COMPANION PLANNER*

No one knows what he can do until he tries.
—Publius Syrus

You've already done an immense amount of work. But having a sensational package and a fantastic group of references won't get you a job. You need an action plan and then action. Knowing what you want to do each day and over the weeks helps you get the results you want. Make your plan; then work your plan.

File your master action plan, monthly planners, and weekly planners in this section. Maintaining your plans and goals provides visual reminders of your activities. In addition, the plans serve two purposes: (1) they allow you to see where you are going and (2) they provide you with the means to measure your progress. Use your action planner to keep on target.

File the following forms in this section:

- FORM 25: Action Plan
  Complete a new action plan each time you begin a job hunt program.

- FORM 26: Monthly Planner
  Use this form or any other monthly calendar. Post each month of the job hunt on the wall or your refrigerator so you can view your plans and progress daily. It is important to plot and visually review your Action Plan on paper. When the job search is completed, file your action plans and monthly calendars in the ACTION section of your *Companion Planner.*

- FORM 27: Weekly Planner
  Use this form or any other weekly planner for making your plans for the week. From your weekly plan you will write your daily "to-do" lists.

- Yearly Planner
  Use a twelve-month preprinted calendar to aid you in planning and seeing the whole year. A plastic twelve-month calendar allows you to change plans often. Hang this calendar on a wall or on your refrigerator.

- Other Documents
  Daily to-do lists.

AN AGGRESSIVE ACTION PLAN

This time, like all times, is a very good one, If we but know what to do with it.

—Emerson

Following is an aggressive action plan for implementing a progressive, fast-paced job search. Obviously, it's a full-time job to find a job. If you are unemployed, you should plan to work a minimum of forty hours per week on your job hunt; fifty or sixty hours would be even better. If you are employed, your schedule and time frames will be considerably different. It may take several months to find the right job.

ACTION PLAN — Page 1 of 2

Tasks to Complete	Target Date	Date Completed
Develop Action Plan Review finances—Establish budget/cash flow Complete Monthly Planner Complete Weekly Planner	Day 1 Monday Oct 9	
Work on self-assessment exercises. Update data file.	Day 2 Tuesday Oct 10	
Complete self-assessment exercises. Complete update to data file Choose job objective and employer environment	Day 3 Wednesday Oct 11	
Write resume draft. Make reference list and write scripts.	Day 4 Thursday Oct 12	
Call or write references, and make a record. Review job application procedures.	Day 5 Friday Oct 13	
Finalize resume and print. Assemble profession package—select three interview outfits, pack briefcase and portfolio. Review progress and prepare new weekly schedule.	Day 6 Saturday October 14	
Play—rest—enjoy family. Forget about job hunting.	Day 7 Sunday October 15	
Review marketing plan. Make Network List—100 names minimum Write and practice marketing (network) scripts.	Day 8 Monday October 16	
Write interview script. Practice interview (Videotape, if possible). Contact agencies—state, school, federal, placement, private.	Day 9 Tuesday October 17	
Letter-Market—Write and mail network letters. Read the Sunday classified ads. Respond to appropriate ads with cover letter and resume.	Day 10 Wednesday October 18	

© 1995 Harris Espérance Incorporated · Form 25/95

Figure 10-1   FORM 25, Action Plan, page 1 of 2.

COMPLETE FORM 25, ACTION PLAN

Begin your planning and preparations when you first learn or decide that you need to hunt for work. Having six months' lead time if you are working or in school is very beneficial. This time frame allows you plenty of time to take care of the necessary activities.

An action plan helps you establish your time priorities. Use Form 25, Action Plan, to set all target dates for a successful job search.

If you do not look at things on a large scale It will be difficult for you to master strategy . . .
—Miyamoto Musashi

Job hunting usually takes longer than most people realize. There are resumes to write, references to call, letters to mail, and a host of other activities to take care of. The quicker you get started, the faster you will find employment.

Here are some guidelines to keep in mind.

- Establish dates for all tasks. The dates may change as time passes, but it is imperative to begin the plan with targeted completion dates for all tasks.

- When dates change, revise the plan; then complete a new action plan.

- File your action plan behind the ACTION PLAN divider in your notebook.

ACTION PLAN		Page 2 of 2
Tasks to Complete	**Target Date**	**Date Completed**
Tele-Market (call 50 people from Network Complete a record for every call. Schedule Interviews. Research companies who are interviewing you.	Day 11 Thursday October 19	
Tele-Market (call 50 more people). Make records; write follow-up letters. Schedule interviews. Research companies.	Day 12 Friday October 20	
Review interview script. Tele-Market (call friends for Group-Market party). Research employers. Letter-Market	Day 13 Saturday October 21	
Play—rest—enjoy family. Forget about job hunting.	Day 14 Sunday October 22	
Tele-Market (call more people). Schedule interviews. Research employers. Interview and review interview, make record.	Day 15 Monday October 23	
Review interview and interview record. Write thank-you and follow-up letters. Prepare Group-Market presentation. Host a Group-Market evening at home.	Day 16 Tuesday October 24	
Tele-Market (call more people). Schedule interviews. Research and interview. Write thank-you follow-up letters.	Day 17 Wednesday October 25	
Receive job offer. Negotiate offer. Accept or reject offer. Write acceptance or rejection letter. Accept offer. Write acceptance letter.	Day ?	
Give notice to employer. Write letter of resignation. Write thank-you letters to other potential employers and references.	Day ?	
(First Day of Work)	Day ?	

© 1995 Harris Espérance Incorporated   Form 25/95

Figure 10-2 FORM 25, Action Plan, page 2 of 2.

COMPLETE FORM 26, MONTHLY PLANNER

NOT I—NOT ANYONE else, can travel that road for you, You must travel it for yourself.
—Walt Whitman

Form 26, Monthly Planner, helps you with the long-term planning of your job search. It allows you to set time frames for your job hunt. An effective and successful job search often takes several months.

If your job hunt will take several months, complete a monthly planner for all months. Use as many forms as necessary to match your plans.

Figure 10-3 is an example of a monthly calendar filled in for an aggressive job search.

File this form behind the ACTION PLAN divider in your notebook.

Priority Tasks	MONTHLY PLANNER				Month of: October, 1995		
	Sunday	Monday	Tuesday	Wednesday	Thursday	Friday	Saturday

Action Plan
Financial
  planning
Six month
  calendar
Weekly
  planner
	1	2	3	4	5	6	7

Self Assessment Data File Job Objective Resume Reference List Reference	8	9 Action Plan Finances Monthly Planner Weekly Planner	10 Self-Assess. Data File	11 Self Assess. Data File Job Objective	12 Resume draft Reference list and scripts	13 Call/write references Review job applications	14 Final resume and print Attire/briefcase Portfolio Weekly Planner

Scripts
Network List
Market Scripts
Interview attire
Briefcase
Portfolio
Interview
  script
	15
	R & R
	Enjoy family
		16
		Review plan
		Network list
		Network script
		Practice script
			17
			Interview script
			Video
			  interview
			Contact
			  agencies
				16
				Letter-Market
				Read ads
				  send resume
					19
					Tele-Market
					Make records
					Schedule
					  interviews
						20
						Tele-Market
						Make records
						Schedule
						  interviews
						Follow-up
							21 Call friends
							Research
							  employers
							Review interview
							  script
							Weekly Planner

Practice
  interview
Tele-market
Letter-market
Group-market
Write thank-
  you letters
	22
	R & R
	Enjoy family
		23 Tele-Market
		Schedule
		  interviews
		Research
		  companies
		Interview
			24
			Review
			  interview
			Thank-you
			Follow-up
			Host party
				25
				Tele-Market
				Schedule
				  interviews
				Research
				Interview
					26
					Tele-Market
					Research
					Interview
					Follow-up
						27
						Tele-Market
						Research
						Interview
						Follow-up
							28 Call friends
							Research
							  employers
							Review
							Interviews
							Weekly Planner

Stay positive Eat right Sleep well Exercise	29 R & R Enjoy family	30	31				
Affirmations	I am an insurance account executive. I enjoy calling employers. Tele-marketing is fun for me. I exercise and eat properly every day. I love job hunting.						

© 1995 Harris Espérance Incorporated   Form 26/95

Figure 10-3   FORM 26, Monthly Planner

Efficiency is doing things right. Effectiveness is doing the right things.
—Stephen Covey

Use your whole day. Your schedule should begin at 6 A.M. and end in the evening. If your hours vary, adapt the times. If you are employed, be creative with your schedule. Use your lunch hour to network. Attend a 6 A.M. breakfast meeting. Visit the employment office at noon. Call prospective employers on your break. Join a professional club and attend meetings in the evening.

Each Sunday set aside an hour to review the week and to establish next week's agenda. This planning should be your first priority. It takes most people longer to get a job than it should, because they often spend their time doing other things. Doing other things is more fun. Unfortunately, it's also the best way to stay unemployed.

Consider the following activities as you prepare for your job hunt:

- Transfer unfinished items to next week's schedule.

- Update your network lists.

- Put action in your plan. This is no time to take it easy!

File this behind the ACTION PLAN divider in your notebook.

Weekly Planner					**Week Ending**		**October 14, 1995**	
PRIORITIES	**TIME**	**SUN**	**MON**	**TUE**	**WED**	**THUR**	**FRI**	**SAT**
Action plan Finances Self-Assessment Data File Job objective Resume Reference list Reference script Call references Interview attire Briefcase Portfolio	6:00	Exercise Meditation	Exercise Meditation	Exercise Meditation	Exercise Meditation	Exercise Meditation	Exercise Meditation	Exercise Meditation
	7:00	Breakfast with family	Breakfast with family	Breakfast with family	Breakfast with family	Breakfast with family	Breakfast with family	Breakfast with family
	8:00	Trip to beach with	Read C10 Work on	Read C1 Do self-	Complete Self-	Review C5 Revise	Contact references	Finish resume
	9:00	family	Action Plan	assessment exercises	Assessment Exercises	resume	Call and write letters	
	10:00		Monthly Planners		Complete update of		Make records	
	11:00		Weekly Planner		data file			Print resume
	12:00	Lunch at Joe's'	Lunch with Lin Chu	Lunch with Fred	Lunch with Yukio	Lunch with Alice	Lunch with Randy	Lunch with Terry
	1:00	Shopping at OL Center	Review C16 Work on	Review C2 Update data	Complete Form 13	List references	Contact references	Select interview
	2:00		Financial planning	files	Job Objective		Call and write letters	attire.
	3:00					Reference scripts	Make records	Pack briefcase
	4:00							Assemble Portfolio
	5:00	Drive home				Review C6	Read C7	Weekly Planner
	6:00 On	Eat Pizza out	7 School play	Read C3 & 4	Insurance Assn. Mtg.	Take kids to see Grandma	Take kids to football game	Take wife to dinner
Affirmations	Job hunting is fun for me. I enjoy calling employers. I am an insurance account executive. I exercise daily.							

Form 27/95

Figure 10-4   FORM 27, Weekly Planner

There is nothing so degrading as the constant anxiety about one's means of livelihood. . . . Money is like a sixth sense without which you cannot make a complete use of the other five.
—**William Somerset Maugham**

Taking a good, hard look at your finances can be a very sobering event. But it's imperative to know how you are going to handle the finances, particularly if you are about to lose your job or source of income. If your income becomes reduced or is interrupted, you will handle the stress better if you have developed an ongoing financial plan. The following three forms will help you to prepare a financial plan. To complete an analysis of where you stand financially, begin by listing all your assets and liabilities.

COMPLETE FORM 41, ASSETS AND LIABILITIES

You may need to prepare detailed listings of information on separate sheets before summarizing the information onto this form.

You may find that a columnar pad is more suited to your needs. If this is true, create your own form.

Involve the whole family in the financial planning process. Go over the budget figures and cash flow projections with them. Their contributions can boost your morale and sense of self-worth, as well as reduce the budget blues. Their positive support is of great value to you.

There is more information on how to complete this form in Chapter 16. If you need more help, study that chapter.

File this form behind the FINANCIAL MANAGEMENT divider in your notebook.

ASSETS AND LIABILITIES

ASSETS	12/31/___ Actual	12/31/___ Projected
Liquid Assets		
Marketable Investments		
Non-Marketable Investments		
Personal Assets		
TOTAL ASSETS		
LIABILITIES		
TOTAL LIABILITIES		
NET WORTH (Assets less Liabilities)		

® 1995 Harris Espérance Incorporated   Form 41/95

Figure 10-5   FORM 41, Assets and Liabilities

COMPLETE FORM 42, INCOME AND EXPENSES

It is not that I spend
more money than I earn.
It is just that I spend it
quicker than I make it.
—Author Unknown

There are many financial considerations associated with a job hunt. If you are unemployed, your income will be greatly reduced and the stress of job hunting may become overwhelming. Spend time with your financial planning. Get help if needed. Involve the whole family. Their support is critical. A financial planner can assist you if necessary.

Cut expenses immediately. Get help from your spouse or accountant. Don't wait for a financial crisis before taking action. Contact creditors to let them know your situation. If you are in great financial difficulty, contact your local Consumer Credit Counseling (CCC). CCC is a nonprofit service organization that provides free counseling. CCC can help you restructure your payment schedules and avoid bankruptcy.

If this income and expenses form doesn't meet your needs, create your own using a columnar pad.

Record the actual figures for last year's income and expenses in the first column; then project figures for next year.

File this form behind the FINANCIAL MANAGEMENT divider in your notebook.

INCOME AND EXPENSES

INCOME	12/31/___ Actual	12/31/___ Projected
Wages		
Self-Employment		
Unemployment Compensation		
Interest, Dividends, Rents, Royalties, Fees		
Child Support, Social Security, Pensions		
Annuities		
TOTAL INCOME		

EXPENSES	12/31/___ Actual	12/31/___ Projected
Housing (Mortgage or Rent)		
Utilities		
Furnishings, Maintenance, Upkeep		
Groceries		
Clothing, Upkeep		
Personal (Health, Beauty)		
Transportation		
Insurance (Car, Home, Liability, Medical, Life)		
Savings, Other Investments		
Retirement		
Taxes		
Credit Cards, Loans		
Contributions, Gifts		
Licenses, Fees		
Recreation, Entertainment		
Education, Subscriptions, Memberships		
TOTAL EXPENSES		
TOTAL INCOME LESS EXPENSES		

© 1995 Harris Espérance Incorporated   Form 42/95

Figure 10-6   FORM 42, Income and Expenses

COMPLETE FORM 40, CASH FLOW STATEMENT

If your outgo exceeds your income, then your upkeep will be your downfall.
—Author Unknown

Money doesn't come and go in steady streams. There are property taxes due in November; there is the annual car insurance premium due in April. And on it goes. It helps to put together a cash flow projection so you will be prepared for the big payments. This way, there will be no big surprises. If you want to project the full year, use a 13-column form.

It is useful to project a **cash** flow to determine how much lead time you have until you must have a new job. This time frame helps determine the goals you should set for the job hunt. Once you determine the time frame and set your goals, activate your plan with determination and a positive belief in yourself.

File this form behind the FINANCIAL MANAGEMENT divider in your notebook.

CASH FLOW STATEMENT						Date March 1
MONTH	March	April	May	June	July	August
INCOME						
Wages						
TOTAL INCOME						
EXPENSES						
TOTAL EXPENSES						
Surplus (+) Deficit (–)						

° 1995 Harris Espérance Incorporated   Form 40/95

Figure 10-7   FORM 40, Cash Flow Statement

Even though work stops, expenses run on.
—Marcus Porcius Cato

It costs money to job hunt. It's important to budget for these costs and to keep track of these expenses for your tax records. Check with a tax accountant on the deductibility of expenses. Keep accurate records.

COMPLETE FORM 43, JOB SEARCH EXPENSES

Typical expenses include the following:

- Stationery
- Postage
- Printing
- Secretarial or word processing assistance
- Travel
- Long-distance telephone calls
- Answering service or machine
- Newspapers
- Directories

You can tell by the "Totals" figure in the example that job search expenses add up quickly. Be sure to keep complete and accurate records; keep receipts for all expenditures.

File your completed form behind the FINANCIAL MANAGEMENT divider in your notebook.

JOB SEARCH EXPENSES

Page ___ of ___

Date	Description	Miles	Amount
3/10	Stationery		$ 15.98
3/12	Postage		32.00
3/16	Printing		24.98
3/16	Answering Machine		59.95
3/19	Trip to Bend—Interview: Alex Seymour at Seymour's & Co.	96	27.84
3/19	National Business Employment Weekly Subscription		24.00
3/24	Trip to Redmond—Interview S.E. Johnson	54	15.66
2/21-3/19	Long-Distance Phone Calls (bill attached)		36.24
TOTALS			**$236.65**

© 1995 Harris Espérance Incorporated   Form 43/95

Figure 10-8   FORM 43, Job Search Expenses

LAND INTERVIEWS
A Marketing Game

Anyone who proposes to do good must not expect people to roll stones out of his way, but must accept his lot calmly, even if they roll a few more upon it.

—Albert Schweitzer

Landing interviews is a matter of marketing yourself. The job hunters who find employment quickly are those who work hardest on their marketing plans. They make an effort to contact as many people as possible in a short period of time. Here are a few stories about how some of them acquired their ideal jobs.

Jimmy was clearing tables at McDonald's one sunny lunch hour. In a chance conversation with some senior citizens, he mentioned that he was looking for an accounting job and would complete his degree in three weeks. A woman who reminded him of his grandmother spoke up. "You should call my son. He's looking for a new employee." Jimmy followed up on her suggestion and got the job. He was exactly the person the woman's son was looking for.

Myra read an ad in the local newspaper. "That's my job!" she said. The position had benefits and flexible hours, and it would utilize all her skills. She talked to her boss about making the change. Her boss said, "That's a great company to work for. Let me send them a letter of recommendation." Myra told me later she felt as if she had the job even before she walked in for the interview.

Bob needed a summer job to help with college expenses. He wrote an achievement resume and went to visit employers he felt could pay the wages he needed. Even though the unemployment rate was over 15 percent in his hometown, before the week was over three companies had made him job offers. The job he took was created just for him.

Katie was looking for a middle management position in personnel or safety. She set up a meeting with an aquaintance, the general manager of a local manufacturing facility. Her intent was to get job leads and advice. While talking with Katie, the general manager recognized that his company was in need of a person like her. Before the meeting was over, Katie was offered a new job—a new position based on the credentials in her resume.

As you can see, landing an interview can lead in many different directions. The one common denominator for successful job seekers is that they take action to get other people involved in their quest. The more people you talk to, the sooner your job search will end.

THE EMPLOYER'S TABLE

You can't win if you're not at the table.
—**Joan Didion,** *Play It as It Lays*

The goal of this chapter is to get you into an employers' offices for interviews. In other words, you must get to the employers' offices to get a job offers. Otherwise it's impossible to get hired. The exercises in this chapter are designed to get you there in the quickest and most efficient manner. You will learn that most people get jobs through personal contact. So don't ruin your chances with improper preparation. Follow each exercise carefully.

HOW PEOPLE GET JOBS

Approximately 20 percent of the jobs in the published job market are found through

Advertised openings	10%
Agencies	<u>10%</u>
	20%

Approximately 80 percent of the jobs in the hidden job market are found through

Direct mail	5%
Personal contact	<u>75%</u>
	80%

This breakdown follows the Pareto Principle, otherwise known as the "20/80 Rule." Let's examine this rule in relation to jobs and job hunters.

THE PARETO PRINCIPLE—THE 20/80 RULE

The Rule:

- 80 percent of the job hunters look at 20 percent of the job openings. They use the published job market almost exclusively.

- Only 20 percent of the job hunters look at 80 percent of the available job openings. These job hunters concentrate on the hidden job market.

In other words, if there are 100 job hunters looking for work, 80 of them will apply for 20 published job openings, and only 20 job hunters will apply for 80 unpublished job openings. You should be able to figure out where to spend the majority of your time. But first, let's examine each of the methods.

Let us examine each of these sources to determine what will work best for you.

ADVERTISED OPENINGS—10 PERCENT

Job hunters find jobs 10 percent of the time through advertised openings. These advertised openings can be found in

- Newspapers
- Trade publications
- Clearinghouses
- Executive publications
- Computerized job banks
- Bulletin boards.

Points to Remember:

1. At least 80 percent of the available jobs are not advertised. Don't rely too heavily on this method.

2. The higher the wage, the lower the probability the job will be advertised.

3. You'll have lots of (poor) competition. Many qualified applicants may be poorly represented. Improve your chances for interviews by addressing the employer's needs, tailoring your resume to those needs, and writing an outstanding cover letter.

4. Respond to ads even if you don't meet all the requirements and qualifications. If you feel you can do the job well and would enjoy the work, respond.

5. Be careful of blind ads—it may be your job that's being advertised! Some newspapers will screen responses to eliminate this problem. Check it out first; don't get caught in this trap.

6. Get mileage from one ad, from one resume. Identify other employers that match the ad you are answering; then send each of these employers a cover letter and your resume.

7. Key media for professional and management jobs include the following:
   - Sunday editions of the *New York Times, Los Angeles Times,* and the *Chicago Tribune*
   - *The Wall Street Journal*
   - *The National Business Employment Weekly*. Twelve issues delivered first class cost about $52.00. Call toll-free 1-800-852-2200

8. The *Gale Directory of Publications* provides addresses of all newspapers and magazines in which you might have an interest.

AGENCIES—10 PERCENT

Job hunters find jobs through public and private agencies 10 percent of the time. The following list indicates some agency sources and guidelines to consider when you select an agency.

State Agencies:

- These agencies are listed in the telephone book under "Government Offices and Schools, State Offices, Employment Division."

- They are located in most cities.
- They provide nationwide network.

Federal Agencies:

- These agencies are listed in the telephone book under "Government Offices and Schools, Federal Offices, Office of Personnel Management–Federal Job Information Center".
- They provide a nationwide network.

Private Agencies:

- These agencies are listed in the Yellow Pages under "Employment Agencies."
- Job hunters should select only "employer paid" agencies.
- Their application form is a contract—READ IT CAREFULLY!
- Services, fees, and reputations vary widely; thoroughly check each agency out.
- Many specialize in handling only executives or medical, financial, or other specific fields.
- Agencies will usually request "exclusive handling." Don't give it.
- Their loyalty lies with the person who pays the bill, usually the employer.
- They depend on rapid turnover; therefore, they have little or no time to assist the job hunter.

College Placement:

- These offices are located on most campuses.
- They are available to students and alumni.
- Their services and effectiveness vary widely.

Executive Recruiters:

- These services are excellent for highly marketable individuals.
- Appearance and first impressions are very important and key factors.
- Many offer many attractive opportunities.
- Job hunters should contact them prior to needing employment.
- The initial contact should not reveal present earnings.
- Follow-up is crucial.
- Job hunters should be sure they're dealing with "search" firms, not a counseling service.

Points to Remember:

1. Be selective in choosing an agency. Check out its reputation, and interview your prospective placement counselor.
2. Seek only "employer paid" placement agencies, not "applicant paid" counseling services.
3. Read all contracts carefully.
4. Remember that agencies work for employers, not for job hunters.

5. Insist that the agency always contact you prior to distributing your resume or providing your availability.

6. Keep in touch. Create a friendly, working relationship with the agency.

DIRECT MAIL—5 PERCENT

Direct mail accounts for about 5 percent of the job offers. It requires an exceptionally prepared cover letter and resume. It needs to be targeted and sent to a person who has the power and authority to hire you. This person needs to be in a position to even be able to create a job just for you.

Direct mail allows you to

- Project your best image.

- Avoid initial disclosures of any liabilities.

- Have independent contact free from outside competition.

- Pick any field you wish.

- Contact top executives who have the authority to create positions and offer attractive compensation packages. In large organizations, chief executive officers or presidents rarely hire or screen applicants. Identify someone who can hire you—a vice president, regional manager, department head, or supervisor.

Points to Remember:

1. Carefully select organizations that meet your career and life goals. Large mass mailings waste your time and money. Instead, focus on a few employers at a time.

2. Identify a person who can hire you. This should be done with a telephone call. This ensures that you have current information. Using periodicals can prove to be disastrous; often the information is out-of-date.

3. Personalize your cover letter. Address the one person who can hire you. Speak to the company's needs.

4. Contact recently promoted executives, successful alumni, and all your references.

5. Include this line in your cover letter if confidentiality is not an important issue to you: "If you have no openings at this time, please feel free to share my resume with others who may need a person with my qualifications and abilities. Thank you."

6. Follow up on your initial contact. If you wrote in your cover letter that you would call on a certain day be sure to call then. If you receive no response, send another letter and then follow up with a call.

PERSONAL CONTACTS—75 PERCENT

Personal contacts account for 75 percent of the jobs obtained by job hunters. A conversation with your neighbor, even a passing contact to a stranger, may lead you to an employer's door and a new job.

Because most jobs are obtained through personal contact, let's look at who you know who can be contacted about getting a job. Who really is a contact? Everyone!

Employers (Present and Past):

- Your boss, the boss's boss, peers, subordinates, department heads
- Personnel manager, other employees, company officers, board members

Professional Associates:

- Clients, customers, sales representatives, insurance agents, auditors, government officials, vendors
- Members of professional organizations
- Doctors, lawyers, dentists, clergy, accountants, bankers, real estate agents, insurance salespersons
- Office staffs of professionals—receptionists, secretaries, clerks, salespersons

Community Associates:

- Members of community, political, and social organizations
- Neighbors, friends, family members
- Gas station attendants, mechanics, waitresses, grocery checkers or boxers

School Associates:

- Instructors, department heads, presidents, principals, counselors
- Superintendents, fellow students, alumni

Now that you know how jobs are found and that personal contacts account for more job opportunities than all the others combined, let's look at ways to make and increase personal contacts. Let's create a network of contacts for you to use in the job hunt.

ASK FOR WHAT YOU NEED—THE SECRET TO MARKETING

Change and growth take place when a person dares to become involved with experimenting with his own life.

—Herbert Otto

"Ask and it shall be given unto you." All of us have heard this saying. But how many times have you asked and not received that which you had asked for? For most of us, the answer is "many, many times." The problem is not that we shouldn't ask, but it is in the mechanics we use to ask. Anthony Robbins, author of *Unlimited Power,* provides us with the correct mechanics for asking. Here is what he tells us to do:

1. **Ask specifically.** Your messages, your asking, are often mixed up and unclear. You do not know exactly what it is you want. If you ask for more money and receive a quarter, then you have received what you had asked for: "more money." Perhaps you had more money in mind. In order to get what you want, you must know the details: what, how much, when, how, and why.

2. **Ask a person who can help you.** This may sound simple, but how many times have you asked and not received because the person you talked to could not give you what you wanted. Think about it. If the person you are asking doesn't have what you want, you are wasting valuable time and resources—yours *and* theirs. Find someone who has what you want; then go ask that person.

3. **Create value for the person you are asking.** When you ask someone for something, there needs to be a reason for the person to give you what you want. For any number of intrinsic reasons, the value may be just a good feeling for doing a good deed, or it may be for financial gain. It's not the reason that's important, but the fact that you have created a value for the person; therefore, there is impetus to give you what you need.

4. **Believe fervently in what you are asking.** Belief is contagious. If you believe strongly in what you are asking for, it is likely that another will believe in it as well. But if you believe halfheartedly that you deserve something, it is also likely that few will believe in you. Your belief must inspire others to act.

5. **Ask until you get what you want.** How many times do you have to ask? How many people do you have to ask? The answer is "until you get what you want." Asking until you receive doesn't mean that you ask only one person. It may mean asking hundreds of people. It may mean altering your method of asking. It may mean reevaluating your want, creating a new value, and finding more people to ask. You need to analyze your asking method, evaluate the results, adjust your presentation, and try, try again until you get what you want.

USING THE NETWORK RECORDS SECTION
OF THE *COMPANION PLANNER*

A filing system is not just a place to store papers; it's established and maintained for easy retrieval of information.

Once you begin to contact your network (by making phone calls and writing letters), you will need a method to file your records. This is where the NETWORK RECORDS section of the *Companion Planner* comes in. This section contains the following forms and documents.

- Form 28: Network Contact List
  This list should begin with one hundred names—a wealth of people to contact. Listed below are the people and companies you should include.

    Potential employers (a minimum of 12)

    All prior employers, former bosses and other key employees

    Personal references

    Professional associates

    Community associates (clubs and association members)

    Business associates

    School associates

    Friends and neighbors

    Family members

- Form 29: Network Contact Record
  Keep a detailed record of every major conversation. Attach additional pages to each contact record if necessary. Keep these records in alphabetical order.

  - Script(s) or Clusters
    Write master scripts for the various types of conversations you'll be having and keep them in this section. Plan out what you want to say. Be sure you have listed the various closing options. Be sure to ask for job leads and additional referrals.

  - Additional Dividers
    You will quickly learn that you need to add alphabetical dividers to this section to keep it organized. You may even choose to make individual dividers for major contacts. All this may seem like a lot of work, but it's worth it when you need to find information in a hurry. A filing system is not just a place to store papers; it's established and maintained for easy retrieval of information.

NETWORKING TIPS

In life, very few worthwhile things are done alone.
—Robert Half

Networking works best when it is a give-and-take relationship, one where you think about what you can do for the other person as much as what they can do for you.

1. **Meet as many people as you can.** Everyone's a potential contact! Attend business meetings and social functions.
2. **Introduce yourself first.** Act as the host, not a guest. Walk over, stick out your hand, and say hi.
3. **Tell everyone you are job hunting,** unless you're employed and need to keep it a secret.
4. **Ask questions.** Inquire: "Do you know anyone who might . . . ?" Volunteer: "May I help?" Pyramid: "Do you know someone who . . . ?" Spot Opportunities: "A recent news article made me wonder if you could use someone with my abilities."
5. **Use key contacts sparingly.** Don't abuse them with constant contact.
6. **Be prepared to help.** Sooner or later you'll be asked. Networking is a two-way street.
7. **Keep in touch.**

8. **Review your contact list regularly.** Separate the productive from the unproductive. You don't have time to be involved with everyone you meet.
9. **Give your resume to your contacts.** Always carry several copies with you in case you meet someone interested in your abilities unexpectedly.
10. **Prepare a list of people to contact.** Begin with a minimum of one hundred names.

COMPLETE FORM 28, NETWORK CONTACT LIST

Keep writing names until you have a minimum of one hundred. Everyone is a potential contact.

Your objective is to record one hundred names. Don't judge your contacts or evaluate whether or not they can help you. Just list and then call everyone. Build your list through referrals. Consider making six different lists—one for each of the following sources.

Potential Employers

Label a page "Potential Employers." Now list as many potential employers as possible. If you know who you should speak with (the person who can hire you), record that name. List a minimum of twelve employers.

Potential Employers	NETWORK LIST					Page __ of __	
Name of Contact Company/Address Affiliation	**Telephone Number**	**Result of Call**				**Result of Letter**	
		Date	Call Back	Left Word	See Record	Date	Reply
1. Town & Country Animal Hospital. 525 SE Division, Columbus, OH 43207 Dr. Andrew Mikes	614 555-9823						
2. Cedar Mill Veterinary Hospital, 143 SE Park Columbus, Oh 43207 Dr. Alicia Williams	614 555-4308						
3. Capital Hill Cat Clinic 1983 Barbur Blvd Columbus, OH 43208 Dr. Pat O'Brien	614 555-1952						
4. Animal Heart Clinic 1210 Hayden Drive Columbus, OH 43208 Dr. Beverly Childress	614 555-7308						
5. Barclay Small Animal Clinic, 865 Murdoc Road Columbus, OH 43207 Dr. José Ortega	614 555-8712						
6. Watkins Animal Hospital, 43 Watkins Rd Columbus, OH 43207 Dr. Barry Doxler	614 555-9966						
7. The Mobile Pet Clinic 78 Ranchero Avenue Columbus, OH 43207 Drs. Jim & Sally Curnow	614 555-2409						
8. Bird & Aviary Practice 4550 SW Lombarde Columbus, OH 43207 Dr. Masaharu Kasahara	614 555-7566						
9. Animal Eye Clinic 8739 SW River Road Columbus, OH 43207 Dr. Kerry A. Greenley	614 555-3351						

© 1995 Harris Espérance Incorporated   Form 28/95

Figure 11-1 FORM 28, Network Contact List

Prior Employers

On another page list the names of work associates.

Business Associates

List clients, customers, vendors, buyers, suppliers, sales representatives, auditors, insurance agents, government officials, and any other associates. Obtain and use the membership list from your professional organizations.

Community Associates

List the names of members from community organizations, including all political, religious, and social groups. And friends, family, and neighbors.

Professionals

List your doctor, lawyer, accountant, dentist, banker, realtor, insurance agent, and other professionals.

School Associates

List the names of your instructors, fellow students, and school administrators. Get a copy of your school annual or an alumni list.

Keep writing names until you have a minimum of one hundred.

File this form behind the NETWORK RECORDS divider of your notebook.

Your objective is to get other people involved as quickly as possible.

UNDERSTAND TELEPHONE CONVERSATIONS

The impression you make is usually a lasting one, so you will want to make sure your voice and manner always show you at your best. Every phone call has three parts: preparation, conversation, and follow-up. Each part is vital to your success.

The Preparation:

- Get organized. Then you won't forget important points.

- Script your conversation. Use a telephone cluster. It makes conversations flow. Plan what you want to say so that you will sound prepared and natural.

- Have a pencil, paper, and calendar handy to write comments and book interview appointments.

- Keep your resume at hand. It helps you to articulate your skills and career objective.

The Conversation:

- Establish rapport. Your opening comments and voice tone set the tone of the conversation. Your voice portrays your attitudes. It is the most obvious means by which the listener can judge you; so sound as good as you really are. Be alert, pleasant, natural, and expressive.

The objective of telemarketing is to get other people involved in your job search as quickly as possible.

- Put a smile in your voice. This can be easily accomplished by putting a smile on your face before dialing the number. With that smile, think positive thoughts about the person you will be speaking with. Imagine that person smiling at you and happily giving you the information you desire.

- Identify yourself immediately; then state the purpose of your call. For example: "Good morning, Mr. Chan. This is Sue Wong, and I'm calling to find out about your company's hiring procedures. May I take a few minutes of your time?"

- Listen closely. Listen to the speed and representational clues. Is the person speaking rapidly? Should you increase your speaking rate? Is the person using a preponderance of auditory words? Are you matching his or her words with auditory words? Speak clearly and slowly enough so your words can be understood. Match the other person's speech patterns.

- Use the person's name often. In a direct conversation, listeners hear astutely the first five words said immediately after hearing their name.

- Show that you are listening intently by being interested in what the person has to say. Respond appropriately to remarks. Put yourself in his or her shoes.

- Close with a friendly ending. Thank the person for his or her help. Be the one to hang up last after saying good-bye.

The Follow-Up:

- Make a record of the call.

- Write a thank-you note or letter, and enclose your resume (see the Exercise 11-4 on letter marketing).

- Complete all agreed upon tasks. If your contact recommended that you call someone else, make the phone call immediately.

- Keep in touch periodically. Calling the same employer daily is inconsiderate. Use common sense—do not become a nuisance.

- Return calls immediately. Unreturned calls are irritating. Prompt responses are appreciated.

Follow these tips in your telephone conversations:

1. **Be friendly.** Get to know who answers the phone. Ask for his or her name and job title; then write it down on your record form.

2. **Ask for the full name, appropriate courtesy title, and correct job title** of the person you're calling. If the person you're calling has a secretary, get his or her name, job title, and courtesy title. Verify the spelling and pronunciation. You may also ask the receptionist or another employee for this information.

3. When placing the call, **ask for the person by first and last names.** You may eliminate the courtesy title here.

4. Upon reaching your party, **identify yourself.** State the name of the person who referred you, if appropriate. Then state the purpose of your call; for example, "I need your help." Don't be shy or beat around the bush.

5. **Remember why you're calling**—to get job interviews, to get leads about jobs, and to get referrals.

6. **Be prepared to state the job you want** and your qualifications. Keep your resume at hand for quick referral.

7. **Offer to be of help** to the person.

8. **Make a detailed record** on Form 29, Network Contact Record, and/or Form 30, Employer Record, whichever is appropriate.

9. **Send a thank-you letter** with a copy of your resume to all prime contacts.

10. **Follow up.** Let your contact set the schedule. Record the date and time on your weekly planner. Be sure to adhere to calling back within the agreed time.

PREPARE TO ANSWER QUESTIONS

Telephone conversations often end up being informal interviews. Be prepared to respond to questions concerning your employment, work habits, skills, and references. Here are a few typical questions that could come up when you call an employer. You'll find more information on how to answer these questions in the next chapter.

1. Where have you worked, and what dates were you employed?
2. What jobs did you hold? Describe the job qualifications and duties.
3. What was your salary?

Your ability to succeed in selling yourself doesn't depend on what happened in your past, but on how you see your future. Convince yourself that you will be successful and you'll convince others as well.
—Dorothy Leeds, *Marketing Yourself*

4. How long have you known   (name of reference, etc.) ? What was your relationship?

5. Why did you leave? Were you fired? Would you please describe the circumstances of why you left your last employer?

6. What are your major strengths and weaknesses?

7. How did you get along with your boss? the boss's boss? peers? subordinates? other department personnel?

8. How was your attendance?

9. How was your safety record?

10. How did you handle deadlines?

11. Tell me about your outstanding achievements and specific results.

12. Who can provide additional information?

SCRIPT YOUR CONVERSATIONS

Working the phone is the quickest and fastest way to get an interview. Over the phone you want to sound confident, professional, and prepared. The best way to achieve this is to write a script for each type of conversation.

Ultimately, you want to talk with the person who can hire you. If this person is not available, ask for the personnel manager or a secretary or a receptionist. Often this person can provide you with the information you need.

Here is how you want your conversation to go:

- First, ask about the company's hiring policies and procedures.

- Next, ask for the names of key personnel. Get their job and courtesy titles. Check the spelling and pronunciation.

- Finally, ask about job opportunities.

- Close with a thank-you. Say good-bye and hang up.

- Don't waste time in idle gossip or small talk. Stick to business. Use your script.

When writing your script, use this list and the following scripts as guidelines.

Script #1: Conversation With Receptionist or Personnel Department

SAMPLE OPENING STATEMENTS

- Good morning! May I speak to   (first and last names) ? Thank you.

- Good morning, Ms. Jones (use courtesy title and last name). This is (your first and last names) . Ken Birkby mentioned that you may be able to help me. I'm currently looking for a new career opportunity and would like a few minutes of your time. Is this a convenient time? When may I call you back? Thanks.

- Hi. This is   (your first and last names) . May I ask with whom I am speaking and your position? Thank you. I'm looking for work, and I'd like to know what your company's hiring procedures are. With whom should I speak? Thank you.

- Good afternoon. Can you tell me the name and job title of your personnel manager? Thank you. May I speak with him/her?

Script #2: Conversation with Employer's Secretary

OPENING STATEMENTS

- Good morning. May I speak with Elaine __(use first name only)__, please. Thank you.
- This is __(your first and last names)__. Larry Anders suggested I call Elaine __(use first name only)__. Is she available? Thank you.

BODY STATEMENTS

- I have recently completed my degree in __(state major)__ with an emphasis in __(state minor/specializations)__. I'm looking for work in __(state field)__. (Now state how your education and/or experience will benefit this company. Give two or three examples. Your resume will help you here.)

The purpose of every call is to get a job interview, job leads, and referrals.

- I'm looking for a position in __(state field of interest)__. My qualifications are __(state experience/education/work history/achievements)__. (Now present three examples of how your qualifications will benefit the company. Use your resume to help you.)
- I've worked for __(state work history, including employers and job positions)__. (Now provide two or three specific examples of how and why you can be of benefit to this company. Use your resume as a guide.)

CLOSING STATEMENTS
To Request a Meeting:

- I believe my work experience and education would be of value to you. May we schedule an appointment on Monday or Thursday to discuss exactly how my qualifications might fit your needs?
- I'd really appreciate your advice on how to __(improve my job search, determine the appropriate person with whom to speak, etc.)__ May we get together briefly today or tomorrow? (Suggest alternative times to meet; give your contact a choice.)

To Drop Off a Resume:

- I know you're busy __(person's name)__, but would it be alright if I dropped by with my resume? I'll only take a few minutes. Would tomorrow or Thursday be best for you? (Note the two choices given.)

To Extend a Luncheon Invitation:

- __(Name of person with whom you're speaking)__, I'll be in town on Wednesday and the following Monday. Would you be available for lunch? That would give us the opportunity to get to know each other without taking time from your busy schedule. Would one of these days work for you?

To Get Referrals:

- Do you know anyone who may be hiring someone of my experience and background? May I use your name when calling? Thank you.
- Are there other companies or individuals you could recommend I call?
- Is there anyone else you can think of that could help me?

To Get a Personal Introduction/Referral to "Mr./Ms.?"

- __(Person's name)__, I have a couple of names in your company (industry), and I wondered if you might know them. The first person is __(name of person and employer)__. (This technique helps you get personal referrals.)

Script #3: Conversation with the Person Who Can Hire You

OPENING STATEMENTS
- Good morning, _(courtesy title and last name)_ . This is _(your first and last names)_ . Sheral Mason (name of network reference) mentioned that you are looking for a _(job title)_ .
- Ms. June, this is _(your first and last names)_. I'm looking for work in the _(field or industry)_ . I would like a few minutes of your time to discuss employment opportunities with you.
- Mr. Lanning (use courtesy title and last name). I'm in need of your help. I'm looking for work and thought you might know of someone who might need a _(job title or field of interest)_ . Do you have a few minutes to talk?

BODY STATEMENTS
- I have recently completed my degree in _(major)_ with emphasis in _(field of specialization)_ .
- I am currently employed at _(name of company)_ and am looking for advancement in the _(field or industry)_ . I have just completed _(major project)_ with exceptional results. Your company is expanding in this area, and I believe my background and experience may be of interest to you.
- I have recently left _(former employer)_ as their _(job title)_ . I worked for them for _(number)_ years. Some of my major projects include _(describe two or three successful projects)_ .

CLOSING STATEMENTS
To Set Up an Interview or Meeting:
- May we get together on Wednesday or Friday to discuss how I may be of value to your company? (Always suggest two meeting times to give the contact a choice.)
- I'll be in town on Monday and Tuesday. Would you be available for lunch? That would give us time to get to know each other.

To Get Job Leads and Referrals:
- Do you know any companies that are hiring people with my background? May I use your name when calling? Thank you.
- Is there anyone else you can think of that I might call? May I use your name when I call? Thank you.

To Drop Off a Resume:
- I'll be in town on Friday, may I drop off my resume at your office? If you are available, may I stop in? I'll only take a few minutes of your time. Thanks.

Be sure to mind your telephone manners—the call could turn out to be an interview. There is always time for telephone courtesy. Treat every call with importance; you may be talking with your next boss.

CLUSTER YOUR SCRIPT

Follow these guidelines:

- Write the person's name you are planning to call in the center of a blank page. List the telephone number below the name, and then draw a circle around it.

- Next, write down each of the main topics you plan to discuss. Draw a circle around each topic, and connect it to the center circle.

- Now go from each circle and make additional notes that pertain to the circle. Continue this until you have captured all the ideas you plan to discuss.

- Use this pictorial script when you make your call. Change colors of ink pens, and make notes on your cluster as you talk.

- When you complete the conversation, transfer the notes to your network contact record. Attach your cluster to the record.

Here's a sample cluster for the conversation script from the previous page:

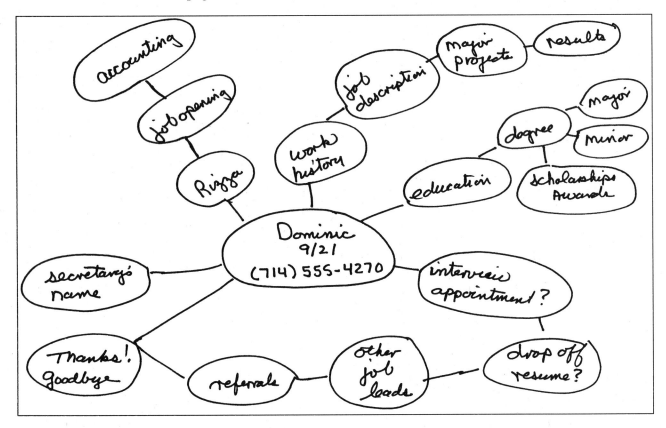

Figure 11-2 Cluster

CALL A FRIEND FIRST

A friend is, as it were, a second self.

—Cicero

When calling your friends, remember that your objective is to get job leads and referrals. The first person you call should be someone you are comfortable talking with, a friend or a business associate. This will help build your confidence and your telephone skills. Start with someone who will support what you are doing and who will help you in your search. After building your comfort zone, call the strangers and the people on your list that present challenges. Do not avoid calling the difficult ones.

Complete Form 29, Network Contact Record

- Cluster each call. A cluster is a pictorial script. It flows easier than a written script. You can make notes on the cluster and transfer the details to your network contact record. I use a pencil for the cluster and a red ink pen for the my notes.

NETWORK CONTACT RECORD

Contact Name/Job Title/Courtesy Title	Work Phone
Ms. Susan Adler, Veterinary Assistant	614-555-9823
	Home Phone
	614-555-8396

Employer	Referred by
Town & Country Animal Hospital	
525 SE Division	No one - Personal friend and neighbor.
Columbus, OH 43207	
614-555-9823	

Home Mailing Address	Secretary/Spouse/Other Names
	Secretary: Ms. Sally Jones
76943 Williamsburg Road	Husband: Mr. Kerry Adler
Columbus, OH 43208	Kids: Brandy, Mercedes, and Chelsea

Conversation Notes

- Company is growing and needs another veterinary assistant.
- Dr. Andrew Mikes (owner) is willing to train.
- Required Qualifications : love animals, work well with nervous pet owners, excellent communication skills, good sense of humor, proficient on computer especially WordPerfect 6.1.
- Desired Qualifications: two-year degree in animal husbandry or similar program, two-year's work experience in vet's office.
- Drop in and pick up application. Application may be taken home.
- Dress appropriately when stopping in. Look professional. Doctor's fussy about personal appearance.
- When you return application, doctor will review, if time. Be prepared to be interviewed on the spot. Otherwise, an appointment will be made.
- Hopes to fill position within three weeks.
- Best time to drop in is first thing in the morning.

Referrals (Name/Job and Courtesy Titles/Company/Phone/Relationship)

- Dr. Beverley Childress, Owner of Animal Heart Clinic. 614-555-7308 - Personal friend and former school mate.
- Ms. Katsumi Yano, Secretary, Bird and Aviary Practice. 614-555-7566 - Fellow Toastmaster
- Ms. Lupé Garcia, Vet Assistant, Barclay Small Animal Clinic. 614-555-8712. Attends same church.

© 1995 Harris Espérance Incorporated   Form 29/95

Figure 11-3   FORM 29, Network Contact Record

- Each time you make a call, make a detailed network contact record of the conversation. Attach your phone cluster. This record will prove invaluable as your job search proceeds.

- Use Form 29, Network Contact Record, to capture the main points of the conversation.

- File Form 29, along with your phone cluster and any other notes, in alphabetical order behind the NETWORK RECORDS section of your notebook.

- When the number of records becomes cumbersome, add alphabetical or individual name dividers.

CALL A STRANGER

Strangers need not to be strangers for long. You can get a referral to almost anyone you need to contact. Ask your friends if they know this person, or if they know someone who might know someone. In this way, when you speak to the stranger, you can say, for example: "Antonio Perez suggested I call you. He thought you might be able to help me." This helps to break the ice and put the stranger at ease.

If you need to go through a secretary to reach this person, you can say, "May I speak to Jim? Tell him it's Randy calling," or mention that a mutual friend suggested that you call. (Be sure you have a mutual friend; don't get caught lying.) When talking to the secretary, get his or her name. Spell it correctly and check the pronunciation. Always be polite.

NETWORK CONTACT RECORD

Contact Name/Job Title/Courtesy Title	Work Phone
Ms. Katsumi Yano, Secretary	614-555-7566
	Home Phone
	614-555-6663

Employer	Referred by
Bird & Aviary Practice	Ms. Susan Adler, Veterinary Assistant
4550 SW Lombarde	Town & Country Animal Hospital
Columbus, OH 43207	
614-555-7655	

Mailing Address Work ✓ Home	Secretary/Spouse/Other Names
9843 Rusty Lane	
Columbus, OH 43208	

Conversation Notes

- No positions available here at this time.
- Can stop in and pick up application and take home-to be returned when convenient.
- Applications kept for six-months.
- Recommended that I join the Toastmaster's Club. Meets at 6:30 A.M. every Tuesday at Salisbar's Restraurant, off Sunset Blvd.

Referrals (Name/Job and Courtesy Titles/Company/Phone/Relationship)

- Drs. Jim and Sally Curnow, The Mobile Pet Clinic (Owners), 614-555-2409 - Former neighbors
- Ms. Alice Cooper, Secretary, Animal Eye Clinic. 614-555-3351 - Friend
- Mr. Antonio Perez, Veterinarian Assistant, Cedar Mill Veterinary Hospital, 614-555-4308 - Neighbor

© 1995 Harris Espérance Incorporated   Form 29/95

Figure 11-4   FORM 29, Network Contact Record

Complete Another Network Contact Record

Keep these tips in mind:

- Your purpose is to get a job interview, job leads, and referrals.

- Cluster each call.

- Make a record. Keep detailed notes. Note the date, time, and purpose of the call.

- File these records in alphabetical order behind the NETWORK RECORDS divider in your notebook.

- When the number of records becomes cumbersome, add alphabetical or individual dividers to your notebook.

USING THE EMPLOYER RECORDS SECTION
OF THE *COMPANION PLANNER*

Once you begin to contact potential employers, you will need to keep records. The EMPLOYER RECORDS section of your notebook serves this purpose. The following forms and documents are kept there.

- Form 30: Employer Contact Record
  Make a detailed record of each potential employer you contact. File the record in alphabetical order in the EMPLOYER RECORDS section of the *Companion Planner*. Attach all supplemental information on the employer to this record.

  - Form 31: Interview Self-Evaluation
    After each interview, complete a Form 31, Interview Self-Evaluation. File this form with the appropriate Form 30, Employer Contact Record. The complete record is stored in the EMPLOYER RECORDS section of the *Companion Planner*.

  - Form 32: Employer Rating Matrix
    Use Form 32, Employer Rating Matrix, to analyze each offer you receive. If you receive more than one job offer, rate each of the employers. Then compare the offers. File Form 32 with the appropriate Form 30, Employer Contact Record.

- Other Documents
  You may choose to file **copies** of other important documents in this section. Some of the possible documents include:

    Cover letter and resume sent to each employer

    Company annual reports (If possible, obtain two or three annual reports on each company you are seriously interested in. This is important for your analysis of each company.)

    All letters and correspondence

- Alphabetical Dividers
  If your job hunt is broad and cumbersome, add alphabetical dividers for each employer to make each file easy to locate. If you accumulate a large amount of information on a particular employer, set up a separate small three-ring binder.

CALL THE EMPLOYER

Be not afraid of life. Believe that life is worth living, and your belief will help create the fact.
—William James

When you telephone an employer, your objective is to get an interview. Failing this, you want job leads and referrals.

Use the telephone; it is the quickest and easiest way to learn about a company. Ideally, you want to talk to the person who can hire you. If he or she is unavailable, ask for the personnel manager. If he or she is unavailable, talk to the secretary or the receptionist. Usually he or she will be glad to provide you with all of the information you need. Be sure to ask for the name and position of the person with whom you are speaking. Also ask for the correct spelling, pronounciation, and preferred courtesy title.

If you need to go through a secretary to reach this person, you can say, "May I speak to Jim. Tell him it's Randy calling," or mention that a mutual friend suggested you call. (Be sure you have a mutual friend; don't get caught lying.) When talking to the secretary, get his or her name. Spell it correctly and check the pronunciation. Always be polite.

EMPLOYER CONTACT RECORD	Page 1 of 2

Employer	Phone
Animal Heart Clinic	614-555-7308

Address

1210 Hayden Drive, Columbus, OH 43208

Directions to Company

- Go down Columbia Blvd. to Hayden Drive, turn left three blocks on right.

Contact Person (Name, Courtesy and Job Titles)

- Dr. Beverly Childress, Owner, Veterinary

Hiring Policies and Procedures

- Come in and complete application. Drop in at any time, receptionist will give you application.
- Applications will be kept for six months.
- If opening occurs during the six months, applications will be reviewed, and if qualified you will be called in for an interview.

Referrals

- Dr. Andrew Mikes, Town & Country Animal Hospital. 614-555-9823 - Fellow veterinarian.
- Dr. Alicia Williams, Cedar Mill Veterinary Hospital. 614-555-4308 - Fellow veterinarian.
- Dr. Pat (Patricia) O'Brien, Capital Hill Cat Clinic. 614-555-1952 - Fellow veterinarian.

Information Checklist: _Annual Report _Value Line _Dunn & Bradstreet _Standard & Poors _Moody's _Who's Who _Forbes _Employee Newsletter _Advertisements/News Articles _Benefit Booklets _Training Programs _Promotion Policy _Other _____

Results of Contact
✓ No Openings, No Applications Being Taken   _ Send Resume/Letter of Application
✓ Come In and Fill Out Application   ✓ Referred to Ms. Sally Adler
_ Mail Thank-You Letter and Enclosed Resume—Sent to _____
✓ Other Attached resume to job application.

Figure 11-5 FORM 30, Employer Contact Record, Page 1

Complete Page 1 of Form 30, Employer Contact Record

- Make a record. Use Form 30 to keep detailed notes of your conversation. Attach extra pages to this form, if necessary.

- Cluster each call. File each cluster with your employer record.

- File the records. File this form behind the EMPLOYER RECORDS divider in your notebook.

- Keep the records in alphabetical order according to employer name.

- When the number of employer records becomes cumbersome, add alphabetical or individual dividers to your notebook.

- Remember, your objective is to get a job interview, job leads, and referrals.

Overcome fear, behold wonder.

—Richard Bach,
Running from Safety

Your first call isn't necessarily the first company on your list. Review your Form 28, Network Contact List, and **choose the employer you least want to work for first.** By doing this, the stakes are lower. Therefore, your stress level is lower. This provides you the opportunity to become comfortable with your script before calling the more important employers.

Here are some tips when calling an employer.

- First, inquire about the company's hiring procedures and policies.

- Next, ask for the names of key personnel. Next, get their job and courtesy titles.

- Finally ask about job opportunities.

- Then thank the person for helping you. Say good-bye and be the one to hang up last.

EMPLOYER CONTACT RECORD   Page 2 of 2

Employer   Animal Heart Clinic

Person Responsible for Hiring Decision

Dr. Beverly Childress

Job Titles I Might Qualify For
- Veterinary Assistant
- Bookkeeper/Secretary
- Receptionist

Description of Job
- Assist veterinarian in animal health care duties
- Prepare treatment room for examination of animals
- Hold, restrain, and comfort animals during examination, treatment, or inoculations
- Administer injections, perform venipuncture, apply wound dressings
- Clean teeth, take vital signs of animal
- Prepare animal for treatment and set up equipment, hand instruments and medical supplies
- Perform routine laboratory tests
- Care for and feed animals. Bathe and groom animals.
- Assist with research projects in commercial, public health, or research laboratories.
- Inspect products or carcasses to ensure compliance with health standards.
- Assist veterinarian in artificial insemination of animals.

What I Can Do To Improve Hiring Possibility

- Complete veterinarian degree program
- Volunteer at local Humane Society

Description of Business
✓ Profit _ Nonprofit _ Not-for-Profit _ Government _ Public _ Corporation ✓ Partnership
_ Co-Op _ Other _ Union ✓ Nonunion Employees: Hourly _8_ Salaried _4_ Total _12_
Annual Sales $ 1,500,000 _____ Annual Production_____

Employer Benefits
✓Major Medical ✓Vision ✓Dental ✓Life ✓Disability ✓Retirement 10 Vacation Days 8 Holidays
_Credit Union ✓Profit-Sharing ✓Education/Training _Stock Options _Car _Expense Account
_Membership Dues Other _____

Probable Salary Range
- Veterinarian Assistant: $25,000 to $32,000
- Bookkeeper/Secretary: $18,000 to $23,000
- Receptionist: $16,000 to $19,000

© 1995 Harris Espérance Inc.   Form 30/95

Figure 11-6   FORM 30, Employer Record, Page 2

Complete Page 2 of Form 30, Employer Record

Be sure to do the following as you call each employer:

- Make a detailed record for each call.

- File each record along with the phone cluster in alphabetical order.

- When you've accumulated a large number of records, add alphabetical dividers to your notebook.

- If an individual file becomes massive, put it in a separate notebook.

- Remember, the purpose of every call to the employer is to get a job interview. Failing this, you want job leads and referrals.

Your objective is to get help with your job search.

Your objective in letter marketing is to get help with your job search. There are several reasons why a person might choose to write letters instead of telephoning. One reason could be cost. If you are relocating, it may be costly to make long-distance phone calls to that location. A letter campaign can get the show on the road quickly and inexpensively. Another reason could be that you are a skilled writer and have had exceptional responses from your letters. Even though direct mail produces only 5 percent of all jobs, it may be worthwhile to pursue in this case.

A NETWORK LETTER FROM A GRADUATING STUDENT TO A FORMER BOSS

Another advantage of letter writing is that it allows you to conceal potential liabilities that could be noticed over the telephone. For example, if you have a speech impediment, a telephone conversation could result in your being dropped from consideration. In approaching the employer by mail, this impediment goes unnoticed. You get the employer's interest first; then you can handle the impairment later.

Try a letter-marketing campaign. Target your friends, associates, employers, and even strangers. You may be surprised at the results you get. If writing is your forté, organize a letter-writing campaign.

JANICE JOYNER

3589 N.W. Fir Street   Redmond, OR 97756   503-555-3297

August 10, 19xx

Mr. Robert Swanson
Vice President, Procurement
Tektronix, Inc.
Post Office Box 1000
Wilsonville, OR 97070-1000

Dear Mr. Swanson:

Following the downsizing of Tektronics and the elimination of my position as Procurement Agent in 1993, I moved to central Oregon. At that time I hoped to find a similar position in the Bend area. What I found was a scarcity of good jobs. Rather than risk further frustration and discouragement in a futile job search, or relocate again, I decided to return to school.

At the end of June I will receive an associate of science degree in business from Central Oregon Community College. My emphasis is in computers and business writing. I am proficient with both the MacIntosh and IBM environments. I have developed excellent skills in programming and software applications. My computer and business-writing assignments have contained many comments of "very good" and "excellent."

After adding two years of business education to my sixteen years of hands-on experience in electronics, I feel uniquely qualified. I've enclosed my resume so you will be fully aware of all my business and education background.

In early July I will be free to relocate and would like to stay in the Pacific Northwest. I really want to be back in procurement again and would like to return to Tektronix, especially to your department. If any positions become available, I am interested. If this isn't possible, I would appreciate hearing of any other procurement positions open or pending. If you hear of any job leads, please let me know. Write or call me collect, and I will follow up directly.

I appreciate any assistance or ideas you can give me. I am eager to put my education and experience back to work.

Best regards,

Janice Joyner

Janice Joyner

Enclosure: Resume

Figure 11-7   Network Letter from a Graduating Student

The more people involved in your job hunt, The faster you will get hired.

RELOCATING? Try a letter-market campaign.
SKILLED WRITER? Letter-market friends, associates, strangers, employers.
DISABLED? Try letter-marketing.

Who to Write

- Former employers and business associates

- Professionals and community associates

- Old and new friends and neighbors

- Everyone on your network list. If you don't call, write.

A NETWORK LETTER TO A FORMER SCHOOLMATE

Here are some ideas of what to do.

ROBERT D. GRAHAM

1616 N.E. Elm Street   Bend, OR 97701   503-555-6893

May 10, 19xx

Dear Greg,

   Arizona looks great! Thanks for the pictures of your spring break ski trip. Living so near a ski area like Mt. Bachelor, it never occurred to me that Arizona has good skiing. How does the snow compare to Mt. Bachelor? Looks like you got a pretty good suntan in just a few days--or have you been to the tanning salon? All kidding aside, you look great!

   I'm finishing my last term at COCC. Around the middle of June I'll receive an associate of applied science degree in business technology with an emphasis on information systems management and a certification in computer-aided drafting and design (CADD). This summer I will be looking for a job using my new knowledge and skills.

   That's where you come in. As much as I like living in Bend, I realize I will probably need to relocate to find the work I want. My sister asked me to stay with her in Seattle and look for work there. I appreciate her offer, but I don't like Seattle's climate. I like a dry climate, and I know Phoenix has that. Can you tap into your network at school and at work and get the names of some companies or individuals involved in information systems management or CADD?

   I've enclosed my resume, which you are free to pass on to anyone who might be interested. Make as many copies as you need!

   You can see from my resume that I stayed with the grocery store where I went to work the first summer out of high school. Besides stocking shelves and bagging groceries, I designed two small remodeling projects for the store. They were projects for my CADD class, but the good news is that the store used them! One was for two new express check-out stations. The other was for enlarging the magazine display area. In addition to the satisfaction of seeing my designs materialize, I received a store bonus and an A+ for the class.

   I plan to continue living with my parents and working at the grocery store until I have another job lined up. You know what they say, "Don't quit your job until there's another one in the hopper." Write me or call collect at the same old address and phone number.

   Thank you, Greg, for any help you can give me in the way of names and addresses or any new and better ideas.

Cheers!

Bob

Enclosure: Resume

Figure 11-8   Network Letter to a Former Schoolmate

- Get in touch with former classmates, neighbors, and old friends. These people know someone who can help you. Don't hesitate to ask.

- Write to all your friends. Announce your intentions.

- Write to your former work associates. Let them know what's going on in your life.

- Write letters to others in the field you are planning to enter.

- Don't sit around waiting for something to happen. Make it happen. Letter-Market!

- Keep copies of all your letters in the appropriate NETWORK RECORDS section or the EMPLOYER RECORDS section, and a copy in the LETTERS section.

Talent and merit alone will rarely get you past the smiling receptionist, the protective secretary, the wary agent, the routine hiring or admissions screening. A personal introduction to someone on the inside will.

—Barbara Sher,
Wishcraft: How to Get What You Really Want

Suppose you want to meet Toshio Takado from Boston, Massachusetts. Mr. Takado is a stranger, a person you have never met. What can you do? Get in touch with him through mutual acquaintances. How? That's what group marketing is about. Getting people together in a group and asking for their help and ideas.

How many people would you have to go through to reach Mr. Takado? Mathematically, it has been proven that within five contacts, you will have the personal introduction you are seeking. Here is a little more background on this theory.

It's a small world—all of us have heard that phrase. Well, Stanley Milgram, a psychologist, set out to prove it. He conducted what is known as the "small world experiment." Mr. Milgram contacted 160 people at random, provided each with a set of instructions, and asked that they get a folder into the hands of a specific person. Each person was given the name of the target person and a little more information, such as where he or she might work. Each person was then asked to pass the folder to an acquaintance (someone they knew on a first-name basis). This was to repeat itself until the folder reached the target person. How many people handled the folder before it reached its target? On the average, it took five intermediate acquaintances.

This experiment, along with several other similar experiments, proved that if you get fifteen to twenty people in a room and ask them to help you contact anyone in the United States, that within five or six contacts, you will have a personal introduction to that person. This technique will likely work as well for contacting anyone in the world. So how do you group-market? Host a group marketing party?

GROUP-MARKET AT A CLUB OR ORGANIZATION

If you are a member of a club or organization, you have a ready-made group. If you belong to a church or synagogue, ask to make an announcement or if you can have five or ten minutes of meeting time. Tell the group what it is you need, and ask that they contact you after the meeting. Follow up on all the leads and suggestions that each person makes.

If you belong to a club, ask to be the program. Spread the word. Tell everyone you're conducting "a small world experiment." The program can be a brainstorming session—a joint "needs and wants" party. If you plan on a brainstorming session, review the rules for brainstorming. Be sure to have a blackboard or flip chart available to write down all ideas. Explain that the wildest idea is acceptable; no idea should be rejected.

HOST A GROUP-MARKETING PARTY

It is easy to get a group together. Just decide when, where, who, and the purpose. Then start calling everyone. Call enough people so you get at least fifteen to your party. Make it fun. People enjoy doing something new and different. Ask a variety of people. If you are shy, friends, neighbors, and family will do. The key is to host the party and ask for what you need. Here are some more specifics.

Set a Date, Time, and Place

- The date and time must be convenient for the people you want to invite. It could be during the lunch hour at a local restaurant or campus activity room. You could ask everyone to bring a sack lunch for the party. It doesn't have to be an expensive get-together. You can offer to supply coffee and soft drinks.

- The party could take place on the weekend or during the week after work. Be creative, and set a time that will work for the people you want to invite.

- You can host this party at your house. It can be fun to get a group of diverse people, sometimes total strangers, together on a small world quest. If your home isn't a good place, consider your local recreation center, a community center, or a room at your church or synagogue. If you scout around, you can often find a room to use without charge.

Decide Who and How Many to Invite

- Who to invite depends on the situation, the time, and the setting of your experiment. It is smart to ask people from a variety of backgrounds and ages. Variety is the spice of life, so invite a wide range of personalities and abilities. Ask a few of your friends. Suggest that each person bring along another interesting friend.

- You want fifteen to twenty people at your small world party.

Set the Rules

Barbara Sher, author of *Wishcraft: How to Get What You Really Want*, offers these rules when you're hosting a big group of people:

- Be as specific as you can about what you need.

- Do not offer anything you are not truly willing and able to give.

- If you can provide what someone else needs, or use what someone has to offer, raise your hand and give your name. Write down each other's names, and get together after the formal part of the meeting is over.

Determine How to Ask

Now that you've gone to all this work, you want to be sure to get out of your party the things you need. Use the steps outlined on page 267, "Ask for What You Need—The Secret to Marketing." These steps are recapped below.

- Ask specifically.

- Ask someone who can help you.

- Create value for the person you are asking.

- Believe fervently in what you are asking.

- Ask until you get what you want.

CHAPTER 12

INTERVIEW LIKE A PRO
Win-Win Encounters

Our greatest glory is not in never failing, but in rising every time we fail.
—Confucius

Brian had scheduled the interview of his dreams, so I was helping him through a practice interview. I asked him, "Why do you want to leave your current employer?" Brian started telling me all the bad things that were taking place at work. I had heard rumors of poor employee morale at his company, but as a potential employer, it was the last thing I wanted to hear.

After allowing Brian to express himself, I asked, "How do you think an interviewer will react to your answer?"

Brian thought for a moment, then said, "Well, it's all true. You've heard the stories, haven't you?"

"Brian," I said, "that's not the question. The question is, how do you think an interviewer will react to your answer?"

"Oh," he said, "I see what you mean. There's probably a more positive way to answer this question. Now that I think about it, the reason I really want to leave my current employer is because this new job is perfect for me. It fits my interests, skills, and background. It's the job and field I most want to work in. It's exactly what I have always dreamed of doing. I'm qualified for it and excited about it, and I would do a terrific job for the employer."

"Now that's more like it!" I said. "That answer is what an interviewer wants to hear. It's truthful and filled with facts and reasons to hire you."

As you prepare for the interview, listen closely to all your answers—and listen from an interviewer's perspective. While your answer needs to be truthful, it also needs to be something an interviewer wants to hear.

Answering all interview questions in a positive, honest manner is key to getting job offers. You can improve your interviewing techniques by learning and understanding more about the interview process. In this chapter we'll examine the basics of interviews and methods for improving your techniques.

USING THE INTERVIEW INFORMATION SECTION
OF THE *COMPANION PLANNER*

This section of your notebook holds preliminary interview information. File all documents pertaining to interviews here. If you find helpful newspaper and magazine articles on interviewing, file them here. The more you know about interviewing, the more confident you will be during an interview.

When you script answers to probable interview questions, file them here. When you make a list of appropriate questions to ask during an interview, file them here. Here are some helpful hints for scripting an interview and for listing appropriate questions.

Interview Script

Draft an interview script to guide you through your interview. Well-thought-out responses will make you more comfortable and build confidence during the interview.

Select interview questions that are typically asked and other questions that might give you difficulty. Write out a positive, honest answer for each question. Then practice your answers. It isn't necessary to memorize each answer, but it is important to know what you plan to say.

Review this script prior to each interview.

Evaluate each answer and the accompanying reaction of the interviewer(s) after each interview. If you received a negative response, review your answer and rewrite if appropriate.

Questions to Ask

Make a list of job-related questions to ask. Questions concerning wages and benefits should be left until the employer brings them up or until a job offer has been made. Important questions to ask may include:

- Why is this job open?

- Why did the last person leave?

- How many people have held this job in the past three years?

- Where do you see this job in the next two to three years?

- Have the job functions changed much in the past three years? How?

- How and by whom will my job performance be rated?

- Where do you see the company's future in the next five to ten years?

- Is there anyone else I can talk to about the company's future?

- How would you describe my supervisor's management style?

- Do you have any company literature that I can read?

THE TEN COMMANDMENTS OF INTERVIEWING

1. **Tell the truth.**
2. **Be yourself.** Relax and forget all the things you're supposed to do. Forget all the practice. Go on automatic pilot.
3. **Speak well of others**—former employers, bosses, coworkers, peers, company products and services.
4. **Maintain eye contact** (but avoid a constant stare).
5. **Ask appropriate questions.** Focus on the job itself and the employer's expectations. Refrain from asking about pay, pensions, unions, vacations, retirement, and fringe benefits. Save these questions until the employer expresses an interest in hiring you. Your research should have provided most of these answers.
6. **Do not press employers for your standing.** This puts them on the defensive and is detrimental to successful interviewing.
7. **Do not intimidate or become a threat to the interviewer.** Employers always say they want to hire people better than themselves, but most of the time they don't really mean it.
8. **Do not act bored or, on the other hand, too curious.** Avoid looking at your watch or reading papers on the interviewer's desk.
9. **Find out what will happen next.** Find out when the hiring decision will be made. Should you call back? When?
10. **Close with a smile, a handshake, and a thank-you.** Leave immediately. Don't linger!

TYPES OF INTERVIEWS

The purpose of every interview is to get a job offer.

There is no such thing as a standard interview. They come in all sorts and types. Let's look at the four basic interview types that you will encounter.

THE TELEPHONE INTERVIEW

This type of interview is often used for preliminary screening. Employers will try to probe the information you have given them. They seek to eliminate you from a person-to-person interview. This is a time-saving device for the employer

To avoid being quickly eliminated, prepare carefully and thoroughly. Here are tips for handling the telephone interview:

1. Train family members to handle incoming phone calls properly. Poor handling may cause you to miss the message or make a poor impression on the caller. Teach them to record the caller's name, the time of call, the date, and a detailed message.
2. Keep a phone message pad, pencils, and paper by the phone.
3. Have your resume readily available.
4. Be ready to answer basic interview questions. Have your interview script at hand.

THE ONE-ON-ONE INTERVIEW

Although this type of interview is what many job candidates expect, it is becoming more and more uncommon. Companies prefer to share the hiring decision with several people—it is part of the participative management style. This type of interview, however, features just you and the interviewer. The interviewer may be the hiring decision maker or a preliminary screener. Find out which.

A GROUP INTERVIEW

The group may consist of two or more people. They may be informally seated, or they may be arranged in a panel. There may be a primary interviewer, or there may be a totally unstructured interviewing process. When in a group setting, generally speak to the person who asks the questions. But bear in mind, if the question asker is just a facilitator, such as a personnel manager, you will want to direct your answers to the hiring decision maker. Make eye contact with all group members, if possible. Often the group members do not have a copy of your resume, so always bring extra copies to hand to each person present. This helps those present and also demonstrates preparedness.

THE SERIAL INTERVIEW

Always have extra copies of your resume with you; you never know how many people will be interviewing you.

This type of interview procedure may or may not be planned. The serial interview happens when the person interviewing you feels that someone else in the company may be interested in what you have to offer or may be of greater help to you. Sometimes you are interviewed by the wrong person. Sometimes the company wants several people to interview you so the company can have a broader analysis of your abilities. Provide each person that interviews you with a copy of your resume.

A serial interview may include people from all levels and departments within the organization. It may include company officers, board members, superiors, peers, and subordinates. Be prepared for all of them.

Always have extra copies of your resume with you when you're interviewing. You never know how many people you'll be talking with.

Before you interview, it is imperative to do research. You want to know as much as possible about the job, the company, your prospective supervisor, and the interviewer.

WHAT YOU NEED TO KNOW

Research is what you do when you don't know what you're doing.

1. **Job Description** of the job(s) you want.
2. **Description of Business:** Look at the company's main products or services (annual sales dollars and production volume). Find out whether these have changed significantly in the past two to three years. What is the ownership (public, private, co-op, profit, nonprofit)?
3. **Key Personnel:** Identify the person who can hire you—the decision maker. This may include the personnel manager or director of human resources. This may also include the company president, CEO, CFO, CIO, department heads, peers.
4. **Management Style/Company Philosophy:** Find out the company's mission statement, company history, organizational structure. Is the company union or nonunion?

   Find out the morale of employees right now and why—employee turnover rate.
5. **Wage/Salary Ranges:** Look at industry salary surveys.
6. **Company Culture:** Is there a dress code (uniforms, dresses, suits and ties, casual)? Is the company involved in outside activities, politics, the community?
7. **Size and Location(s) of Organization:** Find out the number of plants, offices, locations. Find out the number of employees in the company and the location and department where you would work.
8. **Employee Benefits:** These may include insurance, retirement, vacation, holidays, profit sharing, expense accounts, car, training/education assistance, child-care assistance, commissions.
9. **Hiring Policy:** What are the procedures? Do you register with the state employment agency? Do you just stop in and pick up an application?
10. **Industry Standing and Reputation:** Look at the company's stock value (whether it's going up or down), financial condition (whether it has changed recently), competitors, growth prospects.

WHERE AND HOW TO FIND IT

Visit the Library

Your library is your greatest resource for information; if you need help, ask the librarian.

- Consult the *New York Times Index,* business periodical index, and the college placement annual.

- Study trade and business directories and magazines, almanacs, yearbooks, telephone directories, and local, regional, and national newspapers.

- Use computer databases, and review the *U.S. Government Manual*.
- Read useful publications. These may include:
  - *Dictionary of Occupational Titles*
  - *Occupational Outlook Handbook*
  - *U.S. Government Manual*
  - Trade and business directories and registers: Standard and Poor's, Dun & Bradstreet reports, Value Line reports, *Encyclopedia of Associations, Thomas Register of American Manufacturers*, Directory of State Manufacturers
  - Trade and business magazines: *Forbes, Business Week, Fortune, Working Woman, U.S. News and World Report, Purchasing Today, Professional Safety, Personnel Journal*
  - Who's Who directories
  - *Gale's Directory of Publications*
  - Annual reports from public corporations
- Use local, regional, and national telephone directories
- Study local, regional, and national newspapers
- Research salary surveys
- Read books about the company

Call, Visit, or Write the Company

The company is the best place to get current and accurate information. Most employees and executives are approachable, but be considerate of their time.

- Contact people employed by the organizations you want to work for. Request annual reports, sales catalogs, and press releases. Check with the public relations department for all available information on the company.

- The information you want includes annual reports, house publications (employee newsletters, sales brochures, and advertisements), benefit booklets.

- Ask the personnel office, the receptionist, and current or former employees for help.

Visit the Chamber of Commerce

Chambers of commerce maintain an assortment of information on the community and its employers. Chamber directors are storehouses of valuable news.

    Call coworkers from your current and former employers. Telephone your banker and accountant, friends, family, and neighbors. Talk to colleagues, business associates, community leaders, teachers, classmates, your college placement director, reference librarians, alumni, and industry experts. Everyone is a potential source of information.

If you don't ask, you won't receive.

Stop at State and Federal Government Agencies

- There are numerous other state and federal government agencies—check them out. Find out what's available in your area. You may qualify for a special program and financial assistance.

- Your state employment service can provide you with statistical data, wage surveys, and a variety of other information. Get salary surveys, job leads, job descriptions, and names of companies and key personnel.

Contact Your Banker, Stockbroker, Insurance Agent, Accountant, Doctor

- Your banker or stockbroker can provide you with financial information, such as Value Line reports, annual reports, and credit reports.

- Your insurance agent or accountant may refer you to a company.

- Your doctor may just know an employer who needs someone like you.

Visit the College Campus

Anyone can use the services of your local college. Most of them have career libraries and placement centers. They have a wealth of information that can be very helpful.

SYNOPSIS OF LIBRARY REFERENCE BOOKS

Do your research. It's to your advantage to know as much as possible about the organization before you call. Your time and effort will pay off in job offers. Listed below are some of the resources available at most public and college libraries.

Dictionary of Occupational Titles:

- Lists over twenty thousand job descriptions in 1,371 pages.

- Fourth edition, revised in 1991, has two volumes and 1,404 pages of information.

- Published by the U.S. Department of Labor, Employment and Training Administration, Washington, D.C.

- Found in most local libraries.

Occupational Outlook Handbook:

- Describes 850 occupations in thirty-five major industries.

- Found in most local libraries.

- Published annually by the U.S. Department of Labor, Bureau of Labor Statistics.

- Provides descriptions of work, working conditions, employment statistics, training and other qualifications, job outlook, earnings, and a list of related occupations.

U.S. Government Manual:

- Contains detailed listings of all government agencies.

- Includes narratives of an agency's purpose, history, locations, and application procedures.

- Includes the following contents: Declaration of Independence; Constitution of the United States; legislative branch; judicial branch; executive branch; departments of executive agencies; independent establishments and government corporations; guide to boards, committees and commissions; commissions; selected multilateral organizations; selected bilateral organizations; Peace Corps.

- Available for purchase from the Superintendent of Documents, Government Printing Office, Washington, D.C. 20402 and at Government Printing Office bookstores located in major cities.

- Found at most public and college libraries.

Research will pay off in big dividends.

Standard and Poor's Register of Corporations, Directors and Executives:

- 345 Hudson Street, New York, NY 10013—three volumes.

- Volume 1: *Corporate Listings.* 2,419 pages. Alphabetical listings of thirty-seven thousand names, titles of officers and directors, annual sales, number of employees, some division names, principal and secondary businesses. For company/industry cross-referencing, the Standard Industrial Classification codes are listed for public firms.

- Volume 2: *Directors and Executives.* 1,600 pages. Alphabetical listings of seventy-five thousand individuals serving as officers, directors, trustees, partners, etc. Includes their principal business affiliations with official titles and business and residence addresses. Year and place of birth, college, year of graduation, and fraternal memberships are listed when available.

- Volume 3: *Indexes.* 805 pages. Divided into six color-coded sections.

Thomas Register of American Manufacturers:

- Published by Thomas Publishing Company. One Penn Plaza, New York, NY 10001—published annually. Twenty-one volumes.

- Volumes 1–12: Products and services listed alphabetically.

- Volumes 13–14: Company profiles listed alphabetically with addresses, zip codes, telephone numbers, branch offices, asset ratings, and company officials. Brand names and index included in Volume 14.

- Volumes 15–21: Catalog file bound alphabetically by company name and cross-referenced in the first fourteen volumes. Inbound traffic guide included in Volume 21.

Dun & Bradstreet Million Dollar Directory:

- 99 Church Street, New York, NY 10007.

- Lists corporations with sales of $1 million or more. Similar to *Standard and Poor's Register of Corporations, Directors and Executives.*

Who's Who Directories:

- Biographic data on seventy-two thousand influential people.

- Each entry provides name, address, position, vital statistics, education, family status, career and career-related activities, civic and political activities, and writings.

Encyclopedia of Associations:

- Published by National Organizations of the U.S. Gale Research Company. Book Tower, Detroit, MI 48266.

- A guide to over twenty-five thousand national and international organizations. Three volumes.

- International organizations: Four volumes; more than three thousand entries.

- Regional, state, and local organizations: Seven volumes; over fifty thousand entries covering the following subject groups: Trade, business, and commercial; agricultural and commodity; legal, governmental, public administration, and military; scientific, engineering, and technical; educational, cultural, welfare, health, and medical; public affairs; fraternal, foreign interests, nationality, and ethnic; religious; veteran's, hereditary, and patriotic; hobby and avocational; athletic and sports; labor unions, associations, and federations; chambers of commerce and trade and tourism; Greek letter and related organizations and fan clubs.
- Found at most libraries.

Gale's Directory of Publications:

- Gale Research Inc, Book Tower, Detroit MI 48226.
- An annual guide to newspapers, magazines, journals, and related publications—two volumes with over 2,000 pages.
- The professional's directory to print media published in the United States and Canada.
- Includes economic descriptions of the states, provinces, cities, and towns in which all listees are published.
- Includes fifteen separate, classified, custom-made maps on which all the publication's cities and towns are indicated.
- Found in most libraries.

Directory of Oregon Manufacturers:

- Published by the State of Oregon. Economic Development Department. 595 Cottage Street NE, Salem, OR 97310.
- Listings by county, city, and manufacturer.
- Information includes addresses, phone numbers, key officers and titles, employment numbers, and products by code designations.
- Found in Oregon libraries, chambers of commerce, and economic development agencies.

Most, if not all, states have similar listings of manufacturers. Check your local library, chamber of commerce, and/or state economic development agency.

You need to be prepared to answer basic questions with positive, honest, and straightforward answers. The only way you can guarantee confidence while interviewing is to plan, or script, your answers. The questions and suggestions that follow will help you with your responses.

File your script behind the INTERVIEW INFORMATION divider in your notebook.

Listed below are thirteen questions you may be asked during an interview. Some of the questions are inappropriate interview questions, but they are presented here to prepare you for the unexpected. Employers may ask inappropriate questions in ignorance of the law, or through carelessness. You must be ready to handle proper and improper questions. Now let's examine each of the questions.

TELL ME ABOUT YOURSELF

This question is often asked at the beginning of an interview. Your answer should take two to three minutes, with a maximum of five minutes for those with ten or more years of high-level experience. Here are three approaches you could take:

1. **Cover the four major areas of your life:**

15–30 seconds	**Early history.** Provide a general background; for example, where you were born and raised, areas of activities or interests.
15–30 seconds	**Education.** Cover high school, college, military school, and any other training relevant to the job. Highlight relevant courses and training that match job requirements. State your major and minor (areas of specialization).
30–60 seconds	**Work history.** Begin with your earliest jobs. Briefly describe what you did and why you left. Finish with the last job.
15–30 seconds	**Why you and why this company.** Explain why you would be good for the company and why you want to work for the company.

   By using this approach, you are trying to find some common ground. When an interviewer identifies with you (going to the same school, from the same state, etc.), you build rapport and credibility.

2. **Begin at the bottom of your resume and work your way to the top.** It never hurts to repeat your resume. Sometimes even your interviewer may not have read it. Repetition helps to reinforce your highest qualifications, especially since you have worked hard to capture your true essence and abilities on this piece of paper.

3. **Make a high-powered sales pitch.** Select two or three experiences that make you uniquely qualified for this job. Explain why you are the best candidate for the position.

WHAT ARE YOUR MAJOR STRENGTHS AND WEAKNESSES?

If you are asked about your strengths and weaknesses in the same question, talk about your weaknesses first, then end with your strengths. Following are three possible ways to respond to this question.

1. **Review and use the comments made by your references.** This will bring credibility and believability to your answer. You may say:

   "My last boss, Dave Williams, always said I was bullheaded. This is true. But if I hadn't had the perseverance to hang in there, the job would never have gotten done. Dave is one of my references; I'm sure he'll confirm what I say."

   Another applicant answered this way: "Jenny told me I didn't smile enough and was too serious, which has been true. I have been working on this. So now I smile more and try not to take life as seriously. I appreciated her comments; they have helped me a lot."

2. **Translate your weaknesses into strengths.** Look for their opposites.

   Too many jobs = varied and broad experiences, ability to make changes

   Too young = energetic, ambitious, ready to learn, not set in your ways

   Stubbornness = tenacity

   Moody = calm and quiet

   Slow, bogged down = detail minded

   Obstinacy = perseverance

   Unmotivated = easygoing

   Too old = mature and experienced

3. **Perceive weaknesses from the employer's point of view; then explain why this shouldn't eliminate you from being hired.**

   For lack of experience: "I know that I've not been in this field before, but I have many transferable skills that are very relative to this position. (Now name three specific skills that transfer to the position.)

   For lack of degree: "I know you are looking for a person with a master's degree in accounting, but I'm sure that when you look at my job history and skill levels, you will agree that my experience more than compensates for the degree. Here is what I've done . . . "

   Other weaknesses to consider include being the wrong sex, being married or single, being too young or too old, and having health problems or a physical disability. Your past work history can be a weakness if you have held too many jobs, have experience in a different field, or have too much or too little experience. Even your personal appearance can work against you if, for example, you are overweight by twenty pounds or more.

   Take the time to resolve any problem for the employer, and you won't be automatically eliminated from consideration. It's worth the effort.

WHY DID YOU LEAVE YOUR LAST JOB?

Scripting an honest and straightforward answer here can help you get a job. You must be comfortable with your reply; otherwise, your body language, voice tone, and eye contact may send out negative signals.

The first answer that pops into your head is not always the wisest and best answer. Give your response serious thought. Tell interviewers what they want to hear—a positive, honest reply without hesitation or guilt.

There are only two reasons for leaving a job; however, these two reasons can elicit many causes.

Always say good things about your prior work experiences. There's always something good to say if you sincerely think about it.

1. You quit (voluntarily or not). What caused you to quit needs to be examined carefully. Was it because you couldn't get along with your boss, or because you wanted to move up in your career, get a promotion, higher wages, improve your working conditions (hours, benefits, etc.)? Select a reply that's honest and positive, one the employer will want to hear.

2. The company terminated you. This includes being fired, being laid off, or retiring. Companies terminate people for many causes:
   - Company, plant, or department closure, downsizing, reorganization, or restructuring
   - A downturn in the economy
   - The loss of or failure to acquire a large government or private contract

Select a reason that's honest and positive—a reply that your previous employer will support and one the potential employer will want to hear.

WERE YOU EVER FIRED?

Employers appreciate honest answers. Some interviewers will also have been fired and will empathize with you. Do not lie; your body language will likely give you away. You may want your answer to be something like this:

"Yes, and it's probably the best thing that ever happened to me. I have learned a lot from the experience and am far better off than before. I have a letter of reference from my former boss. Would you like a copy?" (Stop here, but be ready to explain this answer in detail if asked. You may not have to say anything more.)

"Yes, the company decided to reorganize (restructure) the department, and I got caught in the process. Losing my job has allowed me to assess my career and make changes I've wanted to make for a long time. I have a letter of reference from my former boss. Would you like a copy?" (Stop here, but be prepared for some probing questions from the interviewer. A word of caution: Make sure your past employer will confirm your reason for termination.)

You commit instant suicide when you give negative answers about prior employers, bosses, or jobs, no matter how true the statements may be. Spend time with this question, and find a positive way to respond. This answer may make the difference in whether or not you get a job offer.

WHERE DO YOU SEE YOURSELF IN THREE TO FIVE YEARS?

This is when the time you spent on goal setting really pays off. You know where you're going for the next ten years. Find an answer that satisfies the employer's question but doesn't harm you in the process. Saying you want the boss's job may not prove to be the right thing to say.

DO YOU HAVE ANY HEALTH PROBLEMS I SHOULD KNOW ABOUT?

This question will probably be phrased as follows: Are there any reasons that you may not be able to perform the job duties or be at work on a regular basis? You may say:

"None. I have no health conditions that would affect my ability to do the job. I'm quite healthy. I enjoy exercising daily and maintain a balanced diet. My attitude is good, and I'm enthusiastic about working here."

"I did have some health problems last year, but that problem is resolved now. It won't affect my attendance or work performance."

ARE YOU MARRIED?

Personal questions come in many forms. For example: How old are you? Do you have any children? Are you planning a family? Are you planning on marrying? Have you ever been arrested? How much do you weigh? What does your spouse do? Are you renting? What was your military discharge?

For help answering these types of questions, read Exercise 12-3, "Handle Illegal Questions."

WHAT PROBLEMS DO YOU HAVE GETTING ALONG WITH OTHERS?

Always say something positive. Relay genuine, specific compliments. Turn negatives into positives. Review what was said when you called your prior employers and references. You may say: "None. I get along quite well with everyone." (Stop here; you've answered the question. Let the interviewer probe further if he or she wants more information. Be prepared to respond in depth with a positive example concerning a tough relationship and situation.)

If you are pressed for a broader response, try: "I found my boss a real challenge to work with. She is slow paced, and I like to move faster. Working with her, I learned to adjust my pace and communicate better with others who work slower. Actually, I learned to value her differences because I learned so much from her. Pace is not a signal of intelligence, ability, or effectiveness. It's just another way of functioning."

WHAT QUALIFIES YOU FOR THIS JOB?

This is the place to sell yourself. But before you answer this question, you want to know what is most important to the employer. If you haven't discovered what will be expected of you in the first six months, ask. This information will let you direct your answer to a specific need of the company.

For example, if the company interviewing you is experiencing problems with employee morale and low production, you may respond: "My understanding of people will allow me to build trust between management and workers quickly, which will result in productivity increases. I'm skilled at team building, quality circles, and cooperative work circles. I have a charismatic personality that people follow easily."

WHAT SALARY DO YOU EXPECT?

Read "Know What You're Worth" in Exercise 13-3. If you have done your research on this question, you know the answer. Here are some typical ways to handle this question.

- Respond with a question: "What range do you have in mind?"

- Respond with a range: "Around $32,000 to $40,000. What do you have in mind?"

- "Before I can respond, I need to know more about the . . . job requirements, benefits, travel requirements, etc. Does the company provide a company car for travel? What expenses will be covered?"

WHAT DO YOU KNOW ABOUT OUR COMPANY? THIS JOB? THE INDUSTRY?

This is where your research pays off. Script a broad answer; for example: "I studied the past three years of the company's annual reports, read (name of book about company) , and talked to (names of several company employees and industry specialists) . From these sources, I've learned . . . " (Be specific here. Discuss the elements that come closest to affecting the job you want. For example, if the company has expanded with new operations and you are an expert in leverage buyouts, talk about this.)

DO YOU HAVE REFERENCES? WHO ELSE CAN PROVIDE INFORMATION ABOUT YOUR WORK?

If you completed the work on references in Chapter 6, this question is easy. You may say: "I've prepared a list for you. I've selected six references from various areas of my life. I've provided each reference with an authorization to release information. In this way, I believe you will find each person more than willing to provide you with a balanced view of my skills and background."

AREN'T YOU OVERQUALIFIED FOR THIS JOB?

There are three reasons applicants are labeled "overqualified": (1) undermarketing, (2) overpricing, and (3) interviewer intimidation. Let's look at each of these reasons:

Undermarketing

This occurs when you apply for positions below your experience, education, and/or skill level. Consider these questions:

- Is your education, experience, and/or skills greater (or perceived greater) than generally expected for the position. If your answer is yes, find out why.

- Do you have a false concept of the jobs available at your level? Be assured that there are job opportunities at all levels. It is estimated that the annual national employee turnover in corporations is 25 percent. No employer or job is exempt from turnover. Even small businesses and sparsely populated communities provide opportunities.

- Have you lost confidence in yourself? If so, do you unconsciously apply for positions below your abilities? When you do this, you wave a red flag in the employer's face. Employers are immediately suspicious—something could be wrong. You don't fit, and they know it. Consequently, they shy away from you.

To avoid undermarketing, restructure, broaden, and enlarge your job hunt. Then apply for those positions at or slightly above your experience level.

Overpricing

This generally happens when applicants change careers, industry, size of employer, or move to areas with a lower cost of living. It also occurs when job hunters have incorrect wage information.

- Analyze wages by job, industry, geographic location, and economic factors. Ask your librarian for assistance. Question state employment service personnel about wage levels. Seek information from your friends working in similar positions. Query local employers.

- Know the wage scales for the job you want. Then review your wage requirements. If you are priced higher than the industry or area norm, anticipate being overpriced. Prepare to discuss and explain your wage requirements during the interview. Identify the causes for the disparity. Provide evidence as to why you're worth the higher wage. Explore ways to offset the wage difference, such as performance bonuses, contract work, or additional fringe benefits.

Eliminate the overpriced label with up-to-date, accurate salary information and creative solutions to higher-than-standard wage demands.

Interviewer Intimidation

This generally occurs when the person vacating the position does the interviewing. Human nature plays a role here.

- The desire to hire the best candidate is offset by the "he's-better-than-me—I-could-look-bad" syndrome. Key statements that characterize intimidation include "You wouldn't want this job," "This work would really bore you," or "You are clearly overqualified for this position."

- When interviewer intimidation occurs, proceed with extreme caution. Do not argue or attempt to change the interviewer's mind. Politely ask to speak to a higher executive about other opportunities. If the interviewer refuses to help, tactfully approach the official on your own.

By understanding these reasons, you can adjust your job hunt procedure and prevent being classified as overqualified. These guidelines will help:

1. Apply only for positions at or slightly above your experience and skill level.
2. Price yourself within the market range, or provide evidence to justify your higher-than-standard salary request.
3. Recognize interviewer intimidation; then seek an interview with another official.

RECOMMENDED READING

Read *Knock 'Em Dead with Great Answers to Tough Interview Questions,* by Martin Yate. This book includes answers to more than two hundred interview questions as well as suggested responses for many interview situations. It covers stress interviews, salary negotiations, how to dress, and body language.

Your goal in an interview is to get a job offer, not to offend or educate an employer on the legalities of an interview question.

Some questions are commonly considered illegal questions, and an employer should not ask them. I like to refer to these questions as being "unwise." The legality of the question should be left up to the courts. Let's look at some topics that border on being illegal and are definitely unwise.

QUESTIONABLE AREAS

- **Marital Status:** The interviewer should not ask if you are single, married, divorced, engaged, or living with someone, or if you date or see your ex-spouse.

- **Children:** You don't have to reveal how many children you have, their ages, who cares for them, or whether you plan on having more kids.

- **Age:** An employer should not ask your age, birth date, or other obvious questions that may be used to determine age.

- **Physical Data:** Weight and height are generally off limits for job requirements unless it has a specific relationship to the job. Health and medical history is another area that causes employers concern, but that is unwise for them to inquire about.

- **Military:** You are not required to provide information concerning what branch of the military you served in or the type of discharge.

- **Criminal Record:** An employer should not ask you if you have ever been arrested, convicted, or spent time in jail or prison. Some jobs do have requirements concerning these areas; in these cases, you may be asked if you can be bonded.

- **Housing/Finances:** An employer should not ask if you own, rent, lease, or are buying. You should not be asked where you bank and whether you have checking or savings accounts.

- **Sex:** In an interview, your sex is generally apparent, but unless sex is a bona fide occupational consideration, employers cannot specify a preference for a male or female.

These questions should not come up during an interview, but often they do. Sometimes an interviewer is naive and unaware of the potential liabilities of such questions. Other times, employers choose to ignore the potential of libel suits because they want the information and figure it's worth the risks.

WHAT TO DO WHEN FACED WITH ILLEGAL QUESTIONS

You can decide after the interview whether you want to work for a company that asks about your personal life, as well as whether you want to contact the Equal Employment Opportunity Commission.

What should you do when faced with these questions? Here are some suggestions:

1. Answer the question, and ignore the fact that it is inappropriate or illegal. This may be your best choice. Your intuition of why the question is being asked will provide you with guidance.
2. Say: "I don't think that's relevant to the job requirements."
3. Ask: "How is this relevant to the job?" or "Why do you ask that question?"
4. Contact the Equal Employment Opportunity Commission. This takes time and results in your spending time on negative activities. Consider your real goal; that is, to get a job offer.

In most cases, answering the question and ignoring the legality issue is probably your best course of action. Your goal in an interview is to get a job offer, not to offend or educate an employer. You can decide after whether you want to work for a company that places such values in areas of personal concern, and/or whether you want to contact the Equal Employment Opportunity Commission.

Ask these important questions: Why is this job open? Why did the last person leave this job? Where do you see this job in three years? Where do you see the company in three years?

Sometime during the interview you will probably be asked, "Do you have any questions?" This question is generally asked toward the end, but I have heard stories of interviewers asking this as their very first question. So be ready to field it professionally.

The right answer is yes. Always have some questions ready to ask. Make a list of questions, and file it behind the INTERVIEW INFORMATION divider in your notebook. Keep the following guidelines in mind:

1. Take a copy of these questions with you when you go to an interview. You can quickly retrieve it from your briefcase. Referring to a list shows that you have given the subject thought. This usually impresses the interviewer. Having your list also prevents you from forgetting to ask an important question that could slip your mind.

2. Never ask questions that you should know the answers to.

3. Don't ask about wages, benefits, vacations, holidays, or retirement, unless a job offer has been made. Research the company, and ask appropriate questions concerning the job, supervisor, or company.

4. Remember these three important questions:
   - Why is this job open?
   - Why did the last person leave this job?
   - Where do you see this job in the next three years?
   - Where do you see the company in three/five/ten years?

5. Ask these questions about the job:
   - Is this job newly created?
   - How many people have held this job in the last three years?
   - Have the job functions changed much in the past few years? How?
   - Are there established goals for this position? What are they?
   - What accomplishments are expected in the first year?

6. Ask these questions about your future supervisor and work performance:
   - How will my work be judged? Are there established guidelines for review and measurement? How often and by whom? How were these guidelines set?
   - Who will be my supervisor?
   - How would you describe this supervisor's management style?
   - Would this supervisor be described as fast or slow paced? As auditory, visual, or kinesthetic? As task or people oriented? (Be ready to explain any term your interviewer may not be familiar with.)
   - Who does this supervisor report to?

7. Ask these questions about the company:
   - Is there anyone else I should talk to about the company's future?
   - Do you have any company literature that I can read?
   - What is the management style and philosophy of the company?
   - Does the company have an established mission statement? How was it initiated? Does the mission statement effectively provide a basis for future planning and for managing conflicts?

The best way to prepare for an interview is to practice.

The best way to prepare for interviewing is to rehearse your answers in a mock interview. Practice your answers so they sound spontaneous and natural. Your goal is not to memorize each answer word for word, but to memorize it's direction—the general content and intention.

A PRACTICE INTERVIEW

Make a list of interview questions. Include the questions listed in Exercise 12-2, and add all other questions you feel need to be asked.

Ask for help from a friend or family member (preferably someone who has experience in interviewing). You may want to ask two or three people and do a group practice interview.

- Before rehearsing, provide each interviewer with the list of interview questions, a copy of your resume, and a completed job application (Form 24). The interviewer(s) may add as many questions as it seems appropriate.

- Have the interviewer read each question. Answer the questions according to your script. But do not read your answers; answer spontaneously.

- Tape-record or videotape the interview.

- Listen to your responses and make notes of any responses that sound awkward, phoney, weak, or otherwise unsatisfactory. Ask for the interviewer's opinions.

- Revise the answers for all questions that you had difficulty with.

A DRESS REHEARSAL ON VIDEO

Videotaping the interview is the best way to improve your performance. You will see and hear yourself as the interviewer sees and hears you. Most of my students have been pleasantly surprised to see how well they do; as a result, the experience turns out to be a confidence builder. They also find ways to make improvements. Don't get cold feet now. Don't allow fear or modesty to control you or get in the way. This experience is too valuable. Follow these pointers:

1. Dress for the interview. Wear your best interview outfit. Look professional and neat.
2. Answer questions directly without stumbling over words or searching for a response. This is where your scripting and practicing pay off.
3. Act with confidence, and be friendly and pleasant. **Smile.**
4. Maintain good eye contact, posture, and voice quality.
5. Sit comfortably and properly in the chair.

Set Up the Video Interview

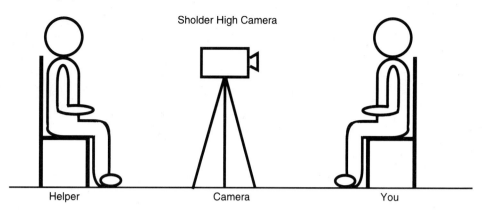

Sholder High Camera

Helper   Camera   You

Establish Question Parameters

- Make a list of difficult questions, and provide them to the interviewer(s).

- Ask the interviewer to prepare a list of questions ahead of time. Do not ask the interviewer for these questions before the practice session.

- Provide the interviewer with a job description and your resume ahead of time. This will help the interviewer prepare questions.

- Make sure that all the tough questions are asked.

Follow These Videotape Procedures

1. If you do not own a camera and tripod, borrow one. Most of us know several people who have cameras. If possible, ask to borrow their equipment and get them to be your interviewer.
2. Your helper should sit directly behind the camera. This allows you to speak directly to the camera.
3. The camera should be placed on a tripod and should be at shoulder height when you're seated. Depending on the lens, place the camera so you fill the picture from head to toe when seated.
4. The room should be quiet and well lit.
5. The camera should be turned on before you sit down. Put a smile on your face and a "win-win" thought in your mind. Walk in, introduce yourself, and shake the interviewer's hand. Wait to be invited to be seated; then sit down.
6. Once the camera is turned on, don't stop. Keep filming until you have covered all the interview questions. This should probably last about thirty minutes.
7. You should close the interview on camera. Stand up, shake hands, say good-bye, and leave. Then shut off the camera.
8. You should sit comfortably and talk to the camera. Make eye contact with it.
9. Nervousness will cause you to speak faster than normal, so concentrate on slowing down your speaking rate.

FORMALLY EVALUATE YOUR DRESS REHEARSAL

After the interview, take time to record your personal reactions. You may choose to review the film several times or to film another dress rehearsal.

You may want to arrange a different type of interview setup, such as having two or three friends interview you at one time. Group interviews are a challenge even to the best of candidates, so a practice session can prove very valuable. Complete Form 31, Interview Self-Evaluation, page 1.

The example in Figure 12-1 was completed by a guest interviewer. The written evaluation provided constructive feedback for the student, who was able to implement the suggestions immediately.

File the practice Form 31, Interview Self-Evaluation, behind the INTERVIEW INFORMATION divider in your note book.

File Form 31, Interview Self-Evaluation, for actual interviews with the appropriate Form 30, Employer Contact Record, behind the EMPLOYER RECORDS divider in your notebook.

INTERVIEW SELF-EVALUATION — Page 1 of 2

Company	Interview Practice	Phone 475-4461
Name and Title of Interviewer	Howard Barker	
Position Interviewed For	Car Salesman	

Check the appropriate description of "how you felt" about the listed aspects of the interview.
E = Excellent   G = Good   M = Marginal (needs improvement)

AREA OF ASSESSMENT	E	G	M
Personal Appearance: Smile, Handshake, Appropriate Attire, Accessories (Briefcase, Jewelry, Purse), Shined Shoes, Grooming (Hair, Breath, Cologne)		X	
Professional First Impression: Handshake, Eye Contact, Posture, Gestures, Facial Expressions	X		
Self-Confidence: Comfortable (at-ease) during interview. Maintained a calm enthusiastic attitude.		X	
Articulation/Expressiveness: Used appropriate words and expressions. Pronounced words correctly.		X	
Responsiveness/Enthusiasm: Responded with appropriate level of enthusiasm (not too quiet, not too loud).		X	
Qualification/Abilities: Presented skills in terms of the job requirements. Described in a positive manner.			X
Strengths: Tied strengths to job and employer requirements.			X
Weaknesses: Presented weaknesses and employment barriers in a positive light. Offset each weakness with a strength.			X
Previous Employers/Bosses: Discussed positively. Described benefits and blessings of employment experiences.		X	
Questions: Asked appropriate questions. Asked specific questions concerning job, company. Avoided questions concerning wages, benefits, unions.			X
Persuasiveness: Expressed interest for job and company. Feel good about presentation and effectiveness.			X
Manner and Chemistry: Established rapport with interviewer. Found common ground. Felt comfortable.		X	
Research/Interview Preparedness: Knowledge of job, company, industry, products, services was sufficient.		X	
Follow-Up: Learned "What Happen's Next." Arranged a follow-up call or interview. Mailed a thank you letter.			X

Other Comments: *Changing vocations/fields of employment is not a negative — think of all the expertise and positives you can bring to a new job from your past.*

© 1995 Harris Espérance Incorporated   Form 31/95

Figure 12-1 FORM 31, Interview Self-Evaluation, Page 1. Courtesy of a guest interviewer

Ask a friend to view the film with you. He or she may be able to see things that you missed. Don't be embarrassed by your performance. Be glad that you have had the opportunity to see yourself in "action." Many times there are specific behaviors, such as slouching in your chair, that you can easily correct.

COMPLETE FORM 31, INTERVIEW SELF-EVALUATION, PAGE 2

After you identify the areas that need improving, list on page 2 of Form 31 the type of improvement that needs to be made. Then list the specific steps that you will take to make the improvement. Follow up your plan with a time period to accomplish each improvement.

You may find that you can make the changes immediately, or that it will take time and some concentrated effort. Whatever the case, begin to make your improvements as soon as possible.

File practice Form 31, Interview Self-Evaluation, behind the INTERVIEW INFORMATION divider in your notebook.

File Form 31, Interview Self-Evaluation, for actual interviews with the appropriate Form 30, Employer Contact Record, behind the EMPLOYER RECORDS divider in your notebook.

INTERVIEW SELF-EVALUATION Page 2 of 2

"M" Marginal Areas Needing Improvement

MARGINAL AREA: Qualifications and Abilities

Improvement Steps: Need to identify and stress what you have. Review your qualifications and abilities. Look for transferable skills — draw from all areas of your work, not just from formal employment. Remember your own buying and selling of automobiles. You've made a bundle with your own deals.

Time Frame for Improvement: X Immediate _ 1 Week _ Other

MARGINAL AREA: Weaknesses and Strengths

Improvement Steps: Find a weakness that the company can identify with. In car sales, it might be the desire to always own the latest and fastest car. Whatever it is, it must be genuine. Identify strengths that will relate directly to the potential employer, for example, your natural gift to identify with people, your ability to relate.

Time Frame for Improvement: X Immediate _ 1 Week _ Other

MARGINAL AREA: Questions

Improvement Steps: Make a list. Know what you want to ask and should ask. Ask questions directly related to the job or the company. Examples: "where do you see this company in three years?" "Why are you looking for a salesperson now?"

Time Frame for Improvement: X Immediate _ 1 Week _ Other

"G" and "E" Areas for Additional Improvements
There's always room for improvement.

GOOD/EXCELLENT AREA: Self-Confidence

Improvement Steps: Don't be so hungry. You try too hard to please. Be yourself. You have a lot to offer an employer: integrity, perseverance, reliability, etc. Capitalize on your strengths.

Time Frame for Improvement: X Immediate _ 1 Week _ Other

GOOD/EXCELLENT AREA: Manner and Chemistry

Improvement Steps: I know it's not easy to be interviewed in front of a class and do all the things that need to be done right. But you will be nervous even in a real interview, so relax. Try taking a few deep breathes. Put a smile on your face. Do your additional preparation and you will do great. Good luck!

Time Frame for Improvement: _ Immediate _ 1 Week X Other Next time

 Form 31/95

Figure 12-2 FORM 31, Interview Self-Evaluation, Page 2. Courtesy of a guest interviewer

There are some important actions to take before every interview. Study these pointers, and make sure you are totally prepared for each employer.

ASK QUESTIONS BEFORE EVERY INTERVIEW

When making the interview appointment, ask the person about the interviewing procedures. Many companies involve several people in the hiring decision. Some companies may even tape the interview. The more you know, the better prepared you will be and the more comfortable and at ease you will be.
Ask these questions:

- What are the normal interviewing procedures?
- Who will be interviewing me? Will there be more than one interviewer?
- How long of an interview shall I expect?
- What time is the interview?
- Where exactly will the interview take place?
- Can you give me directions? Is parking available?
- Do you have company literature that I may read before the interview? (Here are some of the items you want: annual reports, employee newsletters, employee benefit manuals, sales brochures, sales advertisements, company history.)
- Is there a book about the company I could read? Where can I get a copy?

When you are provided with company literature and other useful information, send a thank-you letter to the person who helped you.

PLAN YOUR APPEARANCE

- Prepare three interview outfits. Most companies do not hire at the first interview. Most likely, you will be interviewed at least twice.
- Dress appropriately and professionally (similar to others currently in the position you're interviewing for).
  - Shine your shoes. Sew on buttons, mend hems.
  - Avoid too much aftershave, perfume, makeup.
  - Have a fresh breath. Leave the onions and garlic alone.
  - Radiate confidence with a smile and a positive attitude. Stand straight, walk quickly.

PACK YOUR BRIEFCASE AND PORTFOLIO WITH CARE

- Include twelve copies of your resume.
- Have twelve copies of your reference list.

- Bring at least three letters of recommendation and any other necessary documents. Make three extra copies of each reference letter.
- Carry your weekly/monthly planner. You may need to schedule another interview.

ARRIVE EARLY

Arrive five to ten minutes early for the interview.

OBSERVE YOUR SURROUNDINGS WHILE YOU WAIT

- Do employees seem pressured, uptight?
- Is equipment up-to-date or antiquated?
- Does everyone observe the same dress code?
- Is the manager or secretary nervous?
- Are the offices alive with activity or deathly quiet?
- Are desks sloppy or neat?
- Does the operation appear productive and effective?
- Do employees seem to enjoy their jobs and work environment?

DON'T BE KEPT WAITING

- If you've been kept waiting for an unreasonable amount of time, you may ask to reschedule the appointment. Your time is valuable too. Use your good judgement here.
- Your own schedule and the reason for the long wait should be carefully considered in your decision.

PREPARE FOR SKILL, PSYCHOLOGICAL, AND OTHER PREEMPLOYMENT TESTING

A nationwide trend to create a drug-free, theft-free, and safe work environment has led many companies to use several types of testing. Employers hope to determine whether you are a liar, thief, or substance abuser. They also hope to determine how you will fit into the job and how you work with people.

Testing may consist of a written examination; a performance or skill check, such as a typing test; or a chemical analysis for drugs (through urine or blood sample).

Some companies use only written tests. These tests are attractive alternatives to urine tests, which can cost up to $50 each, are often considered unreliable, and face a growing legal challenge.

Most tests are surprisingly straightforward. They might ask if you have stolen anything from an employer or how many times in the past month you have used drugs. The tests are generally uncomplicated, not stressful, and user-friendly.

Applicants have no recourse but to submit to such testing. If you don't take the test, you won't be hired.

UNDERSTAND THE INEXPERIENCED INTERVIEWER

Not all interviewers are pros or trained, so be patient, understanding, and helpful. If the interviewer gets lost or doesn't seem to know how to begin, you should lead the discussion. Cover each point in your resume and cover letter. Ask questions directly related to the job requirements. Get the interviewer relaxed and talking.

- If the interviewer talks incessantly, wait until there is a lull in the conversation, then lead off with key points in your resume.

- If you are asked a series of questions, answer the last one first, then continue until you have answered all of them.

- If you don't remember all the questions, ask if you've covered everything or for a repeat of the questions.

- Close the interview by finding out what will happen next. Ask if you should call back in three days, when the hiring decision will be made, and when and how you will be notified.

Following is a list of additional interview questions. You may not wish to script answers to all of them, but review the list and script answers for any questions that may give you problems. For example, if you haven't read any appropriate books lately, read one; then you will be able to answer the first question with something like "I've just finished reading *Megatrends 2000,* by John Naisbitt, and found it very interesting"; or "I'm reading *The Seven Habits of Highly Effective People,* by Stephen Covey. It's terrific and I plan on implementing these habits into my daily life."

1. What books have you read recently?
2. What motivates you to put forth your greatest effort?
3. What would you do if you saw another employee stealing, drinking, sleeping, or using drugs on the job?
4. Have you ever failed to accomplish something you set out to do? What was it, and how did you handle it?
5. What was the most important lesson you learned on the job? From your boss?
6. Why do you want to work here?
7. Describe your ideal job/boss/employer.
8. Have you ever stolen anything from an employer?
9. Which do you prefer: working with people, data, or things? Why?
10. What questions do you hope I don't ask?
11. How soon will you be able to make a significant contribution to our company?
12. Would you rejoin your former company? Tell me why.
13. What is your energy level like? Describe a typical day.
14. What did you like/dislike about your last job? Boss? Company?
15. What makes you mad?
16. Are you willing to move/travel to where the company sends you?
17. What did you think of your last boss? Job? Company?
18. What kind of research have you done for your job hunt/interview?
19. What is the long- or short-term future of this industry?
20. Where is the industry weakest? Strongest?
21. What important trends do you see in the future?
22. How long have you been looking for a job? Why has it taken you so long to find work?
23. How long will you stay with this company?
24. How many hours a week do you find necessary to get the job done?
25. What are your greatest achievements?
26. What are your qualifications?
27. How do you organize and plan for major projects?
28. Describe yourself in three words.
29. In what way can you make a contribution to our company?

30. Wouldn't you be happier . . . working for a larger company? Working as a _____?

31. What do you think of this company? How did you make this evaluation?

32. What can you do for us that someone else cannot do?

33. Why should I hire you?

34. What interests you most about this job?

35. What problems have you encountered in your current job? How did you resolve them?

36. Have you identified any problems on your current job that had been previously overlooked?

37. What are you looking for in your next job?

38. How do you handle pressure and stress?

39. Why do you want to leave your present job?

40. What contributions did you make to your last employer? Did you increase sales? reduce costs? develop a product? cut waste?

41. Describe a difficult problem you've solved on the job.

42. How large was the budget you were responsible for?

43. How many people have you supervised? What were their positions and responsibilities?

44. To whom do you report?

45. What would your subordinates/boss/peers say about you?

46. What do you like most/least about the people you work with?

47. What type of decisions did you make on your last job?

48. What will your references say about you?

49. Have you ever been asked to resign? What were the circumstances?

50. Have you ever been fired unfairly? Describe what happened.

51. Tell me how you handle criticism. Describe two situations where you felt your work was unfairly criticized, and tell me how you handled them.

52. How have you changed the nature or content of your last job?

53. How do you spend your free time?

54. How do you spend your time at work? Why?

55. Why aren't you earning more money at your age?

56. Why did you accept each of the positions listed on your resume?

57. Are you applying at other companies? Do they have other pending job offers?

58. Describe your management style.

59. Would you like to have your boss's job?

60. How do you handle praise? Criticism?

61. How do you take directions?

62. Rate yourself on a scale of one to ten. Explain the rating.

63. What makes you worry?

64. What is the most difficult situation you ever faced? What did you do?

65. What are your pet peeves?

66. Tell me about the last time you got mad at work. What caused it? What did you do? What were the overall results?

67. Do you have a resume?

68. Did you have any problem getting here?

69. How have you financed your college education?

70. What makes you laugh?

71. What's your favorite story/joke? (If you claimed to have a good sense of humor or that you were the "Company Comic" be ready with a tasteful story or joke).

72. When and how do you give praise to a worthy employee?

73. How would you handle discharging an employee?

74. Describe a time when your boss got mad at you. What did you do, and how did you handle the situation?

75. We're looking for someone with experience. What qualifies you for this job when you've never worked before? Never worked in this field? Never worked in this industry? And you're so young?

The questions could go on and on. There is no way to list all the possibilities. Analyze your situation, and prepare some tough questions of your own. Preparing and answering practice questions will increase your preparedness for the actual interview. And if you interview like a pro, you'll get job offers.

COMPLETE THE CYCLE
The Follow-Up Process

CHAPTER

13

Nothing's so fatiguing as the eternal hanging on of an uncompleted task.
—William James

The phone rang. It was Cassondra. Her voice was excited and filled with anticipation. She had just completed a job interview and felt that it had gone well. She simply had to share her excitement with someone! She told me she would know in two days whether or not she had the job. Four days later, she called again. This time her voice was sad. She hadn't gotten the job. She had been the second choice and had lost out to someone from inside the company.

This story is a typical scenario for job hunters. There are highs and there are lows. The important part of the process is to keep going. In this chapter, you will learn what steps to take after the interview. Follow-up and perseverance are the keys for getting the job you want. Study each exercise so you will be ready when that job offer comes.

Following up is the key to landing interviews and getting a job. You can telemarket, letter-market, or group-market all you want; but if you don't follow up on the leads or the suggestions of your contacts, the job of getting interviews and a job will never come to fruition.

317

Practice good etiquette . . . leave immediately after the interview. Then as soon as practical, review what happened. Make quick notes. As the day continues, write down the thoughts you have about the interview. Sometime that evening or the first thing in the morning, complete an interview self-evaluation form.

COMPLETE FORM 31, INTERVIEW SELF-EVALUATION, PAGE I

Consider the following questions:

- What did you do well?
- In what areas can you improve?
- What points did the employer emphasize?

Respond to all the areas; then complete the second page.

File this form with the appropriate Form 30, Employer Contact Record, which is kept behind the EMPLOYER RECORDS divider in your notebook.

Figure 13-1   FORM 31, Interview Self-Evaluation, Page 1. Courtesy of a client

You don't have to be sick to get better.

There is always room for improvement. Study page 1 of your form, and select those items that need the greatest improvements. Write out the improvement needed; then specify the exact steps you are willing to take to make the improvement.

COMPLETE FORM 31, INTERVIEW SELF-EVALUATION, PAGE 2

Stipulate a time limit in which you will make the improvement. Sometimes it is a simple adjustment that can be done immediately. Other times, it may take a while to achieve the results you want. But it is important to set a time frame to each step.

Consider the following questions as you review your improvement steps and time frames:

- Have you set a reasonable time frame for each improvement?

- Will you commit to making these improvements?

- Are these improvements really your improvements—ones that you really want to make?

- Does each improvement take you closer to your primary goal of getting a job?

- Does each improvement fit your personality and values?

- Will you really like yourself better after you make these improvements?

File this form with the appropriate Form 30, Employer Contact Record, which is kept behind the EMPLOYER RECORDS divider in your notebook.

INTERVIEW SELF-EVALUATION Page 2 of 2
"M" Marginal Areas Needing Improvement

MARGINAL AREA: Self-Confidence

Improvement Steps: My nervousness showed a lot. I was always laughing. Probably too much. Relax more. Talk a little more slowly. Listen more closely. Smile instead of laughing.

Time Frame for Improvement: _X_ Immediate __ 1 Week __ Other

MARGINAL AREA: Weaknesses

Improvement Steps: Had a difficult time answering my weaknesses. Choose several types of weaknesses that can be turned into positives.

Time Frame for Improvement: _X_ Immediate __ 1 Week __ Other

MARGINAL AREA: Questions

Improvement Steps: Make a list. Know what I want to ask and should ask. Ask questions directly related to the job or the company. Examples: "Where do you see this company in three years?" "Why are you looking for a salesperson now?"

Time Frame for Improvement: _X_ Immediate __ 1 Week __ Other

"G" and "E" Areas for Additional Improvements
There's always room for improvement.

GOOD/EXCELLENT AREA: Research

Improvement Steps: Find out more about the county, the interviewer, and the job. Talk to Julie and Roger. They worked there before and know many of the other employees.

Time Frame for Improvement: _X_ Immediate __ 1 Week __ Other

GOOD/EXCELLENT AREA: Follow Up

Improvement Steps: Be sure to ask what happens next. Put a stickey on my notepad to remind me to ask.

Time Frame for Improvement: __ Immediate __ 1 Week _x_ Other Next time

© 1995 Harris Espérance Inc.   Form 31/95

Figure 13-2 FORM 31, Interview Self-Evaluation, Page 2. Courtesy of a client

CHECK BACK PERIODICALLY—USE THE PHONE

Before you leave the interview, ask when you will hear from the employer next or if you should call again. Don't get discouraged; it often takes longer to make a hiring decision than originally anticipated. If the employer fails to call back, call the day after they were scheduled to call you.

Here are some of the reasons you may want to make a follow-up call:

- To set or confirm another time to meet
- To provide additional information
- To update the employer on new developments
- To check on changes
- To withdraw your name from consideration

Use these guidelines when making follow-up calls:

- Never become a nuisance
- Respect the employer's time frame. If the employer asked you to check back next week, call next week, not this week.
- Know why you're calling. Script or cluster your phone call.
- Be positive, friendly, and to the point. Keep your conversation businesslike and short.

WRITE A FOLLOW-UP LETTER

Few applicants take the time to write letters. Follow-up letters should be used after telephone and in-person contacts with employers, references, and other people helping you in the job hunt. These letters are used to

- Say thanks.
- Introduce your resume.
- Reinforce your image.
- Restate your prime assets.
- Diffuse any employer concerns.
- Update a reference on your progress.
- Confirm your appointment.
- Correct any misconceptions that might have developed during an interview or meeting.

Follow-up is critical to success.

When writing your letters, follow these tips:

- Write in the employer's language, using the employer's terminology.
- Be interested in the employer's problems and in the interviewer personally, if appropriate.
- Enclose your resume if the employer doesn't already have it.
- Keep the letter short and friendly.
- Always close on a positive note.
- Use a postscript at the bottom of most of your letters.

Write a Thank-You Letter After Every Interview

Writing a thank-you letter after each interview puts your name back in front of the employer in a very positive way. It is a reminder of who you are, what you have to offer, and how you conduct yourself, even after the interview. A thank-you letter may be just the thing that gets you the job offer. When writing a thank-you letter, consider these pointers:

- Thank the interviewers for their time and consideration.
- State your continued interest.
- Reinforce your image.
- Repeat your key qualifications.
- Enclose new materials.
- Spell all names correctly.
- Express your thanks and appreciation for the interview in your opening paragraph.
- Sign and date your letter.

Build Bridges

Use all your follow-up contacts to build and reinforce bridges. Following are a few points you should consider during the job-hunting process.

- It's a small world. Always conduct yourself in a manner becoming to the professional you are. Be honest and open. Never speak negatively about anyone you're involved with. It has a way of coming back to you.
- The first-choice applicant may not work out; this could create another chance for you.
- Another opening may develop.
- Employers do not owe you a job.
- It often takes an employer longer than expected to make the hiring decision. Be patient.
- Employers do not have to tell you why they didn't hire you. If you ask why, you will put them on the defensive; and you do not want to do this.
- Keep positive communications going with all employers, no matter what occurs.
- Continue to demonstrate in a positive way what you can do for them, how you can solve their needs, and how well you get along with others. This helps employers know how you will fit into their environment.

Abigail Humphreys

187 Risen Sun Avenue	Home 215-555-9287
Philadelphia, PA 19111-3011	Office 215-555-8931

May 8, 19xx

Ms. Karen Jones, Manager
GRAPHIC ALLURE
2388 Walnut Street
Philadelphia, PA 19101

Dear Ms. Jones:

Thanks so much for the interview Saturday. It was very informative and helpful. I appreciated learning about Graphic Allure and its marketing programs.

I am excited about the possibility of working with you. My education and experience seem to complement your company's goals. I believe that I can meet all your expectations and will be available full-time beginning June 1.

Enclosed is a copy of the marketing project we spoke about. It increased the company sales by 15 percent within sixty days. Feel free to use any part of it if you find it helpful.

I look forward to hearing from you soon. Again, thanks for your consideration.

Sincerely,

Abigail Humphreys

Abigail Humphreys

Enclosure: Marketing project

Figure 13-3 A Thank-you Letter

You're the seller until you get a job offer. If you can hold off the salary issue until the company is determined to hire you, you'll have more negotiating power. You then become a buyer instead of a seller.

RECOGNIZE "REAL" OFFERS

Confusion sometimes happens during the interviewing process. Sometimes applicants mistake an employer's comments for a job offer. The following are examples of some statements that could cause you confusion:

- Are you willing to work weekends or irregular hours?
- I think we have a meeting of minds. Why don't you come back on Monday?
- We'll almost certainly be able to use you two months from now.

   Real offers have these elements:

- A clear statement that says, "We are offering to you the job of <u>(actual job title).</u> Are you interested?"
- A date, time, and place to begin work.
- A definite starting salary.
- A description of the job.
- A description of the working conditions, which should include hours of work, location of work, employee benefits, salary and wage review schedules, vacation and holiday schedules, and moving and/or relocation costs.
- An introduction to your immediate supervisor if you haven't already met.
- A tour of the facility or location in which you will be working.

KNOW WHAT YOU'RE WORTH

Determining your worth is a sophisticated business and a necessary act. You must know what the job is worth to the employer and what it is worth to you. Thomas Paine wrote, "What we obtain too cheap, we esteem too lightly; 'tis dearness only that gives everything its value." In other words, the price you set influences an employer's regard for you and for your work.

   Underpricing yourself makes you appear to be less qualified than you are; overpricing yourself may eliminate you from consideration. So what do you do?

Know What the Job Is Worth to the Employer

Pay rates vary widely for similar and identical jobs depending on the industry, the employer, the economic factors, and the geographic location.

   Industry: The April, 1988, U.S. Department of Labor statistics listed the average weekly wage by industry as the following: construction,

$487.54; manufacturing, $414.91; finance, insurance and real estate, $326.89; service, $287.21; and retail trade, $181.83. Thus, a job in construction would pay more than the identical position in retail. For example, an accountant would receive a higher wage in construction than in finance; a salesperson would earn more in real estate than in retail trade.

Employer: Salaries for identical jobs, in the same industry, vary widely depending on the employer. A grade school teacher would earn a higher salary in an exclusive private school than in a public or parochial school. Similarly, a lift truck driver would be paid a higher hourly rate in a sawmill than in a wood remanufacturing plant.

Economic Factors: Some of the economic factors that affect local pay rates include the cost of living, unemployment rates, the supply of and demand for qualified workers, state workers' compensation costs, the availability of housing, and employee benefits. For example, the oversupply of highly qualified applicants in college communities typically creates depressed salaries, and the high cost of living in Alaska tends to inflate wage scales.

Geographic Location: Geography, according to Webster's dictionary, is the "earth and its life; especially the land, sea, air, and the distribution of plant and animal life including man and his industries." Salaries will vary widely depending on this geography. High wages may be offered to offset undesirable elements, while low wages may be acceptable because of desirable elements. For example, the isolation and difficult living conditions in Alaska command a higher wage than more suitable geographic locations.

Know What the Job Is Worth to You

Only you can decide your worth. John Galsworthy wrote, "The value of a sentiment is the amount of sacrifice you are prepared to make for it." For example, a Bend, Oregon, doctor trades the pressures and high salary of Los Angeles for fewer dollars and the tranquility of a small community.

Your pay request must be balanced between your worth (experience, education, skill level, prior salary, negotiating ability) and the employer's worth (industry, economic and geographic factors).

Consider these factors:

- Do your homework. Find out the wage rates for the job before your interview.

- Don't undersell yourself. Asking for too little can damage your chances of being offered the job as much as asking for too much.

- Be realistic. Take into account that salaries vary according to many factors, such as region, company size, economics, employer, and your experience and education.

- Determine if money is the most important factor; getting the job may be.

Know When to Negotiate

Avoid, if possible, any financial disclosures in the preliminary stages of the interview. If you are asked about your salary history early in the interview, cooperate. Present the information in the most favorable light. Give the value of your entire salary package. Your salary package includes all company paid benefits, such as insurance coverage, pension, number of vacation days, holidays, sick leave, school reimbursements, bonuses, stock options, company parking, company car, expense account, subscriptions to professional magazines, dues to professional organizations. But you will also need to be prepared to split out wages from benefits.

Know the Negotiating Strategies

If an employer offers a pay range of, say, $25,000–30,000 annually, consider these options:

- You can accept the $25,000 if it is appropriate for your skills, experience, education, and prior wages.

- You can bridge the employer's offer. Ask for $28,000–32,000. This keeps you within the acceptable range and prevents you from being hired at the lowest wage.

- You can ask what qualifies a person for the top rate. Demonstrate how you meet these requirements; then request the higher rate.

- You can request a rate higher than $30,000. To do this, you will need to provide evidence as to why you are worth more.

Know Your Lowest Acceptable Wage

- Prepare a barebones budget. Use Form 39 or a similar format. Include all reasonable expenses.

- Don't forget to budget for gifts. There are birthdays, anniversaries, holidays, and all the other important events in one's life.

- Compute your taxes. They are more than most people expect, often equaling a third of your gross wages.

- Federal tax rates vary depending on your marital status and the number of eligible dependents. Check the *Employer's Tax Guide* provided by the IRS for federal tax rates.

- State tax rates vary. Withholding tables can be obtained from your state's Department of Revenue.

- Social Security takes another big bite of pay. In 1995 the annual rate was 7.65%, with 6.20% charged on a maximum of $61,200 earnings and 1.45% on all earnings.

BUDGET WORK SHEET   Date: March 1

Expenses	Month	Year
Housing	$ 495	$ 5,940
Utilities (Phone-Electricity-Gas-Water-Garbage)	125	1,500
Furnishings Maintenance & Upkeep	10	120
Food Beverages, and Other Grocery Items	390	4,680
Clothing and Upkeep	50	600
Personal (Health and Beauty Aids)	25	300
Transportation (Gas, Oil, Maintenance)	125	1,500
Insurance: Life *Currently paid by employer		•
Insurance: Medical, Dental & Vision *Currently paid by employer		•
Insurance: Long-Term Disability *Currently paid by employer		•
Insurance: Automobile	50	600
Insurance: Property and Household	70	840
Insurance: Personal Liability *Included in household insurance		•
Insurance: Other		--
Savings and Other Investments	100	1,200
Retirement *Employer contributes 6% of gross wages to retirement	• 50	• 600
Recreation and Entertainment	50	600
Education	25	300
Contributions and Gifts	100	1,200
Dues, Subscriptions and Memberships	5	60
Loans and Interest Payments	235	2,820
Licenses and Fees	10	120
Property Taxes	100	1,200
Net Before Payroll Taxes	$ 2,015	$ 24,180
Federal Income Taxes		
Other Federal Taxes (FUTA, etc.)		
State Income Taxes *Estimated Total Taxes	• 864	• 10,368
Other Taxes (State Workers Compensation, Unemployment, City)		
Social Security Taxes (FICA and Medicare)		
Total Budget Requirements	$ 2,879	$ 34,548
Rate per Hour (Divide year total by 2,080 hours)		$16.61/hour

© 1995 Harris Espérance Incorporated   Form 39/95

Figure 13-4   FORM 39, Budget Work Sheet

- There may be other taxes to consider as well. For example, in Oregon there is a federal unemployment tax, a state unemployment tax, and a workers' compensation tax. In some cities, there are city taxes to pay.
- Pay special attention to your taxes. You can't afford to underestimate them.

NEGOTIATING GUIDELINES

1. Avoid, if possible, any financial disclosures in the preliminary stages of the interview.
2. Tell the truth about your present salary. You want to state the actual salary and then add the value of the benefits. These might include costs for medical, dental, vision, life, and long-term disability insurance; car; education or paid schooling; travel expenses; meals; parking; stock options; retirement funds; vacation and holiday pay; sick leave.
3. Set an attractive salary goal. If you are looking at a promotion or advancement, a 15 to 25 percent increase in net take-home pay is a reasonable expectation. Watch out for the bottom line. If you are relocating to a higher cost of living area, you may need an even larger percentage increase.
4. Don't lower your goal without first testing the market for a couple of months. You can always lower your expectations.
5. Negotiate a percentage increase; it usually sounds less.
6. Negotiate a review or automatic raise in three to six months.
7. Remember, money's not everything. You may be able to negotiate an extra week of vacation, a higher sales commission, fewer hours, a flexible schedule, or stock options. The options are numerous. It is up to you to be creative.
8. The wage you get to begin work will be the basis for all future raises. It is much easier to negotiate a higher wage at the start, then to significantly increase your earning capacity later. Begin with the highest possible wage at the start.
9. You have the most negotiating power once the employer has decided to hire you. The employer wants you and does not want to go through the whole hiring process again. Asking for an appropriate beginning wage is only part of the hiring game, though. Consider asking for other benefits if you have justification to do so.
10. Never tell an employer you have another job offer at a higher wage unless it is true. This is not the way to negotiate. You must remain truthful. Otherwise, you may lose the job offer altogether.

MONEY IS NOT EVERYTHING

There are many factors to consider besides money. These need to be analyzed, negotiated, and agreed upon. Some of these considerations are listed on Form 32, Employer Rating Matrix.

Complete the Employer Rating Matrix for each job offer. Make sure you are getting those items that are most important to you.

File this form, with the appropriate Form 30, Employer Contact Record, behind the EMPLOYER RECORDS divider in your notebook.

EMPLOYER RATING MATRIX

Employer Name		Date	

Put a check mark by the factors that are most important to you. Six to ten factors should be sufficient for the analysis.

□ Initial Salary	□ Medical Insurance	□ Paid Vacation	□Promotion Potential
□ Commission	□ Dental Insurance	□ Paid Holidays	□Education Allowance
□ Bonus/Stock	□ Vision Insurance	□ Paid Sick Leave	□ Training Allowance
□ Profit Sharing	□ Life Insurance	□ Pension/Retirement	□ Relocation Allowance
□ Travel/Per Diem	□ Long-Term Disability	□ Severance Pay	□ Moving Refund
□ Automobile	□ Geographic Location	□ Company Size	□ Travel Requirements
□ Number of Bosses	□ Private Office	Degree of Privacy	□ Independence
□ Publication Rights	□ Patent Rights	□ Discounts	□Overtime
□ Clothing Allowance	□Job Security	□	□

The next step is to rank these in terms of importance and assign each a weight (or a value for their importance). By using a scale of 1 to 10 you can assign a value to each factor. Some factors may be of equal importance, thereby having the same weight value.

Evaluation Factors				
0-1 = Below Requirements	1-2 = Meets Requirements		3-4 = Exceeds Requirements	
Factor	Weight	Score	Total	Reason for Rating
Total Index Rating				

® 1995 Harris Espérance Incorporated — Form 32/95

Figure 13-5 FORM 32, Employer Rating Matrix

Check out these items before accepting a job offer:

- **Benefits:** Medical, dental, vision, life insurance, sick leave, pensions, vacations, holidays, termination agreements, moving expenses.

- **Job Requirements:** Travel, working hours, overtime, education, reimbursements for expenses.

- **Environmental Factors:** Company size, office size, up-to-date equipment, lighting.

- **People:** What type of people will you be working with, for, and around. Are they people you would enjoy or get along with?

- **Culture and Management Style:** Does the culture fit you? Can you adjust and fit in comfortably with the management style? Do you enjoy the company's outside activities? Will you be able to join in and be a part of the team? What are the dress requirements? Can you afford to dress in a similar way?

ACCEPT THE OFFER

When a job offer is made, do the following:

The main element in landing the job is, believe it or not, how badly you want it. Employers these days put a premium on enthusiasm and zeal because they are fed up with employees who regard their jobs as places to display their wardrobes while waiting for life to begin at five o'clock.

—Barbara Walters

1. **Verbally review the offer.** Ensure that you and the employer are thinking alike. Listen carefully. Ask for clarification if necessary.

2. **Request time to think over the offer only if it is necessary.** You may have another job offer pending and need to check with the other employer. Or you may want to review the offer with your family to ensure their support. Whatever the reason, a request of twenty-four hours to think over an offer is reasonable—a request for more than forty-eight hours is inconsiderate.

3. If you accept the offer, **write a letter of acceptance.** This letter protects you and the employer. It's an opportunity to say thanks and to verify the employment terms.
   Sometimes it is appropriate to ask the employer for this letter. But often employers are hesitant to put it in writing. The higher the wage, the more likely the employer will be willing to write the letter and the more important it is to get the offer in writing. Use your judgement. Don't make extra work for the employer if it is not necessary.

4. If you reject the offer, **write a letter of rejection.**

5. **Send letters to all the other companies you've contacted.** A letter is better than a phone call; it is a permanent record of your thoughtfulness. Thank the employers for their consideration. Tell them you have accepted a job. The extra effort this takes will be appreciated by the employers and may prove beneficial later.

6. **Send a letter to each reference and all the people who have been helping you.** They deserve to know the results of your efforts.

WRITE A LETTER OF ACCEPTANCE

An acceptance letter protects you and the employer. It can prevent misunderstandings and hardships later on. It is your opportunity to show your appreciation and to thank the employer for the job. It is the perfect time to verify the terms of employment in writing.

File one copy of this letter with the Form 30, Employer Contact Record, and another copy in the LETTERS section of your notebook.

Consider the following tips:

- Begin with a short opening paragraph. Thank the employer for the job offer, and accept the position. Express your enthusiasm for joining the organization.

- The body paragraphs should spell out the terms of employment. Include all specified items, especially items that are different than standard company policy. This is important, because the person who made the agreement with you may not be there to back it up if you should need it.

Abigail Humphreys

187 Risen Sun Avenue   Home 215-555-9287
Philadelphia, PA 19111-3011   Office 215-555-8931

May 12, 19xx

Ms. Janet Hankins, Marketing Vice President
GRAPHICS INC.
P.O. Box 1803
Portland, ME 04104

Dear Ms. Hankins:

Thank you for the great job offer. I accept with enthusiasm. I am excited about becoming your Marketing Manager and about joining your team of professionals.

I understand the terms of employment to be:
- Report to work on Thursday, June 1, 19xx, at 8:30 a.m.
- Salary: $32,000 annually with a 2% bonus override.
- Vacation schedule: 3 weeks after 1 year, 4 weeks after 3 years, 5 weeks after 5 years.
- Company-paid benefits include medical, dental, vision, and long-term disability insurance and $100,000 of life insurance. Standard retirement contribution. All benefits effective July 1, 19xx.
- A company car will be provided in 30 days. During those 30 days, mileage will be paid for using my car at a rate of $0.50 per mile.

If I've made any errors in the above, please give me a call. In the meantime, I'm looking forward to my first day with you. Thanks again for this terrific opportunity.

Best regards,

Abigail Humphreys

Abigail Humphreys

Figure 13-6 Acceptance Letter

- The last paragraph should include a disclaimer in case of error. This can save each party from embarrassment. Then you should close with a statement about your enthusiasm for joining the new firm.

After beginning work, do the following:

- Complete Form 8, Employer Record, and move the entire Employer Contact Record file with all pertinent data behind the EMPLOYERS divider in your notebook.

- List your new employer on Form 7, Employer Summary.

WRITE A LETTER OF REJECTION

It is possible to receive a job offer and find out that the job is not suitable for you. When this happens, handle it with care. It is a very small world, and you may be back at this employer's door at a later date.

Write a letter stating your appreciation for the offer. Compliment the company on one or two aspects of its business (make sure the compliment is a deserving one). Then leave the door open for future opportunities.

File one copy of this letter with Form 30, Employer Contact Record, and another copy in the LETTERS section of your notebook.

Consider these tips when writing a letter of rejection:

- In the first paragraph you should thank the employer for the offer, and then you should state your rejection.

- In the second paragraph you should sincerely praise the organization, staff, interviewer, or offer.

- In the last paragraph you should restate your appreciation and leave the door open for future opportunities.

Abigail Humphreys

187 Risen Sun Avenue   Home 215-555-9287
Philadelphia, PA 19111-3011   Office 215-555-8931

May 10, 19xx

Ms. Karen Jones, Manager
GRAPHIC ALLURE
2388 Walnut Street
Philadelphia, PA 19101

Dear Ms. Jones:

Thank you kindly for your offer of employment. However, because the position is part-time, I am not interested at this time. If a full-time position becomes available, please keep me in mind.

Again, thanks for your time and consideration. I really appreciated learning about Graphic Allure and its marketing programs.

Sincerely,

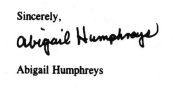

Abigail Humphreys

Figure 13-7   A Rejection Letter

HANDLE THE COUNTEROFFER

It can happen to you. Say you've accepted a job with a new employer and told your employer you are leaving. Now all of a sudden, you can do no wrong. You are the most perfect and necessary employee the company has ever had. Your employer doesn't want to loose you. Or maybe the real reason is that the company doesn't want to spend time and money to replace you. Whatever the reason, your boss doesn't want you to go and makes you a counteroffer—one that's hard to refuse. It is more money than your new job will pay. Now what do you do?

When you receive a counteroffer from your employer, you need to carefully analyze the counteroffer and the reasons you were looking for a different job in the first place.

Seriously consider your reasons for wanting to make a change. If you were unhappy, will anything really change if you stay? Will the company change? It is highly unlikely. Has the company finally realized your real value, or are you just being bought off with a few more dollars? Will the problems that existed before you turned in your resignation actually be resolved?

Compare the offers using Form 32, Employer Rating Matrix. Choose the offer that provides you with the best opportunities.

If you accept the counteroffer:

- Ask to have the counteroffer in writing. The letter should itemize all agreements.

- Call the other employer and explain the circumstances.

- Follow up your call with a letter of explanation. Who knows, you may be back at this employer's door again. Always keep your channel of communications open and honest.

If you reject the counteroffer:

- Write a formal letter of resignation. Thank the employer for the counter-offer, and then resign.

EMPLOYER RATING MATRIX

Employer Name	Date

Put a check mark by the factors that are most important to you. Six to ten factors should be sufficient for the analysis.

☐ Initial Salary	☐ Medical Insurance	☐ Paid Vacation	☐ Promotion Potential
☐ Commission	☐ Dental Insurance	☐ Paid Holidays	☐ Education Allowance
☐ Bonus/Stock	☐ Vision Insurance	☐ Paid Sick Leave	☐ Training Allowance
☐ Profit Sharing	☐ Life Insurance	☐ Pension/Retirement	☐ Relocation Allowance
☐ Travel/Per Diem	☐ Long-Term Disability	☐ Severance Pay	☐ Moving Refund
☐ Automobile	☐ Geographic Location	☐ Company Size	☐ Travel Requirements
☐ Number of Bosses	☐ Private Office	Degree of Privacy	☐ Independence
☐ Publication Rights	☐ Patent Rights	☐ Discounts	☐ Overtime
☐ Clothing Allowance	☐ Job Security	☐	☐

The next step is to rank these in terms of importance and assign each a weight (or a value for their importance). By using a scale of 1 to 10 you can assign a value to each factor. Some factors may be of equal importance, thereby having the same weight value.

Evaluation Factors

0-1 = Below Requirements	1-2 = Meets Requirements		3-4 = Exceeds Requirements	
Factor	Weight	Score	Total	Reason for Rating
Total Index Rating				

® 1995 Harris Espérance Incorporated   Form 32/95

Figure 13-8 FORM 32, Employer Rating Matrix

RESIGN FORMALLY

This is your last opportunity to shine. Your employer has provided you with a job for a period of time, and you need to show your appreciation. Take the time to thank the employer for the job, to build a positive relationship, and to heal any wounds, if necessary.

Write a formal letter of resignation. File one copy of the letter with Form 8, Employer Record, maintained in the EMPLOYERS section of your notebook. File another copy in the LETTERS section.

Follow the points below when you write your letter of resignation.

- Keep your letter upbeat. This is not a time to air your personal grudges.

- Thank your employer for the time you were employed.

- State the effective date of resignation. If you are flexible in that date, mention that too.

- If you are willing to assist the employer after you leave, state this.

Lung Gui Fim
2211 Eleventh Avenue South #207
Manchester, New Hampshire 03103

June 30, 19xx

Mr. Robert Jamison, President
ACME LIMITED
Post Office Box 831
Manchester, New Hampshire 03105

Dear Mr. Jamison:

It is with regret that I submit my resignation as Vice President of Finance and Administration. I have accepted a position of Chief Executive Officer with Tomco Incorporated beginning September 1. My resignation is effective four weeks from today. If this creates any problems, I will gladly work through August 15 or discuss other alternatives.

It has been a pleasure to be associated with this organization and its people. I have enjoyed working with you. You have contributed immensely to my professional and personal growth. I will always be grateful for all that you have done.

It's with mixed emotions that I say "thanks" and "good-bye." I wish you continued success for your company.

Sincerely,

Lung Gui Fim

Lung Gui Fim

Figure 13-9   A Resignation Letter

MAKE JOB HUNTING THE TOP PRIORITY— YOUR NUMBER ONE JOB

Stickability is 95% of ability.
—D. J. Schwartz, Ph.D.

Keep your job search at the top of your priority list. If you want to get hired, you need to work at it full-time if you are unemployed and part-time, but continuously, if you are employed. The more time you spend doing the right things, the quicker you will realize your goal.

Consider these pointers:

- Learn to cope with your family and friends. They can't always be as supportive as you want them to be.

- Seek out a special, supportive family member or friend.

- Devote time to yourself. Take time to exercise and eat right.

- Take time to spend with your family and friends. Plan special days and events.

- Make a plan and use your plan.

- Use your weekly planner.

ENLIST THE HELP OF A SUPPORTIVE FRIEND OR FAMILY MEMBER

Job hunting can become discouraging at times. To maintain your momentum and to keep an optimistic attitude, enlist the help of a supportive friend or family member. This person should be

- Someone you can trust.

- Someone who will see the positive side of all your actions.

- Someone who can encourage you.

- Someone to report in to.

- Someone to review your plans and progress with.

- Someone who believes in you and in your goals.

- Someone who can and will be honest with you.

- Someone who is gentle but firm with you.

- Someone who empathizes, not sympathizes.

- Someone who can keep you on track to reach your goal.

- Someone you can relax and laugh with.

- Someone who is your true confidant, personal cheerleader, and buddy—a genuine friend.

KEEP GOING—NEVER GIVE UP

Consider the words of the poem below when you get discouraged and thing about quitting.

GO AGAIN . . . Don't Quit Now

When things go wrong, as they sometimes will,
When the road you're travelling seems all uphill,
When the funds are low and the debts are high,
And you want to smile, but you have to sigh,
When care is pressing you down a bit—
Rest if you must, but don't you quit.

Life is queer with its twists and turns,
As everyone of us sometimes learns,
And many a fellow turns about
When he might have won had he stuck it out.
Don't give up though the pace seems slow—
You may succeed with another blow.

Often the goal is nearer than it seems
To a faint and faltering man,
Often the struggler has given up
When he might have captured the victor's cup;
And he learned too late when the night came down,
How close he was to the golden crown.

Success is failure turned inside out.
The silver tint of the clouds of doubt.
And you never can tell how close you are,
It may be near when it seems afar.
So stick to the fight when you're hardest hit,
It's when things seem worst that you mustn't quit.
—Author Unknown

HIRED

All labor that uplifts humanity has dignity and importance and should be undertaken with painstaking excellence.

—Martin Luther King, Jr.

Growth and **harmony**—continuous learning and wholeness—are the goals of "Hired." This unit revisits the four zones of your life: personal, social, professional, and financial. You will review the process of bringing a long-term balance into your life.

In the beginning, you learn the basics of corporate life. Then you review your long-term and short-term goals and affirmations. Finally, you examine your finances. "Hired" is the experience in living life to its fullest. As you complete each chapter, you build a stronger pattern for continued growth and harmony.

In Chapter 14, "Climb the Ladder—Tips for Corporate Life," you begin with the first day on the job. You study business protocol and environment. You do exercises in recording achievements, improving job performance, and planning career moves. You learn job tips and suggested business habits. The goal of Chapter 14 is to prepare you for job success.

In Chapter 15, "Manage Life—Tips for Living," you look beyond the job to your total life. This chapter takes you through forming life habits and includes exercises in writing a mission statement, establishing your long-term health and relationship goals, and managing time.

In Chapter 16, "Manage Finances—The Rules of Money," you reexamine your financial goals and learn ways to set and achieve financial independence. This chapter is only a beginning in the realm of financial management. It is up to you to build upon it and follow through.

Once you are hired, it is time to settle into the work and challenge of the real world. Study the concepts of "Hired," and put each of them into daily practice. By the time you complete the last chapter, you will know that this text is not complete. It is still in process with much more to share. But it was time to send it out to you so you could begin your journey into *Hired!* May you enjoy the journey and return each time that life provides the need for a refresher trip.

To work for the common good is the greatest creed.

—Albert Schweitzer

CLIMB THE LADDER
Tips for Corporate Life

Peak performance begins with a mission.
—Dr. Charles Garfield, *Peak Performance*

I'll never forget Hank. The two of us worked together several years ago. Hank had a college education, a great sense of humor, and a good potential future. He had only one fault—the quality of his work was poor. Hank felt that the job he had wasn't important enough to do well. When I asked him why he didn't put forth his best effort, he said, "When they value me enough to give me more responsibility, then I'll do a better job. But since they don't appreciate my capabilities now, why should I put in extra effort now?"

Needless to say, it wasn't long before Hank received a termination notice. I'm sure that he never really understood the importance of doing the very best job possible right now. I never heard from Hank again. But I learned then and there that no matter what the job, you must do your very best now.

This chapter is filled with information about the workplace and suggestions on succeeding. So read on and learn how to climb the ladder of success.

THE FIRST DAY

Questions are the creative acts of intelligence.
—Frank Kingdon

1. **Dress appropriately** for the job and the environment.
2. **Arrive ten to fifteen minutes early.** This is a good habit to develop for every day.
3. **Put on your listening cap.** Listening requires you to put the other person's needs ahead of yours. Listen with your *eyes* as well as your *ears*. Find out what the company's culture is "really" about.
4. **Ask about addressing superiors and coworkers.** Some employees are on a first-name basis, others may prefer the use of courtesy titles. If you must err, err on the conservative side and use the person's courtesy title and last name.
5. **Ask about the telephone.** Learn how the phone system works. Take notes; some telephone systems are very complicated. Find out if there is a company policy on the proper way to answer your phone.
6. **Keep confidential information confidential!** "Loose lips sink ships"—this old adage still merits serious consideration. Always be aware of who's around when you are discussing work. This includes on-the-job discussions, chats over lunch in the company break room or at a restaurant, and conversations at home whether over the phone or in person. Walls do have ears. Children, spouses, and other guests in your home may accidentally repeat conversations they overhear. Be conscious of your conversations about work no matter where you are. Be careful in choosing your confidants.
7. **Do not drink or use drugs,** even if other coworkers are partaking. Alcohol and drugs are taboo in the workplace and at lunch. Nothing will undermine your credibility more quickly than having a few drinks at lunch and returning to work smelling of alcohol. Drinking or using drugs during the workday can be disastrous to a career.
8. **Check the company policy about smoking.** If you are a smoker, be considerate of your coworkers. Find out where smoking is allowed and follow the rules.
9. **Look for positive role models.** Make friends and model your behavior after theirs.
10. **Smile often and stand tall.** Good posture, a quick step, and a smile project self-confidence. The image you project with your body sets the stage for everything you do. It says a lot about you. It is easier for others to accept and follow you when you are poised and confident. Your body tells the story.
11. **Always do your best.** Mediocrity costs—how much can you afford?
12. **Show appreciation.** Little attentions given to others can pay off in big dividends. It costs nothing to give a word of encouragement or to compliment a job well done.

BUSINESS GREETINGS

Shaking hands is an acceptable manner of greeting for both men and women.

- Put a smile on your face and in your eyes. Be friendly.
- Address a female by using her name. Calling her "honey," "dear," or "my girl" is demeaning and inappropriate.
- Using the person's courtesy title (Dr., Judge, Senator) when introducing or addressing a person shows respect.
- Kissing and hugging may be acceptable at business social gatherings. However, in pure business settings, such as offices, restaurants, and conference rooms, it is usually inappropriate.
- If you extend your hand and find yourself in a warm bear hug or being kissed on the cheek, it is best not to overreact. Here are some guidelines to follow:

    Don't kiss or hug anyone you don't know well or anyone you don't want to kiss or hug.

    Take into consideration the occasion, the setting, and the individual. You may choose to just let it slide.

    Extend your hand and step back to avoid being kissed or hugged. This action generally wards off unwanted advances. Always watch the other person's body language.

- Don't feel obligated to kiss or be kissed. If it makes you uncomfortable, give an advance signal by keeping your distance when greetings are being exchanged. Good feelings can be sent with a smile and a phrase like, "I'm really glad to see you."
- If you want your greeting to be a little warmer than the standard handshake, a double-handed handshake will send a warmer message.

SOCIAL COURTESIES

Many men and women often feel uneasy about office protocol. The man is not sure whether to open a door for a woman, and a woman is not sure whether to accept. Neither one is comfortable because they are not sure what is appropriate. This can be resolved by the "offer and refusal technique" suggested by the National Institute of Business Management, Inc. The technique works like this:

- The man continues to offer the kind of manners he feels is appropriate, such as opening the door for a woman or rising when a woman enters the room.
- The female can accept the gestures she is comfortable with and feels are appropriate to the environment, or she can gracefully decline the gesture. For example, if a man opens the door for a woman, she can gracefully say, "Thanks,"and walk through; or she can say,"Thanks, I've got it." If a man rises when a woman enters the room, she can acknowledge with a smile and say, "Please keep your seat."

- Voice tone, facial expression, and stance play an important role in social courtesies. Relax and be natural when accepting or rejecting attentive courtesies. Creating an issue draws negative reactions and attention—exactly what you want to avoid.
- Once your preferences are known, most people will be glad to accommodate you.

TAKING MINUTES

Executives should avoid always asking a woman to record the minutes of the meeting. The woman should not be offended unless the role is meant to be a put-down or if it is abused. If this is the situation, a private discussion prior to the meeting should resolve the issue.

MAKING AND SERVING COFFEE

Ask your staff how they feel about the coffee duties. Find an acceptable solution that fits everyone. Making and serving coffee is a bisexual activity; anyone can do it. It often works best if the men and women in the office take turns making coffee. For the morning brew, the first person to arrive at work usually makes the first pot.

PAYING THE MEAL TAB

The person hosting the meal should pay the bill. Generally, the server will place the bill in the center of the table. If you want to ensure that you receive the bill, speak to the server in private at the beginning of the meal. Ask him or her to hand you the bill. This usually resolves the issue. If, however, the bill is placed in the center of the table, just reach over and pick it up. If it is too far away, politely ask for it.

MEETING AT HOTELS

Hold your business meetings in one of the hotel's public rooms. Holding a meeting in your hotel room is inappropriate and usually makes others feel uncomfortable. If a public room is unavailable or if it is necessary to have privacy, meet the person in the lobby before taking him or her to your room. Ask the person if it is okay to hold the meeting in the privacy of your hotel room. This provides the person with a choice, which usually makes him or her feel more comfortable.

MEETING AT A PRIVATE CLUB

Check out the club before scheduling your meeting there. Make sure that the club's guest rules won't be violated when your guests arrive. It would be very embarrassing to schedule a meeting and find out at the door that one of your members is not allowed in. Know the club's rules and know who is attending your meeting before you schedule it at a private club.

SOCIALIZING AFTER HOURS

One of the best ways to build your network is to meet others after hours in social settings. Many professional organizations hold dinner meetings in

restaurants. You should take advantage of this environment whenever possible. Many business contacts and deals are made during such meetings.

Other opportunities exist at a school ball game, the community summer festival, or a concert. Bowling alleys, golf courses, and health and fitness clubs provide additional opportunities to meet and make business contacts. Your mosque, synagogue, or church may serve that purpose as well.

Your social contacts can keep you informed on new industrial trends, future job opportunities, or even potential layoffs at work. They may give you added sales and profitable tips. They are a wealth of information. Use the social aspects of your life to develop and build an active network of associates. They will come in handy if you are ever in the market for another job.

When attending social functions, observe your superiors, coworkers, and subordinates. You can learn a lot about each person in a social setting that doesn't appear in the hallways of the office or on the factory floor. But, remember that as you are observing others, they are also observing you. Be on your best behavior.

THE THREE "SEXES"

SEXUAL ATTRACTION

It is difficult to keep romance out of the workplace. As more men and women work and travel together, sexual attraction becomes a major concern for the individuals as well as the company. Sexual attraction is a natural and common occurrence. When working with the opposite sex and when considering getting involved with another person, keep these things in mind:

- It is difficult, if not impossible, to keep romantic involvements secret.

- Attraction may be interpreted as favoritism. Coworkers may feel threatened, jealous, or that you are using your relationship to gain favors and promotions.

- Romantic liaisons often misuse company time—how much time are you spending doing company work as opposed to socializing? Romance can interfere with productivity and concentration. Even when you are sticking to business, your behavior is apt to be misinterpreted.

- Assess the risks to your career. Sexual involvements can cost you your job and reputation. Who gets hurt the most, the man or woman? It depends on the company culture and the situation.

- What is the company's attitude toward employee romance? Is the past company history in handing romances a good indicator of how your relationship will be handled?

- Attraction can turn into harassment. Proceed cautiously.

- Attraction can be dangerous. Consider changing jobs, departments, locations, or employers.

SEXUAL DISCRIMINATION

Even though it is against the law, sexual discrimination is still a common occurrence in the workplace. Your best line of defense is to know your rights and then discuss the situation with those involved. Be courteous and open. Listen to the other side. Often there are outside factors affecting the hiring and promoting decisions. It may have nothing to do with your sex.

If you can't resolve the issue, speak to your superiors or consult with the Department of Labor or a labor attorney. Taking the situation to court is not necessarily the best solution to the problem. Court battles are long, costly, and ugly. You spend a considerable amount of time delving into negatives when you sue. It is a choice you can make, but weigh the costs carefully.

Sometimes the best solution is to find a different position in an environment more suitable to your needs. Look at all sides of the issue when you are confronted with sexual discrimination. Look for a variety of solutions. Your career and reputation may be at stake. Proceed cautiously.

SEXUAL HARASSMENT

Sexual harassment can be a threat to you and your company. It occurs when an employer alters an employee's job conditions as a result of the employee's refusal to submit to sexual demands. Know the company policy and follow it.

Employees have been protected by law since 1980 under Section VII of the 1964 Civil Rights Act.

Federal law defines sexual harassment as the following:

> Unwelcome sexual advances, requests for sexual favors and other verbal or physical conduct of a sexual nature constitute sexual harassment when:

- submission to it is made a condition of employment,
- submission to or rejection of it is the basis of employment decisions,
- it is unreasonable and interferes with work performance or creates an intimidating, hostile or offensive working environment.

Confronting Sexual Harassment—What To Do

1. **Tell the harasser that the behavior is unwelcome and that it should stop.** Ignoring the problem usually doesn't discourage the harasser.
2. **Report the problem** if the situation persists to your supervisor, the personnel department, or the harasser's supervisor.
3. **Keep a written record.** Document what the harasser does and says. Take note if there were witnesses. Record how you responded. Indicate to whom you reported the incident and when.
4. **Discuss the situation with coworkers.** Don't suffer alone. You may find they have had similar experiences and can provide helpful advice.

Every great movement must first experience three stages: ridicule, discussion, adoption.
—John Stuart Mill

5. **File an official complaint with the company.** Use the company's grievance procedure. If there's no formalized system, write a letter to your boss. If this does not resolve the problem, inform your supervisor that you are going to take further action by talking then writing, if necessary, to top management.

6. If the aforementioned steps fail, **call the Equal Employment Opportunity Commission (EEOC)** or a private attorney. You will be told what to do next. You may be encouraged to file a complaint. Be ready to do so if the behavior cannot be corrected.

Don't allow sexual harassment to exist. If you are confronted with sexual harassment, take action to have it stopped immediately. Sexual harassment doesn't go away if you ignore it. It needs to be addressed and corrected. If you are guilty of harassment, stop the behavior immediately. You and your company cannot afford to be involved in a sexual harassment lawsuit.

USING THE CAREER MANAGEMENT SECTION OF THE *COMPANION PLANNER*

Reach for excellence.

The CAREER MANAGEMENT section of the *Companion Planner* provides you with a place to keep records of achievements and a list of special projects and improvements. Below is a summary of the documents maintained in this section and suggestions for their use.

- Records of Achievements
  - Maintain a chronological and detailed file of special projects and other personal achievements.
  - Each time you complete a project, make a record of it. Keep specific details. For example, if you saved the company money, include the dollar amount. If you increased production, list the percentage and the volume. Be as specific as possible.

- Form 33: Performance Review
  - Review work performance three months after accepting a new position.
  - Review work performance annually or whenever you feel it's necessary.
  - File review here until next review. Then move the form into the EMPLOYERS section of the *Companion Planner*.

- Annual Job Improvement List
  - Each year, make a list of all the job improvements you want to make during the year.
  - Periodically review the list for progress and additions.
  - At the end of each year, file the old list with the appropriate EMPLOYER file.

Trifles make perfection and perfection is no trifle.
—Michael Angelo

During the year, keep track of all the special projects that you do. They do not have to be major projects. You will find it amazing how many things you do when you begin to keep a record.

Review this list before every performance review. Type it up and take it with you to the review. Present it to your boss and ask for comments.

If you do not keep a record, you will forget the little improvements that you have made during the year. You will not be able to see your growth and contributions to the company if there is no record.

ACHIEVEMENTS - 19xx

Date	Description of Achievements
January 15	Discussed the advantages of installing com-lines on the telephones and designating one person to answer the phones, which I volunteered to do.
	Changes were initiated and completed by February 20. These two changes have reduced the level of noise in the office, added privacy, and created a more workable atmosphere.
	Supervisors and coworkers have told me how much they appreciated the fact that I took the initiative to suggest a change.
February 8	Designed a new log scaling input ticket. New ticket is laid out in the order of entry, saving time and errors in postings. Received compliments on the design and the improved layout.
February 17	Volunteered to study and redesign all major forms for the department. Will keep a detailed record of forms completed and results. This will be a great chance to use my artistic skills.
March 10-11	Received permission to rearrange office on my own time after work. Worked all day Saturday. Turned desk to face the incoming customers. Placed files behind me in easy reach. Put work table on the left, which provides easy access to the rest of the staff. Brought in new pictures to brighten up the place.
	Mr. Story came in on Monday and said: "Wow! Who did this? This is much better. This should have been done a long time ago." Received a $100 bonus for efforts.

Figure 14-1   Achievement List.

Record documented results. If you can prove a $500 monthly savings or a 4 percent increase in productivity, write it in the record.

If you have received an award for your suggestion or a letter of appreciation, attach it to the record.

Keep detailed records of each accomplishment, and then use this record at your annual review.

File your list of accomplishments behind the CAREER MANAGEMENT divider in your notebook.

Give your best to your employer. It's one of the best investments you can make.

—H. Jackson Brown Jr., *Life's Little Instruction Book*, #206

To reach for excellence, review your performance regularly (yearly at the very least). The company you work for may have a standard policy of annual reviews. If it does not, institute your own review program. Use the form provided in the text, or create your own. The important thing is to systematically review your work.

COMPLETE FORM 33, PERFORMANCE REVIEW, PAGE 1

Ask your supervisor to complete the form. Then set a time to meet with your supervisor to compare your review.

Provide a typed copy of your yearly achievement list. You will be surprised at how many of the accomplishments had been forgotten.

When reviewing your performance, use this three-step procedure:

- Review the past.
- Analyze the present.
- Plan the future.

Ask yourself and your supervisor these questions:

- How am I doing? (past and present)
- Where can I improve?
- What promotion opportunities do I have?
- What can I expect to accomplish before my next review?
- How will my work be evaluated?
- What changes are likely to occur in the months ahead, and how will these affect me?

PERFORMANCE REVIEW   Page 1 of 2

Job Title *Assistant Bookkeeper*						Date *March 1, 19XX*
My View			Other			
M	G	E	M	G	E	**Area of Assessment**
	X				X	**Quality of Work** Consider: Attention to quality details of finished products Knowledge and application of current quality standards Reporting of quality problems that repeatedly appear
		X		X		**Quantity of Work** Consider: Volume of work consistently accomplished (within required quality standards) Work performed during downtime periods Concern for production goals and standards Frequency of caused slowdowns or excessively piled-up work
		X		X		**Job Knowledge** Consider: Ability to understand and apply the technical skills to job Ability to adjust and understand changes or new technologies Willingness to learn more about the technical aspects of products or machinery
	X			X		**Communication Skills** Consider: Ability to write concisely, precisely, and effectively Ability to verbally communicate effectively (one-on-one/groups/public/company) Ability to really listen, to withhold comments until other person has been heard
X			X			**Work Relationships** Consider: Ability to get along and work well with peers, subordinates, and management Willingness to work as a team member
	X				X	**Reliability** Consider: Attendance—tardiness (before and after shift, breaks, and lunch periods) General overall conduct including temperament while working Record of following company rules and regulations
	X				X	**Dependability** Consider: Willingness to follow directions and accept position responsibilities Ability to work without constant supervision or correction
	X				X	**Initiative** Consider: Overall resourcefulness on job and willingness to "go the extra mile"
	X				X	**Safety** Consider: Ability to read, understand, and follow safe job practices Willingness to actively participate in safety meetings Avoidance of the "injury/accident-prone" syndrome
	X			X		**Decision-Making Skills** Consider: A working knowledge of decision-making processes Ability to make appropriate and timely decisions Self-confidence in decision making
	X			X		**Leader/Follower Skills** Consider: Ability to lead when required/ability to follow when necessary Ability to motivate others and achieve group unity
	X			X		**Personal Appearance** Consider: Appropriate attire for job Use of perfume/aftershave that is pleasant to be around Pleasant smile, friendly manner, and words of encouragement for others
	X			X		**Overall Evaluation** Consider: Total performance: work and personal habits, enthusiasm, and appearance

© 1995 Harris Espérance Incorporated   Form 33/95

Figure 14-2   FORM 33, Performance Review, Page 1.

Keep these points in mind:

- Ask for feedback from your supervisor or colleagues.
- Establish new directions, goals, and timetables.
- Make a list of goals you want to accomplish for the next year. Identify the projects, changes, and time frames for completion. Your supervisor may have some suggestions to offer.
- File this list with your new achievements listing.
- As the year passes, review your list of goals to ensure that you are accomplishing the things that are important to you and the company.

COMPLETE FORM 33, PERFORMANCE REVIEW, PAGE 2

As you complete the review, put yourself in your supervisor's and coworkers' shoes. See if you can look at your performance from the eyes of your supervisor, your peers, and other company personnel. How would each of them view your work?

File your Performance Review behind the CAREER MANAGEMENT divider in your notebook until the next performance review is completed. Then file it with the appropriate Employer Record located in the EMPLOYERS section of your notebook.

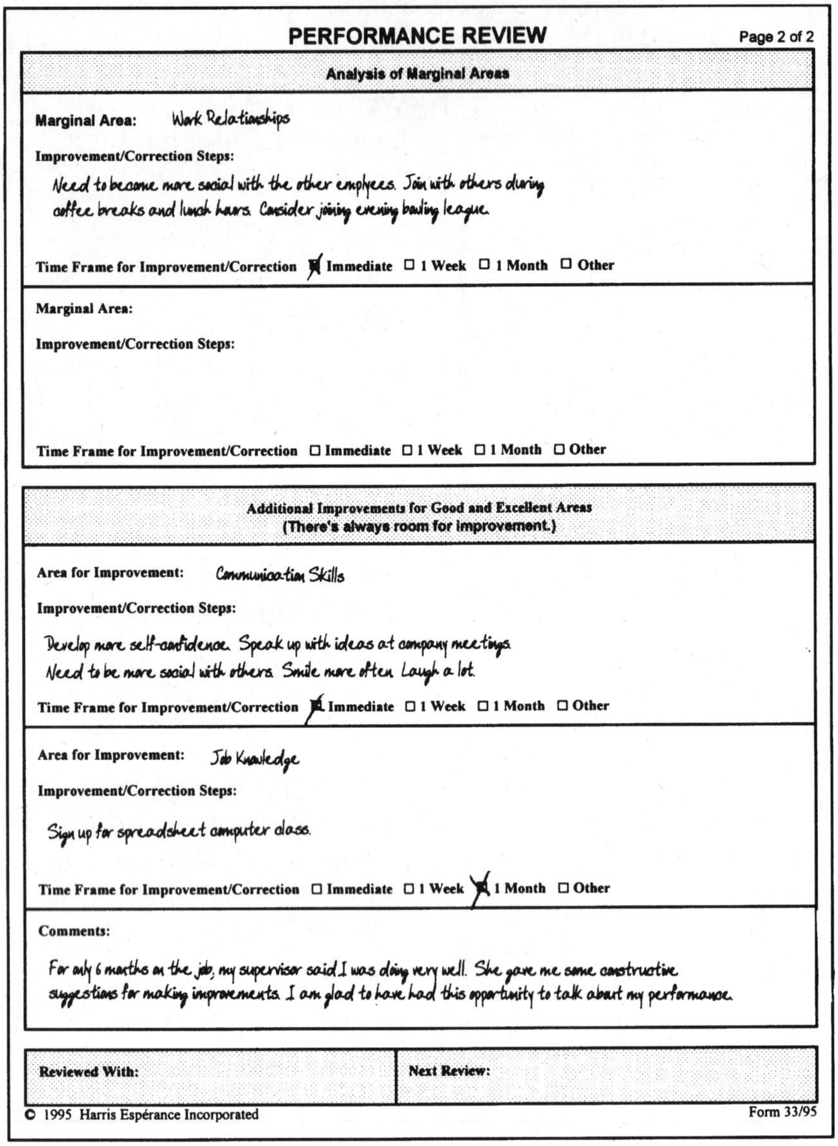

PERFORMANCE REVIEW — Page 2 of 2

Analysis of Marginal Areas

Marginal Area: Work Relationships

Improvement/Correction Steps:
Need to become more social with the other employees. Join with others during coffee breaks and lunch hours. Consider joining evening bowling league.

Time Frame for Improvement/Correction ☒ Immediate ☐ 1 Week ☐ 1 Month ☐ Other

Marginal Area:

Improvement/Correction Steps:

Time Frame for Improvement/Correction ☐ Immediate ☐ 1 Week ☐ 1 Month ☐ Other

Additional Improvements for Good and Excellent Areas (There's always room for improvement.)

Area for Improvement: Communication Skills

Improvement/Correction Steps:
Develop more self-confidence. Speak up with ideas at company meetings. Need to be more social with others. Smile more often. Laugh a lot.

Time Frame for Improvement/Correction ☒ Immediate ☐ 1 Week ☐ 1 Month ☐ Other

Area for Improvement: Job Knowledge

Improvement/Correction Steps:
Sign up for spreadsheet computer class.

Time Frame for Improvement/Correction ☐ Immediate ☐ 1 Week ☒ 1 Month ☐ Other

Comments:
For only 6 months on the job, my supervisor said I was doing very well. She gave me some constructive suggestions for making improvements. I am glad to have had this opportunity to talk about my performance.

Reviewed With:	Next Review:

 Form 33/95

Figure 14-3 FORM 33, Performance Review, Page 2.

AVOID "GETTING USED TO IT"

> Did you know you can get used to anything?... Once you get used to something, you no longer have the drive, the energy, the creativity to reconstruct it the way you know it ought to be.
> —Louis Tice

Do you remember your first weeks on the job? You could hardly wait to make improvements—you noticed projects that needed to be done, programs that could be improved, systems that would increase production. But as time passed, you gradually got used to the way things were when you first arrived. You began to accept things. Those things you noticed that needed changing and improving don't seem to bother you as much anymore. It has become easy for you to let things slide by.

Now is the time to take a fresh look at your job. Are there still jobs that need to be improved or changed? Follow these steps to avoid getting caught in the "getting-used-to-it" cycle.

- Examine your job, your work space, your relationships. Identify items that need changing and improving.
- Make a list of all the things you want to improve in the next year.
- Set a date for starting and completing each project.
- When you notice something that needs to be done, add it to the list.
- Periodically check your list. Check off the completed items. Revise beginning and completion dates, if necessary.

File this list behind the CAREER MANAGEMENT divider in your notebook.

My 199x Improvement List
January 15, 199x

Things to Do	Begin	Completed
Clean out old files	2/01	
Rearrange office	3/15	
Revise procedures for expense accounts	8/13	

Figure 14-4 Improvement List.

Annually, review your long-term career goals. Record these professional goals on page 2 of Form 37, Goals. Look over the long-term plan you completed in Chapter 4. See if you still agree with those plans. If not, make adjustments and then record your new goals on a new form.

File Form 37 behind the LIFE MANAGEMENT divider in your notebook.

REVIEW YOUR PROFESSIONAL LONG-TERM GOALS AND AFFIRMATIONS

GOALS Page 2 of 2		X LONG-TERM ___ SHORT-TERM Date: _____
Professional	**Goals**	**Affirmations**
Job Title or Position Job Description	Become store manager of a large metro jewelry store.	I am a successful store manager. I provide quality service to my customers.
Education Credentials Degree(s) License(s)	Become certified professional jeweler. Complete bachelor's degree in business and finance.	I value and appreciate my employees. I enjoy my work every day.
Employer Size/Type Description	Work for super-large international jewelry company with lots of promotional opportunities. Work for company with wholesale operations.	I am a certified professional jeweler.
Geographic Location Distance from Home	Want to work in Pacific Northwest. Would like store within a 25-mile distance from home.	

Figure 14-5 FORM 37, Goals, Page 2

Ask yourself these questions:

- Are my goals the same this year as last year?
- Do I need to make changes?
- Are the time frames reasonable? achievable? stretching?
- Do these goals blend with my total life goals? If not, why not?
- Rewrite your long-term goals and affirmations if they need changing.

WRITE SHORT-TERM (ONE-YEAR) GOALS AND AFFIRMATIONS

GOALS Page 2 of 2		___ LONG-TERM X SHORT-TERM Date: _____
Professional	**Goals**	**Affirmations**
Job Title/Position Description	Become assistant store manager of a large jewelry store.	I am a successful assistant store manager. I provide quality service to my customers.
Education Credentials Degree(s) License(s)	Register for certified professional jeweler classes. Register for Accounting III class.	I value and appreciate my coworkers. I enjoy my work every day.
Employer Size/Type Description	Stay where I am — get promotion to assistant manager.	I am a certified professional jeweler. I am a college graduate.
Geographic Location Distance from Home	Want to work in Pacific Northwest.	

Figure 14-6 FORM 37, Goals, Page 2

Ask yourself these questions:

- Do these goals blend with my long-term professional goals?
- Do these goals challenge me to reach a higher level?
- Can I emotionally commit to achieving these goals in a timely manner?
- Are these goals fair and equitable to all concerned?
- Have I set reasonable time frames?

Now look a little closer. Identify what you want to achieve in the next year. Write specific, achievable goals. Write goals that make you stretch. Here are some more questions to ask:

Job Goals:

- Do I want to change jobs? Get a promotion?

If yes:

- What job do I want and with whom?
- Will I spend the time to get the new job?

If no:

- What specifically do I want to accomplish in my career this year?

Education Goals:

- What classes do I need to take to improve my skills and effectiveness?
- Should I join a professional organization to increase my knowledge?

Employer Goals:

- Do I want to change employers? If yes, explain why, who, where, and when.

Geographic Goals:

- Do I want to change my geographic location? If yes, explain why, where, and when.

No matter what the job is, it ain't over. You can always quit.
—Peter Drucker

As I've worked with clients and listened to many job-hunting stories, I've come to realize that most people who lose their jobs expect to lose them. They were not surprised the day a "pink slip" was given them. What surprises me is that most people wait for it to be done to them. Let's look at some of the reasons for terminations and examine what you can do about each one.

ACT BEFORE THE HATCHET

Company Downsizing, Seasonal Layoffs

Employees are now notified ahead of time when layoffs are eminent. If you find yourself in this situation, make plans on how to handle the layoff.

- Begin by developing an action plan, such as the one on Form 25 in Chapter 10. This will lead you through all the steps of job hunting.

- Review your finances. Do you need an interim or new job? If this is the case, begin immediately on a job hunt.

- Know what you want. Do you want a permanent job—one to replace where you've been? Do you want a fill-in job until you can return? Do you want a part-time position?

- Know when and where you want it.

- Put action in your plan. Don't wait for the hatchet.

- Ask if you can do consulting for the company.

- Research starting your own business. Be sure to do a thorough market analysis, complete a business plan, and locate finances for operations before committing to this venture.

Poor Performance

Few terminations happen unexpectedly because of poor performance. Generally, your supervisor has spoken to you about your performance and the company's expected performance standards. After you have been given a warning about your performance, find out exactly what you need to do to make improvements and how much time you have. You may want to ask your supervisor for help, training, or a tutor.

If it becomes apparent that you will not be able to meet the company's performance standards, there is still something you can do before the hatchet falls—you can ask to be transferred to another job or department that fits your abilities more closely. If there is nowhere else in the company you can or want to go, begin your job search immediately, before being terminated. Do these things:

- Reach an agreement with your employer. Tell the employer you plan on leaving since you are unable to fulfill the expectations of the job.

- Ask your employer for help in the job hunt. Ask for job leads and referrals.

- Get a letter of recommendation. Review Chapter 6; then draft a reference letter for your boss.

- Keep your relationship on the positive side. You are helping the employer with a sticky problem. You should be able to expect help back.

ACT IMMEDIATELY AFTER THE HATCHET

Personality Conflict

If your termination is a surprise, perhaps the real reason is more of a "personality conflict" that couldn't be resolved. Employers sometimes blame performance because it is easier to deal with than personality conflicts. Take these steps:

- **Accept reality.** The job is over. Get on with your life and a job hunt as quickly as possible.

- **Vent your anger.** It is difficult not to be angry over a job loss, no matter what the cause. It is not something you chose or wanted. However, the anger will poison your whole life if you do not release it in a safe and constructive manner. Here is one suggestion that may help: Host an anger-venting party. Invite several close friends. Tell them you need to clear the air concerning your firing and want to vent your anger by comically attacking it. At the party, roll up old newspapers, get up in front of your friends, and start expressing your feelings, anger, and frustrations about the job loss. Get as ridiculous as you possibly can. Hit the table, desk, or counter with the newspaper. Next ask each of your friends to grab a newspaper and vent their anger at your employer and your job loss. Soon all of you will be rolling on the floor, laughing harder than you ever thought possible. The funnier and more absurd you get, the better.

  Once the anger is relieved, begin brainstorming with your friends on ways to find a new job. Start to think of ways to better yourself beyond the job you just lost. You will be surprised what you and your friends can come up with.

- **Accept responsibility** for yourself and the job loss. It gains you nothing to blame your supervisor or the company for your job loss, no matter what caused it. A job loss is a losing situation for you and the employer. No one owes you a living or a job. You have the skills to do many jobs. You have the skills to seek a better job. Get busy and begin your job hunt. Start with an action plan. Use Form 25 to get you started.

- **Tighten your financial belt.** Don't wait until you are in a crisis or bankrupt to look at your finances. There are many ways to cut expenses if you will just look honestly at the situation. If your finances affect others, ask them to help you. Get everyone affected involved in cutting expenses. Act immediately. If necessary, visit a Consumer Credit Counseling office, a nonprofit international organization.

- **Begin your job search as quickly as possible.** The longer you are unemployed, the most difficult it becomes to find work and stay motivated throughout the job search.

- **Be gentle with yourself.** This doesn't mean to be soft and inactive. It means to accept the fact that you are human and that others have been fired too. You are a valuable asset to your community, to your family, and to your next employer. Concentrate on all your assets, and forget about the negatives. Keep a smile on your face by thinking of all the good and worthwhile things you have done in life.

- **Swing into action.** Put motion in your action plan. Do the things that need to be done on a timely basis. Make phone calls, write letters, and revise your resume. Contact employers; practice your interview.

- **Speak kindly about your former employer and last job.**

- **Look for the positives in the job loss.** Think of the good things that can happen because you now have a new chance. The door of opportunity is wide open. Go out and find your perfect job.

- **Find lessons in the firing.** There are positive lessons to learn from life experiences. The toughest situations can present the best learning opportunities. Learn from this experience, and use what you have learned to better your future.

JOB TIPS

DO YOUR BEST

The work will teach you how to do it.
—Estonian Proverb

The following story is told of a graduate student working for Dr. Henry Kissinger:

> Upon completing his first written assignment, he left it in Dr. Kissinger's office, expecting a critique. A few days later he returned to pick it up. Dr. Kissinger said, "Is this the best job you can do?" The young man winced and said, "Maybe I could change a few things. I'll take it back and see what I can do." He reworded the piece and brought it in again. When he returned a few days later, Dr. Kissinger asked, "Is this really your best work?" "I could probably improve it a little," the student said, retrieving it once more. This time, the student spent hours poring over the piece, working it word by word, sentence by sentence, paragraph by paragraph, and honing it until it was the best he could do. Again, he left it at Dr. Kissinger's office. The student returned several days later. Dr. Kissinger asked, "Are you going to tell me this is your best effort?" "Yes, sir," responded the young man. "This is the best job I can do." "All right," Dr. Kissinger said. "I'll read it now."

Mediocrity costs; how much can you afford?

What does it mean to "do your best"? Does it mean measuring yourself against someone else? Being better than someone else? Coming in first? Always winning?

Doing his best did not mean winning to the man who said, "I do the very best I know how—the very best I can and I mean to keep doing so until the end." This man failed in business at thirty-one, was defeated in eight major political elections, and suffered a nervous breakdown at thirty-six; he was defeated over and over. This man lost many times, but was elected President of the United States of America in 1860. He was Abraham Lincoln. He did his best even though he lost often.

Doing one's best is not always winning—it's persevering. It's picking yourself up and going again. It's continuing on and on and on. It's always striving to reach excellence.

USE NUMBERS TO SUPPORT YOUR IDEAS

A second-class effort is a first-class mistake.

William Thomson (Lord Kelvin) wrote: "When you can measure what you are speaking about, and express it in numbers, you know something about it; but when you cannot measure it, when you cannot express it in numbers, your knowledge is of a meager and unsatisfactory kind: it may be the beginning of knowledge, but you have scarcely, in your thoughts, advanced to the stage of science."

Being able to statistically measure what you have done or plan to do gives your ideas validation. Numbers provide a basis for measurement. When you use numbers, employers listen and proposals get approved.

You don't have to be a financial wizard or an accountant to effectively use numbers. Consider these tips:

- Take a class in statistics, business finances, or accounting. Learn the basics of accounting, cost accounting, and statistical presentations. Adapt the teachings to everyday work situations.

- Become friends with the accountant. Find out what the numbers mean and where they come from. Study department budgets and cost analysis reports thoroughly.

- Develop an understanding of financial reports and how each one reflects and affects the company. Learn about profit and loss statements, assets and liabilities, income and expense reports, budgets, and cost accounting. Your career success depends on it.

- Make every task measurable. Everything the company does is eventually represented in numbers. This may be the job of the accountants, but it is your job to understand these numbers and ensure that the numbers accurately reflect reality. Accounting is not just dollars and cents, it is units of production, hours worked, number of employees, inventory volume, sales volume, ratios, percentages, and years. Every graph is a picture of several numbers.

- Ask questions when you don't understand what the numbers mean.

- Represent your numbers in pictures and stories. Create a graph or chart to visually show what you mean. Talk in ratios and trends. Tell picture stories. For instance, when talking about the volume of lumber cut in a year, you may want to describe it in number of log trucks or in the number of houses that can be built. Stories make your numbers easy to remember.

- Understand the big picture, not just your area. Find out how your department or job fits in and affects other departments and the whole company.

Even if you are not a numbers person, it is smart to understand how to use numbers to prove or disprove a point. Experience and intuition serve you, but when it comes to selling your ideas or making your point, numbers speak loudest. When you make a proposal to management, support your proposition with numbers. Company decisions are always based on numerical projections. Learn and use numbers. It's a smart career move.

ATTEND ONLY NECESSARY MEETINGS

Meetings take a lot of time; thus, the time spent in meetings needs to be productive. To ensure that you're receiving value for your time spent, follow these suggestions:

1. Attend only the necessary meetings. Send another person, if possible.
2. Ask for an agenda ahead of time.
3. Arrive on time.
4. Be prepared. Anticipate requirements. Bring all the necessary papers.

ORGANIZE AND PLAN YOUR MEETINGS

Follow these guidelines for conducting a successful meeting:

1. Establish the purpose.
2. Invite only those who need to attend.
3. Set a date, place, starting time, and ending time.
4. Establish an agenda that includes the purpose, date, place, beginning and ending times, and items for discussion.
5. Send agendas to the participants ahead of time, preferably several days ahead.
6. Post the agenda at the meeting, and set a clock in view of all attendants.
7. Begin on time. Don't reward latecomers by catching them up. This punishes those who arrive on time.
8. Follow the agenda. Be receptive to rearrangement, if necessary.
9. Keep the meeting moving in the direction of its purpose.
10. Allow five to ten minutes at the end of the meeting to recap. This should be on the agenda.
11. Schedule a date, place, and time to handle leftover agenda items.
12. **End on time!** Do this even if you haven't covered all the items on the agenda.

To ensure a successful meeting, it may be helpful to develop a meeting room checklist using categories such as the following:

WHICH ARE YOU?

Are you an active member—
the kind that would be missed,
Or are you just content that your
name is on the list?

Do you attend the meetings and
mingle with the flock,
Or do you stay at home and
criticize and knock?

Do you take an active part to
help your world along,
Or are you satisfied to simply
say that you belong?

Do you ever volunteer to
help the guiding stick,
Or leave the work to just a few,
then talk about the "Clique?"

Come out to the meetings,
and help with hand and heart;
Don't just be a member,
but take an active part.

Just think this over. . . .
you know right from wrong.
**ARE YOU AN ACTIVE MEMBER,
OR DO YOU JUST BELONG?**
—Author Unknown

General	Room Conditions	Equipment
Prepare ahead of time	Temperature	Extension cords
Research audience	Outside noises	Backup equipment
Customize materials	Distracting views/objects	Spare bulbs
Practice and time speech	Visibility	Overhead projector
Visit the location	Audibility	Movie projector
Control the environment	Microphone quality	Video equipment
Enjoy yourself		Chalk and chalkboard
		Flip chart and stand
		Pens and pencils
		Paper

Room

Seating count
Lighting control locations
Heat/AC control locations
Microphone level controls
Smoking and Nonsmoking areas

Miscellaneous

Restroom locations
Telephone
Refreshments
Restaurant locations
Handouts

LEARN HOW TO MAKE PRESENTATIONS

Being able to speak at meetings, to present your ideas to a group, and to run a meeting are critical skills to a successful career. Following are some steps you can take to learn these skills:

- Join Toastmasters. Toastmasters offers complete communications and leadership training programs.

- Learn to make and use visual aids. You can maintain your audience's attention better if they have something to look at. Use flip charts, chalkboards, overheads, props, slides, movies, and videos.

- Learn to operate overhead projectors, video equipment, and movie projectors.

- Control your environment. Make sure your presentation is visible and audible. Inspect all the equipment. Have backup equipment in case of failure. If this isn't possible, have a plan on what to do if the equipment fails.

- Understand your audience. Create a presentation that's meaningful to them.

- Use tasteful humor. When people are having fun, they become more open and receptive. Short humor is best. Long-winded stories lose your audience and the point.

- Organize and customize your materials. Know what it is you want to accomplish.

- Get audience participation. Have them write or do something. Ask a question, and have an audience member respond. Get a commitment from your audience.

- Provide a question-and-answer period.

- Control your time. Set a clock so you can easily see it. Ask an audience member to let you know when it's time for a break. Set a time period for your presentation and stick with it. Even if you haven't completed your presentation, wrap it up quickly; your audience will appreciate it.

- Practice and time your presentation. If it is too long, cut it down.

COMPLETE WHAT YOU START

Nothing's so fatiguing as the eternal hanging on of an uncompleted task.
—William James

Once you start a job, complete it as quickly as possible. Unfinished tasks take energy even when they're siting in a file.

FORM GOOD BUSINESS HABITS

SHOW APPRECIATION

Pave your path to success with recognition and praise of others. People respond positively to you when they are honestly recognized and rewarded. Here are some tips to consider:

- Remember people's names. Dale Carnegie writes, "A man's name is to him the sweetest and most important sound in any language."

- Take time for personal correspondence. Write notes of thanks or congratulations to coworkers or your boss. If you see an interesting article in the paper about someone you know, clip it out and mail it to the person with a note. Let others know how much you appreciate them. This is also a good way to maintain and reinforce your network of associates. You never know when you may need to reach out for help.

- Offer praise for improvements and achievements. Sincere and honest praise is always appreciated. Praise and compliments build rapport and foster good relationships.

- Make the other person feel important. Share the credit with your team members. Don't keep all the glory for yourself.

- Lift others spirits with a word of encouragement. It not only makes them feel good, but lifts your spirit as well.

- Give praise on a timely basis. Do not put it off. Give recognition and praise when due.

KEEP A CLEAN DESK

Cleaning your desk prior to starting work is a form of procrastination. The typical white-collar worker wastes three hours per week looking for misplaced things. That's 150 hours per year or almost four full weeks. To avoid this waste, follow these recommendations:

- Clean your desk at the end of each project and each day.

- Put everything back in its place. In other words, have a place for everything. This is not a stack! The primary purpose of a filing system is quick retrieval, not convenient storage.

- Have only the things you need on your desk for each project.

- Use your trash can. It's the best cure for a cluttered desk.

- Work on only one project at a time.

STRIVE FOR EXCELLENCE, NOT PERFECTION

- Don't wait for perfection. It will never happen.

- Reach for excellence, for your best.

- Set a completion time for each task; then complete it on time.

BE ENTHUSIASTIC

John Paul Getty ranks enthusiasm well ahead of business acumen, ambition, and even imagination. David Schwartz, author of *The Magic of Thinking Big*, writes, "Results come in proportion to enthusiasm applied."

When Mark Twain was asked the reason for his success, he replied, "I was born excited." Talk to successful people, and you will find that enthusiasm is the core of their being. Enthusiasm for what they are doing, for who they are, for what they believe.

Make what you do a passion, not an occupation. Regard each day as important. Maintain a daily interest in your work. Assume two people work at the same job. One works with boredom, waiting for the day to end; the other works with concentration and enthusiasm, finding excitement in the work. Which one is going to do a better job? Which one is going to get ahead?

Enthusiasm applies to more than work. It spills over into your whole life. How do you get enthusiasm? Dale Carnegie advises, "Act enthusiastic and you'll be enthusiastic."

USE HUMOR TO LIGHTEN YOUR LOAD

Laughter is the medicine of the soul. It can ease a pain, reduce stress, and help get things moving in the right direction. Laughter is an opposing force to anger. Anger destroys; laughter unites. Anger is an acid that does more harm to the person possessing it than it does to the person receiving it. Anger is just one letter away from *danger*.

Laugh and the world laughs with you, Cry and you cry alone.
—Ella Wheeler Wilcox

Laugh at yourself. Laugh with others. Use laughter and humor to attract or hold attention. Use it to create expectancy and build rapport. Use laughter to relax a group or audience, or to release the tension inside of you.

Use humor to entertain and inform. You learn better in a fun and lively atmosphere. Tell a story that illustrates your point. Use word pictures to clarify your meanings. It's the stories that are remembered most.

A genuine smile is a laugh. But a full, hearty laugh adds vitality to life.

MANAGE LIFE
Tips for Living

CHAPTER

15

Be not afraid of life. Believe that life is worth living, and your belief will help create the fact.

—William James

Several years ago I attended a presentation about writing positive, present-tense statements for each major goal in your life. I wrote down five specific sentences, but with no time frames. Each sentence expressed a long-term desire as having already been achieved. Looking back, I should have laughed at my audacity. Logically, there was no way these desires could become reality.

After writing my affirmations, I repeated them to myself several times each day. When I had fears and doubts about my future, I would read my affirmation card and repeat each sentence aloud. I did this over a period of several years. As time passed, miracles began to happen. Within seven years of having written those statements, most were realities. Here are the stories of three of them.

My first affirmation was, "I am a college graduate." What an improbable goal! I needed to work full-time, had no way of financing a degree, and lived hundreds of miles from any university. But one day, I saw my answer—an off-campus degree program. Within five years after writing down my goal, I graduated with honors from one of the top private colleges in the nation. I worked full-time and personally paid all of my educational expenses. Coincidence? Perhaps.

Another affirmation was, "I motivate and influence people in positive directions." Again a miracle happened. Within seven years of writing down this goal, I had changed career paths, from accountant, to personnel director, to college instructor—from data and numbers to people.

The third affirmation was "I travel worldwide." Since scripting this sentence, I have visited all 50 states, nine provinces in Canada, seven states in Mexico, and more than 50 other foreign countries. Coincidence? Perhaps.

From broad affirmations, my deepest desires came true beyond my wildest imaginings. Out of my first attempt to set life goals and write affirmations developed the four life zones and the long-term goal-planning forms you find in this book. You, too, may realize your dreams by applying life planning and affirmation writing. In this chapter, you will review the goals you wrote in Chapter 4. Then you will refine each goal and affirmation. So, turn the page and set the tone for the rest of your life.

BEYOND THE JOB—LIFE HABITS

Life extends far beyond any job. To succeed, you must be well-rounded in all that you do. Your daily living habits touch job, health, finances, home, and family. The key to successful living is balance. Let's look at some areas that tend to tip the scale of balance. These areas can affect your job performance and opportunities in positive or negative ways.

Successful businesses, whether an enterprise of one or thousands, manage time, money, people, supplies, and equipment. They manage these items by design, by plan.

Unmanaged segments of your life result in stress. Control time, money, people, communications, health, and education; and you eliminate stress. Following are some habits to form for life.

BELIEVE IN YOURSELF

No job is too big, no goal unobtainable when your belief systems are intact. Your potential is like an iceberg—only 2 percent is visible, the rest is hidden. You have what you need to succeed, just reach deep into your personal reservoir. Begin by taking the first step now.

ENJOY SMALL PLEASURES

To really enjoy life, take pleasure daily in life's small successes. If you don't experience the feeling of happiness in your everyday life, you are unlikely to experience it in the future. Enjoy the big winners when they come. But they come only once in awhile, so take the time to appreciate the little things in life. These small pleasures will carry you through your everyday ups and downs.

EMULATE SUCCESSFUL PEOPLE

Find someone who is successfully doing what you want to do, and then model that person. It is the fastest way to the top. There are many successful role models around. You may even be able to ask one to be your mentor.

Besides finding appropriate role models, read biographies of successful people. You will find common traits. Identify their best traits and the ones that will serve you best. Reproduce these traits in yourself.

BE CREATIVE

Use your imagination. It's free and always at your disposal. It weights nothing, and you can pack it wherever you go. Imagination is stronger than determination. It is more powerful than the will. Trying to "will something away" or "will something into being" only adds more stress to the tensions you already have. Napoleon said, "Imagination rules the world." It's the greatest power you have going for you. Use it.

SET A GOOD EXAMPLE

Actions speak louder than words. It's what you do that counts not what you say. Be aware of what you do and what your actions are saying. It is critical to your success.

ADMIT MISTAKES

The only people who never make mistakes reside in the graveyard. No matter how hard you try, you will still blow it at times. When this happens, take responsibility for the mistake. Admit your error and move on. Dwelling on mistakes and past errors will immobilize you.

THINK WELL OF YOURSELF

It's amazing how many of us have poor opinions of ourselves. Not only do we have a poor opinion, but we beat ourselves unmercifully for our (perceived) imperfections. The happiest day of your life will be when you learn to accept yourself as you are. This doesn't mean that you should stop trying to improve; it just means that you should look upon yourself as a person who is in evolution.

- **Treat yourself as you would your best friend.** There are two sides to you—your worst side and your best side. You have within you the potential to be calm, poised, assured, confident, and powerful. You also have the potential to be the opposite—nervous, afraid, unsure, weak, and limited. Which side shows depends on which side you choose for the moment. The side you express most often depends on how you feel about yourself.

- **Form an ideal picture of yourself and accept that as real,** rather than creating a picture that is less than ideal. Then choose the nature you would like to present.

- **Nourish your ideal self.** Exert a definite effort to develop habits of thinking well of yourself. The more you think well of yourself, the more automatic your thinking and actions become. Yoga masters teach that the brain is like soft clay and therefore subject to impressions. As you repeat a thought many times, the impression or groove becomes deep. Use this thought repetition to give you the power to feel good about yourself and to think well of yourself.

Nothing is so contagious as an example. We never do great good or great evil without bringing about more of the same on the part of others.
—Dr LaRoche Foucauld

The more you like yourself, the easier it is to give up destructive habits—habits you use to punish yourself for not being good enough, for not being perfect.

RELIEVE STRESS

Our bodies are our gardens . . . Our wills our gardeners.
—William Shakespeare

At times the pressure will seem like too much. You can't concentrate. You're ready to explode. Instead of reaching for the aspirin bottle, try one of these instant stress relievers:

- **Say no!** It has been said that the hardest word to say in the English language is no. However, learning to use this word can reduce stress. By having predetermined life goals, you have a controlling factor on what to say yes to. If saying yes takes you closer to your goal, then say yes. If the opportunity takes you farther from where you want to go, say no. Don't say maybe. This leaves the door open for manipulation. When saying no, be diplomatic. Thank the person for considering you. Knowing what your life goals are makes it easy to decide what to say without feeling guilty.

- **Breathe deeply.** Most of us walk around holding our breath. We are so used to doing this that we don't even realize it until, all of a sudden, we let out a deep sigh. We learned to hold our breath when we were children. We held our breath to control our feelings, to keep from crying, to control our anger. Because this is a learned behavior that doesn't serve us well, we can unlearn the bad habit and substitute a new habit—the habit of breathing deeply. Breathe in through your nose and out through your mouth. Concentrate on the changes in your body, how the chest expands and contracts, how the abdomen falls and rises.

- **Sigh.** A sigh relieves tension and signals the fact that you have been holding your breath. Now take six deep breaths.

- **Stretch.** Stand up. Raise your hands over your head. Stretch left and hold 1-2-3-4. Stretch right and hold 1-2-3-4. Repeat this several times.

- **Take a walk.** Even a walk around the office will help. Look out your window. Watch the birds. Notice the sky. Go outside. Breathe deeply for two minutes.

- **Visualize your favorite place on earth.** Right now in your mind, visit Hawaii. Feel the warm sun on your body. Listen to the waves lapping on the sand. Hear the chirps of the birds. Taste the salty water. Smell the sea air.

- **Call a friend.** Phone your most positive and supportive friend. Listen to his or her friendly voice and let it cheer you up.

- **Give a helping hand.** Help someone in need. It will cheer you up and help you to realize that giving is the best way to receive.

- **Hug someone.** You'll enjoy it, and so will they. Hug your child, spouse, neighbor, or favorite pet. Let your warmth and love flow through you to them.

- **Smile.** It's hard to be down while smiling, so keep a smile on your face. A smile will change your thought patterns from sad and negative to happy and positive. It's easy; smile right now, and see how much better you feel.

- **Laugh.** Reach for the joke book in your drawer. Read the cartoons on the bulletin board. Share a joke with a friend. A good laugh will refresh you.

- **Finish a project.** Pick up a task you can finish easily. Then complete it. You'll get a quick sense of accomplishment and a new surge of energy.

- **Change your focus.** Put your concerns to the side. Plan a pleasant event, a vacation, dinner with friends, or playtime with the kids. Think of a special surprise for a friend. Make out your gift list.

- **Sing a cheery song.** Music can lift and inspire. Choose a song that brings vitality and joy to your soul.

- **Exercise.** You may feel too tired to lift a finger, but if you take fifteen to twenty minutes and do some physical exercise, you'll feel renewed. Take a brisk walk. Climb the stairs.

USING THE LIFE MANAGEMENT SECTION OF THE *COMPANION PLANNER*

Life's most urgent question is, "What are you doing for others?"
—Martin Luther King, Jr.

Keep your completed Form 37, Goals, in the LIFE MANAGEMENT section of the *Companion Planner*. Having a permanent place to keep the form gives you easy access for periodical review and revision.

Stay on target with your life goals. Review the previous year's goals and your progress. Then write new goals. To maintain balance and harmony with the four zones of life, review and revise your life goals annually. The first of January is a good time for this project.

This section contains the following documents and forms:

- Mission statement

- Form 37: Goals: Long-Term and Short-Term. The Goals form assists you in the decision-making process and helps you maintain balance and harmony in your life. You should maintain your Form 37 for several years. This will allow you to track your progress and to review and revise annually.

- Form 26, Monthly Planner

- Form 27, Weekly Planner

- Daily To-Do lists

**O, Heart, remember thee
That Man is None, Safe One.**
—Coventry Patmore

Complete this sentence: My mission in life is. . . .

Write as fast as you can. Write everything that comes to your mind. Don't worry about content, order, or spelling. Write until your mind doesn't provide any more ideas. Then sit quietly and see if more ideas come. Close your eyes and visualize your mission. If more ideas come, jot them down. Now lay your mission statement aside. Let it rest for a few hours or a day or two. Then pick it up again, review it, and revise it.

As I was thinking about my mission statement, I began to realize that I had actually formulated my mission statement almost twenty years ago. It was when I wrote what I then considered my "goal card." On this card, I wrote five affirmations. These were the things that mattered most to me. For illustration purposes, I'll share with you my affirmations. See if you can tell which one was and still is my mission statement.

- I am happy.

- I motivate and influence others in positive directions.

- I travel worldwide.

- I am a college graduate.

- I walk and stand tall and straight.

The affirmation that sums up my life's mission is: "I motivate and influence others in positive directions." Everything I do is premised on this statement. It doesn't matter whether I'm involved at work, at home, in the community, or in the privacy of my own thoughts. Because of this mission statement, I can measure everything I do. Today my affirmation statements look like this:

- I motivate and influence people in positive directions.

- I am self-supporting.

- I set a good example in everything I do.

- I am the best me possible.

Behind these mission statements are goals and affirmations. My affirmation for being the best me possible is: "I celebrate today by being my best." For being self-supporting, I use: "I am financially independent," and "I invest wisely."

Because I am a "people" person, my mission statement deals with people. Your mission statement will likely involve a different focus. For example, if you are a sculptor, you may have a mission statement that says: "I improve our world by creating beautiful sculptures."

You, too, may want to review your long-term goals and affirmations. Perhaps hiding among those goals is your mission statement. After spending time with your mission statement, revise it so that it says what you want it to say. Keep your mission statement short, so you can focus on the most important things in your life.

EXERCISE 15-2   Establish Long-Term Life Goals

> Fortunate, indeed is the man who takes exactly the right measure of himself, and holds a just balance between what he can acquire and what he can use, be it great or be it small.
>
> **—Peter Mere Latham**

Life is like walking a tightrope. You take one step at a time, but if you lean too far in any one direction, you will fall. Return to the work you did in Chapter 4. Review your long-term goals, and discover whether you are in balance and in focus.

REVIEW YOUR LONG-TERM GOALS AND AFFIRMATIONS

Using Form 37, Goals, compare your mission statement with your long-term goals, and make sure they are in harmony with each other. Ask yourself:

- Are you spending all your time and effort on the job?
- Are you leaving time for family and friends?
- Are you spending so much time with a club or organization that there's little time to manage your finances?
- Have you gone bananas on an exercise program and forgot your educational goals?
- Are you feeling guilty because something has slipped away?

If any of these situations describe your circumstances, it is time to evaluate where you are, where you want to go, and how and when you want to achieve your goals. You need specific plans for each area.

Decide what you want and where you want to be. Use a full-life time frame. This type of planning provides you with a life direction and focus. It helps you make your daily decisions.

GOALS
Page 1 of 2

___X___ LONG-TERM   ___ SHORT-TERM

Date: ___01/01/XX___

Personal	Goals	Affirmations
Physical Weight, Pulse, Blood Pressure, Cholesterol Level, Personal Appearance	Weigh 138 pounds. Get cholesterol to 198. Improve personal appearance, have it professional and understated.	I am physically, mentally and spiritually fit. I eat only healthy foods. I enjoy exercising daily.
Mental Education, Self-Improvement, Technical Skills, Special Knowledges	Become more computer literate. Improve speaking and presentation ability. Obtain a bachelor's degree in psychology, then a Ph.D. Learn more about diet and nutrition so I can be healthier.	I celebrate today by being my best. I weigh 138 pounds. I always take time to play and rest.
Spiritual and Emotional	Be at peace with my past and myself. Always be enthusiastic. Always be in balance with my personal values. Set the best example possible for others.	

Social	Goals	Affirmations
Personal Relationships Spouse/Partner, Significant Other, Family, Friends, Neighbors	Stay happily married. Be a supportive, loving spouse. Be an understanding friend and family member. Be a helpful neighbor.	I am happy. I am a loving, caring person. I listen intently to others. I enjoy serving my community.
Professional Relationships Work, Business Organizations, Professional Organizations, Other	Be a dedicated and enthusiastic worker. Be totally trustworthy. Be excited and enthusiastic about my work.	I volunteer gladly. I make wise decisions. I am environmentally smart. I support my environment.
Community Relationships Religious, Political, Community, Social	Stay active and involved. Become more globally conscious, locally active. Become more environmentally smart. Serve on local committee that works to improve the community. Become less wasteful, be a wise steward of all resources.	I live and walk my values.

© 1995 Harris Espérance Incorporated   Form 37/95

Figure 15-1   FORM 37, Goals, Page 1

How much of what passes for grief in the world is really nothing more than regret?
—Elizabeth Forsythe Hailey,
A Woman of Independent Means

If you are under extreme stress, if you don't have time for the important things in life, you are probably out of balance. To come back into harmony, look at the four zones in your life and find those areas that need attention.

Annually review your long-term life goals. Make any changes necessary to maintain the balance and harmony you wish to have in your life. Compare your mission statement with your long-term goals, and make sure they are in harmony with each other.

GOALS Page 2 of 2		X LONG-TERM __ SHORT-TERM Date: 01/01/XX
Professional	**Goals**	**Affirmations**
Job Title or Position, Job Description	Become a store manager of a large metro jewelry store.	I am a successful manager. I provide quality service to my customers.
Education Credentials, Degrees, Licenses	Become a certified professional jeweler	I am a certified professional jeweler. I enjoy my work every day.
Employer Size, Type, Description	Work for a super-large, International jewelry company with lots of promotional opportunities in retail and wholesale.	
Geographic Location Distance	Work in Pacific Northwest. Willing to travel 25 miles one way to work.	
Financial	**Goals**	**Affirmations**
Liquid Assets Cash, Money Market Funds, Savings Bonds, Annuities, Life Insurance Cash Value, Other	Have sufficient cash reserves for all emergencies.	I am financially independent. I am self-supporting. I invest wisely. I review my finances monthly.
Nonmarketable Investments Real Estate, IRA's, KEOGH's Other Business Interests	Have partnership in four-plexes. Have a large KEOGH. Have stable and growing retirement funds.	I update my financial plan yearly.
Marketable Investments Stocks, Precious Metals, Mutual Funds, Corporate Bonds	Possess a large, stable, and growing investment portfolio.	
Personal Assets Home, Home Furnishings, Automobiles, Other Vehicles, Fine Jewelry, Furs, Other	Own a large comfortable home. Own second home in the woods. Buy new car. Have quality home furnishings. Own lots of unique valuable art pieces.	
© 1995 Harris Espérance Incorporated		Form 37/95

Figure 15-2 FORM 37, Goals, Page 2

Make sure your life's desires are represented in your goals and affirmations. Laurence G. Boldt, author of *Zen and the Art of Making a Living,* writes:

There is no getting away from problems in this life. You're either going to have the creative problems that come with realizing this vision of yours, or the neurotic problems that arise from suppression of desire. Creative problems, or challenges, test you and spur you to your best. Neurotic problems are simply the murky water of suppressed desire. Let's face it, your deepest desires aren't going away. Talk to people in nursing homes. See if many don't still have the idea of the thing they always wanted to do, but didn't. They are haunted by regret. Their desires didn't go away just because they didn't act on them. Your desire isn't going away either. Honor it, and do your best to give it expression. Keep coming back to it; feed it more and more attention. Let your desire become so strong that no fear from within or obstacle from without can stop your commitment to give your best.

The health of the people is really the foundation upon which all their happiness and all their power as a state depend.
—Benjamin Disraeli

Health management includes your physical, spiritual, emotional, and mental health. Balance is again the key.

To manage these aspects of your life, you must plan time for them. Diet and exercise are critical. Neglecting your personal being is shortchanging yourself.

Consider these health tips:

1. Exercise daily.
2. Breathe deeply.
3. Eat healthily.
4. Meditate and worship regularly to quiet your mind.
5. Build strong and stable emotional spirits.
6. Feed the mind. Read inspirational books. Listen to motivational tapes. Think positive thoughts. Attend educational classes.
7. Develop lasting friendships. Take time for family. Visit friends. Meet new people. Keep in touch.

WRITE SHORT-TERM PERSONAL GOALS AND AFFIRMATIONS

Review your long-term goals and affirmations. Then write short-term goals for the coming year. Ask yourself:

- Are my personal goals in balance with the rest of my life?
- Have I set reachable goals?
- Are my affirmations in the first person, present tense, and positive?
- Have I identified my key desires?

GOALS Page 1 of 2	__ LONG-TERM X SHORT-TERM Date: 01/01/xx	
Personal	**Goals**	**Affirmations**
Physical Weight, Pulse, Blood Pressure, Cholesterol Level, Personal Appearance	Lose 15 pounds (now weigh 138 pounds). Eat low-fat foods, get cholesterol to 198. Walk 4 miles 5 days a week.	I am physically, mentally, and spiritually fit. I eat only healthy foods. I celebrate today by being my best.
Mental Education, Self-Improvement, Technical Skills, Special Knowledges	Enroll in master's degree program. Take computer class. Join Toastmasters. Learn a new word every week.	I weigh 123 pounds. I enjoy walking every day. Water is my drink of choice. I take time to play and rest.
Spiritual/Emotional	Smile a lot. Meditate 20 minutes each day. Do breathing exercises each morning.	I like myself and enjoy being me. I take time to meditate every day. I value and honor myself.

Figure 15-3   FORM 37, Short-term Personal Goals and Affirmations

Your social relationships will affect all other areas of your life. When you are in balance and harmony with the people you live and work with, you are free to concentrate on the other areas of life. Your relationships will be supportive when nourished and attended to; they will be destructive when neglected and ignored. Accept others for what they are, not for what you want them to become.

WRITE SHORT-TERM SOCIAL GOALS AND AFFIRMATIONS

Review your long-term goals and affirmations. Now write short-term, or yearly, goals and affirmations.

Ask yourself these questions:

- Are my relationships in balance with the rest of my goals?

- Do I set enough time aside for my family and friends?

- Is there time to serve my community?

- Are these goals and affirmations what I want today?

- Are there any changes that need to be made?

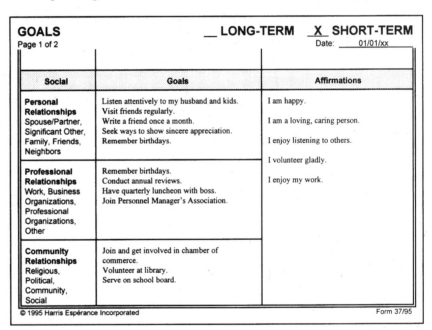

Figure 15-4   FORM 37, Short-Term Social Goals and Affirmations

Work expands so as to fill the available time for its completion.
—C. Northcote Parkinson

To be successful, you must effectively mange your time. It is your only nonrenewable, nonreplaceable resource. Time management begins with plans, "to do" lists, and action. Following are some time-saving strategies to help you manage your time more effectively.

Tools for Time Management:

- Monthly planner
- Weekly planner
- Daily "to do" list
- Clock
- Written short-term and long-term goals

USE YOUR MONTHLY PLANNER

Looking at your short-term annual goals and affirmations, fill in your priorities for each month.

Priority Tasks	MONTHLY PLANNER					Month of: January, 1994	
	Sunday	Monday	Tuesday	Wednesday	Thursday	Friday	Saturday
Review and revise long-term goals and affirmations. Write short-term yearly goals Complete taxes. Review and update all financial reports. Do a budget and 6-month cash flow. Eat healthy. Exercise daily. Smile a lot. Breathe deeply.		1 Review and revise long-term goals.	2	3	4	5	6 Write short-term yearly goals
	7	8	9	10	11	12 Go to birthday party for Ronnie.	13 Review and update budget and financial papers
	14	15	16	17	18	19 Go to beach.	20 Spend week-end with family — relax.
	21 Visit Jane and Bill while at the beach.	22	23	24	25	26	27
Birthdays 12 Ronnie 21 Jane 31 Julie	28 Begin taxes	29	30	31 Call Julie for birthday.			
Affirmations	I celebrate today by being my best. I like to listen. Exercise is fun for me. Today is the best day of my life.						

© 1995 Harris Espérance Incorporated — Form 26/95

Figure 15-5 FORM 26, Monthly Planner

Priorities are important activities. Unfortunately, they usually get put aside for less important, more pressing activities. Important activities include the following:

- Life planning and goal setting
- Exercise
- Building and strengthening relationships
- Eating healthily
- Self-examination

Take your short-term annual goals and affirmations, and fill out your priorities for each month.

USE YOUR WEEKLY PLANNER

Viewing the week in its entirety allows you to see a larger picture and aids in your planning. List your priorities at the left. They are your most important activities. Write the most important affirmations for the week at the bottom of your weekly planner.

Next check your monthly calendar, and transfer your priorities to your weekly schedule.

PRIORITIES	TIME	SUN	MON	TUE	WED	THUR	FRI	SAT
Review and revise long-term goals and affirmations. Write short-term goals. Eat healthy. Exercise daily. Smile a lot. Breathe deeply.	6:00		Review lt goals	Swim	Walk	Swim	Walk	
	7:00							
	8:00							Write annual goals
	9:00							
	10:00							
	11:00							
	12:00			Toast-masters		Lunch with Alex		
	1:00							
	2:00							
	3:00							
	4:00							
	5:00							
	6:00 On				Terry's school play at 7 p.m.			

Weekly Planner — **Week Ending:** January 6, 19XX

AFFIRMATIONS *I celebrate today by being my best. I like to listen. A part of all I earn is mine to keep.*

Form 27/95

Figure 15-6 FORM 27, Weekly Planner

TIMELY TIPS:

Daily To Do List

Write new procedure for hiring

Call Harry about Tuesday's meeting

Write meeting agenda

Finalize quarterly budget.

Prepare budget comments.

Make haircut appointment.

Pick up tomatoes and milk.

Take Kyle to piano lesson at 6 pm

1. Plan your time.
2. Use a weekly or daily planner.
3. Use the little moments.
4. Act, don't just think.
5. Write daily "to do" lists.
6. Prioritize your "to do" list with the highest payoff item as number 1.
7. Complete all the items on your "to do" list.
8. Be assertive. Control interruptions, long-winded callers, and meetings. Establish a time to make and receive phone calls.
9. Begin and complete projects early.
10. Create an ordered environment. Organize your desk and files. Keep everything in its place.
11. Handle each piece of paperwork once.
12. Delegate work. Train others to do your work.
13. Be on time to work, meetings, and events.
14. Periodically update, in writing, your professional and personal goals.
15. Do your most important work during your peak energy hours.
16. Schedule and take relaxation time, free from worry and stress.

As you work at managing your life, relationships, resources, and time, consider the following words by David Keirsey and Marilyn Bates from their book, *Please Understand Me:*

> *If I do not want what you want, please try not to tell me that my want is wrong.*
> *Or if I believe other than you, at least pause before you correct my view.*
> *Or if my emotion is less than yours, or more, given the same circumstances, try not to ask me to feel more strongly or weakly.*
> *I do not, for the moment at least, ask you to understand me. That will come only when you are willing to give up changing me into a copy of you.*
> *I may be your spouse, your parent, your offspring, your friend, or your colleague. If you will allow me any of my own wants or emotions, or beliefs, or actions, then you open yourself, so that some day these ways of mine might not seem so wrong and might finally appear to you as right—for me.*
> *To put up with me is the first step to understanding me. Not that you embrace my ways as right for you, but that you are no longer irritated or disappointed with me for my seeming waywardness. And in understanding me you might come to prize my differences from you, and, far from seeking to change me preserve and even nurture those differences.*

MANAGE FINANCES
The Rules of Money

There is something about making your own money and having control over your life that cannot be duplicated. Knowing that you can take care of yourself, no matter what happens, is so important that it should be a right.
—Rebecca Maddox, *Inc. Your Dreams*

One day a friend loaned me his tape of *The Richest Man in Babylon,* a motivation speech first presented in 1926 by George S. Clason. As I listened to the tape, the truth of wealth became real to me. Out of this first exposure came this chapter—a brief attempt to share with you the secrets of financial security.

My personal journey began with the affirmation "I am financially independent." It is a statement that expresses my desire to be able to support myself always—never to be financially dependent on the state or on others. Although there are no guarantees in life, this statement conditioned me to be aware of my finances and my personal responsibility. After writing and speaking this affirmation continuously over the years, I've watched my financial picture improve dramatically. Another coincidence? Perhaps, but I don't believe so.

I encourage you to get a tape and a copy of *The Richest Man in Babylon.* For further study, read and listen to *Your Money or Your Life— Transforming Your Relationship with Money and Achieving Financial Independence* by Joe Dominquez and Vicki Robin. The books and tapes are available at most bookstores and local libraries.

You, too, can improve your financial status by reading Chapter 16 and by doing the exercises. Compose an accurate picture of your financial state and of your future financial destination. Write a broad, encompassing financial affirmation. Then watch your financial picture change.

WHERE WILL YOU BE FINANCIALLY AT 65?

According to a January 1980 report from the U.S. Department of Health, Education and Welfare, Income and Resources of the Aged, the following statistics exist about 65-year-olds:

For every 100 Americans born 65 years ago

- 29 are dead.

- 13 have annual incomes under $3,500.

- 55 have annual incomes between $3,500 and $20,000, with a median income of $4,700.

- 3 have annual incomes over $20,000.

Why are so many people in the United States of America living in poverty when supposedly they live in the world's richest country? Most of these people spend their life working. Where did all their money go? What went wrong? These people, like so many people today, probably did not save money on a regular basis. They did have a financial plan.

This chapter only begins to plant some ideas about financial planning. It takes work. It takes planning. It takes persistence. Where do you want to be at age 65? On poverty row or living on a comfortable income? If "living on a comfortable income" is your answer, there are things you must learn and practice now to avoid a lifestyle of poverty. Begin by learning the "laws of wealth" as presented by G. S. Clason.

THE LAWS OF WEALTH

G. S. Clason, author of *The Richest Man in Babylon*, presents this advice on money management: The "desire to prosper" is all that's required to accumulate wealth. This desire is not wishful thinking; it is a **burning** desire that fuels the necessity to practice the three laws for accumulating wealth. To ensure a financially secure future, learn and faithfully practice these laws.

HOW TO ACQUIRE MONEY

- Pay yourself **first!** Not less than 10 percent, no matter how little you earn.

- Live off of less than you earn.

HOW TO KEEP MONEY

- Invest your treasure with the greatest of caution.

- Counsel only with those skilled in the ways of money, whose daily task is handling money.

- Don't become greedy. Better a secured investment at a lower rate than a risky investment at a higher rate.

- Exercise a little caution to avoid a great regret!

HOW TO USE MONEY

The beginning is the most important part of the work.

—Plato

- Invest your earnings; don't spend them.

- Let your earnings and your earnings' earnings work for you.

- Acquire your treasure, keep it, and make it grow.

- Then enjoy life's blessings without regrets.

The advice that Mr. Clason gave fifty years ago is just as sound today as it was then.

Learn to manage what you have today so that tomorrow will be brighter. Money management is a life skill that needs attention today. Don't wait until you have enough; start today.

Begin by putting your finances in order. Start with a complete financial picture of where you are today. Put it in writing. Use the forms in the text as a basis for analysis. It is a beginning.

Few employers today offer a full-ride company pension plan. Some employers do offer joint investment based on your proportionate share. These tax-advantaged retirement plans are known as IRAs, 401(K)s, SEPs, and Keoghs. Other employers offer no retirement plan at all.

Financial Management Tips:

- Establish a long-term financial plan. Review your plan annually. Work your plan.

- Look for ways to save money. Buy in bulk. Eliminate cigarettes. Eliminate or limit the use of alcohol and soft drinks; drink water. Eat at home. Pack a lunch. Carpool.

- Study investment strategies with a view toward the future. Take an investment class.

- Invest your money in stocks, mutual funds, bonds, savings accounts, CDs, money market accounts, pensions, real estate.

- Shop for an interest-paying, free, or low-cost checking account.

START EARLY

John and Dave were high school friends. They each had similar jobs, a wife, and three kids. Their incomes for forty-five years were identical, although their financial planning was different. Here is what each did:

- John began investing at age 35. He saved $5,000 a year for ten years or a total of $50,000. At age 65, John's $50,000 was worth $728,962.

- Dave began investing at age 45 and saved $7,500 a year for twenty years, or a total of $157,500. At 65, Dave's $157,500 was worth $561,417.

This example assumes an average growth rate of 10 percent. However, there is no guarantee that your investments will average 10 percent. The story is for illustrative purposes only. Invest in safe secure investments. Don't risk your capital.

USING THE FINANCIAL MANAGEMENT SECTION
OF THE *COMPANION PLANNER*

A lean purse is easier to cure than endure.
—George S. Clason

Having an ongoing financial plan allows you to achieve your financial goals within set time frames. It also assists in making alternate plans when things don't go as planned. Knowing where your money comes from and where it goes is an intricate part of life planning. Maintaining financial goals and records is essential in preserving a healthy, balanced life.

The forms listed below are kept in the FINANCIAL MANAGEMENT section of your notebook:

- Form 39: Budget Work Sheet
The Budget Work Sheet is used to analyze your basic financial needs.

- Form 40: Cash Flow Statement
A cash flow statement is instrumental in maintaining month-to-month smooth operation of a budget. Some months may require withdrawals from savings in order to meet specific expenses. It's wise to plan ahead for large expenditures.

- Form 41: Assets and Liabilities
Prepare detailed listings of information on separate sheets. Then summarize the information on this form.

- Form 42: Income and Expenses
If this form doesn't meet your needs, create your own form using a columnar pad. Add all necessary categories to cover your income and expenses.

- Form 43: Job Search Expenses
Some job hunting expenses may be tax deductible. Keep an accurate record with your receipts. At the end of the year, consult with your accountant to determine the deductible items. Typical deductible items include:

  Resume costs: printing, paper
  Secretarial and/or word processing assistance
  Job placement consulting services
  Stationery
  Postage
  Travel
  Long distance telephone calls
  Answering service or answering machine
  Job-related newspaper subscriptions and purchases

REVIEW LONG-TERM FINANCIAL GOALS AND AFFIRMATIONS ANNUALLY

Use Form 37, Goals, to update and revise your long-term financial goals annually.

```
GOALS                          X LONG-TERM _ SHORT-TERM
Page 2 of 2                              Date:      01/01/xx
```

Financial	Goals	Affirmations
Liquid Assets Cash, Money Market Funds, Savings Bonds, Annuities, Life Insurance Cash Value, Other	Have sufficient cash reserves for all emergencies.	I am financially independent. I am self-supporting. I invest wisely.
Nonmarketable Investments Real Estate, IRAs, Keoghs, Other Business Interests	Have partnership in four-plexes. Have large Keogh. Have stable and growing retirement funds.	I review my finances monthly. I update my financial plan yearly.
Marketable Investments Stocks, Precious Metals, Mutual Funds, Corporate Bonds	Possess large, stable, and growing investment portfolio.	
Personal Assets Home, Home Furnishings, Automobile, Other Vehicles, Fine Jewelry, Furs, Other	Own a large, comfortable home. Own a second home in the woods. Buy new car. Have quality home furnishings. Own lots of unique valuable art pieces.	

© 1995 Harris Espérance Incorporated   Form 37/95

Figure 16-1   FORM 37, Goals, Long-Term Financial Goals and Affirmations

Ask yourself these questions:

- Do these financial goals and affirmations still fit my desires and values?
- Is there a better way to write my financial goals and affirmations?
- Have I looked at the "big picture"?
- Have I adequately prepared for the future?
- Have I set aside enough funds for educational needs for the kids?
- Will there be enough for a comfortable retirement?

File Form 37, behind the LIFE MANAGEMENT divider in your *Companion Planner.*

WRITE SHORT-TERM FINANCIAL GOALS AND AFFIRMATIONS

```
GOALS                          _ LONG-TERM X SHORT-TERM
Page 2 of 2                              Date:      01/01/xx
```

Financial	Goals	Affirmations
Liquid Assets Cash, Money Market Funds, Savings Bonds, Annuities, Life Insurance Cash Value, Other	Maintain a $10,000 liquid cash fund for emergencies. Keep checkbook balanced monthly. Review finances quarterly.	I am financially independent. I am self-supporting. I invest wisely.
Nonmarketable Investments Real Estate, IRAs, Keoghs, Other Business Interests	Draw floor plan for four-plex. Locate and buy property. Get bids on construction. Build by September.	I review my finances quarterly. Saving is fun for me.
Marketable Investments Stocks, Precious Metals, Mutual Funds, Corporate Bonds	Watch stock portfolio closer or transfer stock investments into mutual funds. Save 6% for retirement. Save 4% for educational needs.	I enjoy planning my financial future. I balance my checkbook monthly.
Personal Assets Home, Home Furnishings, Automobiles, Other Vehicles, Fine Jewelry, Furs, Other	Paint exterior of house. Buy new Erté.	

© 1995 Harris Espérance Incorporated   Form 37/95

Figure 16-2   FORM 37, Goals, Short-Term Financial Goals and Affirmations

After reviewing your long-term goals, write your yearly financial goals. These goals need to be more specific.

Set short-term goals for the year.

Be specific in each goal.

Save systematically.

Ask yourself these questions:

- Have I set reachable goals?
- Will I commit myself to this plan?
- Have I been specific about what I want and how I will achieve my financial goals?

File Form 37, Goals, behind the LIFE MANAGEMENT divider in your *Companion Planner.*

Work to become, not to acquire.

—Elbert Hubbard

Reviewing and updating your list of assets and liabilities annually will help you measure your financial progress. Listed below are the items to include in each of the categories on Form 41, Assets and Liabilities.

UPDATE ASSETS AND LIABILITIES ANNUALLY

Liquid Assets:

Cash, checking accounts
Savings accounts
Certificates of deposit (CDs)
Savings bonds
Government securities

Cash brokerage accounts
Cash value of life insurance
Annuities
Credit union savings accounts

Marketable Investments:

Stocks and bonds
Corporate bonds
Mutual funds
Stock options and futures
Commodities
Precious metals

Nonmarketable Investments:

Retirement funds (company, IRAs, and Keoghs)
Real estate
Loans to others
Tax shelters
Trust funds

Personal Assets:

Home
Automobiles and other vehicles
Jewelry and furs
Home furnishings
Personal collectibles
Other valuables

Liabilities

Home mortgages
Credit card balances
Loans (car, college tuition, other)
Income tax liability
Medical bills
Other financial obligations

File your completed Form 41, Assets and Liabilities, behind the FINANCIAL MANAGEMENT divider in your *Companion Planner*.

ASSETS AND LIABILITIES

ASSETS	12/31/__ Actual	12/31/__ Projected
Liquid Assets		
Marketable Investments		
Nonmarketable Investments		
Personal Assets		
TOTAL ASSETS		
LIABILITIES		
TOTAL LIABILITIES		
NET WORTH (Assets less Liabilities)		

© 1995 Harris Espérance Incorporated   Form 41/95

Figure 16-3 FORM 41, Assets and Liabilities

Too many people spend money they haven't earned, to buy things they don't want, to impress people they don't know.

—Will Rogers

Take last year's income and expenses and list them in the first column of Form 42; then project next year's income and expenses. This will help you when you put together your cash flow projections for the next six months.

List all sources of income. Your federal income tax statement will be helpful here.

Review your last year's spending and savings program. See where the money went. Record the actual numbers; then project numbers for next year's amounts.

INCOME AND EXPENSES

INCOME	12/31/ Actual	12/31/ Projected
Wages		
Self-Employment		
Unemployment Compensation		
Interest, Dividends, Rents, Royalties, Fees		
Child Support, Social Security, Pensions		
Annuities		
TOTAL INCOME		

EXPENSES	12/31/ Actual	12/31/ Projected
Housing (Mortgage or Rent)		
Utilities		
Furnishings, Maintenance, Upkeep		
Food, Beverages, Other Grocery Items		
Clothing, Upkeep		
Personal (Health, Beauty)		
Transportation		
Insurance (Car, Home, Liability, Medical, Life)		
Savings, Other Investments		
Retirement		
Taxes		
Credit Cards, Loans		
Contributions, Gifts		
Licenses, Fees		
Recreation, Entertainment		
Education, Subscriptions, Memberships		
TOTAL EXPENSES		
TOTAL INCOME LESS EXPENSES		

© 1995 Harris Espérance Incorporated   Form 42/95

The projected figures provide you with a total picture of what you can expect for the coming year. When you have these figures, you can review your yearly (short-term) goals to make sure that your financial objectives are reachable.

File the completed Form 42, Income and Expenses, behind the FINANCIAL MANAGEMENT divider in your *Companion Planner*.

Figure 16-4   FORM 42, Income and Expenses

Money talks, all right! It says 'goodbye' to me.
—Author Unknown

Prepare a monthly and an annual budget. Form 39, Budget Work Sheet, will help you when you do your cash flow projections.

Use a columnar pad to create your own master budget form if this form doesn't meet your needs.

Compute your yearly needs then divide by twelve to get your monthly requirements.

File this form behind the FINANCIAL MANAGEMENT divider of your notebook.

BUDGET WORK SHEET		Date: March 1
Expenses	**Month**	**Year**
Housing	$ 495	$ 5,940
Utilities (Phone, Electricity, Gas, Water, Garbage)	125	1,500
Furnishings Maintenance and Upkeep	10	120
Food, Beverages, and Other Grocery Items	390	4,680
Clothing and Upkeep	50	600
Personal (Health and Beauty Aids)	25	300
Transportation (Gas, Oil, Maintenance)	125	1,500
Insurance: Life *Currently paid by employer		*
Insurance: Medical, Dental, Vision *Currently paid by employer		*
Insurance: Long-Term Disability *Currently paid by employer		*
Insurance: Automobile	50	600
Insurance: Property and Household	70	840
Insurance: Personal Liability *Included in household insurance		*
Insurance: Other		—
Savings and Other Investments	100	1,200
Retirement *Employer contributes 6% of gross wages to retirement *	50	* 600
Recreation and Entertainment	50	600
Education	25	300
Contributions and Gifts	100	1,200
Dues, Subscriptions and Memberships	5	60
Loans and Interest Payments	235	2,820
Licenses and Fees	10	120
Property Taxes	100	1,200
Net Before Payroll Taxes	$ 2,015	$ 24,180
Federal Income Taxes		
Other Federal Taxes (FUTA, etc.)		
State Income Taxes *Estimated Taxes *	864	* 10,368
Other Taxes (State Worker's Compensation, Unemployment, City)		
Social Security (FICA and Medicare)		
Total Budget Requirements	$ 2,879	$ 34,548
Rate per Hour (Divide year total by 2,080 hours)		$16.61/hour

© 1995 Harris Espérance Incorporated   Form 39/95

Figure 16-5   FORM 39, Budget Work Sheet

Everyone has some type of budget to manage. Learn to manage your own budget, and you will know how to manage a budget at work. The elements of management are the same. Use Form 40, Cash Flow Statement, to show the variations in monthly incomes and expenses.

File the completed Form 40, Cash Flow Statement, behind the FINANCIAL MANAGEMENT divider in your *Companion Planner*.

CASH FLOW STATEMENT						Date	March 1
MONTH	March	April	May	June	July	August	
INCOME							
Wages							
TOTAL INCOME							
EXPENSES							
TOTAL EXPENSES							
Surplus (+) Deficit (−)							

© 1995 Harris Espérance Incorporated   Form 40/95

Figure 16-6 FORM 40, Cash Flow Statement

WORKPLACE INVESTMENT PLANS

Most financial advisors recommend investing your first retirement savings into tax-deferred accounts, such employer sponsored plans as 401(k)s, 403(b)(7)s, SEPs, Keoghs, and IRAs. There is one enormous benefit gained from this type of investment—your account earnings grow faster than in taxable investments. When you invest in one of these programs, your taxes are deferred, thereby giving you more to invest.

401(k)s:

- For employees of for-profit organizations.

  - Maximum annual contribution: Up to 15 percent of compensation, but not more than an estimated $9,235 in 1994.

  - Many employers make matching contributions to their employee's accounts to encourage retirement savings and planning. Typically, an employer may contribute $0.50 for each $1.00 contributed by the employee, up to a maximum of 6 percent of the employee's salary or to a specified allowable maximum.

  - In this type of plan, you generally have a choice of how to invest your contributions. Typically, you will be offered from three to ten plans, depending on the company's plan. Many plans allow access before retirement for education loans and hardship withdrawals. Tax penalties and withdrawal fees may be assessed.

403(b)(7)s:

- For employees of nonprofit organizations, such as public schools and charitable organizations.

- Maximum annual contribution: Up to $9,500, depending on your own maximum exclusion allowance calculation.

- This plan allows you to decide how to invest your contributions. Some plans allow early withdrawals for hardship.

SEP-IRAs/SAR-SEPs:

- For the self-employed and for small business owners and their employees.

- SEP maximum contribution: Company contributes 15 percent of gross salary or $22,500, whichever is less.

- SAR-SEP maximum contribution: In this plan, the employee can also contribute to the plan, but the total contributed to the account by both employee and employer can not exceed $22,500 or 15 percent of gross salary.

- Employees in both plans decide how to invest money, and the plan generally allows early withdrawals.

Keoghs—Money Purchase Pension Plans and Profit Sharing Plans:

- For the self-employed and small business owners and their employees.

- Under the money purchase pension plan, the employer makes a fixed percentage contribution each year of 25 percent of compensation or a maximum of $22,500 per employee. Employees do not make contributions.

- Under the profit sharing plan, the employer contributes a varying percentage ranging from 0 to 5 percent of compensation, but not more than $22,500 per employee. Employees do not make contributions.

- Early withdrawals may be permitted but may be subject to tax penalties.

IRAs:

- All wage earners under the age of $70\frac{1}{2}$ can make IRA contributions.

- Investment is tax deferred.

- Maximum annual investment is $2,000, even if you participate in an employer plan.

Note: Retirement rules and regulations change constantly. Therefore, the information in this section is presented for informational purposes and cannot be considered as legal or tax advice. All investors should consult with their tax advisor to determine the tax consequences and advantages and disadvantages of available plans.

RECOMMENDED READING

APPENDIX A

MUST READ OR LISTEN TO

Cassette tapes are available and highly recommended. These books and tapes can be found in your local library or through interlibrary loans.

- *The Seven Habits of Highly Effective People,* Stephen R. Covey. Simon & Schuster Inc., New York, NY. The best book on life management and effective communications available today.

- *The Magic of Thinking Big,* David J. Schwartz. Prentice Hall, Inc., New York, NY. The wisdom presented here is ageless.

- *The Richest Man in Babylon,* George S. Clason. Hawthorn Books, New York, NY. Principals of finance based on Babylonian parable.

- *Acres of Diamonds,* Russell Conwell. Harper & Brothers, New York, NY. Look in your own backyard for your fortune. A timely and true lesson for today's seekers.

- *As a Man Thinketh,* James Allen. Grosset & Dunlap, New York, NY. A small, well-written volume on the power of thought.

CAREER MANAGEMENT

- *Color Me Beautiful,* Carole Jackson. Random House, New York, NY. Discover your natural beauty.

- *Do What You Love, The Money Will Follow: Discovering Your Right Livelihood,* Marsha Sinetar. Paulist Press, New York, NY.

- *Dress for Success* and *Women's Dress for Success Book,* John T. Molloy. Warner Books, New York, NY. America's best-known clothing consultant tells what to wear and why.

- *Getting Hired: Everything You Need to Know about Resumes, Interviews, and Job-Hunting Strategies,* Edward J. Rogers. Prentice Hall Press, New York, NY. Contains innovative and creative resumes.

- *Guerilla Tactics in the Job Market,* Tom Jackson. Bantam Books, New York, NY.

- *Robert Half on Hiring,* Robert Half. Bantam Books, New York, NY.

Written from the employer's viewpoint. Provides unique insights on how employers make hiring decisions.

- *Knock 'Em Dead with Great Answers to Tough Interview Questions*, Martin Yate. Bob Adams, Inc., Holbrook, MA.

- *200 Letters for Job Hunters*, William S. Frank. Ten Speed Press, Berkeley, CA.

- *What Color Is Your Parachute?*, Richard Nelson Bolles. Ten Speed Press, Berkeley, CA. A practical manual for job hunters and career changers.

- *Who's Hiring Who*, Richard Lathrop. Ten Speed Press, Berkeley, CA. The best book on writing resumes.

- *Zen and the Art of Making a Living: A Practical Guide to Creative Career Design*, Laurence G. Boldt. Penguin Books USA Inc., New York, NY.

- *Professional Presence*, Susan Bixler. Berkeley Publishing, New York, NY.

- *Inc. Your Dreams: For Any Woman Who Is Thinking About Her Own Business*, Rebecca Maddox. Viking-Penguin Books USA Inc., New York, NY.

SPECIAL CAREER NEEDS AND INTERESTS

Check your local library or college library for specialized directories and books to aid you in your job search. You will find an abundance of help available to you. A few examples are listed here.

- *Directory of Special Programs for Minority Group Members*. Garrett Park Press, Garrett Park, MD. Includes career information services, employment skills banks, and financial aid programs.

- *Job Hunting for the Disabled*, Edith Marks and Adele Lewis. Woodbury, NY.

- *Civil Service Tests For Basic Skills Jobs*, Hy Hammer. Arco, New York, NY.

- *How to Pass Employment Tests*, Arthur Liebers. Arco, New York, NY.

- *Practice for Clerical, Typing, Steno Tests*, Maryhelen H. Paulick Hoffman. Prentice Hall, New York, NY.

LIFE MANAGEMENT

- *The Inner Winner*, Denis E. Waitley. Nightingale-Conant Corporation, Chicago, IL. An outstanding audiocassette program on affirmations.

- *Megatrends 2000—Ten New Directions for the 1990's*, John Naisbitt and Patricia Aburdene. William Morrow and Company, Inc. New York, NY.

- *Power Shift: Knowledge, Wealth and Violence at the Edge of the Twenty-First Century*, Alvin Tofler. Bantam Books, New York, NY.

- *The Three Boxes of Life and How to Get Out of Them*, Richard Nelson Bolles. Ten Speed Press, Berkeley, CA. An introduction to life/work planning.

- *Wishcraft: How to Get What You Really Want*, Barbara Sher. Ballantine Books, New York, NY. A unique, step-by-step plan to pinpoint your goals and make your dreams come true.

COMMUNICATIONS MANAGEMENT

- *The Elements of Style,* William Strunk Jr. and E.B. White. Macmillan Publishing Co., Inc., New York, NY.

- *Influencing with Integrity: Management Skills for Communication and Negotiation,* Genie Z. Laborde. Syntony Publishing, Palo Alto, CA.

- *Writing the Natural Way: A Course in Enhancing Creativity and Writing Confidence,* Gabriele Lusser Rico. Jeremy P. Tarcher, Inc., Los Angeles, CA.

- *Unlimited Power,* Anthony Robbins. Fawcette Columbine Book. New York, NY. A unique approach to reprogram your thoughts and behaviors for success. (Cassette tape also available.)

HEALTH MANAGEMENT

- *Perfect Health: The Complete Mind/Body Guide,* Deepak Chopra, M.D. Harmony Books, New York, NY.

MONEY MANAGEMENT

- *Your Money or Your Life: Transforming Your Relationship with Money and Achieving Financial Independence,* Joe Dominguez and Vicki Robin. Viking Penguin, New York, NY.

ANSWERS TO PUZZLES

ONE DOT

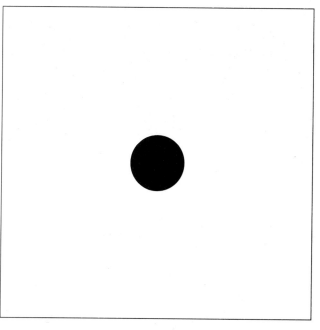

Exercise I: One Dot

Did you write, "A black dot"? That is what most of us see, and we don't look any further. We have our answer. But there is more in the box than just a black dot. What about all the white space around the dot?

Most of us see the obvious, but we need to learn to look for those things that are less obvious, like the white space around the dot.

Another way to do this exercise is to take a self-adhesive dot and put one on your bathroom mirror; put another on a sliding glass door. The dots can serve as a reminder to you to look at your situation from many different directions, to find the answers that are not obvious. In the mirror, there is the reflection and all that it holds. On the glass door, you can view the dot from two totally different sides, each side with its own unique view and answers.

Step back from each situation you encounter in the job hunt. Look for answers beyond the obvious. Ask yourself if there is another way to get what you want.

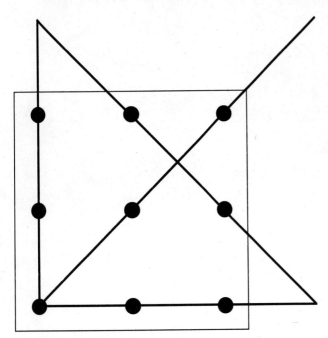

Exercise 2: Nine Dots

NINE DOTS

If you had trouble solving this puzzle, it is probably because you did not allow yourself to go outside the imaginary box defined by the dots. To solve the puzzle, you must go outside the frame of the dots.

This exercise is an example of thinking outside your ordinary mental boxes. It is about discarding old assumptions about life.

If you are to get the job and life you desire, you should use techniques that take you outside the customary strategies that most people use. That is what this book is about. It is to teach you new ways of approaching the old challenge of job hunting.

ACTION WORDS

Accomplished
Achieved
Acquired
Acted
Adapted
Addressed
Adjusted
Administered
Advertised
Advised
Affected
Alerted
Allowed
Amortized
Analyzed
Answered
Anticipated
Appeared
Appointed
Appreciated
Approached
Approved
Arbitrated
Argued
Arranged
Arrived
Ascertained
Asked
Assembled
Assessed
Assigned
Assisted
Assumed
Assured
Attained
Audited

Authorized
Avoided
Awarded
Baked
Balanced
Believed
Bolstered
Bought
Brought
Budgeted
Built
Calculated
Called
Cataloged
Chaired
Changed
Charged
Charted
Checked
Chose
Circulated
Clarified
Classified
Cleaned
Coached
Collected
Communicated
Complied
Completed
Compiled
Composed
Computed
Conceived
Conceptualized
Conducted
Confused

Conserved
Contacted
Contracted
Controlled
Converted
Cooked
Coordinated
Copied
Copyedited
Counseled
Counted
Created
Cut
Decided
Deciphered
Decoded
Decreased
Defined
Delegated
Delivered
Demonstrated
Depreciated
Designated
Designed
Detailed
Detected
Determined
Developed
Devised
Diagnosed
Directed
Disappeared
Discovered
Dissected
Dispensed
Displayed

Disproved
Disputed
Distributed
Diverted
Documented
Dramatized
Dreamed
Drew
Dried
Drove
Dug
Edited
Eliminated
Emphasized
Empowered
Enabled
Enforced
Enjoyed
Enlarged
Ensured
Envisioned
Established
Estimated
Evaluated
Examined
Exceeded
Exchanged
Exercised
Exhibited
Expanded
Experienced
Experimented
Explained
Expressed
Extracted
Facilitated

391

Filed	Interrogated	Originated	Reconstructed	Studied
Financed	Interviewed	Oversaw	Recorded	Summarized
Fine-tuned	Intuited	Painted	Recruited	Sung
Fired	Invented	Participated	Rectified	Supervised
Fitted	Inventoried	Patched	Reduced	Supplied
Fixed	Investigated	Perceived	Referred	Supported
Folded	Invited	Performed	Rehabilitated	Suspended
Followed	Involved	Persuaded	Related	Symbolized
Formulated	Judged	Photographed	Relocated	Synthesized
Forwarded	Kept	Picked	Remembered	Systematized
Found	Landscaped	Pictured	Remodeled	Talked
Founded	Learned	Piled	Rendered	Taught
Fried	Lectured	Piloted	Reorganized	Tended
Gave	Led	Placed	Repaired	Tested
Gathered	Left	Planned	Replaced	Told
Generated	Lifted	Played	Reported	Took
Got	Liked	Possessed	Represented	Totaled
Governed	Listed	Posted	Required	Trained
Graduated	Listened	Praised	Researched	Transcribed
Grouped	Logged	Predicted	Reshaped	Translated
Guided	Made	Prepared	Resolved	Traveled
Had	Mailed	Prescribed	Responded	Treated
Handled	Maintained	Presented	Restored	Trimmed
Harmonized	Managed	Presided	Retrieved	Troubleshot
Headed	Manipulated	Prevented	Reviewed	Typed
Helped	Marketed	Printed	Revised	Umpired
Hired	Mastered	Processed	Risked	Understood
Hypothesized	Maximized	Produced	Rode	Understudied
Identified	Mediated	Programmed	Sauteed	Undertook
Illustrated	Meditated	Projected	Saved	Unified
Imagined	Memorized	Promoted	Saw	United
Implemented	Mended	Proofread	Scheduled	Updated
Improved	Met	Protected	Screened	Upgraded
Improvised	Minimized	Proved	Selected	Used
Included	Mixed	Provided	Sensed	Utilized
Increased	Modeled	Pruned	Separated	Validated
Indexed	Moderated	Publicized	Served	Verbalized
Influenced	Modified	Published	Set	Verified
Informed	Monitored	Purchased	Setup	Volunteered
Initiated	Motivated	Questioned	Severed	Waited
Innovated	Moved	Raised	Sewed	Washed
Inspected	Navigated	Ran	Shaped	Watched
Inspired	Negotiated	Read	Shared	Weighed
Installed	Observed	Readied	Showed	Welded
Instituted	Obtained	Reasoned	Sketched	Wired
Instructed	Offered	Received	Sold	Won
Insured	Operated	Recommended	Solved	Worked
Integrated	Ordered	Reconciled	Sorted	Wrote
Interacted	Organized	Reconditioned	Spoke	X-rayed
Interpreted	Oriented			